I0831922

THE SKIN OF THE SYSTEM

The Skin of the System

ON GERMANY'S SOCIALIST MODERNITY

Benjamin Robinson

STANFORD UNIVERSITY PRESS
Stanford, California 2009

Stanford University Press
Stanford, California

Library of Congress Cataloging-in-Publication Data

Robinson, Benjamin.
The skin of the system : on Germany's socialist modernity / Benjamin Robinson.
p. cm.
Includes bibliographical references and index.
ISBN 978-0-8047-6247-2 (cloth : alk. paper)
1. Fühmann, Franz—Criticism and interpretation. 2. Socialism and literature—Germany (East). 3. Socialism—Germany (East). I. Title.
PT2611.U436R63 2009
838'91409—dc22 2009007179

Typeset at Stanford University Press in 10/13 Galliard

Contents

Acknowledgments

It is a pleasure to thank my friends and colleagues at several institutions for supporting me in this project. Thanks are due to Mariatte Denman and Art Strum, formerly at the Stanford University Introduction to the Humanities Program; Helen Fehervary, Bernd Fischer, Paul Reitter, and Alexander Stephan at the Ohio State University Department of Germanic Languages and Literatures; and Katherina Barbe and Dennis Brain at the Department of Foreign Languages and Literatures at Northern Illinois University. My colleagues at the Indiana University Department of Germanic Studies are a challenging lot. Their good examples, hard questioning, wide curiosity, and sometimes completely unexpected takes on topics I had assumed I understood have been a source of enjoyment and inspiration, and a measure of productive pique. Claudia Breger, Fritz Breithaupt, and Bill Rasch have read and commented insightfully on parts of the manuscript, while Michel Chaouli, Johannes Türk, and Marc Weiner have engaged me on specific issues. Colleagues at the nascent Center for Theoretical Humanities at Indiana have provided an intellectual framework that has been an extraordinary help for me. The Indiana University College Arts and Humanities Institute has supported me with an opportune grant of course relief, and the Office of the Vice Provost for Research with a Grant-in-Aid of Research. My graduate students at Indiana have been a font of adventurous thinking, and special thanks are due to Michael Auer for perceptive comments on manuscript sections.

This project germinated as a dissertation at Stanford University. My advisor Russell Berman and Hans Ulrich Gumbrecht, besides guiding its inception, have continued generously to counsel and support its subsequent incarnations, despite—or for the joy of—substantial differences of opinion. Michael Rohrwasser and Horst Domdey, both then at the Free University in Berlin, read the dissertation and eased my research with their lively seminars. Spirited conversations over the years with David Brenner, Jason Camlot, Erin Carlston, Marzena Grzegorczyk, Dane Johnson, Marcia Klotz, Ross Lewin, Robert McNeill, Leerom Medovoi, Scott Nova, Eugene Ostashevsky, Daniel Potter, John Rosenthal, and Sha Xin Wei ensured that my thinking, whatever its debilities, never became complacent. Edith and Fred Neubauer were kind hosts in East Berlin who opened for me many doors of a labyrinth. At Stanford University Press, Norris Pope trusted this book and brought his wisdom to bear in shepherding it to press; John Feneron, Martin Hanft, and Sarah Crane Newman were always ready with keen eyes and astute advice. Along the way, I have incurred special debts of gratitude to Eva Geulen and Carsten Strathausen for their careful readings of the manuscript. With their kindness, intelligence, humor, and amazing energy, my parents-in-law, Barbara and the late Matthew James, created a second home for me: Barbara jumped in gracefully on crucial occasions to make my work possible, while Matthew was never stinting with ideological sacrilege, cigarettes, or boisterous goodwill. My parents, Valerie and Stewart Robinson, are activists. They cherish the leftist fight and understand how it works through joy, whatever outrages it goes out to meet. They taught me what has been called, in somewhat loftier tones, fidelity to the idea. Such fidelity is not at all disturbed by Stewart's claim to Thomas Münzer's original bran muffin recipe. Fidelity grows close to the absurd in the soil of love—which love goes for my brothers Zachary and Elliott and their families. Then there are the names I write here much as I might elsewhere: as tokens of something too solemn and cheerful to show up for the occasion—yet by a capricious turn, setting them here is my greatest satisfaction: Jennifer James Robinson, who shares in all facets of this work except its errors, and our children Mathilde, Lewis, and Margaret. The book is dedicated to them.

NOTE ON TRANSLATIONS AND PERMISSIONS

All translations from the German, except where otherwise noted, are my own. In the case of Fühmann's work, I have consulted, but not used, the (in any case not very numerous) English translations, since I rely on English equivalents that accurately reflect arguments I developed through reading the German texts. One example neatly suffices to illustrate the (not unfamiliar) problem. Fühmann's exasperated cry from *Twenty-two Days* that "I won't be able to get out of my skin" supplies my book with its primary analytical concept (namely, system boundary, or "the skin of the system"). Leila Vennewitz's English translation, while resourceful, does not help me: "Like the leopard, I can't and never would be able to change my spots." In the case of authors such as Christa Wolf, Franz Kafka, or Karl Marx, authors who are well known to an English-speaking audience through their English translations, I have used those mostly excellent translations. Where I have needed to get at a particular sense of the German, I have either included the German word, or done the translation myself. These instances are marked in the relevant notes. An important exception is the poetry by Trakl, which is connected particularly closely to Fühmann's oeuvre. Despite the fine translations available, I have translated these poems myself in order to ensure that linguistic usages across Fühmann and Trakl remain consistent.

For generous permission to reprint texts and images, I owe thanks to a number of institutions and individuals. An earlier and shorter version of Chapter 2 appears in the collection *A Leftist Ontology: Beyond Essentialism*, edited by Carsten Strathausen (University of Minnesota Press, 2009). Parts of Chapter 7 appear in nascent form as an essay in *The Cultural After-Life of East Germany*, edited by Leslie A. Adelson, which appeared as Volume 13 in the Humanities Program Series of the American Institute of Contemporary German Studies at Johns Hopkins University (2002). My translation of Fühmann's "Dream of Moira," as the epilogue of Chapter 9, is courtesy of Fühmann's longtime publisher, Hinstorff Press in Rostock. The Berlinische Gallerie and the artist Trak Wendisch kindly gave me permission to use his arresting painting "El Coloso" on the book cover. Acknowledgments for permission to use other texts and images appear in the relevant footnotes and captions.

THE SKIN OF THE SYSTEM

Introduction: On Socialist Vacation

> Enjoyment becomes the object of manipulation, until, ultimately, it is entirely extinguished in fixed entertainments. The process has developed from the primitive festival to the modern vacation
>
> —Max Horkheimer and Theodor Adorno[1]

> The ultimate vacation, the denial of reciprocal economy, is itself obtained only by means of an economy.
>
> —Roland Barthes[2]

I. PROSPECTUS

Let's go on vacation! Let's leave the drudgery of work behind. Let's recreate, enjoy, pursue happiness, liberty, and life. It is harder than we might think. Culture, entertainment, erotics—they all seem to lead back to free-market economics. We can pick up almost any volume of cultural criticism today and find the circulation and accumulation of capital written back into our leisure, into the very heart of our escape. A common logic, not ponderous causality, is the formal bond linking the most disparate modes of living in the most disparate times and places. Contemporary historicism, for example, draws together texts from the most obscure corners of experience on the basis of shared figures whose genealogies can be traced to an overarching *Zeitgeist* (episteme), while poststructuralist philosophies separate the order of causes from the order of effects so that, whatever one might say about causality, the effects are all available in a single empire of signs. Even where such homology is criticized as totalizing, it is first stipulated as omnipresent, so that gestures of paradox and subversion may assume rebellious dignity. Despite the diversity of appearances in modernity, and their critical liberation from positivist causality, the name of the game remains interconnection, and its common form is circulation, exchange, traffic. The substantial boundaries of territoriality and temporality have succumbed, even retrospectively, to the virtual globalism of a single, assiduous logic.

But relief is in sight, just on the horizon. There we find socialism, communism: an other system. It is this system, and its otherness, that we want to visit here. To visit and to enjoy—this is a vacation, after all, a voiding, an emptying out of economy in favor of plentitude, sensuality, and relaxation. The only string attached is that we carefully choose a vacation we can afford. For we want to have it and enjoy it too, and to do so we must be realistic and practical, not letting our plans become too fanciful. We want our vacation land to be terra firma, not utopia, found in the travel prospectus of really existing, historical socialism—socialism as grounded first in the Soviet Union in 1917. Why not then visit the most concretely bounded of real socialist lands? Head back over the Berlin Wall, into frontline Cold War rivalries, to the gray German Democratic Republic (GDR)? For this adventure, at first glance so dreary, to succeed in showing us what a true vacation from economy means, we must not shy away from resurrecting borders, recharging antagonisms, and crediting the full existential power of global difference in recent historical time.

2. TRAVEL ADVISORIES

Many astute commentaries on twentieth-century socialist regimes assert that the end of an era—the collapse of the Soviet Union and the socialist states bound to it—is a chance for scholars to reconceive a period so fraught with Cold War tension that an objective analysis had scarcely been possible from within it.[3] In socialism's aftermath, it is contended, we can reconsider the period with an eye toward the dialogues, influences, and enduring structures that extended across military borders and put ideological divisions into question. No longer bound by partisan taboos, we can more accurately assess the epochal similarities of a century universally convulsed by the rise of mass demographics, mass industrialization, mass commodification, mass media, and mass war. The merits of a generous scholarly vantage point are self-evident.

Despite the virtues of such ecumenism, the present study of socialist culture takes the opposite approach, starting with the systematic and historical weight of real and violent border tensions. In this sense, *The Skin of the System* fits into an intellectual tradition that sees social reality as fundamentally agonistic—that is, as based in the inevitable fact of meaningful conflict.[4] It focuses on what made historical socialism *different* from social systems in the industrial West and insists on seeing socialism, as distinctly as we are able, as an *other* system. Only by sharpening our understanding of socialism as something distinct on the horizon of our presumed realities (whether the receding or dawning horizon) can we grasp it in its empirical specificity as a significant choice—a potentially valid response to systemic opportunities and problems—and thus preserve in our thinking some consciousness of socialism's once very persuasive claim to a rationally transcendent, and not just historically conjunctural, content. The Cold War era, as nasty as it was, is therefore not taken as a superseded age of ideological strife, but as a period in which something universal took place with the advent of the socialist alternative.[5]

The historical vantage afforded to us travelers and observers by the end of Eastern European socialism is an important one, although the reasons for its importance are somewhat contradictory. On the one hand, a unique epoch undoubtedly closed with the opening of the Berlin Wall in 1989, and the historical and cultural balance of the socialist era can be assessed, if not teleologically, nonetheless with a sharpened sense of how certain social programs played themselves out in a real historical context. The end of the era—the tying off of its lines of continuity and development, the exhaustion of its potential, at least in that historical embodiment—makes socialism's experience that much more available for a detached empirical description and evaluation. The rare scholarly luxury of having recourse to such relatively stable empiricism in the social and cultural sciences has now become a common scholarly necessity for any credible cultural study of socialism. In this sense, real socialism must be historicized.

On the other hand, the significance of historical socialism's difference is thrown all the more strongly into relief by its absence on the current European stage. No longer there, the distinct bundle of problems, aspirations, unintended consequences, and achievements that were socialism can now be loosed from their tactical mooring in Cold War positions, and understood against the more principled aspects of a fractured modernity. Here, the word *modernity* signifies an epoch in which universalist human aspirations have uneasily converged with the mechanisms and institutions for their social implementation, whether as "good" or "bad" universals, as cyberspace or hydrogen bomb.[6] In this sense, then, I do not restrict my discussion of the socialist culture of the GDR to the relentlessly (and vaguely) invoked desideratum of "historicization," but pursue a speculative as well as empiricist line of argumentation.[7] Modernity is not singular, but riven by rival universalisms that widely exclude each other, as illustrated nowhere more clearly than in the case of socialism. An all too easy acceptance of the factuality of the present globalism's claims to necessity and totality is a dead end in which economic liberalism triumphs because that is simply the way the world is.

As a travel guide into another system, this book takes us on a tour of an alternate form of modernity, one strangely different from the familiar modernity of liberal capitalism. By defining this strange system emptily at first, simply as *other* to capitalist modernity, the book aims to let this system emerge gradually on its own terms. Inevitably, though, such an account sees its foreign soil through the lenses of many other travelers. It aims to describe a new world freshly, but its descriptions also take their place among an existing literature on social alternatives; the distinct way in which it intervenes in that literature should here be remarked to give a clearer idea of what is being embarked upon. While I argue for the possibility of real alternatives in social organization and experience, I do not argue that we get to know and achieve that difference through more or better *politics*. In fact, I hold that the socialist alternative is no political formation at all, but a *system*, with a characteristic arrangement of subsystems. A system, if it means nothing else in the following book, defines an arrangement with *boundaries*. It contrasts with a structure, which operates as an ordering whole. Politics, to the extent that it is a structural feature of human life, will go on as usual, even (or especially) in socialism.

By contrast, an influential post-Marxist literature, developing since the 1980s in part as a reaction against the perceived scientism of structural Marxism, has heralded a "return of the political" in which politics has ever more emphatically been receiving its due as an autonomous sphere of human activity irreducible to economics, technology, or administration. This return of the political emphasizes the infinity of differences in human affairs. Politics here takes the form of disagreement, antagonism, and decision. It takes place not in formalized institutions, such as market, parliament, and judiciary, where disagreement is already subordinated to systemic constraint, but on the streets, in the papers, on the shop floor, in the marginal neighborhoods—anywhere but where order, calculation, and planning reign. It takes place among the uncounted and unlettered. Even when politics appears at the apex of society, its authentic form is the bold stroke, not the capillary action of diffuse suasions and stimulants, sanctions and sedatives. This return of the political often falls together with a celebration of "life"—life not as biology, but as a foundational point of indeterminacy and source of the new, as that which escapes all modes of system and counting (hence, the renewed concern with Hannah Arendt's concept of *natality*, the condition of politics in the unpredictable renewal of life). Politics and politicization become, in effect, not another means for maneuvering in institutional environments, but synonymous with the aspiration for openness in the authentic human life. There are many names associated with this new politics, perhaps the most prominent of which are Ernesto Laclau, Chantal Mouffe, Jacques Rancière, Claude Lefort, Giorgio Agamben, Michael Hardt, and Antonio Negri.

As much as their work finds an echo in these pages, this book is not conceived as a response to a theoretical literature; on the contrary, it is not about that literature, but about really existing socialism, its stories, tasks, and problems. But while I do not polemicize against the new salience of the political, I think that it is nonetheless helpful to note how different the course I pursue is. Where the new political theories dismantle the idea of "specific difference" (a specific otherness *to capitalism*) in favor of difference per se as an endless round of contingencies, it is precisely the sharp smack of one existential difference that preoccupies my subjects. And where the new political focus is based on the primacy of some field of minimal systematization (the political), my study accords primacy to fields of maximum systematization. Theories that value politics as a distinct and self-sufficient field of human endeavor do so because they understand a true politics as less regulated even than language (with its logicist grammar); politics in these theories is essentially an aesthetic field—it is not syntax and phonology, but a purely symbolic rhetoric that, in the last instance, is about itself. Thus, even a communicatively oriented social theorist like Jürgen Habermas is held to shortchange political openness by binding himself too tightly to the rationalist assumptions of linguistic pragmatics.

While that which escapes modernity's "count," and remains indeterminate with respect to our familiar calculations, is likewise at the heart of this study, I do not find the New and Different—the *Novum*—emerging in and aspiring to a minimally structured space of its own, but in a world of systemic commitments and implications. Power, economy, and communication share their universal lessons not in unimpeded discourse, but in more stringent media such as law, money, and bureaucracy. Where choice and decision figure in my treatment of socialism—where political and aesthetic subjectification come into play—is at the boundaries of systems, boundaries that function as indices of transformation, pointing beyond an actual (and even a potential) state. My theoretical ground is not freedom, but the

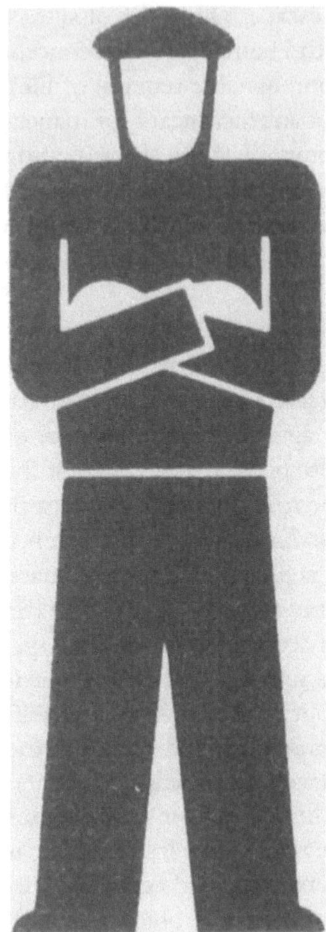

Fig. 1. The New Man in ISOTYPE (International System of Typographic Picture Education) of erstwhile Bavarian Soviet Economic Advisor Otto Neurath. Courtesy of www.gerdarntz.org. Collection Gemeentemuseum The Hague.

universal limits of coercion. Otherness, excess, transformation, and incommensurability refer in the following pages to systemic productions, and what interests me is how they are presented in the media of real socialism. What new and different things do we come to recognize and choose by means of socialism's money, laws, wars, and commands? The New Man or Woman?

When human agency and subject formation emerge as important categories in this study—as they do—they are seen as rare and brief moments of awareness that are just as likely to be disappointments as satisfactions, and certainly not to be welcomed unconditionally as liberations. Awakened by an encounter with a system boundary, social awareness often manifests itself as an inability to distinguish before and after, inside and outside, self and other: as an inability to plan. Such consciousness of change refers to a triggered affect, an unexpected emotional awareness—an ecstasy. However, a new quality of agency is only confirmed—and pleasure in selfhood experienced again—in the feedback arising from devotion to a system for capturing such change. The New Human is not, in the following account, a slumbering giant, a rising voice, and a thundering deliverer from wrong. The New Human we meet here is the patient devotee of transforming social circumstances, the recipient as well as donor of obscure signals groping for some stable pattern that will eventually be recognized not just as new but as new and improved. While politics and freedom play a role for this New Human, what she seeks most is that really existing thing which demonstrates a difference between one politics or another. To the extent that *socialism* names the difference between two great political choices, it cannot itself be a politics. It is rather the object equally of our protagonists' humble patience and agonizing impatience, a matter of solicitude, confrontation, and shock.

In its analysis of socialist culture, *The Skin of the System* combines several broad areas of concern. It is, most explicitly, a study of what insights into socialism the remarkable East German literary loner Franz Fühmann (1922–84) gives us. Not well known outside Germany, Fühmann has an oeuvre conspicuously lacking a "great novel" to secure his reputation. He is, however, an author whose intense combination of mythology, logical conundrums, and philosophical aphorisms with dreamscapes, nightmares, and the sharply etched details of war and bureaucracy qualifies him as a cosmopolitan modernist with the talent and intensity to merit an international reputation. Whatever genre might be used to classify Fühmann, his writings have an aesthetic authority that warrants close reading and sustained critical scrutiny. The choice of Fühmann, moreover, has what is for my purposes an essential aesthetic specificity, one conveyed by contrast with his close friend—and much better known author—Christa Wolf. While both shared a deep commitment to real socialism and an equally deep dissent from those forces more interested in the tactics of institutional self-preservation, they represent strikingly different literary sensibilities. Where Wolf is best known for her interest in the problems of subjective identity—how a person in society can "come to oneself" without at the same time dropping out or away from others—Fühmann is concerned with the problem of securing subjective discontinuities, of preserving the conscious possibility of transformation, of getting outside of one's own well-worn skin.

But if literary exegesis of Fühmann is one armature around which *The Skin of the System* develops, aesthetic questions are neither its only, nor necessarily primary, concern. I want to cite two additional rubrics for the book's subject matter—the relation of science to society and that of literature to economics. The cultural study of science and society has helped complicate a prominent humanistic line of argumentation that treats science as a field of human activity guided by a means-ends rationality, with strict criteria of truth and falsity and correspondingly few measures of moral and cultural value. Like some of this work in "science studies," *The Skin of the System* refuses the dichotomy of instrumental reason versus communicative reason, adopting an approach that sees function and meaning as closely intertwined facts of modern life. Its position can be contrasted to the Frankfurt School tradition of Theodor Adorno and Max Horkheimer, extended most prominently by Habermas, which places emphasis on consensus, normativity, and reflective decision-making. Here the emphasis falls more strongly on institutions, system-bound discretion, and the brief, but inevitable moments of paradox and contradiction that exceed the limits of prior constraints. Even the much-maligned category of instrumental-technical reason finds a sympathetic airing in these pages, since the study, basing itself in postanalytic philosophy and systems theory, situates itself in a pragmatic and utilitarian framework that strives to be broad enough to entertain (though not adhere to) figures as antipodal as W. v. O. Quine and Karl Marx. Such a framework allows us to ask questions about Fühmann's writing, and—through his biographical dilemmas—about the role of technical-rational systems such as cybernetic steering and positive legal jurisprudence in the development of a socialist mentality.

The study of literature and economics has been productively enriched by literary and economic scholars over the last several decades, and the discussion they have initiated is also one that this study joins.[8] The perspective here, however, diverges from that found in the substantial scholarly work articulating and criticizing parallels between the circulation of capital and the circulation of symbolic meaning[9]—the divergence stems from the insistence on a meaningful difference between real socialism and capitalism, a difference that must naturally extend into any parallels between economic forms and symbolic ones. As some sympathetic critics of using economic models to understand culture have noted, the search by cultural analysts for an economic principle prior to and different from capitalist principles often issues in a sort of paradoxicality that winds up making capitalism seem more inevitable than ever. In the spirit of this "internal critique" of economic-cultural studies, this study takes as its theoretical starting point the possibility of systems other than the familiar capitalist system and as its empirical starting point the history of socialism in East Germany. The inevitability of capitalism—and capitalist homologies in the circulation of cultural meaning—is thus ruled out from the beginning.

The challenges of real socialism and the drama of Fühmann's writing are complex and actual—that is, they relate to the empirical world of history and practice. There are, however, certain classical concepts that recur throughout this diversity, concepts related to the difficulty of experiencing transformation as anything more than a fleeting change of names in an unchanging world. These key concepts are marked by such Latin phrases as *tertium non datur* (there is no third), *optimum optimorum* (the best of the best), *differentia specifica* (specific difference), and *unicuique suum* (to each his due), which reappear in different problematic configurations throughout this analysis. In each particular appearance, they turn out to be figures antagonistic to their own universal conceptualization, figures of immediacy and directness in the very literal sense of abolishing any mediating terms. For those on whom these figures suddenly impose themselves as ciphers of real experience, their flash of relevance not only calls forth one affect alone but also evokes in each new situation both an ecstatic longing to stand out as such, as a subject of pure heterogeneous experience, and an indexical longing to register the force of existence plainly, with no special experience of oneself at all. They call on a person uniquely—or call a person forth as unique—that he or she may serve as a sign of universal difference: be a straw in the wind of revolution . . . or, in the less romantic terms of Quine, be the value of a variable.

What reading Fühmann adds to our reflections on the universal problems of social transformation is his overwhelming insight that the *complexity* of transformation—the *improbably difficult* set of historical mediations transformation entails—is engaged only in the event of an experience of blunt *simplicity*. Fühmann's work, it will be seen, turns around the problem of how a world-creating medium and a self-delimiting index can ever be brought to coincide. Or to put it in words of the philosophical canon, how the *tertium comparationis* (a third term for comparison) or *metretike techne* (science of commensuration) can ever coincide with the *novum* or *ex nihilo* (the new thing, never-yet-encountered), since this unheard-of coincidence of universal and particular is the only test of radical change. Fühmann's unique merit as a writer is to lend this abstract problem the tangible, passionate force of his temperament, intelligence, and historical situation in East Germany. The devil, of course, is in his details—and our own—so it will take many careful restatements and refinements of the problem of universal socialist transformation before we begin (I hope) to appreciate its cumulative force fully. Meanwhile, we follow the remarkable path of a Central European writer whose choices and chances put him in the center of the twentieth century's vast and disorienting clash of systems—a brilliant naif, traversing liberalism, fascism, and socialism, trying to experience in body and soul what the meaning of these grand formations could possibly be.

3. ITINERARY

Those commencing this vacation on the heels of our socialist protagonist might find it convenient to know that the book is divided into nine chapters organized into two parts. Part One, comprising three chapters, develops the main theoretical ideas of "other systems." In light of the antipathy of especially leftist social theorists to really existing socialist institutions, Chapter 1 begins with the strategies of cultural studies—from those of Adorno and Habermas to those of Stuart Hall and Richard Rorty—for denying intellectual significance to East European socialism. Against such strategies, I hold that socialism was nothing if not also its practical experience. Yet what did this experience amount to? Having cited academic prejudices, I do not want to make the case easy for myself, so I turn to the exuberant days of the collapsing Wall in the 1980s and 1990s when few were ready to concede that socialism ever existed in the departing mess of the Soviet bloc. The giddy release from socialism's ontological burden is hard to argue with. Socialism's heavy fictions seemed to yield in a magic moment to a reality as free for possibility as any fairy tale. This moment—whether socialism's compendium or contravention—exposes a socialism bereft of power and pretense, a socialism that is not one. Precisely in this afterimage of rigid institutional forms, harsh police measures, legal arbitrariness, arrogant scientism, and, most strikingly, decisive collapse, historical socialism becomes the site for thinking about what is universal in the socialist alternative—about what was or still is there to insist upon. Like the moment of socialism's installation, the moment of its collapse marks it as a system with boundaries, not an idyll of utopian longing. In particular, East Germany—the focus of the book—is not belittled here by adopting the tendency to see it as having been a provincial and parochial backwater of modernity. Rather, in the following analysis East Germany remains an avant-garde, with all the perversity such a claim might imply, an avant-garde that helps us think the future of our own present. This vanguard status is not attributable to some absurd ideological loyalty to the dour martinet of the Eastern bloc, but to the simple conviction that whatever else GDR socialism was, it was real.

Chapter 2 is the main theoretical chapter, explaining in general terms how my analysis of socialism works, how it relates to other traditions—especially that of philosophical ontology—and what it accomplishes that other approaches do not. It forms a self-standing, if condensed and demanding, argument that guides the book's agenda, as well as establishing avenues for further research and debate. In this way, it is the most broadly applicable section of the book, useful to readers who want to engage with the methodological assumptions and implications of this work and to relate it to some of the theoretical literature I have alluded to in this introduction. Drawing on the disparate fields of economics, semiotics, systems theory, and philosophy, the chapter's tasks include the following: explaining what "ontology" has to do with socialism; introducing a set of classical ontological problems reaching from Plato's *Parmenides* to the critique of positivism by Horkheimer and Adorno; using a combination of "internal realism" (Quine, Hilary Putnam) and "systems theory" (Parsons, Luhmann) to reformulate the ontological problems in a way relevant for understanding socialism; showing that this reformulation is especially helpful in distinguishing between "political ontology" (Carl Schmitt, Laclau, Rancière) and something like "economic ontology" (General Equilibrium Theory, Marxism); and, finally, suggesting that a "socialist ontology"—which is the ultimate promise of the book, becoming visible over the course of Part Two—is obliged by its inmost aspirations to generic superiority to chop up its world differently than liberal political and economic ontologies do. Lest this seem too crowded an agenda for one chapter, I want to emphasize that the last item—the socialist ontology—receives no prescriptive formulation, but relies on the disruptive and generative potential of its new synthesis (what used to be called "totality" in the pre-postmodern days). Socialism is not a slick "system differentiation," whereby a new subsystem emerges to resolve a paradox in one or another system—say, the paradox of overproduction in the market economy—but it first appears as something new and incompletely articulated against the background of a vast social "de-differentiation."

Chapter 3 is assigned the task of persuading the reader that my theoretical vocabulary of socialist ontology is also a vocabulary that speaks with and to the literature of really existing socialism. It takes up one of the key contrasts developed in Chapter 2—namely, the contrast between indexical pointing and symbolic mediation, and exemplifies it on the examples of Fühmann and the most famous East German literary figure, Christa Wolf. This pair exemplifies what I call the "skin of the system," to indicate a system's being both an intact whole and a vulnerable body, and the "din of the system," to indicate both a system's physical norms (a pun on DIN, or German Industrial Norms) and their susceptibility to the noise of infinite regression. After showing how what might seem like an abstract and rather technical contrast in fact has aesthetic consequences that might be discerned and appreciated, I pursue an important aspect of Fühmann's poetics to illustrate a related theoretical term—*sovereignty*. This key term I subsequently turn back onto the poetics of real socialism. Sovereignty is such an important notion because it points both to a subjective dimension of intentional selfhood and to an objective dimension of ultimate authority. In Fühmann's poetics, sovereignty becomes an erotic category in the sense that it is not simply a category of individual autonomy—the personalistic authority of the supreme commander—but also a category that in its claim to represent the superlative always relies for its test on an encounter with something worse or better, but surely other. This harrowing and exultant encounter is, for Fühmann, always essentially an erotic encounter, because it is both disruptive of identity and generative. We thus glimpse how Fühmann's rendering of socialism's encounter with antagonistic social forms—a theme of potentially deadening dryness and stolidity—finds an expressive venue in the poetry and philosophy of erotic desire.

Part Two remains in a philosophical register, but takes on board the rich and particular historical experiences of Fühmann, experiences not so much of this or that relationship or this or that episode in his life, but those odd, graphic, highly personal experiences that suddenly, perversely evacuate themselves of specificity in order to take on the cast of the universal—like narrative art in the good old days that promised to reveal eternal human verities in deft little situations, only here the universal truths are often unrecognizably distant from the human. Universality in Fühmann has no guarantee of familiarity, which is exactly its frightening challenge.

Chapter 4, the first of Part Two, is the most descriptive chapter, taking us through the work, biography, and institutional commitments of Fühmann, from his experience reading Georg Trakl as a fascist *Wehrmacht* soldier in the 1940s through his antifascist re-education in prison camp, to his desperate fight against his own sarcasm and self-destructive rage in the face of the GDR's growing institutional absurdity in the 1970s and 1980s. Crucially, Fühmann is presented not as the case study to which the preceding conceptual framework will be applied, but as equally *explanandum* and *explanans*—as both a part of socialism to be explained and as a singularly telling explicator of socialist phenomena. To help readers orient their aesthetic expectations, I place Fühmann's work into a broader context of literary modernism. I also give an overview of his oeuvre, focusing especially on his unlikely travel journal *Twenty-two Days, or Half a Lifetime*, a document of whimsical but unsparing self-interrogation that I return to throughout the book. The life that emerges in his writing is shaped by violent personal transitions, from keen fascist to convinced socialist to what, toward the end of his life, may be called a state of apocalyptic suspense. I address this sequence of ruptures in Fühmann's selfhood not with a theory of psychological trauma, but by way of Fühmann's highly conceptualized perception of the challenge that an existential demand for transformation poses to core subjective needs for boundary and identity.

Chapter 5 addresses Fühmann's Muses, drawing us headlong into a poetics of transformation whose task is not to ascertain just any difference, but to ascertain the true difference a difference makes. Not just transformation, but transformation for the better—in fact, for the best—is Fühmann's concern. A poetics of supercession—a socialist poetics—finds itself only beyond itself, where the ethereal Muses engage the workaday situation of those enunciating their songs. Fühmann's Muses show themselves in just such a material engagement in "Marsyas," a short story based on the Greek myth of the impertinent satyr flayed alive after the Muses judge his music inferior to Apollo's. We see in this story how a realist poetics that is also a socialist poetics leads to a brutal ontologization of formal logic that, ultimately, takes on the illogical form of a physical erotics. Importantly, we see how this erotics is not conceived as an individual bodily experience, but as a *systems erotics* of social transformation. This systems erotics supplies the central figures of Fühmann's experience of socialism, above all the principle of a present and forceful difference: the logical law of the excluded middle, *tertium non datur* (there is no third). This figure, necessary for imagining the sharp boundaries of difference that Fühmann longs to experience as evidence of transformation, describes a kind of skin of the system—that is, the system's outermost boundary that both secures its identity and demarcates its particularity. The flaying of this skin is the fatality that Fühmann explores throughout his imaginative work and relentlessly *un*imagined biography.

After these two chapters have indicated the stakes of Fühmann's dogmatics and poetics, Chapter 6 introduces three rubrics, *camps*, *laws*, and *plans*, which mark historical stations in Fühmann's biography and conceptual stations in socialist transformation. After sketching the broad significance of these terms, the chapter explores the idea of the camp with reference to Fühmann's internment in a Soviet antifascist re-education camp, the *lager' voennoplennych*, where the brutality of containment—of dogma, detention, and discipline—comes together with the lyrical abjection of the unlivable life. Chapters 7 and 8 then continue the program set out here and take up the other two terms. The three institutional realms of camps, laws, and plans correspond, albeit ambiguously, to three competing world orders in modernity: fascism, liberalism, and socialism. Fühmann's own relationship to each order is a central concern of his poetics of transformation. Building on the analysis of "Marsyas," Chapter 6 resituates the bodily torment of the satyr's flaying in the Stalinist prison camp where Fühmann reads Georg Trakl, the expressionist *poète maudit* who first inspired him as a fascist soldier, and whom he continues to read as an elusive constant of his own inconstant life, autobiographically recounting his changing readings of Trakl in his epic critical essay *Facing the Fire Pits*. The camp that emerges in this chapter is both a harrowing instrument of physical orthopedics and a ground-laying, a taking of position, a drawing of sides—the straitened socialist who discovers himself and his Muses in this camp is one who, having confounded all laws of retribution and distribution, is ready to receive the new dispensation.

In Chapter 7, the renegades are already legion, and the walls of the socialist camp no longer exert the force they once did, socialism's unity requiring a renewal through the purer force of law. The promised new law of socialist order, however, remains stubbornly suspended between the emergence of socialism and its catastrophic state of emergency. This suspension becomes grimly apparent in Fühmann's correspondence around the time of several aggressive legal actions against GDR writers in the mid-1970s, and it only intensifies in the letters about his abortive attempt to assemble an anthology of younger, unpublished poets shortly before his death. The idea of laws as an opposite to camps, or, more technically, the opposition of indicative and normative orders, becomes ever harder for Fühmann to maintain, especially as his various goals of sovereignty and system are seen to exclude, repeat, and exceed each other. More and more, the positive law of socialism diverges from socialism's systemic disposition until it is no longer clear which order is more absurd. At that point of disordered expectations, Fühmann becomes keenly attuned to the privative (lacking) case of sense: the maddening *non*sense of real socialist law.

Chapter 8 then takes up the plan, the institutionalized form of providential reasoning that lies somewhere between normative law and factual description and that is—in the guise of the "Five-Year Plan"—the proverbial institution of real socialism. I examine more closely the philosopher Georg Klaus, the leading proponent of cybernetic systems theory in the GDR, whose writings on norms I introduce in the previous chapter. Klaus's cybernetic project aims to find an efficient quantitative measure of the socialist system and in doing so runs up against the problem of maintaining a substantial quality of socialism. The unbiased flow of quantitative commensuration would itself be something so new in human affairs that such a liberated quantity would count as the very quality by which socialism's success could be measured. From Klaus's paradoxes of quantity and quality, we turn to Fühmann's science fiction story "The Heap," which poses the classical Eleatic problem of the *sorites*—namely, when does a quantity become a quality?—and answers it with biting reference to the unresolved problems of GDR socialist identity: sovereign quality and quantifiable system must both yield again to transformation.

Fühmann died in 1984, before the collapse of East German socialism. Chapter 9 draws together some of the key themes from Fühmann's work, reminding readers of the landmarks of socialism from the vantage point of a brief trip to the West, a strange place, if we can picture it, free of socialism's anguished contortions. In the futuristic story "The Street of Perversions," Fühmann's protagonist journeys across the wall to liberal Libroterr. There he is able to glance back at real socialism (Uniterr) from across the horrible ontological dividing line of its immeasurable difference. Right on the edge of that line, I pause to consider an essay on E. T. A. Hoffmann's novella "Ignaz Denner," in which Fühmann asks what happens when the Hegelian dialectic of progress comes to a shuddering halt, not in an exuberant flash of revolutionary energy but in an abject perception of the material inertia of the world. Perversely, though, this moment of belonging to things, while shattering, addresses the fundamental desire—the desire for socialism—whose many forms I have been exploring over the course of this book.

After such difficult travels, after so many marvels and so many desolate stations of transit, we might feel exhausted and ready to return to the border checkpoints where, in Part One, we first got our documents in order. By the time we reach the end—dare I reveal it?—the checkpoints are gone.

Without any border between systems, we are no longer free to leave another system, but *compelled* to return to our more familiar sectors. My hope is, however, that at least some touch of (other) worldliness remains behind from that earlier freedom to go. May you cheerfully avail yourself of it.

Bon voyage!

PART I

BETWEEN NOT YET AND NO LONGER

I confess that in America [East Germany] I saw more than America [East Germany]; I sought there the image of democracy [socialism] itself, with its inclinations, its character, its prejudices, and its passions, in order to learn what we have to fear or to hope from its progress.

—Alexis de Tocqueville

CHAPTER ONE

Utopia and Actuality: What Is to Be Done with Really Existing Socialism?

1. "THE INTERNATIONALE": ONE ICON— TWO STORIES OF FUTURES PAST

> 'Tis the final conflict, let each stand in his place.
> —Eugène Pottier, "The Internationale"[1]

> Come, join in the only battle wherein no man can fail,
> Where whoso fadeth and dieth, yet his deed shall still prevail.
> —William Morris, "The Day is Coming"[2]

In Ken Loach's 1995 Cannes Prize–winning film, ***Land and Freedom***, the protagonists—volunteers fighting Franco in the libertarian-left POUM (*Partido Obrero Unificado Marxista*) militias—sing the workers' anthem, "The Internationale," after a fractious debate over land reform in the Aragón village they have just liberated.[3] The song rallies the multipartisan, multinational soldiers back together again in working-class unity. An anthem, particularly "The Internationale," is a powerful symbol, and the complex emotions of the volunteers—bravado, fatalism, solidarity—are portrayed by way of the song's effect on film audiences who have their own emotional and political associations with the fabled anthem. In the film's screening time, the historically alert audience senses the tragic irony of the volunteers' faith in the fragile unity wrought by the still stirring refrains. The main narrative, meanwhile, goes on to play out the irony as the characters discover through their own actions—"with my own eyes," as the protagonist puts it—how much less charitable events are than ideals. The young comrades-in-arms are led either to tear up their party cards or go their separate organizational ways. Loach's historical fiction makes it clear that the militia members singing the song are ultimately not fighting under the banner of either the Spanish Republic or the Communist Party of Spain. Rather, loosely based on George Orwell's account of the war, *Homage to Catalonia*, the film tells the story of the Barcelona-based POUM militias' efforts to force the pace of revolution by collectivizing the land under their regional control.[4] They are defeated in this project not by Franco's fascists, but by the Communist parties committed to the bourgeois democratic Popular Front of the Spanish Republic. It is a complicated story that leaves intact little of the celebratory unity of the "The Internationale." By the film's end, not a few of the debaters who closed their session on land reform with the song have died, along with the Spanish revolution, at the points of each other's guns.

As material culture, "The Internationale" is a real and even banal thing: a military march existing in sheet music, impromptu performances, recordings, and films. What it symbolizes, however, is not so clear, although it still mobilizes great passion, as the film's extended citation of it indicates. Moreover, if this vague thing it symbolizes might be called "socialism," then it is even less clear whether this reference has any substantial existence in reality or belongs only to the infinitely displaced world of signs. In fact, the difficulty of specifying anything concrete about socialism is what allows the film to negotiate the slippery border between symbolic autonomy and historical reference. For while the main narrative concentrates on the Left's internecine squabbles, taking advantage of the audience's historical knowledge of the twentieth century's failed socialist revolutions to highlight the story's tragic power, the film gives back with the right hand what the left has taken. Thus, the film's framing device accomplishes another aspect of its narrative agenda: to deliver its heroes and their struggles, sacrifices, and symbols from a less-than-heroic socialist history that appears finally to have been discredited by the world-shaking events of the late 1980s. The frame takes the film's story up to the moment of the protagonist's death in a derelict council flat in post-Thatcher England, where his grandniece recovers and identifies with the personal history whose mementos he has stashed away in a little chest. Now—both diegetically and in the theater—the symbols and sacrifices contained in the narrative box are passed on to the audience outside of it. The fire of international workers' revolution escapes its dousing by functionaries and fellow travelers; the martyrs have not died in vain; the valiant culture the film has cited is no longer artifact, but living legacy. Over the hero's open grave, his youthful grandniece recites a few words by William Morris and raises her fist with a group of his loyal comrades.

By salvaging "The Internationale" at the expense of the Comintern,

Loach's film frees the workers' anthem from the betrayals of Stalin and the tainted cultural legacy of "really existing" socialism. A less burdened socialism than that which "really existed"—namely, one whose revolution never happened—can thus become the heroic reference point of the living legacy. From the Loyalists' defensive cry *¡No pasaran!* the slogan now becomes the utopians' untested "Not yet!" *Noch nicht* is the phrase Ernst Bloch used to characterize the glimmering "principle of hope": the workers' future is yet to come.[5] So what has happened in *Land and Freedom*'s switch of the primary reference of "The Internationale"? That socialism which claimed to be really in existence—the socialism of the commissars—is denied as false. That socialism that never existed—the socialism of those who haven't had or have been denied their chance, the socialism of song—is adopted as the true reference of the anthem's refrains. This transformation of socialism is indeed a gain of many degrees of freedom. It has become a "floating signifier," the surplus signification that like the mana of primitive reverence "is the disability of all finite thought (but also the surety of all art, all poetry, every mythic and aesthetic invention)," according to Claude Lévi-Strauss.[6]

At the same time, other stories of fact and fiction besides Loach's can be told about the embattled workers' anthem, ones that, however much latitude we grant them, leave us with less perfect freedom. Admiral N. G. Kuznetsov, commissar of the Soviet Navy, had been a top military adviser to the Loyalist armies in Spain during the crucial years of the Civil War. Alone among the non-Axis powers, the Soviet Union had committed matériel and manpower to the defense of Spain against fascism. Five years after the bloody events in Spain described by Loach's film, the Red Navy under Kuznetsov's command found itself under massive attack in its own waters.[7] On June 22, 1941, the Nazis invaded the Soviet Union, and within two months Hitler's Eighteenth Army had trapped the Baltic Fleet in the harbor of Tallinn. The Red Navy, desperate to evacuate more than twenty-five thousand Soviet troops and civilians from the Baltic republics, was forced to sail east toward Kronstadt through the thickly mined Gulf of Finland under heavy air attack by the German First Air Fleet. In the exodus twenty-eight out of twenty-nine transport ships were sunk, with the loss of over ten thousand lives. A sailor witnessed the transport *Virona* as it went down. At the very last, with the remaining passengers and the crew assembled on the quarterdeck, the sailor heard the sound of singing. They were singing "The Internationale" out over the dark, wreckage- and mine-strewn water. Defiant to the end, the civilian and military personnel on the ship foreshadowed the determination that those who survived the evacuation were to demonstrate in the ensuing nine-hundred-day siege of Leningrad, one of the few modern sieges more costly than Franco's siege of Madrid. Just before the *Virona* slid under water, the officers on deck drew their guns. A brief series of cracks and flashes signaled their final act of loyalty. Whatever other meanings one ascribes to the story—Russian patriotism, respect of naval tradition, fear of Stalin—one can also accord to the same Red soldiers whose treachery Loach decried the rich meaning of the workers' anthem.[8] But whose legacy is the flawed one?

2. INSTITUTIONS VERSUS IDEALS

These two tales of military courage displayed in the name of "The Internationale" bring into focus a problem in cultural studies posed by the end of the Cold War and the collapse of "really existing" socialism in Eastern Europe. The problem, simply stated, is whether critical scholarship should "emancipate" the kernel of real socialism—as a set of utopian ideals carried by an independent popular culture—from the context of a discredited institutional history; or should that institutional history and the culture that emerged with it form a primary basis for our understanding of what was distinctively socialist about "socialist" culture? In the one case, the arts and ethos of Eastern Europe are best served by an approach like Loach's that recuperates their critical negativity from the instrumentalization of state sponsorship, just as Loach salvaged the anarchist spontaneity of the workers' anthem from its duty to maintain discipline along a chain of command. As Adorno put it, "[C]ulture is only true when implicitly critical."[9] In the other case, the question of whether or not Eastern European regimes produced a socialist culture can only be answered by taking seriously their claim to be socialist in the first place, recognizing that their intellectual and expressive symbols, their class and property relations, and even many of their party traditions were those shared or envisioned by the workers' movement. Whereas Adorno demands for true art "separation from the prevailing realm of purposes,"[10] the singing of Kuznetsov's sailors took on its "truth" in their embracing the Red Navy's redness as their own in an affirmative act of "cultural reconciliation." The story of Kuznetsov's sailors might describe only a familiar kind of patriotic gesture—it is hard to read behind the lines of a single episode.[11] But the very fact that it was "The Internationale" accompanying their auto-da-fé hints at how important it is to understand the powerful commitments that made it possible for societies to subsist under socialist government—however they came, and we come, to understand that label.[12]

Nevertheless, it might be objected that this second approach, which critically embraces Eastern European socialism as a systemic effort to realize a socialist society, is an unwarranted narrowing of the culture that may be considered socialist. Surely the socialist tradition is broader than Eastern Europe in the twentieth century. It includes religious and communal communisms as well as workers' and reform movements in the industrial West and Third World; it includes the solidaristic capacity emerging within and against the rule of competitive individualism.[13] As broad and diverse as the tradition is, however, cultural studies would surely not want to mistake breadth with indeterminacy and refuse any specification of socialist institutional forms that have a referential concreteness beyond the play of differences in a culture of modernity. Kuznetsov's sailors understood themselves and their social belonging in a complex and effective network of relationships, and to this network they ascribed the symbolic value of "The Internationale." The "validity" of equating that polyglot anthem with that thick network of logics, intentions, and cross-purposes consists not in its exclusive determination of socialist identity but in its historically real determination of socialism as a governing power.[14] However much this determination weighs down the free-floating signifier with the red sailors' sunken ship, it is one that any future socialism, as a practical designation for an alternative organization of the good life, cannot overlook.

Two otherwise very different traditions of cultural studies—the more positive "culturalist" tradition associated with the name of Raymond Williams and the critical "culture industry" tradition associated with the Frankfurt School—both emphasize that it is the strict specification of some ensemble of practices, meanings, and values that distinguishes the field of cultural studies from more methodologically individualistic approaches focusing on autonomous works of high art.[15] While these traditions have wrestled with the necessity of a concept of "totality" for anchoring their analyses, it is nonetheless characteristic of cultural studies that it proceeds holistically either by defining culture itself as a total field where forces from disparate realms of life come together, or by bringing cultural artifacts into relationship with influences outside of culture as a merely imagined self-sufficient whole (in fact, the imagined self-sufficiency of science is also an important focus of attack by critical theory[16]). In either case, it is some large inter-relation of logics, rather than one strand in isolation, that grounds cultural studies analyses. Thus, even as Walter Benjamin and Adorno, for example, build their inquiries upon the basis of juxtaposed fragments, rather than assuming the perspective of the whole, their juxtapositions suggest a shattered culture's indexical reference to an unrevealable totality. If Adorno, as we indicated above, ultimately emphasizes the critically negative autonomy of true art, then it is his interest in "false" art that makes him a pioneer in cultural studies, for false culture finds its meaning in what Frederic Jameson has called "the common historical situation" to which Adorno's language always makes "monitory allusion: *the* administered world, *the* institutionalized society, *the* culture industry, *the* damaged subject"[17]—and it is some form of this tendentially unified historical situation that interests cultural studies. Together with Horkheimer in their 1944 study of the "culture industry," Adorno even goes so far as to claim that the culture of modern capitalism functions as "a system which is uniform as a whole and in every part," a uniformity that derives from the "absolute power of capitalism."[18] While the work of Williams more positively emphasizes even everyday culture's moment of "relative autonomy" from other social determinations, he is most interested in what he calls the "'social' definition of culture," rather than the "'ideal' definition" that characterizes culture as a progressive realization of universal values.[19] For Williams, culture indicates a "whole way of life" of a people and its inter-related structures, not simply individual or spontaneous expressions, nor simply its most impersonally universalistic side. It is "the signifying system through which necessarily (though among other means) social order is communicated, reproduced, experienced and explored."[20]

It is to such definitions of culture as part of a broadly understood social order that this study harks—but in our case we presume that the social order finds itself in a radically different "historical situation" than the one to which Adorno alludes. If the impetus behind a cultural studies approach to *socialist* culture is the attempt to identify the "signifying system" that allows the culture to be reproduced both as such—that is, as a unitary, well-ordered culture—and as distinctively socialist, then its task would be misconceived were it to concentrate on socialism only as a movement of resistance, emerging unsystematically from both the capitalist and the . . . what would it be called? non-capitalist? state-capitalist? . . . world. The contention here is that a negative, symbolically focused approach, by excluding the actual historical circumstances of socialist governance from its definition of socialism, is ultimately more confining than the historical-systemic approach I argue for, which moves beyond a primarily symbolic realm to include a correlative world of matter, events, and actions.

3. WESTERN VERSUS EASTERN MARXISM

> "Hate the Germans, kill the Germans"—such was, and is, the slogan of common, i.e., bourgeois, patriotism. But we will say [. . .] "Learn from the Germans!" [. . .] Yes, learn from the Germans! [. . .] The Germans personify, besides a brutal imperialism, the principle of discipline, organization, harmonious co-operation on the basis of modern machine industry, and strict accounting and control. And that is just what we are lacking.
>
> —V. I. Lenin[21]

Even as it identifies and affirms materialist and institutional over utopian impulses in cultural studies, my effort to examine real socialist culture as an element of really existing socialism has to contend with the long-standing hostility of cultural studies' Western Marxist tradition to Eastern Europe as its evil twin whose very existence threatens the critical Western spirit. According to the intellectual historian Martin Jay, the term *Western Marxism* was coined in 1955 by the French phenomenological Marxist Maurice Merleau-Ponty at a key moment of the Cold War to demarcate a critical vantage that "was identified solely with a subterranean tradition of humanist, subjectivist and undogmatic Marxism that was the negation of its official Soviet (or Eastern) counterpart."[22] Even Stuart Hall, a founding figure of the otherwise so ecumenical culturalist Marxist tradition, has commented that the critical Left "has, for decades, been trying to define a socialist alternative which was rooted in a profound and unequivocal repudiation of 'the state socialist model.'"[23] Continuing the moral purism of Western Marxism into the post–Cold War period, much cultural studies scholarship propagates a misplaced anxiety that turns it away from a thorough appraisal of the system of culture that maintained (and was maintained by) the socialist societies of Eastern Europe—namely, the fear of sacrificing the critical and emancipatory goals of socialism (along the lines of Marx's famous call for "a ruthless criticism of everything existing"[24]) to the gray normality of the Eastern bloc. Rather than taking the collapses of 1989 as a chance to assess the programmatic contradictions and errant institutional processes that socialist-identified governance entailed, many left commentators embraced the liberal narrative of 1989 as an occasion for vindicating Western Marxism's anxious Cold War demarcations and disavowals: there was, as they suspected all along, never any there there. Thus, in the immediate aftermath of events, historian Geoff Eley reconceptualized socialism as a force that has not served to realize an enduring program of its own, but historically to moderate the worst excesses of capitalism.[25] Philosopher Richard Rorty suggested that "the time has come to drop the terms 'capitalism' and 'socialism' from the political vocabulary of the left."[26] And sociologist Anthony Giddens declared the "death of socialism," "at least as a system of economic management."[27] Even strictly Marxist-identified scholars such as political economists Stephen Resnick and Richard Wolff, although they do not accept the liberal story, conclude that "the class structure that succeeded and failed in the USSR was a particular form of capitalism and not, as is typically held, a socialism or communism."[28]

If socialism was never socialism, not even for the Left, then revolutions in the wake of World War I and the founding of socialist states in the wake of World War II drop out as significant caesuras in the orienting narratives of the twentieth century. That semantic void does not leave us, however, with a clean slate on which to sketch a coming community. Frederic Jameson argues that "we cannot *not* periodize"—that is, that historical meaning isn't conceptual, but narrative, and as such demands epochs and junctures in order to work.[29] Real socialism, if it ever *was* real, could once contest a unitary story of modernity whose "only satisfactory semantic meaning," according to Jameson, "lies in its association with capitalism."[30] But real socialism's retrospective disqualification from reality is a temporal abandonment that allows twentieth-century history to be structured by other events that still command their loyalists. Even if there is no one "grand narrative" to acclaim or dispute, certain past events are reiterated again and again as inevitable components in the constitution of the present: World War I (rather than its revolutionary aftermaths); the rise of illiberal powers (rather than the Great Depression); the Holocaust as a discrete event (rather than a part of a larger conflagration); the heroic liberation of the camps (rather than the pragmatic Yalta order); the fall of the Berlin Wall (rather than its construction). In such orderings of historical time an entire improbable, but all the more striking, episteme of modernity is written out of the twentieth century. Socialist thought either becomes assimilable as "Western Marxist" criticism of modernity, or is curtly discounted as an illiberal curiosity. Meanwhile, the magnitude of the Holocaust structures a tragic drama—as dominant as it is inevitable—for repeated historical narration, and the dancing on the fallen Berlin Wall becomes the epithalamion ending a comedy we still cannot get enough of, wherein all rivals to liberal modernity are revealed to have been mistaken identities. To the extent, which I believe is wide, that some variation on these historical dramas guides our response to both modernity and aesthetic modernism, one central goal of my argument here is to bring about a dramatic restructuring, not only for its own closed effect, but for the ways in which it might restore socialism to its central meaning in the twentieth century.

To complicate my goals further, the Western Marxist tradition underlying cultural studies not only has been hostile to learning from Eastern European socialism but also harbors deep epistemological reservations about the truth claims of science and political reservations about its specialized technical institutions.[31] Focusing on Eastern European administrative systems as one of the realities of real socialism, however, inevitably brings to the study of socialist culture all the implications of economic plans and their scientific-technical exigencies. It thus requires that one have recourse to critical social thought that is not exclusively "humanist and subjectivist," like Merleau-Ponty's Western Marxism, but that also has scientific and technical epistemological concerns in the ambivalent but relevant tradition of Engels's *Dialectics of Nature*,[32] Lenin's admiration for American Taylorism and Fordism, Trotsky's concern for military strategy and tactics, and the East German social critic Rudolf Bahro's conviction that the coming universal laborer will be the socialist cybernetic engineer.[33] In this sense, the cultural study of sciences, developed by philosophers of science such as Otto Neurath, Thomas Kuhn, Hilary Putnam, and Bruno Latour, opens up aspects of historical socialism to inquiries not hamstrung by hasty dismissals of technical-functional thought. This is particularly important because, as the economist Alec Nove has argued, a feasible socialism is, among other things, a complex technical task that, if it avoids coming to terms with the historical difficulties of Eastern European planned economies, risks its own trivialization. "One *must* discuss what sort of economic problems it is reasonable to expect to encounter in any socialism defined with some reference to real-life possibilities."[34] Because that reference to real-life possibilities, and impossibilities, is the heart of this project, the sort of scientific thought on nonmarket economics exemplified by the Pole Oskar Lange in the 1930s and the Hungarian János Kornai in the 1980s cannot be dismissed out of hand as inimical to utopian Marxism's speculations on the conditions for human autonomy.

By contrast, in *Dialectic of Enlightenment* Horkheimer and Adorno treat science as they treat the culture industry—namely, as indifferently subordinated to the heteronomous laws of instrumental rationality. "Science is not conscious of itself," they lament. "[It] is only a tool."[35] This position is a critical inversion of Karl Popper's affirmative view of science as a republic of individuals subjecting their claims freely to a jury of peers.

Jürgen Habermas, carrying on the Institute for Social Research's general dispute with positivist epistemology, develops a sharp separation between "life world" and "system world" based in the last instance not on historical institutional considerations but on the epistemological distinction between (positivist) empirical-analytic reason and (reflective) dialogic-hermeneutic reason. His argument relies on the epistemological difference between constative, descriptive, and logical thought and thought that is reflective, communicative, and normative: "between fact and norm," as his 1996 case for a discursive theory of legality has it.[36] Locating enlightened liberatory practice in the priority of the latter, he lets this epistemological distinction dominate his historical narrative. There must be a real, historical public sphere, distinct from the sphere of dispersed and saturating power that Michel Foucault calls "governmentality," for Habermas's progressive epistemology to find historical confirmation.[37] This epistemologically driven historiography, however, leads to an overly rigid divide between technical and communicative realms. Where Habermas rescues culture from the lockstep to which Horkheimer and Adorno consigned it, he continues to let science languish in its supposed one-sided unreflectivity.[38] While any cultural study of science must share Habermas's assertion that "a radical critique of knowledge is possible only as social theory,"[39] it is not clear that scientific understanding has not proceeded as a social theory and practice all along, with the same ambivalent subservience and autonomy as communicative culture has had in bourgeois society. For Habermas, however, the natural sciences have followed a path of the increasing desocialization and subordination of the individual to the alienated powers of physical law: reality is disclosed to the sciences only insofar as what is observed further promotes the control of objectified (law-based) processes.[40] In this way, Habermas continues to draw a sharp, qualitative line between culture and the sciences.

An approach that instead starts with empirical institutional differences between cultural and technical realms has a harder time being satisfied with the idealized boundaries of Habermas's approach. Shapin's and Schaffer's celebrated study of the origins of empirical science in *Leviathan and the Air-Pump* suggests that the rise of scientific instrumentalism in the seventeenth century represented a victory of Boyle's decentered communities of experimenters over Hobbes's law-based, a priori reason: a triumph of local, pragmatic epistemology over the sort of sovereign rationality that Adorno and Habermas attribute to "the" administered system world supposedly brought about by the dominance of techno-science.[41] Bruno Latour summarizes what he calls "the most fundamental aspect of our culture, since Boyle's day": "[We] live in communities whose social bond comes from objects fabricated in laboratories; ideas have been replaced by practices, apodeictic reasoning by controlled doxa, and universal agreement by groups of colleagues. The lovely order that Hobbes was trying to recover is annihilated by the multiplication of private spaces where the transcendental origin of facts is proclaimed—facts that have been fabricated by man yet are no one's handiwork, facts that have no causality yet can be explained."[42] Allowing for its controversies, science studies demonstrates how in the emergence of bourgeois modernity the boundaries between science and culture were as little fixed as those between state and civil society or market and policy, and to this extent it need come as no surprise that in socialism's case its cultural works grappled similarly with the boundaries of life and system worlds (to borrow the Habermasian terminology). Indeed, we will see that the socialism our writers are trying to think and feel their way through is closely associated with the new production of uncertain distinctions between official and unofficial, plan and chance, spirit and power, scientific validity and subjective authenticity, system and sovereignty.

Only by coming to grips with the profound difficulty of coordinating material, political, and cognitive interests into a governing alternative (with all the uneasy connotations of system and power that "government" conveys), can we recognize socialism as a living project (with all the uneasy connotations of authenticity and collaboration that "life" conveys). A Western, post-Marxist condescension that does not admit kinship with the leftist aspirations of the socialists who sustained Eastern Europe for a good part of the twentieth century seems opportunistic, rather than analytic. "What has distinguished structuralism and post-structuralism," Perry Anderson has written about the privileged theories of postmodern social critics, "is the extraordinary lability of the political connotations they have successively assumed. This external history is essentially one of passive adaptation to the prevailing fashions and moods of the time."[43] Although the adaptability Anderson diagnoses might be attributable to the social position of the academic more than to a specific philosophical orientation, a poststructuralism that has relinquished Marxist concerns with history, objectivity, system—in some critical form—lacks the realist armature for resisting the liberal market triumphalisms that followed the collapse of socialism in 1989. Jacques Derrida himself has noted that "now that Marxism seems to be in rapid decomposition," the stereotypical response will be to save Marx by arguing that "he doesn't belong to the communists, to the Marxists, to the parties, he ought to figure within our great canon of Western political philosophy. [. . .] This recent stereotype would be destined, whether one wishes it or not, to depoliticize profoundly the *Marxist reference*, to do its best, by putting on a tolerant face, to neutralize a potential force . . ."[44] An assessment of the Eastern European socialist experience (with its communists, Marxists, and parties) aims to restore an important part of this Marxist reference and to illuminate what kind of effort is entailed in conceiving and organizing alternatives on a systematic scale.[45]

4. LIBERALISM UNBOUND: NON-EXISTENCE TRIUMPHANT

> Neither Fascism nor Communism turned out to be the ensign of a providential destiny for humanity. They were merely brief episodes, framed by what they had sought to destroy. Produced by democracy, they were interred by democracy.
>
> —François Furet[46]

Of course, the disappearing reference of the socialist signifier suddenly takes on a whole new dimension in 1989. For all my commitment to connecting theoretical thought about socialism with the historical experience of real socialist states, the rapid collapse of those states into oblivion seems to render moot the issue of their status as either instantiations of true socialism or mere simulacra. The intellectual risk, and pathos, of deciding on this existential status vanishes as abruptly as the concrete socialist referent itself. Who is going to launch a missile over a philosophical question? Going a step further than those socialist idealists who concluded that there was no there there, Derrida sees simply no there, asking, "[Is] there *there*, between the thing itself and its simulacrum, an opposition that holds up?"[47] For Derrida, who denies a stable Platonic distinction between idea and instance that would make a real socialism true or false in the first place, the socialist referent was only a ghost all along, and the events of 1989 merely déjà vu. Nothing is gained or lost when the Wall falls, because what began as a specter haunting Europe and which died countless times over its history, could hardly suffer anything different in 1989 as the much attenuated ghost of a ghost of a ghost. Those who are more skeptical about the existence of ghosts, however, might see a qualitative difference in the fate inflicted in 1989. Whether socialism is a ghost or not, the haunting of *capitalism* ceases; its marginal but persistent "what ifs?" become dull and fade away. Capitalism, in principle as susceptible as socialism to the question of whether it is "the thing itself or its simulacrum," seems to be free of demon doubles. Never a ghost for itself, never suspected of being only a simulacrum of capitalism, really existing capitalism is now no longer haunted by a rival either. Spectral nonidentity turns out to have been a terminal problem only for real socialism, which was always its own scariest ghost. While the stake through socialism's undead heart sent it firmly to the grave, for capitalism it meant only that its gaze in the mirror revealed a fleshier and more robust self.

In the face of capitalism's overwhelming presence, I want to turn to the public discourse around the events of 1989 as a way to understand how such presence, indeed omnipresence, indifferently preempts the possibility of other systems. Reviewing the enthusiasm of the liberal triumph, I mark socialism's true site—here at its ending, but just as well at its beginning—as the point where systemic alterity vanishes; where bourgeois modernity sees itself as an immanent transcendence enveloping any rivalry. In real socialism's demise and the popular declarations that it never really existed, we clearly hear the emphatic use of the existential terminology that grounds this study's ontological thematics. Here, in an informal language of nonexistence—socialism was at best a pipe dream, at worst a nightmare—we get our gut sense of why the question of real socialism is a properly ontological question, a question about the very possibility of being other in general. Even as I have been reviewing contrary emphases in the scholarly traditions of cultural studies and Western Marxism, I find in the more casual public discourse of blanket disqualification the roots of the existential analytic that I will undertake. For now, I highlight this existential vernacular only in the negative, as it closed out the last century's great and horrible social projects in its daily papers, journals, and public speeches. It is the burden of this book—starting in the next chapter—to elaborate a positive ontological sense of socialism . . . by which I certainly do not mean a comfortable affirmation.

I also direct our attention here to the country that is our primary focus, Germany, and to the German Democratic Republic (GDR), a frontline socialist state on the border with the West, commonly held to be the most socialist of the socialist states—whatever that might mean. The first article of the GDR constitution proclaimed it to be "a socialist state within a German nation."[48] Sharing the same nationhood with the Federal Republic (FRG), the GDR's difference from the FRG could be construed in principle only as socialist, not national. Either the GDR is socialist, or "the

GDR never existed," as the playwright Heiner Müller formulated the contempt some of his fellow poets held for the reality of his state's socialist promise.[49] Elsewhere in Eastern Europe overlapping national and socialist boundaries blurred the difference between socialist identity and national tradition, making the specifically socialist difference of those countries harder to discern.[50] With the relatively placid accession of East Germany into a unified Federal Republic in October 1990, the ultimate lack of such a specifically socialist difference seems to have been confirmed with as much experimental clarity as is possible with historical events: there was, it seems, no distinct socialist culture in the GDR—despite cultural distinctions—because there was no real socialism. This negative outcome of one of the twentieth century's most intense experiments in forging an alternative to bourgeois liberalism is abstracted from the moment of the Berlin Wall's collapse and held to confirm not so much the *superiority* of the liberal path into modernity but its *singularity:* liberalism is modernity. Hardly an East German constituency, even among the former ruling elite that had so timorously ceded its power after years of reckless state coercion, showed itself interested in defending really existing socialism as an example of real socialism.[51]

Across the political spectrum there emerged in the 1990s a clear consensus holding the real socialism of the GDR to have been deficient modernity or a simulacrum of an unrealizable Idea—in either case, not to have been real socialism at all. This conviction takes on two general forms: downgrading the experience of the GDR to either a merely *provincial* significance, by which I mean local and particular, or a merely *parochial* one, by which I mean improvised and substandard. The presumed provincialism of GDR culture rests on the claim that its residual value is limited to the particularity of the experiences it represents. In a specifically literary context, Ursula Heukenkamp argues for seeing it harmlessly as a "variant of regionalism in German post-war literature." She holds that "the political connotations vaguely binding the concept GDR literature with the legitimacy of the GDR, its culture, its existence as a subject of international law, etc., must be dissolved." In their place there should be "a regional tailoring of the concept of GDR literature."[52] Even Christa Wolf, herself a cosmopolitan ambassador of GDR culture, suggests that an unthreatening provincialism is all that she cares to defend of it, in which it is reduced to playing an essentially therapeutic role for those unhappy souls who lived on its former territory. "What will become of East Germany's forty years of history[?]" she asks in a 1990 speech. "[W]ho will continue to express openly the grief, shame and remorse which I read in many people's letters and see in their eyes . . . ?"[53] Elsewhere she sees her defense of GDR culture against its critics as "the struggle for dignity in a lost cause," here presumably the dignity of those who had tried and failed to make something of lasting significance out of the GDR—with the cause gone, the personal dignity is all that is left.[54] Karl Heinz Bohrer, one of GDR literature's least sympathetic critics, showed himself scandalized more by the meekness of its provincial self-defense than by its aesthetic failings. His mordant commentary offers the last word on real socialist provincialism as he imagines the absurd spectacle of a "Cultural Protectorate, GDR" (*Kulturschutzgebiet DDR*).[55]

The presumption that GDR culture is parochial in nature, the very "metaphor of walled-in and limited life,"[56] holds that it has lasting merit only to the extent that its isolated conventions tended to converge with those of the West. Otherwise, it represents merely accommodation to the unjustifiable demands of an authoritarian state: "GDR literature is nothing, everything worth anything in literature written in the GDR is not GDR literature, but German, European or world literature."[57] In 1989 Horst Domdey argued that the East German writing that flew in the face of damning empirical evidence in order to represent the GDR as an epoch subsequent and superior to capitalism was a literature of "epochal illusion."[58] Stubbornly imagining that it was operating in a qualitatively different society, this literature only failed to grasp the reality of the society's epochal sameness. To paraphrase Benedict Anderson, GDR literature represented an imagined community that turns out to have been merely an epochal illusion—an imagined community that had no business imagining itself as such.[59] But once the epochal illusion is exploded, the supposed epochal continuity of the GDR with the West becomes a default position that itself goes too far for Habermas, who sees such equivalency as "*dangerously* false," since it grants too much epochal legitimacy to the GDR. Thus, in a 1991 letter to Christa Wolf, Habermas insists that bourgeois liberalism is (and was in 1945) the only progressive social form available to post-Fascist Germany. Against those who would take 1989 as an occasion for reassessing the cultural epoch of two Germanys, he argues that there was no symmetry between the FRG's affiliation with the "universalistic, enlightening and subversive features" of the West and the GDR's with the "inhuman praxis" of the East. Real socialism had no rational social mission; it was not a historically equivalent "alternative," but rationally delusive.[60]

When the Wall fell, this GDR parochialism was supposedly swept away at last by a Western "system of accountability." In terms reminiscent of

Marx's description of Napoleon heroically tearing away the antiquated remnants of feudalism, legal anthropologist John Borneman writes that the restructuring of socialist legality "is part of a larger transcontinental process of transformation that is redefining the nature of all political communities, creating rules for accountability and membership as well as new categories of victims and criminals."[61] This transformation depends on relinquishing the "socialist state" enshrined in Article 1 of the GDR constitution in favor of the notion of individual "dignity" enshrined in Article 1 of the FRG constitution—"the dignity of man shall be inviolable." Indeed, the role of a unified Germany becomes nothing less than "to implement a moral world" in an old GDR where there used to be only a narrow society of niches (*Nischengesellschaft*).[62] Borneman sees "an implicit trust in the *Rechtsstaat* as providing the framework in which to experience [one's] freedoms."[63] In keeping with this stipulation of a unique liberal framework for experiencing freedom, the influential literary critic Frank Schirrmacher argued in his 1990 article launching the famous "literary debate" (*Literaturstreit*) downgrading the reputation of Christa Wolf and GDR literature generally, that "Wolf, it seems, has only been able to reflect on GDR society, on the system, its incapacity for freedom and right, in the sentimental categories of a private crisis in a relationship."[64] In other words, her novels provided no narrative categories through which her GDR readers might have experienced, even if only in their imaginations, freedom. Schirrmacher's terms for what the GDR lacked, freedom (*Freiheit*) and right (*Recht*), are, however, the slogans of a procedural liberalism that did not inspire the GDR legal order, such as it was. Instead, the GDR order appealed, through Marx, to the communitarianism of Hegel's *Philosophy of Right*, where "the good," defined with reference to the totality of social relations (*der sittliche Staat*), supplies normative criteria over "the right" (*das abstrakte Recht*).[65] In this sense, Schirrmacher's diagnosis of Wolf, rather than characterizing the ethical experiences she might be drawing on, simply marks her, with reference to the liberal tradition, as ethically deficient.

While a literary critic like Schirrmacher is under no constraint not to retroactively revise his standards, he shares with the post-Wall judicial system a common ontological prejudice regarding the order that in fact (and for better or worse) existed in the GDR. "No country has insisted so much on using criminal law to cope with its communist past as Germany," noted the best-selling author and jurist Bernhard Schlink in 1994.[66] Contrary to Borneman, Schlink believes that Germany's "enthusiasm for penal law" short-circuits the very rule of law it claims to uphold. "The concept of law that uses criminal jurisdiction to paper over the prohibition against retroactive application of the law is incompatible with the rule of law [*Rechtsstaat*]. To apply what ought to be recognized and practiced as law instead of what is [in fact] recognized and practiced deprives the concept of law of an essential dimension: reality."[67] With little or no desire to imagine what the integrity and consistency underlying the GDR order had been, the broad post-Wall reaction to the order's failure can make no sense of the real socialist experience. Nor, for that matter, can it grasp, as did the best GDR writers, the order's consummate *nonsense*—contenting itself instead with attitudes of righteousness, nostalgia, or pity.

While there is no monolithic liberal position represented by German commentators in the aftermath of the Cold War, there is a near negative unity to the shades of difference: socialism's claim to have represented an alternative to capitalism is deception at best, if not something more sinister. GDR socialism turns out to have been an unworkable construction whose most concrete historical realization was a type of Marxist fundamentalist state nominally functioning under utopian principles: "a country with a rotten economy, with a decrepit public vernacular, with cities whose historic districts resemble American slums, and with a falsity in public pronouncements that has long crossed over into ridiculousness," as the author Monica Maron put it in her popular *Du* magazine column in 1989.[68] The phrase "really existing socialism" is either a contradiction in terms or implies a system that, qualified by the demands of its real existence, is not really socialism. Hence, the presumed thinness of the socialist label's reference: if the "social totality" of the GDR was given by a narrowly self-perpetuating totalitarian rule, then one searched in vain for the wealth of systemic correlates that a real socialism could be expected to generate. Beyond the hieratic Marxist ideology there was no technical, moral, aesthetic language for socialism; rather, GDR citizens had only the "anachronism of their own existence."[69]

In his renowned "Theses on the Philosophy of History," Benjamin commented that "only a redeemed mankind receives the fullness of its past—which is to say, only for a redeemed mankind has the past become citable in all its moments."[70] Although Benjamin's thesis more readily suggests that modesty is called for in judging the socialist era than that the turning point of 1989 was a redemption of socialism's guilty past, the latter reading accurately indicates the millennial, "end of history" presumptions common to most commentators of the collapse. Liberalism's victory over socialism has given it the right to cite socialism's moments as finished episodes and read its literature as the dead letters of false prophets. When the border between

East and West disappeared as a material institutional phenomenon (when it disappeared ontically, so to speak), it disappeared also as a meaningful alternative (that is, it disappeared ontologically). Empirical evidence of collapse became in this moment something else—the *revelation* of the truth of liberal categories beyond any partisan commitment or engagement. "If we'd read it a year ago in some Western tabloid," admitted the novelist Peter Schneider in *Die Zeit* in 1990 of the mass of discrediting revelations about socialism, "we'd have dismissed it as witch-hunting."[71] But after the Wall, the news simply expressed the gospel of liberalism's redemption. Its triumph finally resolved the historical anxiety over whether socialism might not have somehow supplied alternate normative criteria for the ideal society. "Mightn't one get the suspicion these days that history itself had decided the contest between socialism and capitalism and declared the latter the victor? And that this victor now speaks to us from up on Mount Sinai: you shall have no other economic system before me!?"[72]

This apotheosis of capitalism, however, finally marks the limit that I want to concentrate on—namely, the limit or boundary that all systems have by virtue of their very coherency. "Systems have boundaries," notes the systems theorist Niklas Luhmann. "This is what distinguishes the concept of system from that of structure."[73] In this sense, the revealed liberalism of the post–Cold War does not see itself as a distinct system, but as a timeless structure, a template for the single global logic at the end of history, whereas socialism, even in its most universal evangelical, most Pauline aspects, conceives itself as a specific system involved in producing its closure. A system can never constitute itself solipsistically, observing only the existential fact of its boundary, because it cannot finally decide whether the boundary belongs inside the system or outside. Real socialism, haunted by its violent, unpredictable emergence after World War I, remained preoccupied throughout its history with its unresolved process of demarcation. One of its most distinguishing characteristics was, in fact, just this anxious production of self-distinction from its world-historical rival.[74] Even the supremely confident Lenin, for example, uneasily apologized for an apparent similarity stubbornly persisting in the socialist difference: "[U]nder communism there remains for a time not only bourgeois right, but even the bourgeois state, without the bourgeoisie! [. . .] In fact, remnants of the old, surviving in the new, confront us in life at every step, both in nature and in society."[75] Meanwhile, capitalism is not concerned with making itself distinct from socialism, but with denying its supposed rival any "difference that makes a difference."[76] From the liberal point of view, real socialism was a failed attempt at modernity with no ontological weight or philosophical significance beyond that of negative experimental results: it was a classic Platonic simulacrum. If, however, it is reasonable to suppose that all systems have boundaries, then at the very point where liberal capitalism has lost its sovereign and self-proclaimed antagonist, *there* the empirical question of its proper boundary opens up again, as does also the more impassioned question whether, from some other side of it, liberal capitalism might itself appear to be a simulacrum of a true order—an order even better than it; maybe, even, the best order of all.

CHAPTER TWO

Other Systems: Mud, Mana, Money

So the century, between 1917 and the end of the seventies, is in no way—as today's liberals claim—the century of ideology, of the imaginary or of utopia. Its subjective determination is a Leninist one. It is the passion for the real, for what is immediately practicable, here and now.

—Alain Badiou[1]

INTRODUCTION TO A METHOD

While the downward revision in socialism's meaning—its depotentialization as a "practical utopia," in Karl Mannheim's phrase[2]—has been the rule since the end of the Cold War, I argue to the contrary that socialism remains to be understood on its own ontological terms. These terms, however, are not readily available on the face of things as a standard for assessing socialism's potential. Although part of the problem I have been diagnosing with the post–Cold War consensus on socialism is its misrecognition of the object whose death it anatomizes as either deficient modernity or a simulacrum of an unrealizable Idea, it would be inappropriate to turn around and insist on the basis of an impervious Marxist orthodoxy that this moribund object, real socialism, has an immortal kernel that transcends the historical moment of the Eastern European collapse. To do so would be to confirm the very suspicion that Badiou is at pains to deny in my epigraph—namely, that the past socialist century was an ideological one in which great significance was claimed for things having little meaning beyond those arbitrary claims themselves, rather than a century that, as Badiou holds, was preoccupied by the full potential of its actual present.[3]

Even as we resolve to begin with the really existing things of socialism themselves, we do so *without* their measure or quality, considering them not as neat "reflections" of a socialist context, but as brute pieces left over from an era when socialism was still enacted as a will, desire, and determination. "I was and am," Heiner Müller noted frankly in a 1993 interview, "a piece of GDR-history."[4] Such lives and their works (that is, their wills, desires, and determinations) are the authentic Mars rocks, the fragments of the Red Planet directing us toward a rigorous conception of the whole. To analyze these Mars rocks without presuming familiarity with Martian geology (areology)—to let them emerge as their own best measure—I start with a premise strong enough to support a vision of an alternate whole and agnostic enough to avoid prejudicing our grasp of it. The premise of my analysis is broadly and simply that *other systems exist*. This premise provisionally suspends a commitment to pointing to what its ultimate reference is—*some this!* (τοδε τι or *hoc aliquid*) in the Aristotelian tradition. While the question of what socialism is cannot be settled except with reference to the distinct system of relations composing a socialist whole in time, we need to allow ourselves room to understand *how* cultural works come to refer to such a systemic whole, which, after all, seems to be out of the range of anyone's immediate perception. Without ignoring the question of the whole, then, I want to emphasize our concern with the idea of reference to it. The question Did socialism really exist in the Eastern bloc countries? is inseparable from the question What sensible thing or event do we refer to when we call it socialist?

Since "existence" and "reference" lie at the heart of our project to grasp socialism in its historical specificity and ontological generality, this chapter's agenda is, accordingly, to trace a workable understanding of *how* really existing socialism is referred to. It is, to be sure, a large agenda that takes us on some remarkable twists and turns in our efforts to bring some order to it. A wide range of elements come together—for real socialism covers a wide range of phenomena—so the reader is encouraged to bear with the chapter's abstraction. Its crucial points are elaborated and emphasized in the next chapter, where I relate them more specifically to the literature of real socialism and the case of Franz Fühmann. In the larger, second part of the book, I then reverse the order of motivation—instead of overall theoretical coherence driving the presentation, the presentation is driven by the patchwork of details, sometimes baroque, sometimes banal, that emerge cumulatively to give, I hope, a better understanding of what real socialism is.

So we do not get lost along the way, I start with a survey of the chapter.

(1) Our agenda opens at a *locus classicus* of ontological thought, an exchange from Plato's dialogue *Parmenides* in which Socrates and Parmenides discuss whether all actually existing things can be said to partake in a more

fundamental kind of being, or whether there are a bunch of phenomena that are too unimportant to participate in a grander scheme and so are left out of order altogether. I compare this classical exchange about "mud, dirt, and hair" with later discussions about the status of the divine emanation called mana, something that seems their opposite in all existential respects. By juxtaposing mud and mana, I establish a way of taking up a classical regression paradox known as the "Third Man Argument": how do actual things participate in a general essence, and conversely, how does a general essence find its instantiations in the actual world? What mediates between the one and the many? On what grounds can we compare a real man with the idea of Man—on the basis of some third kind of Man-ness (perhaps the New Man)? This search for a ground to commensurability is so urgent for us because our goal here is to understand limited, abject, even objectionable, real socialism in the aspect of its most general significance—socialism as neither a flawed individual thing nor a flawless Idea beyond all time and place. If socialism is a general, even universal entity, it is nonetheless so in a historical and functional sense.

(2) My approach to the perplexity of regressing comparative thirds relies on an idea of systems to bring some sense to it, and I give here an initial conceptualization of what I mean by systems ontology, introducing such key terms as medium, element, relation, and equilibrium. This conception of systems takes us from a classical focus on existence to a modern focus on reference, as I consider how a medium gives us its elements and relations. Medium makes its appearance, then, not as a third thing like the Platonic idea, but as the mode in which a system is given. The more we explore the identity of medium and system, however, the more we understand the multiple aspects of such an identity as both an emergent (but incomplete) whole and a self-divided part. To make this multiplicity clear I emphasize not only the symbolic properties of system mediation, in which a world is given through continuous interpretation, but also the referential properties. In this latter sense, a system not only mediates its own immanent identity but also prepares encounters with incommensurable and unrelated things, laying the ground for the cycle of action and reaction that gives it its distinct and contestable quality as a living world. Here my concern is less relationality, understood as the internal production of a third term between two elements, than it is indexicality, understood as a direct encounter between two unrelated things. The term *indexicality*, given its philosophical underpinning by C. S. Peirce, helps formalize our inquiry into how media refer.

(3) At this point, however, after I've set out a basic systems apparatus for

discussing existence and reference, I clarify our project by distinction from what I called in the Introduction "the return of the political," an influential revival of ontological discussion around an assertion of primacy for the category of "the political." My goal here is twofold. First, it is to underscore my concern with reference, encounters, pragmatics—in short, with a special kind of empirical orientation. It is my contention that political ontology overestimates the role of subjectivity, whereas what I emphasize is the continuous creation of subject-object encounters: that political actors are called upon to react appropriately, objectively, to the situations they help foster (or even just find themselves in). Second, I aim to introduce a crucial distinction in the idea of medium, a distinction related to the subject-object divide I just mentioned. I contend that political ontology sees its world on the model of figurative language, which is a medium—and, if you will, a system—with minimal structure and constraint. Figurative language is a generous and creative model for the world, especially in language's wide poetic and rhetorical capacity to name things as it sees fit. My view is perhaps not so generous, emphasizing media that function less as tools of creative subjectivity, but are more equally divided in their capacity as expressive and impressionable. Media are not only symbolic, in the sense of signs circulated by and for interpreters, but are also indexical, in the sense of unambiguously conveying the world's hard boundaries to its inhabitants, boundaries that form around the real things that one might encounter. An example that I explore in detail, since it introduces us more specifically into our discussion of real socialism, is money.

(4) Money is a medium whose workings are considerably more restrictive than those of symbolic language. It circulates, evaluates, and provides users with a sense of identity, but no one would confuse its unforgiving idiom with that of expressive discourse. It is more rigid, more constraining, and, for most people, far less plentiful. Money exchanges are not in principle reciprocal, but involve one participant giving it away and another accepting it—in this sense money is a particularly disciplining medium. In this chapter section, I take us through several versions of "the economic" that are mediated by money, especially the first mathematized version, known as marginal utility, or General Equilibrium theory. I pursue the discussion of money as an economic medium in some detail because it both introduces us to the crucial role of economics in socialism and returns us, by way of a close inspection of medium and reference, to our ontological questions and in particular to the question of whether socialism exists as economy or something else. For it seems that, in the various influential ac-

counts of what makes economy possible, we are faced with an ontological relativity that does not allow for very satisfactory judgment on what economy consists of. In a nutshell, the problem is that socialism has no obvious medium like money and private property in the capitalist system—so how, and to what, do we point to ascertain its reality?

(5) The issue of a specifically socialist economy leads us to the chapter's final segment, where I again rely on elements of the analytical tradition, from Peirce and Neurath to Quine and Putnam, to discuss the way system reference addresses the difficulty of "ontological relativity." This tradition queries what real things our various media commit us to behaving toward as though they exist; asking what really exists by way of how existence is practically and meaningfully referred to. The issues are seen here to involve pointing—the indexical gesture—but not just pointing in the punctual sense of my own limited "here and now," but rather how pointing implicates us in the greater world we are pointing at as a world that points back to us with its laws, loves, and leaders, with bread loaves and lime pits, natural landscapes and mechanical legacies. With the juxtaposition and relation of discrepant things outside of us (as discrepant as mud and mana), there also comes a range of mindsets within each of us, from that of automatic reflex to that of wild initiative, from utter contempt to joyous commitment. This range, a recurrent topic of our later literary analyses, appears here with an invocation of a few modest signs of socialist life.

1. MUD AND MANA: ONTOLOGY AS THE GROUND OF REFERENCE

If we want to talk about socialism in this day and age, we are immediately confronted by the problem that there is little agreement about what it is we are talking about. Because the determination of socialists—and I mean "determination" in the sense of both a determined will and a determinate specification—has no social organization governing it, socialism, if it means anything at all, does so only in an extremely abstract sense. Already that abstraction, that privation, contradicts what we would expect socialism to mean—namely, something we perceive in everyday life as a vindicating force against the alienation, exploitation, and inequality of capitalism. But exactly such a clear everyday meaning for socialism is lacking; or, to put it in our philosophical idiom, there is precious little ontological commitment to the reference of the term *socialism*.

What do I mean by "ontological commitment," a phrase borrowed from the analytical philosopher W. v. O. Quine?[5] The force of shared discursive assumptions in everyday life stems not only from the wide currency of their terms but also from the practical self-evidence of the objects and actions to which they refer in our mutual world, what we might call their *apodixis* or *evidentia*, their showing forth in common sense. Whether we are talking about something so abstract as the cube root of 2 or so concrete as a vampire, we have a reasonable sense of the use of the words in our transactions, analyses, narratives, or conversations. Confronted with a vampire we might disbelieve, willingly suspend disbelief, or, simply astonished, pound a stake through its heart. Whatever the case, we are fairly confident in our manipulations of the monster, and for that reason the word and beast maintain their prevalence among us. We have a sense, that is, of the ontological commitments of our vampire stories, knowing from their practical context more or less when they are gothic tales or jokes or piercing metaphors for everyday consumer society, and we behave accordingly. Quine's argument is that a given unified expression—the winged horse Pegasus in his example—need not have a direct objective reference to be meaningful. Rather, the question of reference can be deferred until we have adequately paraphrased the expression in its context as an "incomplete symbol," thus giving it "its full quota of meaning."[6] Satisfying the question of reference is then a matter of provisionally entertaining provisional symbols in context to see which have objective correlates and which do not. Speaking of vampires, then, does not ontologically commit us to the real existence of the blood-sucking undead—rather, we commit to their objective reference only once we have satisfied ourselves that the incomplete vampire symbol can be contextualized (or paraphrased) to mean, for example, a bloodthirsty exploiter of human desire, which we are all too likely to find in the real world.

Adding Wittgenstein's voice to Quine's, we might say that being ontologically committed is confidently playing a "language game," which Wittgenstein defines as "the whole, consisting of language and the actions into which it is woven."[7] We do not have that confidence when it comes to the stories of real socialism. In spite of the ban Marx cast on the "specter" of communism, the ghosts of historical socialism remain more troubling than the vampires of Transylvania. Was socialism sheer fantasy, was it an experience of deep solidarity, or was it merely the senseless endurance of consumer deprivation and Stasi surveillance? To answer these questions the first thing we need to do is to translate the ontologically contested concept *socialism* into an open-ended description; or more exactly, to take socialist literature as such a description, and analyze the distinct, if unsettled, life form in which that ongoing description tested itself. As Wittgenstein put it, "[To] imagine a language means to imagine a form of life."[8]

But I am getting ahead of myself. I want to take a little more time to clarify why Quine's expansion of the relevant unit of reference from a word, like *socialism*, to a larger analytical unit, like East German literature, is so important for our ontological discussion about what we are talking about when we talk about socialism, and to do that I need to go back to a very old question in ontology. What I want to argue, by way of a Platonic discussion about hair, mud, and dirt, is that trivial things do indeed have their "form" or "idea," that the mundane world of queuing and spying does have its order and system—in fact, these abject things are what will save us from the regress of abstraction in the same measure that the regress of abstraction saves us from their abjection. Nothing, not even dirt, tends to be left out of the grand idea, but this overarching drive to inclusion is checked against the last, stubborn trivialities it meets. The all encompassing idea I am speaking of reveals itself as not a timeless, static concept, but a pragmatic system: a system gives us our mud as surely as it gives us our statespeople. But let us step back to the fundamentals.

"Are you also puzzled, Socrates," asks his archrival Parmenides, "about cases that might be thought absurd, such as hair or mud or dirt or any other trivial and undignified objects? Are you doubtful whether or not to assert that each of these has a separate form [*eidos*] distinct from things like those we handle?" This is a momentous question, because if Socrates accepts that such undignified objects have forms, he risks making the form world simply a double of the temporal world, too rich in entities, and so of no help in discriminating, categorizing, and ranking according to importance or universality. Too rich, but also too poor, since as a double, the form world shares all of the confusion, but none of the actuality, of the temporal world. With this in mind, Socrates denies undignified objects a form. "In these cases, the things are just the things we see; it would surely be too absurd to suppose that they have a form."[9] Here, the proverbial idealist Socrates retreats into a simple positivism: hair, dirt, and mud belong to a nominalist world, where things have no concepts, but are there as positively and accidentally as the singular names we give them. There are no general categories of properties, no predicates to which mud can be subordinated; rather, mud is there, right where I in each instance point, coextensive with my gesture.

The problem with such tactical positivism is clear—it preserves the august order of Platonic forms by ignoring great swaths of the empirical world, leaving our sensual experience to languish in anarchy and abjection—in a sense, denying us, at least us unwashed, access to ideational heaven (the cosmic Politburo). Of course, in the bigger picture Socrates is emphatically not a nominalist, but here, where Parmenides forces him into a corner, he recognizes nominalism's challenge to the universal scope of conceptual thought. To get a better sense of this challenge, we might consider a modern rejoinder to nominalism's perceived over-reaching: Horkheimer's and Adorno's *Dialectic of Enlightenment*, a work dedicated to criticizing the way nominalism fosters an indifferently atomized world of punctual identities.

Horkheimer and Adorno regard the encroachment of trivial stuff that, like God and Popeye, is what it is—that is, self-contained and self-identical, without form or development—as an assault on the open potential of being human. They witness this assault in the decline of once-sovereign mana, an originally Oceanic concept designating the primitive force or substance of all wonder. They argue that when mana was named in the course of humanity's emergence from myth into enlightenment, it lost its unspecifiable power as divine emanation and became subjected to the tautological nominalism of the self-identical concept. "As a nominalist movement, the Enlightenment calls a halt before the *nomen*, the exclusive, precise concept, the proper name," they contend. "Unidentified, volatile *mana* was rendered consistent by men and forcibly materialized."[10] For the sake of functionalism's vulgar reification of the "things we handle," sacred mana is reduced to the individual positivity of mud.

If in the *Parmenides* we saw the idealist Socrates resorting to materialism, here in the *Dialectic of Enlightenment* we see the materialists Horkheimer and Adorno resorting to idealism. We might be tempted to accept their respective ambivalences, and let mana and mud each be what they were meant to be: let mud besmirch our shoes and mana lift our souls in wonder. The trouble with such dualism, however, is that the world loses all ground for rational mediation. We have the pure immanence of mud and the pure transcendence of mana and never the ontological twain shall meet; without any *encounter*, then, how do we decide when one thing belongs on one side and another on the other? As I indicated above, the problem of understanding how a general category can come to mediate the many particular elements of the world is known as the Third Man Argument. In a nutshell, the argument, first made in Plato's *Parmenides* but elaborated by Aristotle in the *Metaphysics*, says that every general measure—assuming that the measure resembles itself (that is, that a standard of a yard is itself a yard, or a paragon of mankind is himself a man)—must be measured against some standard in turn. Each thing, even the most abstract, must meet its measure. The implication, then, is that the measure of the measure, the form of the form, is always pushed out to a more general standard capable of subsuming both the particular being measured and the measuring rod taking its measure. This ever receding and repeating measure of the measure is the guarantee that things are what they are, and yet this guarantee—an unchanging Platonic *eidos* at the end—seems unattainable.

With the regressive structure of the Third Man Argument in the back of our minds, let us return to mud and mana. Our challenge is to find a standard for measuring a shared world while letting this standard be mortal and everyday enough that it may also participate in the changeable nature of really existing things. Plato's forms seem to imply a second, ideal world, apart from the world of change, that we can reach only through arduous philosophical abstraction. Meanwhile, the world of everyday things, the very things we would like to assemble into a commensurable whole, recedes ever further from our increasingly abstract measure. Horkheimer's and Adorno's Critical Theory worries less about the regress of forms per se, than that any formal stabilization at all—especially as devised in modern set theory and logical positivism—saves us from regress only by denying us our potential for change. For Critical Theory, standardization means the standardization wrought by commodity production, which locks everything into its proper slot, achieving a meaningless universality on the terms of deathless Capital. What Horkheimer and Adorno aspire to with their invocation of mana's wonder is a world in which a moving target, an unfixable other, liberates, rather than regulates, our banal things from abject facticity.

Socrates and Critical Theory share a common dread of the self-identical particular, the dumb mud that resists both the enduring elevation of forms and the resourceful flexibility of mana. Where they differ is in Critical Theory's desire for a changeable ontology, resistant to the remoteness built into the regress of Platonic forms. My reason for devising this particular contrast between Platonic formal ontology and Critical Theory's antipositivism is that the elusive concept of mana, with its simultaneous echoes of Platonic *eidos*, vitalistic élan, and political sovereignty, is such an effective touchstone for demonstrating a shared ontological disdain for particular individual things while distinguishing between strategies for escaping their supposedly suffocating positivity—strategies pointing us away from what matters most in our analysis: really existing socialism. *Mana*, moreover, is a term that conveniently, if accidentally, forms a link between thinkers such as Adorno, Claude Lévi-Strauss, and Derrida, all of whom figure prominently in the twentieth century's "reversal of Platonism," a reversal whose roots in Nietzsche pit the defuse power of life against the baleful constraints of formal order.[11]

Citing Lévi-Strauss's research on mana, Derrida argues that the entire course of metaphysics since Plato is disrupted at the moment when "the structurality of structure had to begin to be thought, that is to say, repeated."[12] This thought of the iterative, infinitely substituting "structurality of structure"—modern reflexivity par excellence—in fact canonizes the circular regress of the Third Man Argument not as a devastating critique of ontology but as ontology's very presupposition. Ontology "henceforth" is less the search for the final grounds of cosmic order, and more the tracing out of how philosophy—and ethnography, sociology, and psychology—are each themselves mythopoetical discourses creating their own "reference myths." Ontology becomes the discourse of the dissemination of discourse without end. What would be in that end place, that distant horizon of orientation, is something like mana; but unlike Plato's crystalline *eidos*, mana, as Horkheimer and Adorno indicate, has no fixity, no final status, no ultimate being. Lévi-Strauss simply notes that "the notion of mana does not belong to the order of the real, but to the order of thinking, which, even when it thinks itself, only ever thinks an object."[13] In other words, ontological thought recognizes itself in mana when it grasps mana as no separate entity, but as a thought whose universality consists in its very absence or emptiness, like the empty slot in a sliding tile puzzle that allows all the other pieces to move. Mana is an empty signifier available for various objects to occupy its pivotal spot. "I see in *mana*," Lévi-Strauss continues, "the conscious expression of a *semantic function*, whose role is to permit symbolic thought to operate despite the contradiction inherent in it . . . [f]orce and action, quality and state, substantive, adjective and verb at once; abstract and concrete; omnipresent and localized. And, indeed, mana is all those things together; but is that not precisely because it is none of those things, but a simple form, or to be more accurate, a symbol in its pure state, therefore liable to take on any symbolic content whatever?"[14]

The idea that the ontological regulator is not something frightfully remote, but nothing, only a blank spot, the empty symbol, the measure without any measure, is the idea Derrida canonizes as guiding metaphysics after

Plato. Rather than letting myself be derailed by an extensive engagement with this postmetaphysical tradition, let me juxtapose an unglamorous alternative, associated with an Aristotelian tradition extending to pragmatist thinkers such as Peirce and Quine—namely, that the ontological regulator is *some*thing, not nothing. Lest this something seem too much like a return to old-fashioned ontological substance (*ousia*), let me characterize—in the spirit of Lévis-Strauss's and Derrida's emphasis on mana as a sign—this something also as a sign, albeit a kind of nonsymbolic sign. It is, in our account, an "index," which, unlike the disseminating symbol, confronts us immediately, suddenly as a brute fact.

To clarify the indexical function I intend, I return to Quine, who gives us a workable way to address the paradox of ontological regression first named by the Third Man Argument. Modern-day mana resolves the problem of iteration and repetition by embracing it: the ontological structure of the world is simply incomplete—it is a symbolic circulation, a dissemination without direction or truth. Quine's solution, however, allows for incompleteness while preserving some idea of direction, of a *status nascendi*, or becoming, that as incomplete as it is, for that very reason allows the referential truth of a whole. In short, where mana resolves the problem of regress by emphasizing how the world circulates essentially as figurative language, Quine resolves the problem by pointing at the world as it appears in some one iteration, vast as it is, or another.

Earthly mud, with its tendency to get on our shoes, and heavenly mana, with its sovereign aura, are each things that might or might not *be* in our world. Despite this ontological ambiguity, we refer to them quite blithely in a single discourse. For a "linguistically turned," discursive view of being, that way of discussing might be enough, the full story of our irreducible ontological relativity. For Quine, however, and for us, the complication arises when we want to compare several things from the empirical world of our perceptions to see if they really are mana or mud, and to distinguish one from the other.[15] How, in the case of comparing two things whose referential qualities are unrelated and hard to assess, can we avoid ontological confusion and find a suitable medium for a comparison—for an encounter—even one that issues in a rejection of the reality of one or both of its two terms?[16]

The problem is that we do not want to be prematurely forced into a punctual literalism that identifies mana (or mud) as one thing and one thing only—or as nothing, in which case our use of the word has been otiose. Rather, the challenge is to preserve the vast robustness of the discourse on mana in its holistic possibilities of meaning; and to do so without having to commit in advance to the existence of mana in a naively positivistic sense. Our test of mana and mud—say we want to see which is more volatile in some context—makes use of what logicians call "bound variables" or "quantifiers." These devices, by binding us to an appropriate context, allow us to mediate the differences between our terms.[17] The discourse that gives us *mana*, whatever that might be, is considered a variable function over real quantities of stuff in a given context "out there." If we can find some value out there that satisfies the referential function *mana*, then we can commit ourselves to the existence of one or another entity (that is, to *some*thing) described by our extended (but always unfinished) discourse on mana. We can then see how some mana stacks up against some mud.[18] If it turns out that we find no relevant values to the discursive variable *mana*, we can still tell our stories about it, though without yet making an effective commitment to its existence.[19]

The use of quantifiers enables us to refer effectively to our world and the relations between its contents, without forcing us exhaustively to determine each element in itself as a complete identity. In other words, the infinite qualitative diversity and uniqueness of the world is brought into quantitative homogeneity by our medium of comparison, but only provisionally, in the limited sense determined by that medium. Should we later refine our effective descriptions (refine the relevant values of our mana-function), then we would find and compare other quantities of stuff. Quine puts the case for quantifiers this way: "[T]he seeming name, a descriptive phrase, is paraphrased *in context* as a so-called incomplete symbol. No unified expression is offered as an analysis of the descriptive phrase, but the statement as a whole which was the context of that phrase still gets its full quota of meaning—whether true or false."[20]

Despite the Enlightenment positivism that Horkheimer and Adorno believe reifies modern humanity, Quine thinks that we can decline to close off our discourse about mana with a unified, exclusive, and precise concept. Rather, we can let our discourse extend into infinity, only asking that we have a relevant paraphrase for practical "materialization," or, what amounts to the same thing, commensurable "quantification." This quantification (mana identified as *some* thing) permits us to ask empirical questions about functional, experienceable systems. But because the quantifying paraphrase is provisional, our empirical conclusions are never one-way streets: either we have shown something about reality or we have shown something about the (in)adequacy of our paraphrase of the mana discourse. Our empirical assessment can neither prove something positively about mana nor falsify our claims (as per Karl Popper); rather, we must always discursively adjudicate an equilibrium between our ongoing discourse and our ongoing sensual tribunal.

2. SYSTEMS ONTOLOGY: PRIVATIVE AND PARTITIVE

If I risk being misunderstood in the previous section as suggesting a semantic solution to the ontological problem of our unlikely encounter between mud and mana, then let me forestall that confusion by emphasizing why I have been using the word *medium* rather than *language* in my version of Quine. As I briefly mentioned, whereas a medium—our story's mana, if you will, the elusive quantity that gives us our system—does consist of signs, it consists of signs especially in their operational capacity as indexes, as forceful markers of limits, boundaries, separations, and that indexical power distinguishes our account from one like Derrida's that emphasizes dissemination, circulation, and indeterminacy. Moreover, Quine's affirmation of universal and existential quantifiers bound to a given semantic context interests us for its demonstration of how a medium picks out—and, for all intents and purposes, also *creates*—positive quantities of real entities that confront us in the world as things to which we must react. Only, and this is a crucial point, the entities so created exist not in this or that conversation or expression, but in the entirety of a given medium's universe.

Unlike language in the sense of a figurative, expressive medium, then, the sense of medium I underscore is that which gives us an extended operative system. Medium is not (to begin with) some third thing distinct from system, but is the way a system comes into being as a unity of difference. To mention some relevant cases such as money, law, and police enforcement—but also figurative language—these media both express socialism and make socialism what it is. They are distinct elements of socialism only to the extent that they themselves separate out socialism's distinct somethings—that is, to the extent that they give a functional unity to a functional unity. Let us then, without further ado, fold the concept of medium I have been elaborating into a fuller account of a systems ontology. This latter account will give us the additional terms we need to make sure we are talking about socialism not in a semantic, but an ontological idiom. In other words, they will keep our discussion on track as concerning not what real socialism "said about itself," but what real socialism really *is*.

The idea of a system is in some respects similar to the "disrupted" idea of a structure, but a system also comprehends the temporal dynamic between structures of continuity and agents of change that structuralism neglected.[21] As I underscored at the end of the last chapter, a system, unlike a structure, always has a boundary—it is not an amorphous field of unconstrained analogies, but, existing in limited time and space, it has beginnings and endings. It is also, as our discussion of Quine hints, never in a completed state of self-identity, but always lacks the final equilibrium that it is up to our continuing activity to foster. It is only through such participation that a system tends toward a stable balance between individual units and overall unity as they reproduce themselves and their interactions as an evolving identity through time. Because a system's regulative terms are also its observational terms, a system determines what counts as information about itself. Knowing and being are thus reciprocal actions of systems creation, where being does not imply some way things exist "in themselves," but how they exist to be identified and used by an actor/observer who is an element inside the system. Being is thus always mediated by meaning; in other words, a system only emerges where there is a medium in which it can observe, describe, understand, and choose to reproduce itself as itself.[22]

Such recursive systems are familiar from biology not only in presenting basic life-forms but also in presenting whole evolutionary ecologies. Computer science designates steered environments and artificial intelligence in similar terms, using the language of cybernetics to refer to constructive feedback loops. While such parallels are suggestive, and will be taken up at different points later in the book, here I want to keep our focus on the vocabulary of classical ontology, especially as it contends with two enduring paradoxes of ontological thought: the singular versus the multiple, and change versus stasis. To that end, I want to develop some crucial characteristics of systems with reference to Aristotle's ontology of change, where he answers Parmenides' arguments against Socrates. In particular, I am concerned with the Aristotelian notions of "privation" (*στερησις*) and "some this" (*τοδε τι*). The first term marks for us holism, change, and incompletion; the second term marks positivity, specificity, and multiplicity. While we cite the Aristotelian vocabulary, we do not use the terms in the original sense of Aristotelian ontology to complement each other around an idea of primordial substance, but to suggest the conflicting impulses that together make up the discontinuous, agonistic movement of systems.

Privation is, perhaps counterintuitively, our key holistic term, since it must be understood as a relation internal to the idea of what it is missing.

The grammatical privative, a particle like *dis*-, *un*-, *in*-, or *a*-, marks an incompletion or inversion with respect to a positive whole.[23] For example, "*dis*-equilibrium" or "*un*-precedented" would not make sense if it referred only to chaos or an indifferent event, to a thing that had no disposition toward that which it is wanting. Aristotle introduces this idea of privation in order to maintain the possibility of emergence against the Parmenidean objection that what is not cannot come to be, since nothing comes from nothing; *ex nihilo nihil fit*.[24] Aristotle carefully defines privation as a lack that is *not* nonexistence; it is, rather, existence in the mode of want, shortage, or, to speak with Socrates, *eros*, desire. Privation (*steresis*) is thus distinguished from negation or denial (*apophasis*), defined as the opposite of assertion (*kataphasis*).[25] In this sense, then, privation has an internal relation to the encompassing positive, rather than implying a complete exteriority over and against the positive in the manner of a remainderless negation.

Now, our key positive term is, perhaps just as counterintuitively, one of partiality and multiplicity. Aristotle designates the positive form of substance "this-ness," arguing moreover that a positive presence cannot be formless and indiscrete, but must be "separate and some this" (το χωριστον και το τοδε τι).[26] This sharp positivity, a distinct spattering of mud to the diffuse mana of privation, represents the opposite ontological terminus from Plato's ideal form. For Plato the most general entity, the form, is the final measure of the real, whereas in Aristotle, it is the particular species term that indicates a distinct (*choriston*) and forceful presence (*tode ti*). The very positivity of pointing to Aristotle's ontological ground, however, ensures that "some this" also indicates that *this something* is not also *something else*. In other words, existence in the positive sense implies multiplicity and distinction, and—although this is not Aristotle's drift—it also guarantees us an agonistic world.

For Aristotle, the two characteristics of being, its privative mode and its multiplicity, are what allow change to exist in his ontology without the contradiction that Parmenides, Zeno, and the other Eleatic philosophers claimed change entailed. Something new comes to be, not out of nothing, but out of the immanent privation of form, and it becomes what it is as something that is not something else—that is, as something discrete and formed that can be pointed to. Aristotle situates this emergence from privation squarely within the essence (*to ti ên einai*) of each separate "this." Contrary to Aristotle, however, a system in my account is not given by the continuous emergence of an immanent potential into a fully fledged form. Rather, each lacking "this" is always subject to an encounter with a nonimmanent force, with "some (other) this" that comes from outside its context and stands in no previous relationship with it. These unmediated encounters (or, better, encounters between two media) confront the smooth progress of Aristotelian emergence with the unprecedented force of emergency; they confront system (context) with a strangely coalescing environment. I am *not* saying that a system has no behavioral disposition to actualize its immanent specificity. What I *am* arguing is that a system, as a multiple, *also* meets with a force or event that has no place in it—this force is not simply the empty slot of mana, but another positivity that has not been articulated with any of the system's terms.[27] This positive something—whether an expected something or an unexpected something else—can be compared to a grammatical partitive, as when I ask for *some* water and receive either a refreshing glass or an unimaginable crystal of ice-nine. In the latter case, the humble partitive "some" expresses a definite existential reference, but besides its sheer existence the definite reference is shorn of any definite predication—as though one of Quine's bound variables ($\forall x$ or $\exists x$) were to leap up suddenly with an unheard-of existential truth bound as yet to no context we can specify.[28]

Let me now turn from this Aristotelian ontological terminology back to our discussion of system and medium. As I remarked above, a medium is not *to begin with* some third thing separate from system, but is simply the way a system presents itself. If we speak of a medium as *tertium comparationis*, as a comparative third term, it is nonetheless a third that comes between and relates any two elements, negotiating and simplifying their infinite complexity into the practical balance of unity. A medium in this sense is the internal relationality of the one system, allowing continuous comparison of relevant qualities of system elements in quantifiable terms (that is, finding the common denominator of apples and oranges). This relationality is nonetheless never complete in itself, because if it were, it would give us not a system but a structure—a full, unchangeable whole impossibly remote from the dynamic of everyday historical experience.

At the same time as a medium gives us an *internal* relationality, however, it also gives us a *separate* and *specific* relationality. This specificity—what we have been calling the indexicality of the medium—in turn has two aspects. Since this ambiguity will turn out to be the crux of my argument, I will spell it out clearly. On the one hand, the specifying capacity of the medium detaches or spaces some qualities as discrete and recognizable among all the other qualities toward which the system has no disposition. However imponderable the respective green furies of apples and oranges might be, my taste buds can single out tartness as a distinct quality for comparing them.

A medium thus picks out a system's qualitative variety as a dimension subject to its quantifiable continuity.[29] Apples and oranges are equally at home in the tartness system. On the other hand, this qualitative specification of the system is not just an internal dimension to be reconciled with the quantitative mediation. It is also an externally directed quality of the system as a whole—a boundary separation that marks where the system ends and the environment begins without being able to quantify this boundary in a way that could bring it back into the process of mediation.

In this latter, disruptive sense, a medium is indeed a third thing. It is not the internal relationality of system, but a suddenly external boundary: a limit marking the site of an encounter with some other system. Because it is not related to the first system by any comparative third term, this other system appears under the guise of "two-ness" as an immediate and unprecedented other. As a boundary, the medium is no longer the infinitely displaceable symbolic currency of system integration, but the sign of system multiplicity, of a system having to assert itself against alternatives it cannot fathom on its own terms. In our systems ontology, then, the reassuring *tode ti* of Aristotelian ontology at some point becomes precipitously uncertain. Does our gesturing to "this something!" firmly root our perceptions of an emergent system in its really articulated elements? Or does it on the contrary point to a limit or breach—to a critical system emergency? Can the *tode ti* be incorporated back into the lacking whole, related by a common metric of systemic identity, or does it compel the whole to admit meanings that do not belong and cannot be digested, to regard itself as merely a part and thus make itself vulnerable to the force of alternatives? The *tode ti*, in this latter case, points not to an element, but to the boundary of a system. It is not the empty slot allowing the whole to move, but the bluntly positive imposition of another whole: a real variable bound to a categorically new context.

The ontological juxtaposition of mud and mana with which we began can now be grasped as one that need not—at least not at first—be regarded as systemic incommensurability. Rather, mud might be an element we point to and greet with the wonderment of mana in our progressive articulation of a generous and all-inclusive system. No sooner, however, does the one system present the ultimate terms (the *telos* or *arche*) by which it aims finally to establish itself as sovereign genus, than those same terms define a specificity that disrupts its universal progress. From mud to mana, each iteration of the system counts as an ontological unity, but in the very moment it identifies its sovereign principle, the world-genus speciates itself anew.

3. POLITICAL OR SOCIALIST ONTOLOGY: FROM FIGURATIVE SYMBOL TO REFERENTIAL INDEX

When to the moment I shall say,
"Linger awhile! so fair thou art!"
Then mayst thou fetter me straightway,
Then to the abyss will I depart!
Then may the solemn death-bell sound,
Then from thy service thou art free,
The index then may cease its round.
And time be never more for me!
—Goethe, *Faust*[30]

If I worried at the outset of the previous section that my argument might be taken for a semantic or discursive ontology, here I want to make sure that the argument not be misunderstood as political decisionism or constructivism. It might indeed seem that the inevitable speciation of systems implies, in a political sense, a plurality of sovereignties. Since we have no basis for deciding among these sovereignties on substantive merits, we must simply choose our allegiances. In this view, Quine's "ontological commitment" looks like a subjective commitment to the equal existential status of any semantically justifiable entity. We are all equally placed interpreters in a world that only awaits our choosing our true colors. An ontological commitment to socialism, then, would be tantamount to the revolutionary political act: commitment appears as pure event or effect, without relation to the causal order of facts or logical order of propositions.[31]

In such a view, the bottom line is that in a world of semantic ambiguity, the space of interpretation and the space of politics are coextensive, since, at least *to some degree*, to name what is real is to seize real authority over it. Of course, *delimiting* the degree to which nominal authority is real authority is what interests us; hence, the empirical side of the equation in which our commitment to something exposes us to the force of sensual judgment. In fact, it is at this charged conjunction of interpretation and politics that a socialist systems ontology becomes especially important in order to distinguish between that which exists by virtue of our decisions or observations and that which exists through no virtue of our own. The socialist ontology that clarifies this distinction is necessarily a historical one, one that addresses what is real in the social time of political decisions. Yet however much a discussion of socialism sounds like a political discourse, a socialist ontology must be distinguished from a political ontology per se—that is, from a decisionist ontology that situates the sovereign political act at the root of social being.[32]

In order to clarify the direction of my argument, let me consider how a radically political ontology rules out the possibility of a substantive referent for political activity, and, a fortiori, rules out *empirical* socialism as a substantive reference for *political* socialism. According to Ernesto Laclau and Chantal Mouffe, "[O]nly the presence of a vast area of floating elements and the possibility of their articulation into opposite camps is what constitutes the terrain permitting us to define a practice as hegemonic"—that is, political.[33] The autonomy of "the political" guarantees that its specific, nonrational logic, like the figurative logic of language generally—or like mana—is not reducible to empirical causality. Conversely, the indeterminacy of the empirical world is what guarantees its subordination to a political logic of sense. The political project, in this view, is to establish a provisional bond between linguistic resources of metaphor and metonymy, denotation, and connotation, on the one side, and the indeterminate social realm of identification and distinction, on the other. The important thing is that the floating elements of society that language is articulating—the coalescing or factionalizing political camps, as it were—are completely open to opposed positions. In Carl Schmitt's influential argument for the priority of politics over other expressions of the social such as law and economics, politics is our fate because the existence of an enemy is ontologically fundamental and so, therefore, is coexistence among political rivals. "As long as a state exists, there will thus always be in the world more than just one state." There are no moral, aesthetic, or rational determinants to political rivalry, only the ad hoc "intensity of a union or separation."[34]

In other words, there is nothing in a purely political ontology that would establish a substantive distinction between left and right; rather, the terrain of the political is only called upon to ground contrary camps without ontological prejudice. Socialism is just another politically motivating symbol (like Georges Sorel's "mythic violence" and Rosa Luxemburg's "mass strike") and not in any way—least of all an empirical way—a substantial presence underlying a difference. The whole question of socialist ontology—of really existing socialism—is rejected as an essentialism of the same sort as that which hypostatized such phantasmatic social actors as "classes," "masses," and "history" to such tragic effect over the course of the twentieth century. Instead, *liberté*, *egalité*, and *fraternité*, supplemented by *altérité*, *marginalité*, and *différance*, remain as the "discursive acts" of leftist self-constitution without any empirical beyond regulating them. To their pronouncement we may always ascribe fresh nominal existence, simply not any systemic empirical existence. Such empirical solidity, it is said, would only involve them again with the functional and veridical logics (logocentrism) that had so tainted them in the, ultimately phantasmagorical, real socialist experience.

The extreme consequences of a discursive ontology that sees the world and its politics on the amorphous model of figurative language or rhetoric is brought out by Boris Groys in *The Communist Postscript*. There figurative language is presented not only as the political means to the better world, but as characterizing the end of the world itself. Groys writes:

> By communism I understand the project of subordinating economy to politics in order to let politics act with freedom and sovereignty. The economy functions in the medium of money. It operates with figures. Politics functions in the medium of language. It operates with words—with arguments, programs and resolutions, but also with commands, bans, decisions and regulations. The communist revolution is the rewriting of society from the medium of money to the medium of language. It is the linguistic turn on the level of social praxis. [. . .] The question of the possibility of communism is thus deeply bound up with the question of the possibility of governing, shaping and politically administering in and through the medium of language. This key question can be formulated in the following way: can language as such ever—and if so, under what conditions—exert enough force to be a means of governing society?[35]

Contrary to political-discursive ontology's hasty farewell to real things, my position is that without a specifically socialist ontology, leftist (or rightist) politics remains only a grand or hysterical gesture, without reference to either real subjects or a mutually valid world. Accordingly, socialism cannot be taken as a purely *political* commitment that does just fine without any *indicative* commitment to a logical or empirical world, for such a political commitment would transpire without regard to any demonstrable content. Socialism—as the reference of leftist political commitment—is a real system that is not understandable in an exclusively political ontology, but requires a *systems* ontology to make sense. The corresponding rightist commitment is, reasonably enough, not an immanent political self-reflection negatively revaluing leftist values like liberty, equality, and solidarity, but is a reference to a world in which no systemic organization of these values, as envisioned in socialism, is held to exist (in any modality of actuality or possibility). Both worlds, of course, can contain human minds and bodies for whom pains and pleasures matter, and both can be places where bodies and intentions cooperate and collide. The substantive distinction between worlds, however, can only be made at the systemic level—that is, at the time and place where things and events, individuals and generalities are brought into consequential relation.

When I assert, against the free indeterminacy of a discursive ontology, that I am reintroducing things into a socialist ontology, I want to be clear what I mean by things. On the one hand, I have already indicated that I have an ecumenical sense of things—everything from vampires to mana and mud are invited into my socialist world, at least provisionally. But this ecumenism is not promiscuity, smuggling all manner of unreconstructed "things" back into a long since deconstructed world. Rather, systems ontology gives us substantial, distinct things that are nonetheless not the punctual, individual entities of skeptical, positivist, or decisionist philosophies. These philosophies, from ancient sophism and medieval nominalism through modern logical empiricism, prefer their things small, individual and without generality. Systems ontology, by contrast, gives us big things, general things, without however resorting to the existence of ideal forms or structures outside of time and space. What difference, however, does the scope of things make? It makes all the difference, because what a systems ontology accomplishes is both to give us a world with identifiable qualities (rather than atomic points) and to lend those qualities the capacity to change. While Carl Schmitt was a famous antagonist of positivism in law, he shares with positivism an ontology that has no qualitative robustness. Political ontologies derived from Schmitt see existence articulated by the sheer "this-ness" (the atomic irreducibility, or *hecceity*) of each sovereign decision. Politics comes down to *naming* singular and insubstantial differences that we fight over only by virtue of that sovereign act of naming itself. This *hecceity* of decision or naming is no different than that of a strict positivist's mud or rock, whose properties do not exist as independent universal substrates, but coincide only with *this* mud right here. There is in the cases of both decisionism and positivism an Aristotelian *tode ti* (partitive), but no *steresis* (privative), no bound variable, that would allow for change and becoming. *This* is it, and it is always outside of *that*, never nonidentical, never within a process of transformation. Thus, in a political ontology the act of taking sides is an instance of nothing but itself—with the consequence that that which, in its *negativity* and *agonism*, initially passes as a critique of *positivism* finally ends up in the purely immanent positivism of each decision. To put as sharp a point on it as possible, where positivism holds a punctual ontology of objects, decisionism holds a punctual ontology of subjects. In both cases, the punctuality excludes those systemic ontological frameworks that contain, in the words of Rudolf Carnap, "abstract entities like properties, classes, relations, numbers, propositions, etc."[36]—the very frameworks in which a socialist system is situated.

The allusion to Carnap—the quintessential logical empiricist—supplies us with a convenient point to differentiate our position from that not only of Schmitt but also of language-based ontologies more generally. Although Carnap is interested in language strictly as a medium for logical world-construction, not language in its figurative capacity, that restrictiveness only makes our point more clear—precisely because it is not restrictive enough (that is, not restricted by the force of things in the material sense). Discussing the ontological paradoxes of logical empiricism, Carnap winds up with a surprisingly decisionistic formulation of the problem, noting that "to be real in the scientific sense means to be an element of the system; hence this concept [reality] cannot be meaningfully applied to the system itself. Those who raise the question of the reality of the thing world itself have perhaps in mind not a theoretical question as their formulation seems to suggest, but rather a practical question, a matter of a practical decision concerning the structure of our language."[37] The choice of systems, according to Carnap, cannot ever be an empirical question, because an empirical question is always posed internally to a given system. Thus, when one speaks of the reality of the system itself, one is simply stating an incommensurable ad hoc preference. If, however, a system itself stages its own encounter with its alternatives, if the *tode ti* of reference can also refer to an other system as something more than a blank gap at one given system's limit, but a necessary qualification of it, then we must admit questions concerning the reality of the systems themselves into our ontology. We can ask if really existing socialism is really socialism and vice versa. Systems need not be either insurmountably external to each other—resulting in a pure decisionism at that level—or inextricably internal to each other—resulting in the infinite regress of the Third Man Argument. "In practice," Quine notes, "we end the regress of coordinate systems by something like pointing."[38] Only now it should be clear that this modest gesture of pointing can indicate not only the small empirical elements of one system but also the unprecedented presence of another system. Moreover, such pointing is not only a voluntary action; it is also an involuntary reaction that is not subject—in its primal force—to interpretation.

This two-way force of pointing—in which an indexical sign acts as a conduit bringing the force of what is indicated to bear on its witness—returns us to the question of what allows an ontological commitment (that is, a commitment to what is real) to be something more than a political decision. Why, in other words, am I not content to let the autonomous space of politics serve as the critical arbiter of the social real, rather than the other way around? In discussing what makes an index a distinct sort of sign, Peirce emphasizes that as opposed especially to conventional symbols, "the index is physically connected with its object; they make an organic pair, but the interpreting mind has nothing to do with this connection, except remarking it, after it is established."[39] An index is characterized by a minimal role for interpretation and a maximum quotient of objective force. In a fashion anticipating behaviorism, Peirce writes of the index "forcibly intruding upon the mind, quite regardless of its being interpreted as a sign."[40] This forcible intrusion, it should be emphasized, is not some kind of "forceless force of the better argument," as in either logical empiricism or Habermasian communicative action.[41] Nor is it a linguistic figure in Saussure's or Laclau's and Mouffe's sense, based on an infinite series of differences and catachreses. Rather, the index "is something which, without any rational necessitation, is forced by blind fact to correspond to its object."[42] This element that is in some sense beyond interpretation—beyond figurative discourse, although not beyond all mediation—is what takes ontological priority in the commitment to socialism.[43]

The antinomy that has impressed itself on this discussion of political ontology and into which the index intervenes as outside arbiter is this: one cannot rationally commit to one "thing world" over another (say, to socialism over liberalism) if there is no higher index of reality to decide between them. At the same time, where such an index becomes a basis for real commitment—that is, is part of a working relation larger than any arbitrary decision of my own—it is at least incipiently internal to another system. The externality of plurality stands opposed to the internality of privation. To each side of this opposition there corresponds a contrary affective stance that bears on the degree of conscious will or interpretation demanded from a political actor. In the tense interval in which the index of my commitment is neither an element of one system nor clearly a marker of another system—where my "ontological commitment" is sheerly generic—my subjective pathos tends to the sublime or ecstatic. When, however, my ontological commitment is less a matter of discretion and more a matter of the sensual authority of facts—when one system or another prevails—then my corresponding pathos assumes the cool affect of behaviorism: the things of my world speak for my actions, saying I cannot do otherwise.

The indexical sign—written in neither the book of ideals nor the book of nature—appears in the book of historical social institutions. As a sign based on presence, its ontological significance is explicit, existing in the fullness of both the sensual and cerebral worlds: Hilary Putnam has remarked with deceptive simplicity that "the mind and the world jointly make up the mind and the world."[44] What this fullness entails for us is the patience to heed the interval between an index's force and its meaning—the time it takes to realize its relevance as a sign of system emergence or, contrarily, of system emergency. A political ontology that recognizes only the plentitude of the one moment—in the usurpation of eternity by the present or the sacrifice of the present to eternity—is too impoverished to gauge the reality of real socialism. Rather, we recognize socialism when, as I propose in the coming chapters, a patient observer like Franz Fühmann gestures through the ugly jargon of party-political socialism and demonstrates *this is it!* (τοδε τι!) At that point, and with such a real socialist, we might behold what is real with the cry, "Linger awhile! so fair thou art! . . . The index then may cease its round." In this lingering reality—in Fühmann's reality, which lingers for us—a system emerges in its fullness . . . as subject to the force of its emergency. Our responsibility in the face of this fair apparition, however, is to resist the call to either heaven or hell.

4. MONEY: GE VERSUS THE GDR

> The movements of society are spontaneous and not artificial, and the desire for joy which manifests itself in all its activities unwittingly drives it towards the realization of the ideal type of State.
>
> —Paul Pierre le Mercier de la Rivière (1767)[45]

Let us advance our resistance to damnation or salvation, to any eternity, by here taking up the most venal example of an indexical medium, one that is nonetheless crucial for thinking about the socialist distinction—namely, the economic medium of money. My aim is to make more intuitive some consequences of organizing a world around one medium or another, demonstrating why the ontological stakes involved with the question of medium are so high. Most important for me to bring out is how the mediation I am interested in—whose strict realism I have been emphasizing—expresses a compelling force that, despite its vast coordinating authority, also generates grave ambiguity about its universal scope.

In keeping with my resistance to a discursive ontology, Niklas Luhmann differentiates natural language media, "media of dissemination," from what

Talcott Parsons calls "symbolically generalized communication media."[46] These latter include truth, love, power/law, and property/money. Like verbal language they are means of observing and communicating about social system identity, only they are distinguished by a linkage of information and persuasion much stronger than even the finest rhetorical argument. "One need only remember the significance the language of money possesses for politics and the economy to have a striking example: this language understands the difference between system and environment as the difference between whether one has money or not."[47] In citing money's objective physical relation to the meaning it forcefully conveys, Luhmann invokes characteristics like those of Peirce's index, holding that media such as truth, love, and money are more "motivating" than discursive language in that they force an objective situation upon one with a "blind compulsion" (Peirce) unavailable in the interpretive ambiguity of verbal communication.[48]

Given such emphasis on the objective force of money as a medium, it might seem that the question of socialism's reality could be settled by looking for some hard and fast equivalent to the ruthless capitalist adjudicator, money, along the lines of the adage, Show me the god and I'll show you the man. As a generalized medium, money (god, mana) gives us a rigorously objective world, the economic one, that admits some entities into its consideration and not others. If money could be distinguished without fuss into capitalist money and socialist money, it would stand to reason that the economy mediated by each currency would admit different entities into its ontology—capitalist entities and socialist entities, respectively. The situation would be analogous to two foreign languages. Whether such languages are held to be essentially similar, related by a universal grammar (as per Noam Chomsky), or essentially incompatible, each projecting an internal worldview (as per Benjamin Lee Whorf), in either case the contest between capitalism and socialism would ultimately seem as absurd as fomenting a revolution in French to switch to Chinese: what could possibly motivate such a switch? The absurdity rests on the same boundless linguistic constructivism I have been so keen to deny. The reason for my denial bears reiteration once more: a medium's structural properties do not alone complete its semantic universe.[49] To be coherent, a "socialist medium" needs to refer to socialist things, just as socialist things need an effective medium of reference.

The two-way street of money and economy, then, has to be analyzed more closely to understand how a medium both completes a system and encounters the constraints that undo such completion. Money is traditionally seen as functioning in a threefold capacity as a means of exchange, a means of accounting, and a means of recording and storing value. Systems theorists like Luhmann and Parsons focus especially on the first capacity as the one that distinguishes money from noneconomic media: as a means of exchange, money is given away when it is spent, unlike language, whose use is not dictated by concerns of scarcity.[50] Here, however, we are concerned less with circulation than with reference, so it is the relationship between the third capacity and the first that interests us—namely, how is it that we are willing to exchange on the basis of the values recorded and stored by monetary prices? Or, put the other way, how is it that individually motivated transactions result in an objectively calculable order? Adam Smith coined the famous phrase "invisible hand" to characterize the way in which the private market regulates its own balance without intervention from beyond the economic sphere (presumably by a "visible hand"). If this balance referred only to the first or second aspect of money, it would be no remarkable achievement, but simply a closed accounting book, or, as system designers express it, "garbage in, garbage out" (GIGO), a circuit that, no matter how fancy its bookkeeping, has no relationship to real human participants in the market.[51] To truly complete the economic system, money and prices have to have reference beyond a closed circle of balanced commodity exchange (that is, supply equaling demand) that in itself has no reference to human choice and preference.[52]

The theory of General Equilibrium (GE), first elaborated independently by William Jevons, Carl Menger, and Leon Walras in the 1870s, is what was able to account for the enormous referential power of prices. It mathematically extended the economic sphere beyond the gray calculations of the "dismal science" and into the rosy playgrounds of hedonism where unrelated economic participants act rationally (or pragmatically) to maximize their consumer pleasures. Using the concept of marginal utility, GE explains the systematic nature by which the equilibrium price of a good is reached on the basis of a differential calculus that determines the additional quantity that a participant in the free market still desires of some one good instead of another with each infinitesimal increase in its price. The effective demand of real economic agents could thus be observed through GE as an invisibly coordinated regulating force within the autonomous whole of the capitalist economic system, money serving as the coordinating medium not only for accounting and exchange but also for the personal calculus of pleasure optimization under appropriate economic conditions.

Money, as we see, becomes a means to evaluate and preserve socially articulated needs and pleasures in their specific construction as effective demand. Effective demand is not, however, demand per se, somehow articulated without respect to a medium. Individuals, even vast communities, can be starving and at the same time powerless to affect the economy. If they have little access to money (or credit), then their needs go effectively unexpressed, and as far as the economy *casus strictus* is concerned, they are not constituted as agents at all.[53] Their subjectivities (and reproductive necessities) are not registered as values in the monetary economy. Their deprivation might be structured by any number of factors other than properly economic ones. Yet despite the morally forceful label "need" adhering to their situation, there is no singular essential reference point to it, say, in a natural physiological sense, although there is *also* a physiological sense of need. Some formulation of their needs might find alternative recourse in a politically or culturally effectual medium, such as votes (that is, representation in the political franchise) or signs (representation in a symbolic domain). But here, too, there are systemic conditions that shape the way values are registered and preserved, as the history of suffrage in its many forms demonstrates or the culture wars over literary canon formation.[54] One can thus see, in the case of money, how a medium is not merely a constraint on the exercise of a pre-existing reality, but reciprocally creates that reality as a systemic fact, distinct and apprehensible as some one and not some other fact. Money, as the universal equivalent of a commodity economy, creates the standards of what is "socially necessary" for an economic agent to materially reproduce itself—whether that agent is an individual, household, or firm.

It is clear that money thus mediates one particular reality, economic reality, and that economic reality is not unique, but excludes certain sorts of agency and agents, *homo oeconomicus* being distinct, for example, from *homo suffragans*. But let us come back to the question of why we cannot, with a few modifications of money's properties, use it to articulate some other reality—a socialist reality. On the basis of our argument that a medium articulates a unified reality only by also carving up reality in some particular, nonunique way, it might reasonably be the case that money need only be tweaked to find itself articulating an improved economic system we might then call socialism—for if it is nothing else, socialism is surely also an economic system. According to the orthodox liberal economic theory that gave us the conception of money we just outlined, however, we are out of luck. The essence of money is one thing and one thing only—the rational dynamic of the medium of exchange per se—and there is only one system that works with it. Money is the index of the liberal capitalist real. This stark ontological conclusion is, on the face of it, a stunning setback to any attempt to apprehend another system to liberal modernity, as well as a contradiction of our claim that a medium gives us not only unity but, equally, the possibility of a plurality. It implies two courses for us. First, we will play out the reasoning of formalized liberal orthodoxy, GE theory, to see why it expresses its economic ontology so strongly. Second, we will see how three prominent alternative economic theories give us utterly different ontologies. This survey of a total of four fundamental theories will then throw us back onto the territory where we began the chapter—Quinean ontological relativity and the need to carefully scrutinize what is "out there" as a prerequisite for making an ontological commitment among our theories.

Since GE remains more uncontested than ever after the fall of the Soviet bloc, I take its ontological claims about economic equilibrium as a reasonable orientation point for inquiring into socialist ontology. According to GE, an economy is the unified interrelation of all economic agents through the medium of money. In precapitalist economic formations, money was not yet the sole medium for coordinating distinct parts of the production and exchange process in an articulated whole, and, lacking such a conduit for closure, these formations were not strictly economic systems at all. Only with generalized commodity exchange and the universal equivalency of money does a distinct economic system emerge.[55] In eighteenth-century France the Physiocrats pioneered terminology adequate to the emergence of a national economy as an interrelated whole. Through the movement of prices they observed how the value of land, for example, rippled through the monarchy to affect things as diverse as urban wages and royal tax receipts that recursively affected the value of land. It was this more or less closed circular causality that demarcated the economic as a system.[56] The Scottish Enlightenment around David Hume and Adam Smith shared this insight into the compelling power with which a closed system of causality shaped and articulated distinct but coordinated elements of the world. With Smith, one could for the first time speak persuasively of the sovereign individual, rather than the divine sovereign, because individuals, on the basis solely of self-interest expressed in private property values, could generate from inside out an order that was coherent, comprehensive, and rationally related to one's actions. The monuments of this era remain the sovereign individual (with no necessary intentions beyond self-interest) and the invisible hand of automatic coordination (laissez-faire)—and with their economic testament, Locke's civil contracts assume pride of place before absolute sovereigns of state.

In the course of the late nineteenth century, GE came to express the economy's processes and balances in precise mathematical terms, codifying its systemic integrity and normal state. That mathematical formalization, with its various underlying assumptions about profit-maximizing firms and utility-maximizing consumers, informs most economic science and policy today.[57] To function with such mathematical efficiency, GE rests on three propositions that I want to keep in mind: there is a state of compatibility among diverse economic interests coordinated through an economic system (that is, equilibrium *exists*); these interests can assume they are all playing the same game (equilibrium is *unique*); and interests tend to converge on such a compatible state (equilibrium is *stable*). In each of the three antagonistic economic views I now consider, the reality of these conditions is contested. The third proposition, which requires an inherent economic stability, rather than an intentionally directed one, is the most controversial. In the versions of GE espoused by Ludwig von Mises, Friedrich Hayek, and Milton Friedman, the economic *as such* requires that the third proposition apply autonomously, without intervention from the noneconomic sphere.[58] In other words, independent actions must be coordinated by inherent economic forces—Smith's "invisible hand"—or those actions are not economic and talk of a system is nonsense. For Smith's force to apply, therefore, actors need to be motivated by clear economic interests they can calculate on the basis of common market prices and by no other interests besides. The only requirement for setting the whole in motion is that each participant owns property, be it just a day of labor power, whereupon the interest in meeting the maximization criteria of marginal utility follows—with the net effect being that the economy balances supply and demand at equilibrium prices, allowing further transactions to continue on the same basis. But it is only if prices are left free to find "their own" equilibrium, that property owners can continue to choose rationally among available alternatives for satisfying their desires and thus keep the whole in motion. Considering whether socialism can meet these criteria, Mises writes in 1920 that "without economic calculation there can be no economy. Hence, in a socialist state wherein the pursuit of economic calculation is impossible, there can be—in our sense of the term—no economy whatsoever."[59]

These strong conceptions of the properly "economic" leave either capitalism or socialism without systematic economic existence. As I indicated, we are in exactly the sort of ontological impasse described by Quine. If we accept GE—and there are compelling empirical reasons to do so—then we cannot countenance socialism in our economic ontology. If we persist, however, in trying to understand whether seventy years of socialism really existed—and there are also compelling empirical reasons to do so—then we need another paraphrase of (another medium for) the economic order. In the 1930s, partly in response to the "socialist calculation debate" launched by Mises's philosophical interdiction of socialism, the Polish economist Oskar Lange began to address the problem of how economic calculation might be possible in a system that through political negotiation, rather than through money, decided on its equilibrium states, where *homo oeconomicus* converged with *homo suffragans*.[60] This politically steered equilibrium gives us our first alternate economic ontology. For Lange, socialism did exist, because a stable equilibrium existed that was called into being not by market prices but by a material balance reached through trial and error controlled by mathematical models. "Any mistake made by the Central Planning Board in fixing prices would announce itself in a very objective way—by a physical shortage or surplus of the quantity of the commodity or resources in question—and would have to be corrected in order to keep production running smoothly."[61] The announcement of economic mistakes in a physically objective manner, Lange believed, is a far more obvious and compelling index than prices, whose significance, despite their mathematizability in GE theory, is still subject to interpretation by biased interests. According to Lange, the physical balance of surplus and deficit could in principle be achieved by a democratic planning board with fewer successive calculations than a market required, a market and its prices being merely a primitive analogue computer that was being superseded by nascent digital technology and its direct quantitative inputs. The 1965 East German publication of his *Totality and Development from a Cybernetic Point of View* played an important role in overcoming official ideological skepticism of computer steering and cybernetics in the GDR, lending momentum to the 1960s reforms known as the New Economic System, and influencing the key East German proponent of cybernetics, Georg Klaus, whom we will discuss in Chapter 8.[62]

Although deeply influenced by Lange's cybernetics, the next view I consider sought a more radical reconceptualization of economics than Lange, indeed one fully outside GE assumptions.[63] The Hungarian economist János Kornai, considered by many "the only scholar who . . . attempted a general theory of the socialist economy," does not aim to extend the world of the economic on the orthodox terms of either GE or Marxism.[64] Rather,

Kornai develops a theory of the economic based on information and values not strictly mediated by money, thereby mooting GE's preemptive disqualification of socialism from the realm of the economic. He characterizes socialist economies as "economies of shortage"—in other words, nonequilibrium economies—suggesting an economic ontology that undermines the first postulate of GE theory: that equilibrium exists. In a work pointedly titled *Anti-Equilibrium*, Kornai argues not only that socialist economies are nonequilibrium economies, but that there are in fact no equilibrium economies anywhere, and that GE's discrimination between the formalizable market economies of the West and the administrative (non)economies of the East is untenable. Again, the distinction is untenable, not because, as Lange hoped, planned economies *can* be guided by GE, but because even market economies *cannot*.

Because there is no significant private ownership, socialist economies cannot rely on prices to generate the information their participants need, raising the problem of understanding how socialist economic reproduction is systematically mediated. Goods and services are exchanged and accounts formally balanced, but money does not serve as a reliable measure of value. Firms, for example, do not have to attract scarce investment capital on a competitive stock exchange, but have state-subsidized budgets that prohibit bankruptcy. They thus do not buy inputs according to a marginal utility calculus; instead, a central planner must assume that each firm's demand for any available input is infinite.[65] In fact, since prices are nowhere determined at a level that balances demand with supply, serving simply as conventional markers for accounting, it is not only firms but all economic actors who have potentially infinite (budgetless) demand. The ensuing generalized shortage of goods lends the socialist economy its typical phenomenal forms: hoarding and queuing. The planner's task should thus not be conceived as chasing a GE fantasy of the perfect set of market-balancing prices, but as rationing a general shortage of producer inputs and consumer goods.

The planner's task is complicated by another factor besides the lack of monetary valuation; without private property, it is not clear what subjectively motivates individual economic actors. As a consequence of collective ownership, *legal* property agents ("the People," as in *Volkseigene Betriebe*, or "People's Owned Firms," the legal form of incorporation in the GDR) are not equivalent to *economic* property agents. As Jadwiga Staniszkis argues,

> of the three moments of material reproduction—that is, work, capital, and material assets—[the latter two] have ceased to be identified with anyone's actual in-

> terest and have at the most become "theoretical interests" resulting from knowledge concerning the requirements of the production process. As such, [. . .] they have little motivational power. This rift between the requirements of material production and the map of actual interests, together with the systemic absence of a wide range of information which can only be generated by the market, represents the main barrier to the state and the party having real control over the economy.[66]

While Kornai agrees that socialist economic actors have few motivations as unambiguous as monetary incentives, he recognizes that "there exist some deeper-lying motives, which have a stronger and more lasting influence on management's behavior. Of these I stress that most people *identify themselves with their job*."[67] The Nobel Prize–winning economist Amartya Sen has likewise addressed this apparently nebulous issue of identification, phrasing it as a dilemma about the proper proportion of reason (as an autonomous rational calculus) and identification (a desire to become unified with something) in economic choices:

> Does a person identify with anyone else in deciding on what objects to pursue and what choices to make? Is the idea of social identity vacuous when it comes to explaining behavioral regularities, since no identification is involved other than with oneself? A good deal of economic theory has tended to proceed as if that is indeed the case.[68]

Kornai is ultimately interested in formalized systems, but by insisting on the importance of identification, he understands socialist economies as controlled by a heterogeneous, but systematic, combination of bureaucratic power, social symbolism, material balances, and, to a lesser extent, money.[69] According to Kornai, these factors can be apprehended and socialism systematically reproduced using diverse incentives—all of which find a place in a socialist ontology. Ontologically, however, the system is not perfectly consistent and free of contradiction, and therefore there is no single medium through which efficiency can be optimized—that is, through which the socialist economy can come into itself as its own pure form. "The tradition of economics has accustomed us to the concept that everything can and must be 'optimized[.]' . . . But that is a naïve, wishful day-dream[.] . . . It seems to me that it is impossible to create a closed and consistent socio-economic normative theory which would assert, without contradiction, a politico-ethical value system and would at the same time provide for the efficiency of the economy."[70]

Kornai's polemic against equilibrium sets forth nonequilibrium terms that include capitalism and socialism as possibilities in one theoretical universe.[71]

While Kornai recognizes differences between the two systems, he reduces them to distinctions along a single continuum of economic forms. By contrast, the orthodox socialist view which I now consider maintains a strong ontology of socialist difference, thus sharing the exclusivity of GE ontology, only with the opposite polarity. For tactical reasons, Eastern-bloc Marxists considered the Cold War stalemate between two separate but relatively stable worlds a moment of "peaceful coexistence."[72] "In the framework of this cooperation the two social systems will compete with each other and demonstrate which can achieve the most for the German people," proclaimed an open letter from the East German party Central Committee to West German workers in 1960.[73] On an analytical level, however, the outcome of this competition was a foregone conclusion. GE's bourgeois ontology, based on the supposedly efficient mediation of money, was self-contradictory and, hence, nugatory. In the *Grundrisse*, Marx traces how bourgeois wealth in monetary form—the very index that in GE correlates the emergence of the economic as such—"appears as its own mediator" and subordinates, in its drive to universality, all other economic actors.[74] "Note," Marx observes, "that money becomes an end instead of a means and that capital, as the superior form of mediation, everywhere establishes the inferior form, labor, simply as a source of surplus value."[75] In other words, monetary capital loses its medial character and becomes an absolute end, riding roughshod over all other social considerations and encountering other identities only as limitations to be overcome, until "the universality towards which it is perpetually tending finds limitations in its own nature, which at a certain stage of its development will make it appear as itself the greatest barrier to this tendency, leading thus to its own self-destruction."[76]

The target of the Marxist critique is liberal faith in "capitalist production as the absolute form of production."[77] Marxism might concede to Mises that the market price-index is the most generalized measure of commodity exchange (and the basis of labor exploitation). But the commodity economy is only one form of economy, not the whole of the economic; and this very particularity leads to capitalism's overcoming. Capitalism is seen as a species of the genus "economy." In the superseding socialist economy—or better yet, one should now drop the ontologically limited idea of socialism as an economic species and simply say "socialism" as a new genus—instead of capital serving as "the absolute form of wealth coinciding absolutely with the development of productive forces," labor-time steps in as the new mediator. But the mediation by labor does not mean simply putting labor-money in the place of capital-money and letting the rest of the social transformation follow mechanically. There is an important second element to Marx's view of how socialist productive relations will be mediated—namely, by socialized labor as a conscious historical actor. Ernest Mandel writes that "between the growing economic contradictions of the capitalist mode of production on the one hand, and the collapse of capitalism on the other hand, there is a necessary mediation: the development of the class consciousness, organized strength and capacity for revolutionary action of the working class."[78] The new ontology of socialism thus measures itself by an index more vital and compelling than GE's frugal money—regarding labor both as spatio-temporal quantum for economic calculation and as conscious actor pointing toward collective decisions on the basis of labor-time information. Completing our parallelogram of ontologies, then, Marxian economics holds GE theory to be not only inapplicable to socialism, but, except as ideology, simply inapplicable. Socialism might exist *coincidently* at the same moment as capitalism, but *systematically* it negates and supersedes capitalism's contradictory laws of development. In this view, GE theory has no place, whether west of the Wall or in Lange's extension of it eastward, and neither does Kornai's theory, which denies GE only to squeeze capitalism and socialism into one neutral language of economic description.

5. THE FLICKERING SIGN OF THE NEW: BETWEEN BEHAVIORISM AND DECISIONISM

> From moment to moment the hedonimeter varies; the delicate index now flickering with the flutter of the passions, now steadied by intellectual activity, low sunk whole hours in the neighborhood of zero, or momentarily springing up toward infinity.
>
> —Francis Y. Edgeworth (1881)[79]

At this fourfold ontological impasse, we see the danger of making a hasty commitment to a single, unambiguous index of the real—neither an empiricism, marshaling the facts and figures of Dow Jones and GDP, nor a constructivism, creating a guiding light by virtue of a militant discourse, gives us an obvious sign of discretionary truth. Waving the Red Flag or storming the Winter Palace does not peremptorily decide the debates we have been reviewing and suddenly make an economy *work*. Once again, but now at the institutional level of socialist economy, our problem is this: if the ontological is a matter of commitment, commitment for its part, in order to be anything other than decisionism, is a matter of ontology. Our position at this point resembles that which begins Peirce's lectures on pragmatism, in which he plays out an example of a marginal utility calculation, only to conclude that such calculations cannot be undertaken out of the blue: "[It] is obvious that it must be of the nature of a *real fact* and not a mere *state of mind*."[80] It must therefore be accompanied by a survey of real options given by an unprejudiced type of knowledge that "simply opens its eyes and describes what it sees."[81] To ground this evidence Peirce resumes his focus on those singular facts of nature that speak louder than words ever can, revealing a cardinal order of existence lacking any property other than "unicity" or a *hecceity* (this-ness). "An index does not describe the qualities of its object. An object, in so far as it is denoted by an index, having *thisness*, and distinguishing itself from other things by its continuous identity and forcefulness, but not by any distinguishing characters, may be called a *hecceity*."[82]

For such a momentous *hecceity* to serve as a pure, unprejudiced index for prudent action, and not just a blank slate for a momentary fantasy, we need to ask whether beyond sheer existence, its opaque promise can present an equilibrium state that is also *unique* and *stable*—that is, whether it refers to, and coordinates, a larger universe of given things—a practical reference that, as we have seen, is also the chief challenge to GE theory. Just as we cannot grab a balanced equation out of the sky and expect it to stand alone as truth, we also cannot point to an isolated fact of simple existence and have it anchor our equations. What we come back to, then, is my key point about the scope of our objects of reference. Simplicity is always the result of a complex and extensive process in time.[83] Our reference must be to other *systems*: we need to understand our guiding indexes not as points, as this or that perception, but as fundamental existential challenges, shaking our individual and collective being to the core.

To forestall the confusion to which existentialist rhetoric is prone to give rise, let me make clear that in the following pages our readings of socialist literature won't miraculously decide the ontological ambiguity of competing world systems. Such manifestation has never been the point of my project. Rather, I aim to extend the prospect of an ontological encounter long enough that we can pursue a real socialist, Franz Fühmann, as he struggles to make a commitment on (and to) his system's own terms. This commitment will never be like the punctual ones of decisionism or empirical positivism. Or, I should say, there will be plenty of those sorts of commitments along the way; they turn out, through no lack of faith and good will, to be fickle commitments, however, and not reciprocated over the distance.

What animates Fühmann's work are not the small devotions, but the large ones that endure through betrayals and transformations. I therefore do not want to nurture false expectations that hidden somewhere in the writing of real socialism we find the occult formula of true ontological commitment surviving the collapse of 1989 unscathed. On the contrary, what we find is only patient and detailed attempts, crises, retrenchments, stock-takings, renewed efforts, and galling disappointments. *Only?* This combination of receptivity and initiative, patience and impulsiveness is the very stuff of ontological commitment. Let me then, in this last chapter section, turn to the indexical sign again, with special attention to the emotional affects that are bound up with the subjective experience of it, affects ranging from piety to profanity, laissez-faire to exuberance.

In a seminal 1951 article, credited with inaugurating the postanalytical turn away from Carnap's propositional positivism, Quine argued against the supposition that we can fit any signifying system piece by piece to a single, punctual apprehension of reality, but need something larger to satisfy our referential requirements.[84] Would a single noun, for example, correspond to a physical state at a point x, y, z in time t? Or would the fit be made between a whole sentence and such a state? Quine suggests that, indeed, neither an isolated word nor a statement can be tested against reality: "[O]ur statements about the external world face the tribunal of sense experience not individually but only as a corporate body."[85] To make his case—and to help us make ours—Quine introduces considerations of economics and equilibrium. We are tempted to believe, he argues, that we can separate the discursive (or logical) from the factual (or empirical) and, once they are neatly disentangled, bring the two into an economical relationship with each other by means of a univocal index (à la Ockham's razor). The hitch, Quine argues, is that there is no *one* such relationship or economy of referential thrift. "In logical and mathematical systems either of two mutually antagonistic types of economy may be striven for, and each has its peculiar practical utility. On the one hand we may seek economy of practical expression—ease and brevity in the statement of multifarious relations. . . . Second, however, and oppositely, we may seek economy in grammar and vocabulary."[86] The one economy is akin to the expressive richness of Shakespearean diction, the other to the standardizing power of binary code—even in the most technical language, however, it would be hard to determine strictly to which economy one belonged. Is, for example, Quine's use of "mutually antagonistic types of economy" literal, in the sense of our preceding discussion of marginal utility, or is it figurative? The difference in ontological commitments between any such economic axes requires that we recognize a relativity that cannot be resolved into any purely logical or any plainly observational system of signs.[87] "Total science is like a field of force whose boundary conditions are experience," he writes. "A conflict with experience at the periphery occasions readjustments in the interior. . . . But the total field is so underdetermined by its boundary conditions, experience, that there is much latitude of choice as to what statements to reevaluate in the light of any single contrary experience. No particular experiences are linked with any particular statements in the interior of the field, except indirectly through considerations of equilibrium affecting the field as a whole."[88]

Quine's figure of a general equilibrium brings us to a mental equilibrium index as another important measure for the ontological realism I am after. Just as a functional system is the existential condition for an equilibrium among objects, so is conscious equilibrium the condition for fitting thinking subjects into the order of objects.[89] When all is said and done, even with regard to the compelling vigor of indexes, what a social system produces is conscious acquiescence in and affirmation of its forces. We endure around our balances, we do not endure when all reference to balance is lost. This consciousness of being in dynamic time is just the flip side, the subjective side, of the same objective processes for which the medium is the conduit. The question is how, with what strength and sentiment, Quine's "corporate body" of equilibriated statements relates to the "blindly compelling" index that guides political action out of the wilderness of inconclusive disputation.

At the height of the Cold War, Nobel prize–winning economist Tjalling Koopmans and his collaborator John Montias sought to cut through their era's doomsday tension by means of a signifying system that was beyond all interpretation and thus suited for resolving fundamental economic disputes between capitalism and socialism. They claimed that "for an objective comparison, the descriptions of the systems being compared should be couched as much as possible in system-free terms. . . . The ideal is that the *primitive* (undefined) terms entering into these definitions be few in number and universal in applicability and prior meaning."[90] Like revolutionaries who seek to overcome the false division of subject and object and the alienation and reification of the modern individual, these two economists aimed to tether our ever more hyperbolic thoughts to our modest things. But similar as their aspirations are, their sensibility could not be more different from that of the radical revolutionary's. Their affect is postrevolutionary and level-headed, looking for empirical confirmation of real socialism's merits (or lack thereof), whereas the agitators' affect is prerevolutionary and ecstatic, relishing in an apocalyptic tone. Whereas the former flee politics and its wearying stalemates, the latter embrace politics and its vital self-determination. This enormous discrepancy in affect interests me because it points toward the twofold encounter with the system I have been delineating: the holistic, privative side, and the multiple, partitive side. If equilibrium is the ideal state of system self-sameness, where subject harmonizes with object, then its marker will inevitably be conflicted. On the one hand, it will give the privative case of equilibrium—that is, *dis*equilibrium—striving patiently to develop its immanent potential. On the other hand, it will give the nonsingular case of identity—that is, self-difference—striving violently to rupture its own constraints. Sometimes it will give both: a "coming-to-oneself" (J. R. Becher) and a "getting out of one's own skin" (Franz Fühmann).[91] In any case, there is no authentic choice between the calm of artisanal holism or the pathos of apocalyptic sublime, but they are intimately tied to each other through the temporality of the socialist determination they reference. In this sense, then, Koopmans's and Montias's soothing objective terms promise to justify (and leave in peace) the violent revolutionary event, just as the revolutionary event relies on such terms to organize its emerging identity.

Unsurprisingly, Koopmans was a colleague of Oskar Lange's at the Cowles Commission for econometrics in the 1940s, and Montias—an art historian as well as economist—trained directly in the material balance tradition founded by the Vienna School logical positivist Otto Neurath.[92] Neurath, perhaps the key philosophical figure in the material balance school of economic thought and a major voice in the "socialist calculation" debate started by Mises, had early become convinced that a socialist economy might outperform capitalism by avoiding the crisis-laden market system.[93] In the nineteen-teens, Neurath tried to devise a moneyless means for optimal planning that balanced "objective properties" of economic inputs directly, without the mediation of prices, by conceiving the inputs as "natural kinds" that might, accordingly, relate to each other naturally, on the principle that, as Shakespeare said, "one touch of nature makes the whole world kin."[94] In 1919 he put his convictions to the test as the director of Central Planning in the short-lived Bavarian Soviet, and he was Lenin's first postrevolution mentor for thinking about the practical problems of nonmarket economic organization.

While Neurath's plans came to naught in the White Terror that elim-

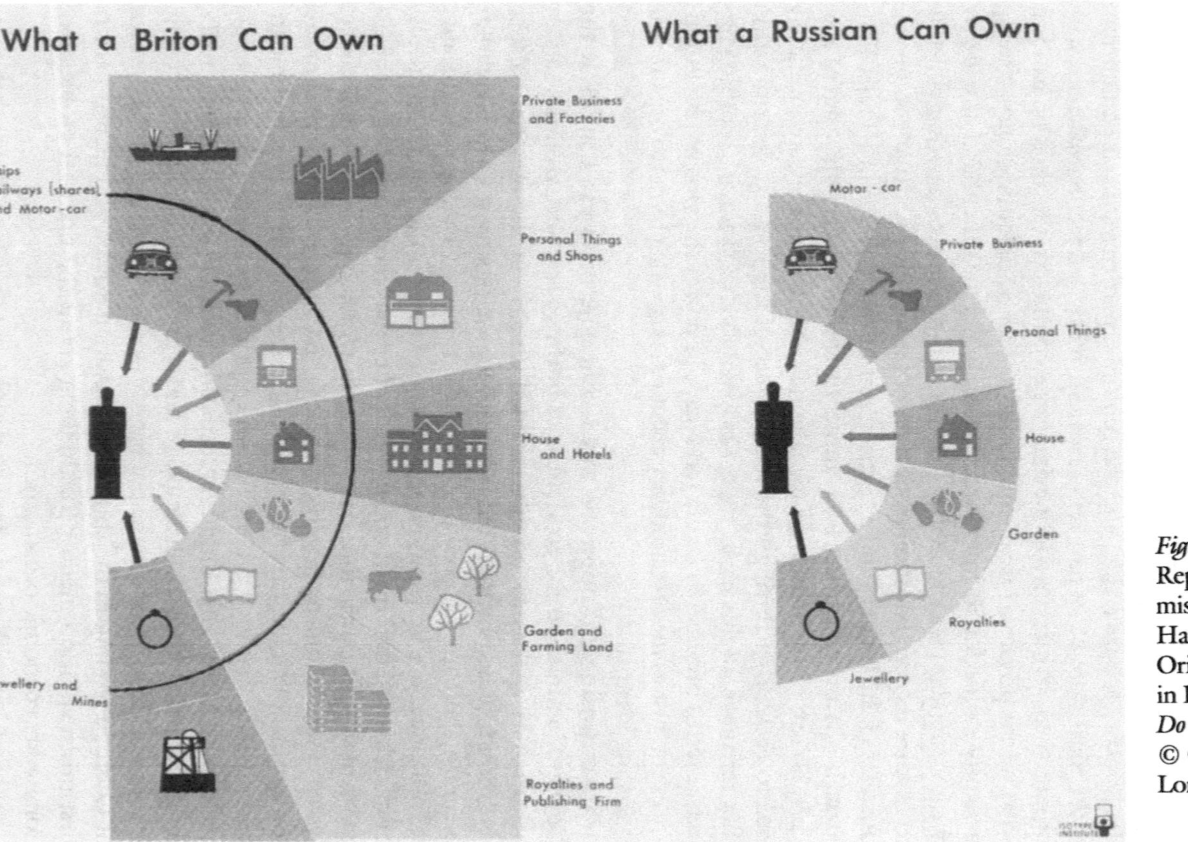

Fig. 2. ISOTYPE chart. Reproduced by permission of Chambers Harrap Publishers Ltd. Originally published in Ralph Parker, *How Do You Do Tovarish* © George C. Harrap, London, 1947.

inated the Bavarian Soviet, his career continued in a telling way: he developed a pictorial language called Isotype that he claimed preselected no particular properties, but let the things to which it referred speak for themselves without any need for interpretation. Drawing his semiotic theory from the work of Charles Morris, a Peirce scholar and semiotician close to the Vienna School, Neurath held that an Isotype united icon and index, *qualia* and quiddity.[95] The idea was not to invent a universal logic that captured empiric reality—that goal belonged to the other logical positivists such as his erstwhile colleague Carnap. On the contrary, Neurath's idea harked back to the Renaissance traditions of *ars combinatoria* and encyclopedism, to the *clavis universalis* that sought to know the world directly as it spoke through its things, not as it was appended to a questionable discursive logic.[96] In other words, Neurath harked back to an era before Kant's "Copernican turn," when things still held their authority before the mind. At the same time, he allied himself with the utilitarianism and behaviorism that characterized technocratic liberal utopias since the Enlightenment. In the late eighteenth century Jeremy Bentham had dreamed of an index called the "political thermometer" that would add up "the greatest happiness of the greatest number," and his nineteenth-century utilitarian follower F. Y. Edgeworth envisioned a similar device for coordinating social felicity with the simple compulsion of a sum that he called a "hedonimeter." Even in the roaring, revolutionary 1920s, after the bloody suppression of his economic experiments, Neurath still supposed, without a hint of irony, that "it is easy to imagine a thoroughly empirical 'felicitology' on a behavorialistic foundation, which could take the place of traditional ethics."[97]

Neurath hoped that his Isotype would guide social interactions in an idiom that was as close to things as it could get. Like an iconography, its symbols resemble the objects they represent. At the same time, their size and distinction are generated by statistical tabulations that function analogously to snapshots—as simple, transparent indexes of quantitative material distributions.[98] Anticipating user-friendly, culture-blind computer interfaces, he describes Isotype as a "picture-text style which should enable anybody to walk through the modern world that is beginning to appear about us and see it as he may see a landscape. . . . The aim is to trace the origin of 'modern men' and depict their behavior and achievements, without presenting any social or economic theory. . . . An international picture language is combined with a world language."[99] Like Peirce's index, each Isotype sign is a "thisness," a particular and compelling institutional fact reduced to its most generic and generative universal force.

In actual experience, however, Isotype seems all too banal. We recognize its figures from toilet doors and roadway exits around the world, but it hardly seems to compel momentous social choices. As easy as it is, however, to turn away now at the eleventh hour, and search the horizon for grander events and brighter signs of wonder, I do not want to dismiss Neurath's technocratic behaviorism and Koopmans's and Montias's cosmopolitan goodwill. Indeed, I share their embrace of some generic index as the measure of the socialist real, just as I share the more heroic pathos of the century's revolutionaries and their explosive dialectical images. As all-inclusive as my socialist index is, however, it cannot be closed off around the finality of either a great thing or a sovereign decision: the rivalry of indexes entails a trial of revelation and a plurality of ordeals. In a secularized modern world, where all prophecy must be proved in public practice, commitment to the existence of socialism is not a commitment to the sign of redemption per se. Rather, it is a commitment to a system that coordinates the holistic progressive pathos—in ecstatic as well as everyday forms—to some vast and robust balance of material goods. Leftists, to be sure, like rightists, will concern themselves passionately with the void of pure antagonism and the plenum of the decisive event. But at the end of the day, after the barricades and red flags, a leftist has to own up to the everyday weight of the socialist burden. At that point, only the real objects a leftist carries can be an expedient against the distortions of capital; and as Dean Swift noted of the Laputans, a people who had foresworn the vagaries of discourse for the certainty of things, "[If] a man's business be very great, and of various kinds, he must be obliged in proportion to carry a greater bundle of things upon his back."[100] In the past century this awkward bundle of things made leftists alternately ridiculous and terrible, leaving today's left with a sorely tested dignity and an ambiguous legacy of compassion and violence—one it prefers to forget in its utopian moments. But only by taking a historical socialist ontology seriously as a contemporary challenge will it succeed in doing better. It must take its mud with its mana.

CHAPTER THREE

The Skin of the System and the DIN of the System: A Poetics of Sovereignty and System

> Given the abstract concept of boundary—the concept of the difference between system and environment—one cannot decide whether the boundary belongs to the system or to the environment. Viewed logically, the difference itself is some third thing [. . .]. Viewed from the system's perspective, boundaries are 'self-generated'—membranes, skins, walls and doors, boundary posts and points of contact.
>
> —Niklas Luhmann, *Social Systems*[1]

I. RÉSUMÉ

Our inquiry now deposits us at the doorstep of East German literature—in particular, the life and work of the enigmatic and philosophically-minded socialist author Franz Fühmann—with several riddles to unravel in the course of gaining admission to the realm of the socialist real. Let me in a few words reformulate the key conclusions of the preceding chapter to see where we stand and how the rest of the book will proceed. The socialism whose real existence we are after is not conceived as a politics that starts and ends with the constitution of free subjects, but as a system that coordinates subjects and objects in a specific way to specific effect. As such a coordinating system, its goal is not to maximize political openness and fluidity, but to create operative closure around certain principles of egalitarian coordination. Politics—as the decision on the exception, in Schmitt's famous definition of the sovereign[2]—is not eliminated, but it is made system-specific, related to the limits of systemic commensurability. The system, in other words, minimizes the opportunity for sovereign decision by striving to re-enter every presented exception back into the system. In this way, the specificity of the system, which also gives the specificity of its exceptions, always seeks to lose itself in the general. The predicates of socialist difference strive to achieve the indifferent generality of the whole (to be the very genus of the social). This progressive tendency describes two sovereign tension points—and thus potentially political moments—inherent in the system, that of its qualitative speciation at the origin and that of its generic supremacy at the end.

A system, I argued, has two necessary qualities: it produces the *unity* of commensurability and compels the *plurality* of some one measure and not another. We come to know the existence of a possible system when we encounter a powerful medium whose functioning can likewise be designated in a twofold way. First, the new medium acts as an *index* in the sense that it is simply, suddenly there for us as a distinct *novum* in our universe, as a sign indicating the potential of another world directly adjacent to our hitherto complete world. Second, the new medium acts as a *symbolic means* of coordination between subjects and objects that only now have come to be matters of interrelation. In the first case, as an index of an opportunity, the medium does not mediate; rather, it stands immediately juxtaposed to us as a disruptive figure of either/or, now/never: either we try to realize an exception or we try to accommodate it to the rule. In this indexical sense, the medium compels a *reaction* from those who encounter it. In the second case, the medium mediates—it is the classic *tertium comparationis*, the third term with the rational potential to relate the exceptionality of any other two. A system thus ranges over an infinite multiplicity of its own devising and also occasionally comes up against that infinity's exterior in the blunt smack of an outside boundary. This external indexical smack is a sharp derangement of subject-object relations that invites us to make a decision, one whose apparently sovereign freedom (or sovereign violence, which here amounts to the same thing) is subject to an objectifying temporality in which it achieves, or fails to achieve, a simplified order that is not only new, but better.

As violent as such a smack is—Peirce describes the index as a shrill whistle piercing into a reverie of self-sufficient sensation[3]—my use of the indexical sign deliberately inflects my discourse away from a psychoanalytic one of trauma and a political one of decisionism to one of pragmatic realism.[4] How boring! Yet, as we have seen, the issue is important because if the real represented by the indexical smack is held only to disrupt symbolic ordering with no character of its own, it can always only figure negatively and violently, exposing the emptiness of any consummation without indicating another sequence (or temporality) of progress.[5] What gets lost in the rhetoric of trauma is the idea that the same disruptive index, the same novel medium, acquires its existential force over us precisely because it promises to mediate a new whole, to become a new and improved functional standard for organization. Meanwhile, the strictly heterogeneous real—the real of recent radical political theory—only puts order into constant flux to assure the autonomy of the political realm. This radical politics' highest reality—its *ultima ratio regnum*, as it were—is the recognition that the political has no positive reality other than itself: it is pure medium without system, where "the system" would only figure for it as a binding centripetal force. Boris Groys, as we have seen, has supplied this *ultima ratio* with its *reductio ad absurdum*. The fantasy of Groys's "communist postscript" consists in imagining a social space completely rewritten from its articulation in restrictive media like money, power, law, and erotics to its open dissemination in the most general and unsystematic medium of figurative language. Or, as Giorgio Agamben puts it, "[P]olitics is the sphere neither of an end in itself nor of means subordinated to an end; rather, it is the sphere of a pure mediality without end, intended as the field of human action and of human thought."[6]

As a dream of medium without system, the new political ontology abolishes the constitutive tensions between system and sovereignty. By contrast, in the literature of real socialism that Fühmann exemplifies, the medium and its endless proliferation of "Thirdness," as Peirce characterized the nature of symbolic circulation, is always confronted with its inherent "Twoness," Peirce's term for the nature of indexical reference.[7] In its ongoing articulation of the world, the medium inevitably also prepares the site where the world encounters its boundary. A social medium is strictly not self-sufficient, "a means without end" in Agamben's phrase, but is also always an index for something outside of itself. That outside figures as both another sovereignty and another system, as both a violent *creatio ex nihilo* and supervening order of commensuration.

2. FÜHMANN BY CONTRAST TO WOLF: CHRISTA WOLF'S IDENTIFICATION WITH IDENTIFICATION

> It wasn't ordained by the good Lord that a typewriter sheet has to measure 210 by 297 millimeters. [. . .] For the first time you realize the presumption of naming one's own measurements DIN, meaning Das Ist Norm—this is the norm.
>
> —Christa Wolf, *Patterns of Childhood*[8]

Before giving a more conventional literary-biographical introduction to Fühmann at the beginning of Part Two, I want to introduce him into this theoretical context by sketching a heuristic contrast between him and the best known East German writer, Christa Wolf. This contrast sharpens our sense of how the theoretical terms I laid out in the last chapter relate to a writer whose work is so saturated with its particular context that the prospect of my theoretical terminology meeting his literary language might seem farfetched. Fühmann and Wolf make an illuminating contrast not only because of the intelligence of their critical commitment to GDR socialism and the intense friendship that ensued through their loyal dissidence but also because they instantiate opposite literary sensibilities whose divergent paths follow closely just the disjunctions of media and equilibria I have been elaborating in the previous chapter. Where Wolf is concerned with the mediated identity of selfhood and the desire for an authentic, stable equilibrium of social belonging, Fühmann is concerned with the multiplicity of mediated worlds and the nonuniqueness of any equilibrium. Fühmann's writing figures socialism under the grammatical sign of the deictic partitive—socialism is *some* one thing, not another. Harking back to the Aristotelian τοδε τι or *hoc aliquid*, this deictic partitive functions as the index of the recalcitrantly empirical world. Its partiality and multiplicity drive Fühmann's narrative quests with ever increasing violence beyond the limits of identification into excess, transgression, and, ultimately, rupture. Wolf's writing figures socialism under the grammatical sign of the privative (or internal negation)—socialism is always a lacking state of *dis*equilibrium or *im*balance. Harking back to the Aristotelian στερησις or *privatio boni*, this privative functions as a mediating symbol whose infinite relativity always calls for an interpreter. Its restless incompletion turns her novels ever inward in a process of groping—the *tâtonnement* or *Abtasten* of a feedback loop[9]—searching for an immanent measure or standard around which a stable identity might converge. The intensity of both writers' work points toward the radical otherness distinguishing the system whose presence they are trying to grasp. Whether in an impossible rupture or an impossible identification, an image of unity and sovereignty flashes up now and again fleetingly through their writing.

Let us turn to Christa Wolf and briefly see how the themes of her work tie in with the arguments we have been developing about the reality of socialism. Wolf epitomizes a narrative ambition complementary to Fühmann's: instead of a paradoxical identification with change and plurality, Wolf looks inward into her characters and their social milieu in search of "the very inmost part, where the nucleus of the personality develops and consolidates," as she put it in her influential 1968 statement of socialist poetics, "The Reader and the Writer," an essay called the "founding document" of critical GDR literature.[10] A substantial body of literary study has linked Wolf's work closely with this theme of interiority, especially with issues of feminine subjectivity, the difficulty of achieving a coherent narrative voice, and the importance of spiritual depth in a modern world of technological alienation and military violence.[11] Like Fühmann, Wolf begins her literary reflections with a society transformed by "the revolution that does away with private property in the means of production" (196). Wolf proposes that "one should ask oneself whether the emergence of a new kind of society does not confront the writer who deliberately commits himself to it with tasks radically different from simply modifying the content of old literary patterns" (202). This firm starting point—the new kind of society—is the "established fact" (202) from which Wolf's controversial, because explicitly relativist, socialist realism begins. How are its tasks "radically different" from those of old literary patterns?

According to the structuralist critic Tzvetan Todorov, "the minimal complete plot consists in the passage from one equilibrium to another. An 'ideal' narrative begins with a stable situation which is disturbed by some power or force. There results a state of disequilibrium; by the action of a force directed in the opposite direction, the equilibrium is re-established; the second equilibrium is similar to the first, but the two are never identical."[12] Todorov's structuralist impulse is comprehensive and ahistorical, seeking "the codes and conventions which make . . . meanings possible."[13] Wolf's problem, however, is that the new world her writing is announcing is not complete and ahistorical, but characterized precisely by its unprecedented newness. "A change has occurred in one's perception of the world that even casts doubts on the unimpeachable memory; we see 'the world' once more—but what do we mean by the world?—in a different light" (177). The "equilibrium states" through which she might refer to her world are simply lacking. Disequilibrium is not a brief passage in her plots between stable starting and end points, but the existential condition of her writing. Historicizing an a priori narrative grammar like Todorov's, Wolf comments on the development of the modern plot [Fabel]:

> [T]his construction, built on an extremely solid foundation, was bound to show up most clearly in those plots that ended in tragedy—typical for the bourgeois novel; and the dying hero also bequeathed to his heirs some unquestionable constant values: reality, whatever might be understood by this, and space and time as its immovable coordinates. The unrivaled optimism of this mechanism, not to be doubted even by those it crushes, is obvious: I perish, but it remains

> and moves. This had a function, it encouraged understanding and imagination, stimulated ability, exposed contradictions without endangering the substance and, in every case, engendered reality. (195)

Against the immovable "coordinates" in which the bourgeois novel functions, described so neatly by Todorov as an equilibrium equation, Wolf suggests that socialism has introduced an inevitable relativism that leaves behind "a mechanical attitude to the world in favor of a dialectical one" (195). Emblematic for Wolf of this new attitude is the physicist responsible for "the uncertainty principle" in natural science, Werner Heisenberg. The new writer, like the subatomic relativist, must be guided by an "urge to go forward into those still uncharted regions in which the structure of the moral world of man living in society is open to question, a feeling perhaps similar to the cautious groping of the atomic scientist when he ventures to develop provisional pictures of what goes on inside the atom. We are fascinated, not without reason, by an adventure that takes the outward form of extremely exact, delicate and probably, through constant repetition, monotonous measurements" (200).

The heroic relativism of Wolf's new socialist writer, however, encounters the unheroic problem of any relativism taken to its logical extreme. As each provisional system of values gives way to the next, no system has any meaning for any other until the din of an infinite regression finally drowns out the possibility of a shared world. Plato first played out the absurdity of such absolute relativism in the Socratic dialogue *Theaetetus*, where he demonstrates the incoherence of Protagoras' famously plural notion that "each man is the measure of each and every thing."[14] For no matter how precise each person's measurement of each thing, the measurement would be obsolete as soon as it was taken, since, as Socrates notes, nothing "even appear[s] the same to yourself, because you never remain in the same condition."[15] As a result, says Socrates, reducing Protagoras' idea to absurdity, "we must not admit the expressions 'something' or 'somebody's' or 'mine' or 'this' or 'that' or any other word that brings things to a standstill."[16] The basic indexicals of empirical reference are impossible. The world that the socialist writer, tossed onto terra incognita, would want to point to as "something," as "this" world, this new world, vainly regresses—it is a "constant repetition" that does not converge on a stable picture of an atom, or consolidate the "nucleus of the personality," but explodes into meaningless noise.

Reflecting on this problem of trying to stabilize "a pattern of experience" in her life, Wolf comes across a banal, but disturbing childhood memory:

> I remember the can of Libby's milk that confused me as a child, the paper band on which a smiling nurse balances another can of Libby's milk with that confounded nurse on it, now very small, with the ever-present can balanced on her hand . . . and so on ad infinitum, no longer to be seen but, and that was the horrible suggestion, on which tinier and tinier nurses went on holding out cans of condensed milk to the consumer. This thought irritated me because the entire effort of imagination led to nothing, the funnel down which one had forced one's imagination to creep finally ended up in empty space. (179–80)

This infinite regression represents the potentially ruinous disequilibrium with which the new socialist plot begins—or fails to begin.[17] The task of the writer is not to return the tenuous story of socialism to a balance like one that had existed earlier, before the revolution doing away with private property, but to assess the new story, to see where it is tending, to be sensitive to its immanent disposition. "If questions of reference of the sort we are considering make sense only relative to a background language, then evidently questions of reference for the background language make sense in turn only relative to a further background language," Quine argues about the relativity of existence and experience. But he seems to see a handy way out that Plato denied was possible in such a relativistic world: "In practice of course we end the regress of coordinate systems by something like pointing."[18] Indeed, as we suggested, the socialist narrator would like to point at the relationships in which she and her characters are embedded and exclaim, like Miranda, "Oh, brave new world that has such people in it," but the problem is that, without a pre-existing equilibrium to give the world its identity as a self-compatible and coordinated whole, there is nothing recognizably there to point to.[19] Unable to point directly at the world, Wolf points at change itself as an index of something—socialism—that only exists as a possible tendency eventually reconciling her state of disequilibrium. "A change has occurred[;] . . . the unease [*Unruh*] is observable" (177, translation modified). The *un*ease is observable.

Here, in Wolf's foundational document of GDR literature, we come across two of the central themes of her writing. First, there is the disequilibrium of the socialist narrative. This disequilibrium bears a privative relationship to equilibrium, just as the observable unease with change bears a privative relation to an as yet unperceivable ease. Wolf's writing seeks to determine whether the disequilibrium of her experiences will become the balanced identity to which the experiences bear such a profound internal relation of lack; whether palpable unease will eventually turn into the ease of a "new way of being in the world." Since the lacking equilibrium or ease—the stable state—cannot be pointed at directly, it has to be referred to *in*directly. Such indirect pointing—given the technical name "deferred ostension" by Quine[20]—is the way that we point to a meter to say that our car has gas (or does not), and this meter and its metrics constitute a second key socialist theme of Wolf's writing: the desired, but deferred index of the socialist real. Unlike the case in Fühmann, the index never strikes directly in Wolf, but always leaves space and time for interpretation.

"Prose makes people, in a double sense," Wolf contends at the end of her essay, describing prose as the crucial medium for consolidating socialist reality, a medium more promising for her than money, whose black and white rigidity she sees as holding little prospect for equilibriating socialism. "It breaks up deadly simplification by displaying the possibilities of living in a human way. It serves as a store of experience and judges the structures of human societies from the point of view of productivity. It can compress and save time by playing through on paper the experiments facing mankind; here it coincides with the standards of socialist society" (212). These flexible socialist standards we might call the improved DIN of the system, where D*eutsche* I*ndustrie* N*ormen* (German Industrial Norms) are the fixed physical standards by which the engineered German economy reproduces and optimizes itself as a quality-controlled system. At the same time, if the literary meter of ease and unease, balance and imbalance, begins to point away from a stable value, then socialist prose will not issue in new and higher standards for the coming society, but only in noise, in the din of a fading future, in an ever smaller nurse holding an ever smaller can of milk.

3. SOCIALISM BEYOND SYSTEM: FRANZ FÜHMANN'S DESIRE FOR THE OPTIMUM OPTIMORUM

> I won't be able to get out of my skin anymore and I never could . . . *Still*, to escape one's skin.
>
> —Franz Fühmann, *Twenty-two Days*[21]

Let us now anticipate the contrary direction of Fühmann's work and how it relates to our conceptual apparatus, deferring the details of his oeuvre and biography until Chapter 4.[22] "From where does one start in drawing up a balance?" Fühmann asks in his 1973 "Lebensbilanz," his midcareer assessment of his life up to that point, *Twenty-two Days or Half a Lifetime.*[23] "Of course, from 'my function'—but who is to guide one to it?" In a famous slogan, Quine comments that "to be is to be the value of a variable"; but, he goes on to caution, this existential function serves only "in testing the conformity of a given remark or doctrine to a prior ontological standard."[24] That standard, as Fühmann's work demonstrates, is especially elusive in a real socialism that is based on a claim of radical otherness to prior social systems such as Weimar liberalism and Nazi fascism. But at the midpoint of his career, in 1973, the lack of a starting point for assessing the balance of his life is becoming alarming. In the subsequent dozen years until his death in 1984, his search for the variables identifying his social function (to realize "socialism"?) and the values balancing it (those of the "New Man"?) becomes only more desperate and intense—but never leads him to a firm answer. Instead, it draws him along a path of increasingly perverse, violent, and dysfunctional stories to the limits of his literary medium, where he arrives again at the ancient Eleatic paradoxes of transformation whose disabling contradictions it had been his life's work to overcome. "My vain attempts . . . to describe that which is called transformation!" he sighs. "It is the experience of my life, for twenty years my theme, but it is really still just an intention . . ." (99). One generation before Socrates, the Eleatic philosophers Zeno and Parmenides, the founders of ontological thought, held the view that everything is one unchanging whole (*το εον*), that transformation and plurality are unreal. Even motion, according to Zeno's best known paradox, is impossible, for in moving from one point to another, one must always pass the halfway point, and, since there remains always another half to traverse, one never arrives at one's goal. Revisiting these ontological paradoxes in the writings of his remaining half a life, however, Fühmann never finds the classical balance of the single Parmenidean substance—the structure and stasis of the whole—but is compelled to the opposite conclusion: *only* transformation and plurality are real.

How was Fühmann to know that the halfway point marked by his book was actually closer to the end of his career in the ungentle hands of colon cancer and the end of socialism in capitulation to capitalist West Germany? Yet in the face of inevitable uncertainty, he initially hazards a voluntaristic answer to the question of the right vantage for assessing the balance of his life, entertaining the idea of a self-sufficient Archimedean standpoint (*που στω*) outside the partial functions of one system or another. He tentatively ventures that the "sovereign decision of the individual writer" (85) establishes a center of gravity around which the writer's world revolves, the poet being, in Novalis's words, "the self-consciousness of the universe."[25] Such sovereign capability, Fühmann surmises, depends in turn on the uniqueness of a writer, "and this indispensability should also be the starting point of society" (85). But his sovereign hopes promptly stumble upon that first surmise, for who qualifies as irreplaceably unique in the brutal context of the twentieth century? He reminds himself that, although his function as a young soldier in Hitler's war happened to be telegraphing from the front and not gassing inmates at Auschwitz, "you would have functioned in Auschwitz exactly as you had behind your telegraph machine in Charkow or Athens: that's why you were there, my friend" (207). "An equal sign between you and [Auschwitz guard Oswald] Kaduk? Yes . . . your transformation begins in the moment that you see Nuremberg as your own case" (210). Only by grasping the universal comparability and interchangeability of elements in a system—that is, only by apprehending the system as a specific unity—is another system imaginable. Transformation emerges as a consequence of being some one thing and not another. His own plurality appears by way of this insight into his larger identity, and only in the multiplicity of such identities is the stasis of one system or another, be it fascism or something more benign, escapable: "[B]eing open toward every direction: the decisive conjunctures of life, points of possible transformation, but also possible non-transformation, and the sum of the avenues between such open points, all this is biography" (114).

Like the openness and totality of the biography to which it refers, the linguistic medium itself in Fühmann's view is plural in its relationship to its "boundary conditions, experience" (Quine). "Could it be," Fühmann asks, "that in the various aspects of its primary meaning a sentence is in each instance false, but in the totality of all its aspects true?" Like the earlier hypothesis of a sovereign decision, this question puts forward the romantic hypothesis of a "Universalpoesie."[26] If such a sentence exists, he infers, "then the concept of the optimum belongs to the concept of a declarative sentence: with regard to all its aspects—optimum exactness. Could one say: optimal univocity?" (193). This idea of an optimum is a crucial idea in Fühmann's writing, reappearing in different contexts and guises as a hope for a balanced perspective (the most meaningful one—and in that superlative sense no longer a perspective, but an ultimate truth) achieved beyond the merely provincial optima of a given system. The essential point Fühmann is making is that for any claim to universality, one needs singularity—a single scale relating every part over which to optimize meaning as exhaustive and impartial. Absolute optimality thus belongs to a conception of an ultimate medium—whether that medium is money, love, law, language, or some as yet unheard-of thing remains an open question.

This ideality of an absolute optimum is recognized as mathematically untenable in General Equilibrium accounts of the liberal economy. In a central GE tenet, the equilibrium characteristic of the money economy is established at what is known as a "Pareto optimum."[27] Pareto optimality describes an optimum with respect to variables mediated in a single, existing system of interrelations, and it expresses the point where their values are maximized. In a liberal economy, a state is defined as Pareto optimal if, given available capacities and supplies, there is no other state that satisfies at least one consumer to a higher degree and none to a lower. It is a local optimum over a given set of alternatives that are not compared as independently subsisting cardinal values, but ranked as *relative* preferences (ordinal values) by pleasure-maximizing consumers. Importantly, a Pareto optimum, the only one available in GE, is *not* the universal optimum per se. It is the best equilibrium state to which an existing system is disposed. It has no way to refer to optima to which the system has no immanent disposition.

Returning to Fühmann's observations about language and its possibilities of meaning, we can follow how this same notion of a local (Pareto) optimum fails the optimistic desires of Fühmann's own writing. An optimum, in its constitution through a single scale, is never a true *optimum optimorum*—the best of the best. When Fühmann reflects on the idea of the superlative, he notes that a superlative is by definition a singular and a conclusion, not a multiple and new beginning. "The best" is always just one thing and the last thing in a series. "Each use of the superlative," he observes, "is a piece of pessimism: here is the peak, from here nothing goes any further." The singularity of "the best"—the optimum—defeats the possibility of something "better" through the stasis of its own conclusiveness: "Superlatives set terminals: to this point and no further! What goes beyond it is a new quality and starts again with the positive!" (97). Fühmann's plots begin by seeking something that goes beyond the best and the most, as a foundational, albeit still partial element of another sequence—and in the escalating narrative violence of this quest to found a final series, his protagonists come to recognize the impossibility of their desire and the consequent plurality and incommensurability of their foundation.

If a Pareto optimum is the only optimum available to an economy in the view of orthodox economics, then GE serves as a foil for Fühmann's desire for an *optimum optimorum*. Where GE purports to identify the monetary economy with a rigorous mathematical relation, Fühmann's desire to transgress that relation leads him to identify with difference from economy, and the content of that difference is socialism, as the equilibrium relation's negation and supersession in the absolutely new. The merely ordinal relation of GE theory is surpassed in the cardinality of the unconditional best. Fühmann's literary identification with socialism thus takes on the form of an identification with difference from economy.

Because identification, as we have seen in the discussion of media, is itself a quasi-economic process of finding a unique balance, an identification with difference from economy is necessarily also a paradoxical formulation. The violence of this paradox was a central theme of the French surrealist and "anti-economist" Georges Bataille, whose work proposes a state of egalitarian consumption in a realm outside of and prior to conventional liberal economics of scarcity.[28] For Bataille the goal of life, which he called "sovereignty," is excess beyond all utility, including the utility of reproduction—sovereignty is a pure eroticism rather than a calculating economy, or, as he grandly put it, it is "a freedom for which, instantly, everything is resolved, *everything is rich*—in other words, everything [. . .] is commensurate with the universe."[29] This Bataillean excess and abandon, like its thrifty and husbanding opposite, GE, also serves as a foil for Fühmann's desire to identify socialism as something that can be experienced and written about as a really existing difference.

As the GDR abolished private property, capital, and the money-price system in its founding years, it transgressed the orthodox taboos of economic identity. "Would the communist society," Fühmann wonders, "be the society without taboos?" (174). Without taboos of thrift and measure, is one left with only the erotics of sheer unbounded drive as a beyond to economics? But in what sense could one speak of any existence uneconomically, as pure means or pure ends? These typical Fühmann conundrums are those of what I call the "systems erotics of socialism," the passionate dialectic by which Fühmann writes of his commitment to socialism as a search for an *optimum optimorum* that takes the form of an identification with difference from economy, an evisceration of and desire for all the achievements of self-ordering.

Using a theological rather than libidinal analogy, Niklas Luhmann makes a similar point about how fundamental this movement of self-supersession is to the identity of socialism:

> In *religious* cosmology the devil had the function of introducing moral difference into the world. Observing God, the devil wouldn't think of soaring to the level of God the Lord, since that would mean: desiring to be better than the best, and to be one as The One. . . . In *capitalist* cosmology this law repeats itself. Capitalism's incontrovertible economic success cannot be outdone. . . . When socialism

makes the attempt, it fails; which it might have recognized by normal scientific means. Meanwhile, however, the moral difference is made use of. Whoever morally rejects capitalism owes his position to the devil; and socialism, should one want to speak of it well—that is, badly—is in this sense of the devil's party.[30]

4. SOVEREIGNTY BEYOND PERSON: THE EROTICS OF DISTINCTION

A sudden blow: the great wings beating still
Above the staggering girl, her thighs caressed
By the dark webs, her nape caught in his bill,
He holds her helpless breast upon his breast.
How can those terrified vague fingers push
The feathered glory from her loosening thighs?
And how can body, laid in that white rush,
But feel the strange heart beating where it lies?
A shudder in the loins engenders there
The broken wall, the burning roof and tower
And Agamemnon dead.
Being so caught up,
So mastered by the brute blood of the air,
Did she put on his knowledge with his power
Before the indifferent beak could let her drop?
—William Butler Yeats, "Leda and the Swan"[31]

If in this chapter and the previous one, I have been criticizing the way the "new political ontology" values sovereignty at the expense of system, the remainder of the chapter comes back to sovereignty as the unfulfillable genus, as the desired One, the Best One, the *optimum optimorum*, that is always divided again by the specificity of its systemic boundaries. In this sense, I want to be clear that by arguing for (if not exclusively in) an analytic idiom of pragmatic realism, I am not dedicating myself only to the "delicate and . . . monotonous measurements" Wolf admired in the subatomic scientist. Rather, the ecstasies and intensities hinted at in political ontology return in Fühmann's writing to qualify the system, just as the system qualifies the sovereign. As contrasting as their narrative arcs and affects are, Wolf and Fühmann are both writing about the conflict between sovereignty and system in socialism. They desire the sovereign essence of their socialist commitments—the self-sufficiency of belonging to the best there is—but they can locate it only by affirming their system's difference, by constantly dividing the ontological unity whose consolation they seek.

Modern political philosophy is far from unanimous about what sovereignty actually means. I want to consider briefly three distinct aspects of sovereignty before returning to the sense that I see as most relevant to Fühmann's writing. In the work of Carl Schmitt, who remains the touchstone for contemporary discussion, sovereignty is the personal element in politics. It is the guarantee that politics cannot be separated from the subjectivity of its leaders. To say that sovereignty is the highest power, underived from anything else, does not distinguish for Schmitt what sovereignty actually comes down to—which for him is the decision on the state of exception. This fateful decision can have no objectivity, since it applies by definition to what lies beyond any shared system of rules. It is nothing other than the demand that personality, or, in another idiom, *life*, be accorded its full political due.[32] This insistence on the personal, in the idiom of life I have alluded to, continues in the work of Giorgio Agamben, who seeks his own synthesis of what real life, before its bifurcation into biological life (*zoe*) and religious-juridical life (*bios*), demands from a future politics.

Although both Schmitt and Agamben want to save the personality from the system, respecting sovereignty is the solution for Schmitt, whereas it is the problem for Agamben.[33] In Agamben's account, sovereignty characterizes a state's exceptional origin in the very effacement of its origin, wherein sovereign authority banishes its founding scapegoat (the unacceptable sacrifice) from any self-accounting. The scapegoat figure, which Agamben calls the *homo sacer*, is produced as the immanent exclusion constituting both the juridical and religious orders. Such an exclusion grants these orders—the bases of the modern state—the ability to dispose over their discounted misfits as "mere life." Not the decisive leader, but the concentration camp is Agamben's image for what sovereign power comes down to: in the name of order, sovereignty degrades the disorderly into unworthy and indifferent life.

Agamben's account leads us from Schmitt's personalism to the second of three main aspects of sovereignty as it is currently discussed—namely, its status as the obscure origin of state authority, as both a universal law-giving property and an exceptional property of standing above the law. This is Hannah Arendt's theme in *On Revolution*, where a state's sovereign constitution makes it simultaneously an exception to any pre-existing authority (violently born out of the ruins of the *ancien régime*) and an object subordinated to its own new authority (in violation of its founding exceptionality).[34] Arendt puts the vicious circle, whose clearest formulation she traces to Abbé Sieyès, this way: "[T]hose who get together to constitute a new government are themselves unconstitutional, that is, they have no authority to do what they have set out to achieve. The vicious circle in legislating is present [. . .] in laying down the fundamental law, the law of the land or the constitution which, from then on, is supposed to incarnate the 'higher law' from which all laws ultimately derive their authority."[35] Rather than the necessity of personal leadership, what comes to the fore in Arendt is the necessity that sovereignty not be hypostatized as an absolute origin (*arché*) beyond all procedure. Indeed, as much as Arendt wants to preserve the personal deliberative element of politics, system returns in her account as the only way to secure the ongoing legitimation of the exception.

The third theme, finally, is symmetrical to the second—not the paradox of origin (*arché*), but that of finality (*telos*).[36] This is the theme of Bataille's *The Accursed Share*, where sovereignty "has little to do with the sovereignty of States," but is a quasi-economic notion distinguished by "the consumption of wealth, as against labor and servitude, which produce wealth without consuming it."[37] In Bataille, as we saw in the section just above, the paradox is that the aspiration to sovereignty, in order truly to refer only to itself as its own end, cannot be subordinated to any other end, yet the very process of sustaining and reproducing itself implies subordination to the means of its perpetuation. Where Arendt wants to solve the problem of how eruptive revolutions establish new authority binding in perpetuity (the "perpetual union" of the American Articles of Confederation), the anarchic Bataille recoils at the infinitely reciprocal bonds of perpetuity as precisely the burden that sovereignty needs to shuck off. "We may say, in other words, that it is servile to consider duration first, to employ the present time for the sake of the future, which is what we do when we work."[38] For Bataille, sovereignty can ultimately only be an act of useless immolation (*inutilité*).

As much as these various understandings of sovereignty illuminate crucial issues in Fühmann's writing, the challenge in my own use of the term is to express the positive differential that matters for Fühmann, the decisive *quality* of socialist sovereignty. Sovereignty for our purposes is not a personalistic property, but a property guaranteeing system distinction—it is the substance of a difference. Neither the origin nor end of politics, sovereignty hovers, like system, around the limits of important decisions. In this sense, even the freest, most unencumbered action is always a reaction; while even the most servile reaction harbors active initiative. By emphasizing only the latter half of the equation, the new political ontology portrays politics as both supremely generative and an end in itself. For Ernesto Laclau, as we have seen, the sovereign is approximated by the "empty signifier" to which the political contest strives to assign a proper name. "Identification with the empty signifier is the *sine qua non* for the emergence of a 'people.'"[39] But since such popular identification cannot ever be complete, "there is no beyond the play of differences."[40] The inevitability of interpretative play in political contestation is what enables hegemony and lends politics its generative force. What matters in Fühmann's stories, by contrast, is precisely what does indeed lie beyond the play of differences—namely, the difference that makes a difference. Identity is not a-morphous, but results from a meta-morphosis as sharp as the scalpel separating it out as *some*thing new. Tough boundaries and unforgiving changes, the signs indicating superiority and inferiority in social progress, have shaped the history of real socialism Fühmann is narrating.

In this chapter's epigraph Niklas Luhmann reminds us that "boundaries are . . . skin." Fühmann, who calls transformation his lifelong theme, imagines the way transformation violates boundaries as a process of getting out of one's skin. As Luhmann notes, while the skin seems to be self-generated from one point of view, from another it seems imposed; and from a third point of view, "one cannot decide whether a boundary belongs to the system or to the environment."[41] Another way to put Luhmann's dilemma here is to say that it is not universally evident whether the sovereign sets the boundaries—decides, in Schmitt's language, between friend and foe—or whether the sovereign has the boundaries imposed, and is hardly sovereign after all. Without a system commitment, the very idea of decision is jeopardized. The ability to make a sovereign decision is a result of systemizing real options, which bring in turn a liability to succumb to the system's judgments. It is just this dilemma of the skin that Fühmann sees enacted with brutal logic upon Marsyas, the hapless satyr flayed alive by Apollo in the classical Greek myth. What is at issue for Fühmann is whether the infinite playfulness of the satyr can ever encounter the otherness of its boundaries, whether it can—to hark back to Zeno—ever actually get anywhere, "beyond the play of differences." By the same token, he wonders whether Apollo's particular judgments are not always betrayed by their abstractly universal form. Can Marsyas ever get out of his skin? Can Apollo ever embrace his own embodiment? The harshness of Fühmann's mythical vision seems to confirm the supposed inability of socialism to reform, let alone transform. Singular and uncomprehending, socialism, in Fühmann's bloody figures of evisceration, appears captive to its inability to shed its straitening skin.

But reading Fühmann's work as focused on socialism's immoveable body would be the wrong reading. What stands out is the challenge posed to the singularity of sovereignty by actuality of *other* systems, by the *plurality* of choices that might make a difference. Socialist sovereignty in Fühmann is not a pure presence, without reference to anything else—it is not simply a name or an icon of itself—but emerges through a quest for the *reference*, for the specific quality that makes socialism worth embracing as the new, and best, body politic. On the face of it, however, such plurality seems worlds away from the stereotypical image of the grim Berlin Wall, armed borders shielding Communist Party functionaries resisting mounting pressures to reform their hide-bound system. Plurality's enormous ideological significance seems instead to belong to the "open society" of the liberal West. Besides denoting multiplicity, plurality connotes a process of liberal integration: *e pluribus unum*, in the motto of the Great Seal of the United States. It connotes tolerance, diversity, and the peaceful coexistence of differences. In its received liberal sense, plurality is surely an inappropriate word for an oeuvre conspicuously lacking in reassurance. Fühmann's dark affinities with Romanticism, Vitalism, and Decisionism—movements associated with conservative names such as Novalis, Schopenhauer, Nietzsche, Heidegger, and Jünger—suggest at first glance what historian Fritz Stern ominously called German "illiberalism" and what Lukács summarily dismissed as "the destruction of reason."[42] While East German avant-garde dramatist Heiner Müller had no qualms about provocatively affirming Carl Schmitt's influence on him, in Fühmann's writing the decisionist elements remain reluctant, only to explode with the overpowering necessity of a story's irrational development.[43] Fühmann's work tends to extremes, challenging the integration of difference in favor of its disruption, supersession, and renewed eruption. To get out of one's skin means for Fühmann not to reinvent oneself through a fresh-faced makeover, but to ground oneself in the singularity and sublimity of difference from everything familiar: to stand alone.

If, against common sense, I maintain the concept of plurality as the touchstone of Fühmann's socialist realism, it is because the lonely sovereign sublime appears in it again and again not as a cipher of mystical self-sufficiency, not as pure symbolic representation with no reference, but to vouchsafe the real substance of the distinction between socialism and capitalism: that they qualify as alternatives to each other, that they supply grounds for a choice between them, that system plurality is substantial and not cosmetic, that socialism is some one thing and not something else. Thus, the role of sovereignty in our discussion of Fühmann stands in contrast to a nostalgic *corpus unum mysticum*—or, as we will see, the chivalric amorous union—whose ripe symbolism flourished in the fin de siècle literature of decadence and *Jungendstil* that nonetheless influenced Fühmann, and whose theorization in Ernst Kantorowicz's 1957 study *The King's Two Bodies* continues to inform contemporary analyses of sovereignty. Examining "the halo of perpetuity" gracing a medieval king, Kantorowicz observes that while authority is embodied by the mortal king, his physical death does not entail a discontinuous interregnum.[44] Rather, the problem of orderly succession is resolved by postulating two bodies for the king, a mortal body [*corporis naturalis*] and a body politic [*corpus mysticum*]. Whereas the mortal body dies, the body politic functions as corporation in perpetuity, passing on the majesty and dignity of the royal institution from one sovereign to the next. Drawing upon Kantorowicz by way of Claude Lefort, Julia Hell's study of East German literature, *Post-Fascist Fantasies*, characterizes its foundational narratives as ideological fantasies of two bodies: an antifascist father's body and the sublime communist body.[45] Focusing on the patriarchal iconography of party leaders, on the symbolism of red flags and martyred dead, Hell's reading of GDR literature accords socialism no specific difference; socialist society in Hell's analysis has no reference beyond the symbolism of its own sovereignty, in which self-sacrificing antifascists endlessly battle fascists over the empty space of the sublime father.

Fühmann's portrayals of the dilemmas of socialist sovereignty cannot be contrasted more strongly. His growing aversion to the pious pageantry of red flags and heroes, to talismanic words like "the people" and "socialist fatherland," is what drives his quest for a qualitative difference beyond the ancient symbolism that the new socialist states heavy-handedly sought to appropriate for themselves. The turbulent socialism of rational plans and irrational choices that emerges in Fühmann is worlds away from medieval corporations and stately rituals of majesty; worlds away from the homogenous community called forth by a leader's glorious martial decisions. Already in his 1965 antiwar story "King Oedipus," Oedipus' patricidal drama is displaced by the more subtle one of Teiresias, "who knew everything and didn't speak for fear of what was to come."[46] If GDR literature could only produce antifascist negations of fascist fathers, then its emerging conflicts would omit the very third term that would constitute the coming socialist order. Fühmann's literary test thus becomes whether socialism's unique drama can be told in the idiom of its future, in the positivity of its difference—rather than in anxiety-filled rehearsals of its Red Army–aided rupture from fascism. Depicting neither the long-suffering perpetuity of a body politic, nor the rejuvenating pageantry of a royal succession, Fühmann's stories instead pursue a distinct articulation (or catastrophic disarticulation) of a qualitative socialist difference. As Brecht wryly warned rhapsodists whose visions stopped at the glory of revolution, "[T]he struggles of the mountains are behind us, before us lie the struggles of the plains."[47]

For the purposes of our readings, then, sovereignty is not the opposite of plurality, but the quality which ensures that multiplicity is *not in name only*. What is sovereign is the positive difference—the *differentia specifica*—between capitalism, fascism, and socialism. In their process of mutual qualification, however—and here is the rub—socialist sovereignty aspires to unqualified difference (difference without economic constraint): for what gives socialism its weight as a practical (if risky) choice is its potential to supersede and exclude capitalism as an inferior organization of modern experience. Fühmann's violent fictions are not intolerant or chauvinist, as are some of their gloomier literary antecedents, but their topic is the intolerant metabolism—the diabolism—that regulates the relationship of difference to order and sovereignty to system. Distinction, change, and progress loom as frightening, even apocalyptic processes of separating and dividing, beginning and ending that require "a step into the unknown that has nothing comparable in previous experience, a new dimension."[48]

The commitment to "a new dimension" that characterizes Fühmann's own work is conceived by him along the lines of an *erotic* commitment. In his 1975 poetic credo, "The Mythical Element in Literature," Fühmann evokes for his readers the radiant horror surrounding a first sexual coupling, noting that the mysterious other one, like a new system, is "the enemy who will cut an unimaginable wound (*Wunde*) in the self, but this wound, as you vaguely suspect—or, better yet, as something in you knows—this wound is simultaneously the gate opening up onto the miraculous (*Wunderbare*)" (93). A primordial sexual myth like Leda and the Swan, endlessly and stubbornly varied throughout the mythic corpus, captures the tension of sovereignty and system so much more acutely than any didactic realism could, precisely because "the real career and status designations" (95) of socialist society cannot encompass a reality large and significant enough to understand itself. While such precise designations point to "our familiar way of being" [*unseres vertrauten Daseins*], they cannot point beyond that self-enclosed familiarity to any difference that truly makes a difference. They cannot capture the adversarial impulses of familiar affection and strange carnality that motivate a determination of, and commitment to, what is real. Conventional realism operates with one coordinate system, and so lacks the torsion, the productive skewing, that only the possibility of two unrelated coordinate systems somehow relating to each other can have. "Myth," in Fühmann's view of its achievement, "reproduces a contradiction [. . .]; in one aspect that we need recognize as essential, myth corresponds to life" (95). As general as its problematic is, the erotic myth of Leda and the Swan directs readers to the privation and superfluity of real experience in a way the punctilious ethics of a nominalist realism cannot. In Zeus' seduction (or rape) of Leda (or Nemesis),

> there is no bad and good in neat separation, in fact there is neither good nor bad at all, there is not even question and answer, here there is only one thing that could help, and that is experience, and this is exactly what is missing. Threat and temptation, fear and longing, terror and attraction, submission or refusal: every first amorous union is suspended between such poles. (94)

Just as the *corpus unum mysticum* of sovereignty is sundered by Fühmann's pursuit of a qualitative reference for socialism's difference, so we see that the amorous union is torn between poles of contrary affects, between the irreconcilable choices presented in a first sexual encounter. Rather than resolving these oppositions into a perfumed unity of tender affection, into a transcendental incorporation, Fühmann's poetics is committed to the realism of irreducibly carnal erotics. Fear and desire, commitment or rejection—the erotic union, just like the sovereign socialist aspiration, is always divided and self-transgressing. This erotics of sovereignty, then, is the counterpart to the pragmatics of system that together inform Fühmann's socialist realism.

5. SOCIALIST SWAN SONG?

In *A Lover's Discourse*, Roland Barthes writes about the skin as an organ of love, the surface of the beloved body and the flat palm of the caressing hand; in fact, according to Barthes, the discourse of the lover itself forms a sensitive skin enveloping the lovers. "Language is a skin: I rub my language against the other."[49] Skin to skin. In this very personal essay, Barthes massages the contours of sentimental love to make its language more supple. It is a language of desire as deficiency and need for an other; a language wherein the lover forever lacks the resources to equal the adored beloved adumbrated in his adoring discourse. "He praises the other for being perfect, he glorifies himself for having chosen this perfect other; he imagines that the other wants to be loved, as he himself would want to be loved, not for one or another of his qualities, but for *everything*. . . ."[50] It is a privative, if not ultimately private, language, in which the yearned-for plenitude of love—where everything is rich and commensurate with the universe—always winds up maddeningly *im*perfect. Insofar as the couple still love each other, they are always robbed of their hoped-for Eden, always fleeing or pursuing the all-encompassing bliss of devotion, deprived of rest by every ruse of their insecure identities. "Love," as Socrates says, "is the love of something which love hasn't got, and consequently lacks."[51]

In Barthes's *Sade/Fourier/Loyola*, by contrast, the language—the skin—of tender love gives way to a sharp, vehement discourse.[52] The love invoked is not gentle and affectionate, neglecting no pledge that might nurture the cozy equilibrium of union. Its rhetoric is not of shortage and want. Rather, love there is erotic love, violent and transgressive. Its rhetoric is one of excess, itemizing possessions until nothing counts anymore—for all that positive order taken together explodes in an ecstasy of material belonging. The whole, intact surface articulated and caressed by the lover's sweet words is now ruptured, slit, flayed. Pleasure respects no limits and crosses over the threshold of pain. The erotic union, as opposed to the tender one, violates inside and outside, self and other, one and all in the transgression of any singular envelope for life.

The contrast we drew between Fühmann's figuration of multiplicity and excess and Wolf's figuration of privation and lack does not, of course, pertain to an intimate language of romantic love, but to the collectively passionate discourse of socialism. The writers' passion for socialism, however, lends love's powerful affect to their expression of it. Just as we desire in these pages to grasp socialism—its truth, its identity, its difference—so does the literature we analyze also desire it, cherishing each identifying mark and relishing every bloody difference. Lest this desire, so unbounded, be taken as utopian or aleatory—as if socialism were a cost-free game, were vain and for nothing, the shell game of political tacticians and the daydream of poets—it should be remembered that socialism both lacks and has in abundance a heap of real objects and demands a system for parceling them out. Its defiance of utility-maximizing individualism and the balanced equations of GE characterizes a particular systematicity that is, maybe, nothing in particular. But if, or, *especially* if it has succeeded in the unlikely project of being nothing in particular (that is, of being everything in general, like mana itself), then it has succeeded absolutely in achieving a complete, specific difference from the liberal world that triumphed over its challengers at the end of the twentieth century. For the liberal world *is some*thing in particular. Although deposed by a frustrated and sullen populace, and disposed of by imperialistic market machinery, socialism nonetheless reminds the new millennium what its coming limitations and encounters might look like. The record of trial and error launched by socialism's strange difference from economy is "what remains" in excess of the no-longer-really existing particularity of socialism. Attested so passionately by Fühmann, socialism's special antieconomy echoes the more general one cited in our introduction:

> [T]his economy is not appropriative, it remains "excessive," it says only that unconditioned loss is not uncontrolled loss: loss must be ordered in order to become unconditional: the ultimate vacation, the denial of reciprocal economy, is itself obtained only by means of an economy: Sadian ecstasy, Fourierist jubilation, Ignatian indifference, never exceed the language that constitutes them: isn't a materialist rite that one beyond which there is nothing?[53]

Between the *noch nicht* [not yet] and *nicht mehr* [no more] of socialism's various utopian and materialist rites comes *nicht*s [nothing]. Were we to take a brief cabalistic turn, however, we might arrange things so that, between *nicht mehr* and *noch nicht*, we would read *mehr noch* [yet more]. "The Internationale" has a similar, but simpler economic calculus: "[We] have been naught, we shall be all."

The three chapters of Part One have introduced us to the agenda of an ontological study of real socialism, and, finally, to a socialist literary maverick who explores this ontology with single-minded—though indeed polymorphous—fascination. My hope is that this agenda, besides guiding Part Two of this study, might contribute to charting a course for keeping socialist culture in the canons of intellectual life; and that a revived concept of socialism, one not merely derivative of debates from the nineteenth and twentieth centuries, might illuminate the open-ended paradoxes generated by the last century's socialist order, a social configuration usually understood in terms of Cold War rigidity. Even more, I hope the agenda supplies some persuasive reasons for finding socialism "itself" to be a still pressing question of our contemporaneity. The very possibility of systems like the free-market economy implies the possibility of "other" systems; and the empirical experience of nearly three-quarters of a century of real socialism actualizes that possibility as a practical task of intellect and imagination. Combining the possible and the actual, universal sense and specific reference, in a careful consideration of alternatives to the present order allows us to keep such grand, but gladly embraced, hypostases as equality, justice, welfare, and free play from becoming dead letters—and that vitality, after all, is socialism's enduring desire.

PART II

PLURALITY AND THE OPTIMUM OPTIMORUM

[She] saw her world plunged into death, and saw again this Thing the old nurse bared to her, and seeing it, was overcome with emotion, at once a ridiculous languor and a monstrous sign, and sensed, barely loosening her limbs, the sweet perfection of her hale, ageless body and sensed in the appetite of the swelling also the swelling of her appetite, and felt her breasts tauten and felt blood again and desire, and their gazes met, mortal and divine, descended from one mean, and in the deathless eyes the old nurse saw the shimmer of a smile bloom . . .

—Fühmann, "Baubo"

CHAPTER FOUR

Diabolical Transformations: A Necessary Comrade

I. WHY FÜHMANN?

> His writing is not *about* something, *it is that something itself.*
> —Samuel Beckett on James Joyce[1]

> Poetry here succeeds in grasping a process of most intractable—because as compact as it is nuanced—human reality, and it does so as simply and inexhaustibly as the figure √2 or log 2 grasps a number that, as precise as it is, cannot be expressed in decimals.
> —Fühmann on Sarah Kirsch[2]

Although esteemed in reunified Germany, Franz Fühmann is not well known internationally, and the interpretive weight I put on him and his work asks for some legitimation. For an answer to the question, Why pick up Fühmann in the first place? there is no better place to turn than a 1994 speech by Christa Wolf dedicating a new Franz Fühmann Elementary School near Potsdam. Wolf suggests to the assembled children and teachers that one should read him "because immersing yourself in Fühmann's books, you'll be encouraged to take yourself seriously."[3] Fühmann himself fills out the picture of such seriousness in a 1979 plea to the GDR chief of party and state Erich Honecker: "I ask for only this one thing: to take my writing as it is intended: seriously, and originating from deepest sympathy for the development of our socialist democracy."[4] Seriousness in the sense conveyed by these quotations should not be confused with humorlessness or self-righteousness, but suggests a quality of weightiness fundamental to classical ethics. For Aristotle the weighty person, the *spoudaios*, lives with a sense of the importance of a life defined by both its contemporary relationships and its orientation toward the best possible completion.[5] Even as the *spoudaios* becomes the *eiron* (the ironic fool) in the anything but classical tribulations of the socialist experience, Fühmann insists on a classically imagined balance in conducting his authorship with respect to its public and to public authority—although this balance remains as elusive as any of its constituent elements.

As I claimed at the outset of Chapter 2, my aim here is to understand the Red Planet of real socialism by looking at some of its surviving fragments—it won't do, then, simply to frame Fühmann for a wider audience in the familiar terms of the Western literary tradition; rather, I must discover him in his irruptive specificity as a chunk of magma spewed from the Martian geology. At the same time, I need not make an exciting project of interplanetary exploration sound stingy by withholding details of Fühmann's life and work, as though the times and places of his earthly itinerary would corrupt the grander mystery of the other system I am after. On the contrary, I trust the Red Planet to hold its own here, and without fearing that Fühmann will be domesticated by the familiar routines of the "author function,"[6] I want to sketch an overview of what he wrote and who he is. After all, given the plentitude of Mars rocks eroding indifferently into the landscape of cosmopolitan literature, a reader might still harbor skepticism about the choice of Fühmann.

Part of the reason for Fühmann's relatively modest reception in Germany as well as abroad is surely his failure to reassure readers with what Frederic Jameson calls "the ontological consolation of the *Hauptwerk*."[7] Fühmann's central theme of transformation finds its expression rather in the "ceaseless metamorphoses which make up the life of an idea in time,"[8] metamorphoses that are conveyed especially well by the experimental and fragmentary essay form, a provisional genre that characterizes not only Fühmann's variegated oeuvre but also key individual works from his breakthrough Hungarian journal *Zweiundzwanzig Tage oder Die Hälfte des Lebens* (*Twenty-two Days or Half a Lifetime*) to his stunning readings of E. T. A. Hoffmann's tales as allegories of real socialist experience. As the democratic reforms of socialism inspired by Khrushchev's 1956 reckoning with Stalin failed to take hold, Fühmann found himself unable to continue writing in the poetic genre that had inaugurated his youthful literary career. In a 1980 interview he recalls how, "at that time [the late 1950s] I concentrated on prose and began from afar to steer toward the essay because I felt that it was the medium in which above all I could find my way to myself."[9]

Although Adorno, in "The Essay as Form," considered the ability to create literature without the consolation of a closed and monumental work to be a mark of courage and adequacy to the alienated bourgeois context, Fühmann experienced it in his rival socialist context as inadequacy—as a fatal foundering (*Scheitern*).[10] In 1983 he subtitled the fragments of his incomplete final work ***Im Berg*** (***In the Mines***), "Report on a Foundering" (***Bericht eines Scheiterns***),[11] and in a letter to Christa Wolf from April 1982 he writes of his growing dejection as "this feeling of paralysis, of being-an-object, of helplessness, of bound hands, and not only in my own case: I hear ever more unbelievable things about this Democratic State. . . ."[12] The lack of completion and closure in his own work is intimately linked by Fühmann to the GDR's wider failure to secure its ontological distinction from alternative historical formations. Thus the pathos of literary defeat that he declares in his final testament from July 1983 (a year before his death) expresses not so much a personal romantic pathos, but his more sober estimate of the failure of the social project to which he devoted his life: "I have terrible pains. The most bitter is that of having foundered [*gescheitert zu sein*]: in literature as well as in the hope for a society like that of which we all once dreamed."[13]

Despite this harsh testamentary self-assessment, Fühmann's literary legacy is a lasting one, whether demonstrated by his influence on German poets from Uwe Kolbe to Elke Erb, novelists from Wolfgang Hilbig to Volker Braun, and graphic artists from HAP Grieshaber to Barbara Gauger, or by the intellectual rewards of a close reading of his work. In a similar sense, the legacy of the society he dreamed of, and its devastated realization in the socialist state to which his writing intimately referred, can be dismissed only if one ignores a persistent, often violent current in the modern aspiration for change. I would go so far as to say that if one accepts, as Fühmann did, the self-description "progressive" in politics, one assumes a terrible burden of responsibility whose weight is no place more effectively narrated than in Fühmann's work.[14] Kant noted that if the individual human being is its own highest end, then progress—whose purview is the species and its future—inevitably violates the inviolable dignity of the individual: the dilemma of progress is that it is an end outside of any given human as end in itself. With a view toward progress, Kant allows that even war, "in spite of the most horrible tribulations which it inflicts upon the human race, is nevertheless one more incentive [. . .] for developing to their highest degree all the talents that serve for culture."[15] Unsurprisingly, then, Hannah Arendt found herself wondering in her Kant lectures whether a commitment to human progress also commits one to the criminal violation of individual human dignity.[16] In the sense of so fundamental a dilemma, then, it is the relationship of defeat and potential running through Fühmann's realism, rather than the singular experience of failure, that defines an aesthetic legacy unique in its portrayal of the historical limitation and unlimited emotional rigor of progressive social metamorphosis.

Fühmann wrote in an amazing range of forms, from his early poetry to his German renditions of Czech and Hungarian modernists, and his retelling of ancient Greek myths and epics. He wrote children's literature, dramas, screenplays, dream journals, reportage, and works in many other forms. "How many years will it take to see through even the first steps of assembling a workable catalogue of the ideas we absolutely must carry forward?" Uwe Kolbe asks in his eulogy for Fühmann: "How many directions of his complex oeuvre will now lie fallow for years: the mixing of mathematical logic, semiotics, semantics, game theory, psychoanalysis, and insights into a poetic methodology that can only be wrung from time?"[17] Outlining Fühmann's prose oeuvre here, I highlight those segments of his work that form the focus of my own contribution to Kolbe's catalogue. After his turn to prose in the 1950s, Fühmann first began writing war stories based on his experiences on the Eastern fronts, and those stories, collected in *König Ödipus* (*King Oedipus*), established his reputation as a writer engaged in coming to terms with the Nazi past.[18] This reputation was consolidated with his 1962 volume *Das Judenauto: Vierzehn Tage aus zwei Jahrzehnten* (*The Jew's Car: Fourteen Days out of Two Decades*)—a series of interlocking episodes taking place on fourteen symbolically freighted days from the 1929 market crash to the 1949 founding of the GDR. Fühmann meanwhile sought also to heed the so-called Bitterfeld path, the official policy calling for a literature of and for the new socialist factories of the GDR. In 1961 he published his reportage on the Warnow shipyards *Kabelkran und blauer Peter* (*Cable Crane and Blue Peter*). A collection of stories about the fantasies and repressed desires of a Bohemian childhood appeared in 1970, *Der Jongleur im Kino* (*The Juggler at the Movies*), marking with its strong Freudian undertones Fühmann's clear move away from the terrain of Bitterfeld socialist realism. Then, in 1973, his travel journal *Twenty-two Days* announced his break with any creative writing that set ideology before poetics. After the appearance of *Twenty-two Days*, Fühmann could only be considered a dissident writer, albeit one who remained scrupulously loyal to the socialist aspirations of the GDR. His final long work was the 1982 hybrid study of the expressionist poet Georg Trakl, *Vor Feuerschlünden* (*Facing the Fire Pits*), in which he analyzed Trakl through the autobiographical lens of his encounters with the poet in distinct phases of his own dislocated life. In

1982 Fühmann was also finally able to see his interest in psychoanalysis make some headway in the GDR, when a volume of Freud essays he edited, *Trauer und Melancholie* (*Mourning and Melancholia*), became the first collection of Freud's work to appear in the GDR.[19]

Between Fühmann's two longest works, *Twenty-two Days* and *Facing the Fire Pits*, and continuing up until his death in 1984, a remarkable series of short stories were published that, along with those two essays, are Fühmann's primary legacy. They rest on a rich fund of literary traditions—classical mythology, biblical tales, science fiction—and range thematically from closely observed satires of Communist Party bureaucrats to reflections on torture, sexual fertility, sexual loyalty, and historical impotence. At the same time as they demonstrate a classical formal discipline—sharply defined setting, unity of action, economy of prose—they also use citation, parody, and mixed genre forms that echo the essayistic structure of modernist riddles like those of Borges or Kafka. Perhaps the most pointed characterization of Fühmann's short-story style comes from Christa Wolf, who describes how "the most insane dramas take place in fragments of seconds, the most insane reversals of emotion in moments. This monstrous distension generates the effect a scientist experiences through a strong microscope, enlarging, distorting, intensifying, often almost beyond credibility."[20] In Wolf's description of him we can identify another clear antecedent—namely, Heinrich von Kleist, whose style has been described by J. Hillis Miller in words reminiscent of Wolf's, and that could equally well be applied to Fühmann: "[U]niquely Kleist's own . . . are the brutal violence, the laconic abruptness with which episode follows episode, the decisive role of unlikely happenstance, and most of all, the telling of the story with the distinctive Kleistian rapidity of staccato tempo and rhythm."[21]

The tension between Fühmann's commitment to engaged and realistic writing, on the one hand, and high modernism, on the other, led to a productive experimentation unique in the literature of real socialism. While scholars of postmodern literature such as Linda Hutcheon and Harro Müller locate the specificity of postmodernism in its avoidance of modernism's textual hermeticism and its resulting readiness to employ modes of historical reference characteristic of essay forms,[22] I sidestep the modernist/postmodernist distinction in favor of emphasizing a literary distinction that emerges from Fühmann's mixture of modernist rigor and realist reference to the specific experience of socialism. The improbability of this mixture comes out in an early work of Fühmann before he began consciously grappling with it as a formal challenge. In the various episodes from his 1962 story cycle *The Jew's Car*, he negotiates a line between ideological didacticism and narrative obliquity. In the best known title episode, for example, the consciousness of a child who resorts to an anti-Semitic lie to cover up an ostensibly innocent childhood exaggeration is narrated without any intrusive authorial comment, ending simply: "Jews. Jews Jews Jews Jews. They were the guilty ones. I hated them." The last and most didactic episode, *Zum ersten Mal: Deutschland* ("For the First Time: Germany"), however, falls into an ideological mawkishness that Fühmann came to regret. He described it later as "a change from self-irony to an affirmative pathos that inevitably had to produce the discrepancy in quality between the first and last story."[23] While Fühmann correctly assesses this chapter's "lapse of style," its very awkwardness illuminates the governing tension of Fühmann's work long before he was ready to accept this tension as precisely the formal challenge he was seeking. Observing the protagonist's return from a Soviet camp to divided Germany in 1949, the episode describes the first test since leaving prison of his commitment to settle in the newly formed GDR—and his free and conscious affirmation of the decision. Returning to his family in Weimar, the re-educated POW has a layover in Berlin and decides to visit his only acquaintance there, a literary partner from earlier days who happens to live in West Berlin. Not surprisingly, the Western acquaintance is dismayed by the narrator's plans to settle in the GDR. In order to persuade the aspiring writer that his future lies in the West, his acquaintance shows him his library:

> He merely pointed to the shelves, and there they stood in rank and file, the witnesses to his freedom: Eliot, Camus, Pound and many others whom I didn't know, and among them, look, there were Binding and Jünger as well, and they I knew indeed. I read the titles and authors, and my acquaintance waited quietly. Finally he said: "Well!"—"Well!" he said, "you're surprised, aren't you? You won't find those in the Russian Zone!"
>
> "Certainly not Binding and Jünger," I said, "and a good thing, too!"[24]

Ignoring the narrator's clearly expressed ideological preferences, the friend appeals to the narrator's aesthetic identity as a writer:

> "You know, you ought to write a dance of death, that would be the sort of thing you could do well—a horrible, demonic dance of death ranging over the whole apocalypse of our times," he said and finished his Nescafé. "The whole apocalypse," he repeated and set his glass down, "the loneliness of the human creature, the despair, the mercilessness, the thrownness . . ."[25]

The protagonist, of course, ignores his friend and leaves for the East, boarding a train car filled with a People's policewoman and her children and a contingent of workers from, of all places, the uranium mines at Wismut. He leans out of the train window and composes a socialist realist ode on a farmer returning to collectivized land: "See and grasp: he'll leave the land no more!" The irony of Fühmann's juxtaposition of such aesthetic sentiments would be all too easy to mock retrospectively—but the grim humor is not merely the result of history's corrosive effect on pious hopes. On the contrary, Fühmann's work is built on a gradual intensification of this contrast between modernism and the realism of an alternate modernity.

The force of Fühmann's later stories comes from their uncomfortable embrace of not only the reviled quintet on the West Berlin decadent's shelves—Eliot, Camus, Pound, Binding, and Jünger—but also Joyce, Kafka, T. Mann, Seghers, Benn, Brecht, Barlach, Freud, and Trakl, all authors to whom Fühmann refers with varying degrees of explicitness and urgency.[26] The West Berliner's formulation of "the loneliness of the human creature, the despair, the mercilessness, the thrownness," imputed both to modernist authors and to the narrator's latent talents, echoes the programmatic realist who decisively influenced Fühmann's aesthetic development, Georg Lukács. Lukács characterized modernism with nearly identical words, though for Lukács they were pejorative rather than laudatory. Writing of "the theory and practice of modernism," Lukács points to Heidegger's *Geworfenheit* (thrownness-into-being). "A more graphic evocation of the ontological solitariness of the individual would be hard to imagine."[27] As an antidote to such despair of the external world, Lukács holds up realism. Although he recognizes different historical phases of realism, he sees it generally as resisting modernism's tendency to dissolve objective society in subjective stream-of-consciousness narratives. In its specific socialist phase, he continues, "socialist realism differs from critical realism, not only in being based on a concrete socialist perspective, but also in using this perspective to describe the forces working towards socialism *from the inside*. Socialist society is seen as an independent entity, not simply as a foil to capitalist society, or as a refuge from its dilemmas."[28]

This aspect of Lukács's contemporary realism is what comes to most torture Fühmann because the very idea of an interior and exterior to socialism—a socialist system separated from a distinct environment by a firm skin or boundary—is impossible for him to presume. On the contrary, Fühmann gives narrative form to his participation in the GDR in order to uncover the extent to which his real experiences are socialist experiences: his desire is to avoid merely *presuming* that socialism is what it posits of itself. Lukács holds that the insistence of modernists like Kafka and Musil on the "ghostly" aspect of reality is an ideological choice to "attenuate" reality in their prose.[29] Yet Fühmann's attempt to heed the call for a realistic interior perspective on socialism propels his most haunting inquiry: is the "independent entity" known as the GDR a *real* socialism, a distinct reality from inside of which he can write? And is the socialist Fühmann a *real* socialist, a coherent subjectivity whose perspective is "concrete"? The apocalyptic modernism in Fühmann is thus less passionately colored than the empirical realism—and that inversion lends his writing its powerful distinction. It is just because he commits himself to socialism, like his *Jew's Car* protagonist who turns against his friend's exhortations to move to the West and write an apocalyptic literature, that Fühmann finds his way to a demonic modernism not as an epigone of decadence, but as a socialist realist. "Every age," he writes in a 1978 letter to Christa Wolf, "brings forth the writers and artists it must, or the other way around: if one struggles against one's time, one's talents come to nothing. Apparently this epoch wants a bitter literature, even if we don't. Gradually, I do. Gradually, I want to write evil. Only, then, consistently.—It's a screw without an end."[30]

2. REAL SOCIALISM BEGINS AT HOME

> Alas, where do I find, when
> Winter comes, the flowers, and where
> The sunshine
> And shade of the earth?
> The walls stand
> Speechless and cold, in the wind
> The weather vanes are clanging.
>
> —Friedrich Hölderlin, "Half a Lifetime"

Born in 1922 to a middle-class pharmacist's family in a Bohemian village in the recently independent Czechoslovak Republic under Tomás Masaryk, Fühmann was sent off at age ten to receive a Jesuit education at the elite Kalksburg convent school outside Vienna.[31] Returning prematurely to Bohemia four years later in 1936, he became at fourteen a youthful enthusiast of Sudeten Nazism, joining the SA when Germany annexed the Sudetenland in 1938 and volunteering for the fascist *Wehrmacht*, where he was eventually assigned to a telegraph company in 1941 and served a long four years on Soviet and Greek fronts. Captured by Red Army troops near the German-Czech border the day after the German capitulation in May 1945, he was reeducated in Soviet prisoner of war camps and subsequently embraced

Stalinism as the antithesis of his earlier fascism. Returning from a Latvian prison camp in December 1949 to the new socialist Germany founded that October in the Soviet occupation zone, the twenty-seven-year-old Fühmann took up administrative functions in the National Democratic Party of Germany (NDPD), a sham-pluralist bloc party intended to coax former members of Nazi organizations and middle-class soldiers (like Fühmann) into the hegemony of the Socialist Unity Party (SED), the ruling Communist Party of the GDR. He quickly established his credentials as an up-and-coming party-line writer, finding favor in the early 1950s from the once-expressionist and then doctrinaire-classicist poet Johannes R. Becher, head of the Cultural League for the Democratic Renewal of Germany, and finding symmetrical disfavor in an early 1960s assessment by the influential West German critic Marcel Reich-Ranicki.[32] Describing himself later as having been torn between "poetry and doctrine,"[33] Fühmann, whatever considerable talents he lent to his poetry, surely gave doctrine its due through the mid-1960s, self-critically dating his "real entry into literature" only to the 1973 publication of his meditative Budapest diary, *Twenty-two Days*.[34]

Unsurprisingly for a GDR writer of his generation, Fühmann has been retrospectively classified as both collaborator (*Mitarbeiter*) and victim (*Betroffener*) by the 1991 Federal German Law on State Security Documents (StUG).[35] As a secret informer (*GI—Geheimer Informator*) from 1954 to 1959, he reported to the Stasi under the code name "GI Salomon," although he never supplied any information and was consequently dropped; while in 1977 an extensive operative process (*OV-Operativer Vorgang*) was initiated against him under the code name *OV Filou*.[36] As is often the case with the Stasi, the two code names fit Fühmann surprisingly well: both wise Salomon and puckish Filou. Some episodes of his earlier conformism to authority he later sought to reverse, others he did and could not. Thus, a short story from 1974 critical of party stereotypes, "Bagatelle, rundum positiv" ("A Trifle, Largely Positive"), satirically reflects the self-deceptions characteristic of his own enthusiastic 1961 labor reportage, *Cable Crane and Blue Peter*, which had credulously hailed the heroism of workers at the GDR's Warnow shipyards.[37] On the other hand, also in 1961, he was largely responsible for a negative official assessment of the young Brecht-protégé Heiner Müller's play *Die Umsiedlerin* (*The Refugee*), which led not only to the play's being banned but also to Müller's marginalization in officially recognized East German culture.[38] Without ever publicly disavowing this condemnation, he bitterly alludes to it eighteen years later in a 1979 protest letter to General Secretary Erich Honecker, in which he reminds the chief of state and party that "works that today count among the firm legacy of socialist literature," among which he prominently cites Müller's play, "all these works were once condemned as 'harmful' and 'hostile,' even counter-revolutionary[.] . . ."[39]

There is, in short, little exemplary in Fühmann's experiences of conformity and adaptation from prewar fascism through postwar Stalinism. While his short story collections about his youth, *The Jew's Car* in 1962 and *The Juggler at the Movies* in 1970, recall childhood desires, anxieties, and resentments boiling over grotesquely in a cauldron of Jesuit, nationalist, and Nazi authoritarianism and prejudice, their autobiographical protagonists are reminiscent of adolescent monsters in the work of Géza Csáth or Arthur Schnitzler, chroniclers of an earlier, not necessarily fascist, generation of the Habsburg psyche.[40] Fühmann was neither a Nazi monster, nor did he take any special initiatives to distinguish himself in opposition to nationalist fascism. "One was simply part of things," he notes, "if one didn't happen to have a completely class-conscious communist as a father or come from a very religious home."[41] In the logic of the events of which he was thus a part, one thing led to another, culminating in the violent cataclysm of world war and holocaust. Fühmann's initially reactive commitment to socialism was thus not born of proletarian subjection in the factory and communist class-consciousness in the party hall, but, as he writes in the early 1960s in *The Jew's Car*, it was a baptism of the fire he witnessed as a soldier on the Eastern front. Or, as he later told West German students conducting a survey of authors in 1971, it was an insight arrived at through Auschwitz: "I belong to a generation that came to socialism by way of Auschwitz."[42]

Regardless of his individual innocence of war crimes and crimes against humanity, he recognized himself as a willing part of the National Socialist machinery that had made fascist atrocity possible. "There are no 'innocent' world views," stipulates Georg Lukács,[43] whose work, Fühmann writes, represented "my first encounter with Marxism, with dialectics, with materialism."[44] Or, as the officer protagonist of his war story "König Ödipus" ("King Oedipus") puts it: "[T]he new era was on the march to bury the old, which already made one guilty by simply belonging to it."[45] Fühmann's Stalinism responded to an intellectual decision to give a collective way of formulating his volition during the Third Reich precedence over any exculpating experience of individual innocence. For him, recognizing his collective implication in the machinery of fascism meant pursuing a collective remedy, whether through his efforts as political activist or creative writer. "I don't see literature as an extra-social realm and an end in itself," he wrote to the same West German students to whom he told of Auschwitz's transforming effect on him. "I consider the idea of an 'independent author' or a 'truly independent author' categories of an ivory tower aesthetics."[46] Reflecting on their common postwar orthodoxy, fellow GDR writer and eventual dissident Erich Loest recalled that "Fühmann was no exception then; it was to his and my satisfaction to feel and speak like many others, like, if possible, everyone."[47] Clearly, neither Fühmann nor his literary protagonists are likely to resemble Ken Loach's immaculate film hero with whom this study began, shredding his Communist Party card to save his ideals from being conscripted into the ranks of republican Spain's (and Stalin's) disciplined soldiers of revolution. Rather, Fühmann's serial loyalties to collectivist movements have left behind a literary legacy that traverses the calculations of the human cost to conscious participation in the twentieth century's conflict-ridden history.

Fühmann's developmental trajectory might sound less like conscious engagement and more like a never adequately reflected process of mechanical action and reaction, where, never sovereign over his own decisions, he just propagates old totalitarian mindsets under new symbols, the very reproach that Reich-Ranicki made against him in 1963. "Thanks to the new salvation dogma," wrote Reich-Ranicki, "he could continue the struggle he once began in the ranks of National Socialism—only under other pretexts, on other planes and with different goals. [. . .] He had only been 'repurposed' in the 'antifascist school': thus he wrote Hitler Youth-poems with FDJ [the communist youth organization] insignias."[48] In Reich-Ranicki's view, the distinction between old and new Fühmann was just a conventional one of changed flags and insignias—an insubstantial distinction between fascism and postfascism as variations on the symbolism of battle-hardened fathers and führers. The colors changed, the apocalyptic values remained—"their flag was ablaze in the enemy's midst, and after it they rode," as Rilke painted the timeless battlefield.[49] We see in Reich-Ranicki's early criticism of him an exact source for Fühmann's anxiety that the socialist difference might be a difference that makes no difference, that socialism might be sovereign only in the medieval sense of the ritualized pageantry of statehood—its distinction going no deeper than its lumbering May Day or October 7th anniversary parades. Stung by Reich-Ranicki's comment, however, Fühmann continued moving beyond defensive anxiety to a consuming artistic desire to locate, and meaningfully depict, precisely what was substantial in his own transformation to socialism. "He was right," Fühmann concedes a decade later; "he pointed to the right spot; not to a sore spot, which one finds on one's own, no, to one that one believes healed[.] . . . My thanks to him, but: shouldn't it have been a friend who pointed it out[?]"[50]

In *Twenty-two Days* Fühmann uses his biography to contrast a merely mechanical process of transformation with the deeply contradictory one he felt literature—and socialism—should be grappling with. "What happened to me in Kalksburg [the Jesuit boarding school he attended as a child] was also a transformation—and how! I went in a naively pious, deeply religious and God-fearing kid, and I ran off after four years a convinced atheist: black box, input and output."[51] This merely formal model of input/output relies on a blind causal system to do the work of conscious apprehension. It leaves the newly minted atheist without any substantial moral or political development—still a credulous and timorous child, he is ready to substitute Sudeten fascism for Jesuit authoritarianism. But Fühmann's literary goal is consciously to grasp the qualitative element of transformation as lived experience rather than system postulate. His own (and Reich-Ranicki's) analogy with religious upbringing suggests to him an ethnographic reflection on transformation. "Can one define transformation as a transition to another value system (other values or also other priorities for old values), as a process that closes off the old value system with a self-assessment and begins a new one with a purge (self-criticism, confession, expiation, atonement, punishment, ritual, etc.)? That would explain many remarkable phenomena in our camp."[52] An ethnographic model for the intellectual and emotional catharsis apparently necessary for thorough transformation between value systems, however, strikes a suspicious note with Fühmann: the intellectual insistence on cathartic transformation, tragic emotion, and heroic pathos underlies some "remarkable phenomena," as he delicately puts it, in the GDR political psyche. He impatiently interrupts his own academic train of thought to return to the phenomenology of empirical experience. "But why play with concepts? My life *was* after all a transformation."[53]

The emphatic location of an empirical starting point for his narratives of transformation in his own life experience marks a crucial development in Fühmann's literary biography because it affirms the validity of personal experience—whether that experience counts as representative of social experience generally or not. "I had a concept of overcoming the past which, while honorable enough, was very narrow, and I even choked off my own song. But there is no deleting from history, not a single aspect and not a single emotion [. . .] Not a 'It never happened,' nor a 'As if it had never happened,' but only a 'That's the way it was, and it is past' is the secure foundation on which to build something new."[54] Since this autobiographical and historical deixis is so important for Fühmann's oeuvre, it is worthwhile to distinguish it carefully from what it is not. First of all, his self-affirmation cannot be read as a retreat into privacy, where personal states and private ends assume priority over social ones. Rather, it finds its significance in Fühmann's growing conviction that broad social commitments must be justified on the basis of individual perceptions—no matter how initially limited or personal, these perceptions cannot be off limits. He repeatedly mulls over the implications of Erich Honecker's solemn 1971 declaration that "there can be no taboos in the realm of art and literature"[55] for his own increasingly unorthodox literary practice, reflecting throughout his Budapest journal on what it might mean to write without taboos—a paradoxical reflection on limitlessness that I elaborate in the following chapters.

Secondly, he is aware that the individual and chance perceptions of his life are also not those of a class-conscious proletarian, the privileged identical subject/object of communist revolution in the orthodox Marxist worldview. Few intellectuals (if anybody) could boast such a generalized perceptual standpoint; on the contrary, it was, for most who assumed it, an acquired, or as Fühmann was later to formulate it, a "delegated" experience.[56] The only figures who seemed to Fühmann and his generation legitimately able to claim this standpoint of simultaneously universal and individual experience were the veteran communists of the Weimar-era KPD (German Communist Party). Examining memoirs of veterans such as Franz Dahlelm, Walter Ulbricht, and Erich Honecker, the historian Catherine Epstein concludes that they did indeed live their party-line commitments as individual experiences. Their lives describe an almost recursive process whereby choices are guided by a political understanding and the consequent experiences are then interpreted back through the same lens, creating a hermetic and propulsive model for communist personal identity. "KPD members lived the communist ideal: they practiced the tough rules of revolutionary activity, they depended on the brotherhood of their fellow comrades, and they felt themselves to be active agents in the unfolding drama of History. Their experiences confirmed their Leninist belief that they were the chosen avant-garde of History. [. . .] During the next forty-five years, they would tenaciously cling to the values and political lessons that they had learned during the Weimar and Nazi eras. They would apply these views to their rule of East Germany and, in the process, fundamentally shape the character of GDR politics."[57] Such constantly embroiled veterans of the KPD could hardly be expected to foster a variegated culture of phenomenological perception; theirs was the big moment of anticapitalist revolution, not the little episodes of socialist construction.

Fühmann recognizes in *Twenty-two Days* that the personal experiences that matter most to him cannot be dismissed as objectionable simply because they are individual, even eccentric, nor be affirmed simply because they embody (or once strove to embody) the party-and-class-conscious perceptions delegated by the veteran communists in power. According to the literary historian Werner Mittenzwei, the intellectuals who like Fühmann immigrated to the GDR in the early 1940s, and inevitably lacked the impossibly synoptic proletarian standpoint the party would have them assume, came instead for one of two more mundane reasons. They either "felt themselves obligated to a socialist society or saw in it a new, laudable experiment."[58] That is, they fit into either the quasi-religious, cathartic mindset of guilt and redemption that Fühmann saw as responsible for some "remarkable phenomena" in the socialist camp, or they fit into the more practical mindset of willing labor power: technocrats, bureaucrats, pragmatic idealists. Arriving in divided Germany from a Latvian prisoner-of-war camp, the young Fühmann seems to fit well enough into the category of those obligated by guilt, his early writing, especially his 1953 poetry-cycle *Die Fahrt nach Stalingrad* (*The Journey to Stalingrad*), reflecting a socialist commitment that responds to the carnage he witnessed as a soldier. After the Eichmann and Auschwitz trials in the early 1960s, Fühmann started foregrounding the disabling guilt his generation felt for the Holocaust as another, even deeper, reason than Stalingrad for his obligation to socialism. Such powerful guilty affect led many Germans, not only socialists or those drawn to the GDR, to adopt a heroic and cathartic view of history in which the German nation would redeem itself only on the basis of a radical, self-conscious rupture with the past and a recommitment to a totally new future.

Yet these passionate intuitions of guilt and obligation, as he realizes in *Twenty-two Days*, are insufficient to give specific definition to the real socialism to which he had been committing himself through highs like Sputnik and lows like the crushing of the Prague Spring: a sustained socialism is not a matter of sublime emotional attitude. In his 1982 essay on the expressionist poet Georg Trakl, *Facing the Fire Pits*, he describes his discomfort with the way Johannes R. Becher, the presiding spirit of the GDR's literary rebirth out of ruins of fascist pomposity, had so eagerly availed himself of nationalist words like *Volk* and *Vaterland* in the name of revolutionary renewal. "They underwent a sort of miracle of Lazarus, even such degraded ones as 'heroism' and 'hero.'—Their resurrection transpired under the sign of truth."[59] The heroic language (and vague epistemology) of the GDR construction period—an elevated emotional tone already then on the wane since its zenith in the early 1950s—decisively loses its affective power for Fühmann. *Reference*, however one is to understand its complex intellectual power,[60] becomes the linguistic item taking first place in Fühmann's literary agenda. By the early 1970s he is explicitly understanding socialism as a deliberate empirical experiment in transformation, one that begins with a rigorous, even ruthless, dissection of himself. "Could one say: transformation is that process in the individual sphere that has become historically necessary for society?"[61] This new understanding differs from that of Mittenzwei's experimentally minded intellectuals of the late 1940s in that Fühmann finds himself, with decades of sobering empirical experience behind him, in the midst of an experiment that is yielding increasingly questionable results, not only in terms of society but also in terms of his psyche. It suddenly no longer seems even halfway credible that a cathartic commitment, no matter how sincere or how willfully blind, will transform those of good will to the spontaneous perception of class necessity. Instead, the question of choosing socialism must, according to Fühmann, be faced not only more consciously, but with a different kind of consciousness—that is, patiently, deliberately, and with unsparing emotional candor.

This keener awareness of a dialectic of introspection and empirical analysis, of individual choice and social necessity, makes him at once more critical of the GDR and more eager to identify any real substance inhering in the socialist transformation that the GDR posits itself as representing. Thus, as I elaborate in Chapter 6, Fühmann's commitment to socialism moves away from traditional categories of socialist or postfascist epistemology. "True" proletarian affinity is not a possibility for this pharmacist's son and Nazi soldier; and guilt over Auschwitz—even though he also announces such guilt in *Twenty-two Days* as the primary motivation of his generation of socialist writers—is no longer enough to mark a substantial transformation from old to new. Fühmann's project—again, as he puts it, "his true entry into literature"—distinguishes itself as an experiential search for the qualitative difference represented in the socialist sovereignty of the GDR. Grasping this transformation to socialism requires practical participation in his society, but such a requirement cannot be reduced to obedience and sentimentality, which would only reenact the same sterile process of conformity. "I know," he comments again to the 1971 high school interlocutors to whom he had written about Auschwitz, "that 'serving and wanting to serve one's society with literary means,' like any social phenomenon, has its own specific problems and its specific inner contradictions. I know that this engagement is a process."[62]

A process with inner contradictions cannot, however, be a traditional rational process with formal expression in classical logic, since the axiom of the excluded middle—*tertium non datur*, an axiom that, as we shall see in detail, haunts Fühmann's imagination—does not admit contradiction into its ontology. What exactly this individually lived process of engagement is, however, and how it relates to the social experience of socialism, is Fühmann's artistic drama. If his idiosyncratic drama does not fit neatly into the mode of either the cathartic or pragmatic intellectual, it nonetheless expresses the intense pathos of Fühmann's hopes and disappointments and the analytical logic of his participation in the socialist experiment. It is a drama that admits contradiction into its ontology at the same time as it excludes moral absolutes, submitting the emotional catharsis of its denouements to uncompromising intellectual appraisal. Even in his early writing on fascism and the war, it is not the obvious criminals and monsters that present him with a literary challenge. Rather, individuals caught in crime, cruelty, and violence—in a real sense guilty, but not juridically condemnable—draw him, and he depicts their errors not as sins to be atoned for in ceaseless mea culpas before a jealous God or Party, but as experiential facts to be plumbed for their applicability and relevance to the socialist aspiration. Does the fact of a young man's Nazi enthusiasm obligate him to disavow subsequent social commitment? Is Cartesian skepticism the only appropriate expiation for provincial fascism? Or on the contrary, does true expiation demand a symmetrical countercommitment to the communist movement so vigorously persecuted by the Nazis? Is Marxist orthodoxy the epistemological standpoint of the authentic expiator? Whatever the answers, Fühmann does not narrate the frequently autobiographical errancies of his literary characters as mechanical lessons, but struggles with them as dilemmas of public culture. New values and questions develop in Fühmann's work from his practice within a social system whose radicality perforce begins as merely a postulate of difference. They start by recognizing the everyday violence of choices inherent within this system; they end by measuring the distance between the everyday and extraordinary. As Fühmann observes of Trakl's poetry, so it might be observed of his own writing, that it is "a process, not a result, [. . .] anyone who feels affected by it [*betroffen*] is free to find himself in its image, and that means recognizing what is happening to him"—*tua res agitur*: it is your thing at stake here.[63]

CHAPTER FIVE

Tertium Non Datur: *The Systems Erotics of Socialism*

Écorché/flayed: the particular sensibility of the amorous subject.
—Roland Barthes, *A Lover's Discourse*[1]

Man encountered himself
And found,
There are two sorts of human, and
The order of one
Is not the order of the other.
—Johannes R. Becher, *The Great Plan*[2]

I. THE UNHEARD-OF BEGINNING: INTRODUCTION TO A SOCIALIST FLAYING

Echoing the claim by Johann Wolfgang Goethe, the father-figure of German bourgeois literature, that the dramatic novel is an "unheard-of event" (*unerhörte Begebenheit*)[3], Johannes R. Becher, the father-figure of East German socialist literature, begins his 1950 journal *Auf andere Art so grosse Hoffnung* (*Another Way So High a Hope*), chronicling the GDR's first full year of existence—a year for Becher of sublime and unspeakable promise—with the observation that "an 'unheard-of' sentence should stand at the beginning, but searching for such an 'unheard-of,' one loses oneself in mannerism, and one begins as though in a conversation—utterly not 'unheard-of,' but as though just tossed off, obvious, often heard and indeed: human."[4] While he professes the desire to begin—and to see the German socialist epoch begin—with Goethe's 'unheard-of,' Becher's ultimately contrary desire instead anticipates Michel Foucault's inaugural address at the Collège de France: to begin "freed from the obligation to begin," amid an ongoing stream of language in whose flow an author impassively stands, both speaking and spoken.[5]

Becher's designation for this alternative to a sublime origin—the ordinary "human"—is not so far removed from Foucault's "post-humanist" skepticism as it might seem. In neither view is an author a wellspring of sovereign identity, but just the medium, or even just the function ("the author function"), of prevailing circumstances: the epic of the Greek polis arising out of the Achaean victory over Troy; the novel of bourgeois individualism declaring its universal genius on the wings of French revolutionary *liberté*; or the sober realism of the proletariat assuming long deferred responsibility for Germany's future. History's epochal events are the "ponderous, awesome materiality" whose naked contingency discourse seeks to clothe, to provide with a skin, whose uncertain contours it seeks to reveal and secure.[6] Like the constitution of a sovereign new regime that I discussed in Chapter 3, the Muses must both announce the new and declare it timeless, must simultaneously initiate and enforce the taboos of the prevailing order. They are the guardians of institutions, who "solemnize beginnings, surrounding them with a circle of silent attention," at the same time as the unheard-of violence of instituting is made to flow into the babbling brooks of daily life.[7] This is the inescapable conundrum of Muses at every real beginning: to be both monstrous and human, different and the same. Seeking the Muses to inaugurate an unprecedented era, Becher at the threshold of really existing socialism, like Foucault at the dawn of his posthuman age, discovers that language is unequal to the awesome "unheard-of" it is called upon to proclaim: either high mannerism or low banter, the medium alone capable of revealing transformation's disruptive power regulates it in the very moment it is to be unbound.

Fühmann, who knew how roughly Becher was treated by the Muses inspiring his great proletarian hopes, does not evoke the Parnassian Nine in their finest hour. His story "Marsyas," one of four stories with Greek mythical themes written between 1976 and 1978 and published together in the 1979 collection *Die Geliebte der Morgenröte* (*The Beloved of the Dawn*), is a bitter reckoning with the Muses of his era, treating one of the most shameful moments of their classical legacy.[8] Fühmann cites Diodoros and Apollodoros as his sources for the myth in which the hapless satyr Marsyas, wandering along the beaches of Phrygia, comes across a double flute that Athena had invented only to discard with a curse. Unaware of the flute's origins, Marsyas picks it up and begins playing it (or, alternatively, it begins playing itself in memory of Athena's divine music): the strange sound is beautiful and irresistible. Made complacent by the praise he receives from all who hear, the satyr challenges Apollo to a musical competition, flute versus lyre, in which it is agreed that the winner may do with the loser as he sees fit. Judging the competition, the Muses decide in Apollo's favor, whereupon Apollo does his will and remorselessly flays the satyr alive.

These marvelous events on the shores of ancient Phrygia might seem remote from the daily grind of life in the prosaic GDR. Indeed, Fühmann's story touches on the timeless themes of identity and transformation that had been preoccupying him at least since *Twenty-two Days*: can one transform consciously, is there a place from within one's own skin from whence one can vouch for substantial change, and is the flux of change ever compatible with the identity of order?[9] Written in the aftermath of the dissident singer-songwriter Wolf Biermann's expulsion from the GDR in 1976—an event (discussed in Chapter 7) that both traumatized and politically mobilized a key segment of East German artists, permanently unsettling the intelligentsia's already uncomfortable ideological truce with the state—"Marsyas" was nonetheless "no encoded political story." "In 'Marsyas' there was no didactic intent," Fühmann asserts in a 1980 interview, dismissing interpretations that narrowly historicize "the artist's problematic," which Fühmann considers both too general and too immediate for the political idiom.[10] "I hear in much modern Art the cry of Marsyas," is Oscar Wilde's emblematic formulation in *De Profundis* of the artist's problematic.[11] Echoing "the Phrygian Faun's" howl in his persecuted aestheticism, Wilde inscribes the satyr's legacy in modern art's refusal to submit to social norms: "[B]etween my art and the world there is now a wide gulf, but between art and myself there is none." In the same vein, Fühmann insists that there is no coy political intention hidden between the lines of his "Marsyas," but only "utterly direct involvement and dismay [*Betroffenheit*]." "When I want to say something directly, I say it," he declares. Surely, as Fühmann's dedication of the story to the highly political West German author Heinrich Böll or the simultaneous appearance of another Marsyas story by the angry young GDR rebel Thomas Brasch hints, even the most direct of artistic intentions cannot escape the web of historical and literary contextualization. But it seems most promising to begin by taking Fühmann at his word—here, the repeated word *direct*—and attempt literally and sensibly to hear the "unheard-of" hallowing of the institution of the socialist project.

Fühmann's story differs strikingly from both classical versions of the myth and subsequent retellings by a subtle, but decisive shift of protagonist: from sensual Marsyas to the unreachable Muses themselves. A face-to-face confrontation between satyr and god becomes a story about a confrontation between systems and mediums. In the classical versions, the Muses are a third party, implacable judges of the contest between god and satyr. In Fühmann's socialist version the drama is their own as they assume an equivocal role between impartial judges and implicated bystanders to an event they are unfit to judge. The Muses are benumbed auditors, "bestowers of speech" who are left speechless in the face of the competition between the satyr, playing Athena's double flute, and the god, meeting him with the lyre. "They couldn't, the bestowers of speech, say what happened, though it did happen, and happened before their ears, and happened to them: they didn't grasp it.—The unheard-of.—" (360)

What happened is unheard-of. But at the same time it is only a musical competition, essentially just a comparison. Why should the drama of comparison ever be so terrible that it lend itself to the Muses' speechlessness, a horror beyond words and representation? It seems the opposite would be the case, that comparison would be a measured act, implying contact and proximity, with Marsyas merely "presenting his art to experts for judgment and measurement," as Brasch puts it in his version of the story.[12] But the horror that silences the Muses (and not Marsyas, as in Brasch) indicates another realm than that of measurement. It hints at violence, the absolute, the irrational and unrepresentable: the realm that Georges Bataille describes as giving rise to humanity's most fundamental prohibitions, a realm, in other words, that rules out in advance the possibility of comparison.

"The horror that gives rise to prohibition," Bataille writes in his unfinished magnum opus *The Accursed Share*, ". . . is not consistent with 'more or less.' . . . A horror so sick does not tolerate any degree. It is based on 'all or nothing.'"[13] The competition the Muses witness seems to have the full effect of the existential horror Bataille describes, as though it had nothing to do with two like things, worthy partners, meeting in a measured contest of "more or less." It is something, rather, so unheard-of that "all the sisters' rules of speech tremblingly shattered in an incomprehensible shudder" (360). If the effect on the Muses is so unlike that which one would expect from a competition, how does one conceive what they are witnessing? What lies at the root of their terror? The literal "unheard-of event" is not Marsyas' gruesome torture, whose physical violence may indeed be incomprehensible, but precedes it: the musical competition itself disables the Muses. This competition, not its brutal resolution, transgresses a taboo so fundamental that it threatens to undo the boundaries of intelligible experience. The true nature of the competition thus eludes the grasp of interpretable speech, the Muses' grasp, presenting itself in a realm that Bataille calls the erotic.

For Bataille the erotic plays a philosophical role whose importance goes beyond its normal connotation of individual pleasure. It marks off a space of ecstatic experience that cannot be brought back into the intelligible ambit of human consciousness. A student of Alexandre Kojève's deeply influenced by Kojève's account of Hegel, Bataille seeks to escape the finality of Hegel's absolute consciousness, where the historical tasks of humanity are complete and human essence achieved. Kojève emphasizes the centrality of desire (*Begierde*) in Hegel, tracing desire's fortunes through the Master and Slave dialectic to "the perfect Man, fully and definitively 'satisfied' by what he *is* and by what he *knows* himself to be."[14] The objective and subjective conclusion of desire in the completed historical act of becoming is precisely what Bataille rebels against. In the place of Hegel's absolute consciousness—at the point of Man's full satisfaction—Bataille sets the utterly heterogeneous experience of erotic desire, deeming it beyond the reach of all dialectics of history, law, and economics.

The erotic starts as horror in the face of a natural plenum that is immeasurably "other." Other than what? is the inevitable question, and eroticism consists in the unstable constitution of that "what." In other words, eroticism initiates a fundamental process of demarcating the "what" of human specificity against the "what" of generic nature. A vague, incomparably intense dread of nature leads to a prohibition that marks off "man" as nature's negation (the gendered anthropology belongs to Bataille). By prohibiting certain sorts of sexual contact that otherwise occur spontaneously in the animal world, he sets a border between himself and nature.[15] Bataille cites Lévi-Strauss's claim that the incest prohibition "is the fundamental step because of which, by which, but above all in which, the transition from nature to culture is accomplished" (31). But prohibition is only the first step of a subject/object differentiation. The fact of prohibition draws attention to the present value of the so delimited object: if the object were not desirable, why would the force of prohibition be necessary? Thus, the revulsion that leads to prohibition simultaneously anticipates the attraction that leads to transgression. As a conscious perversion of the morality of prohibition, the erotic allows the subject to recognize the object as desirable, subject and object emerging as such across a boundary of sexual charge. "There would be no eroticism if there was not also a respect for forbidden values. But there would be no complete respect if the erotic deviation were neither possible nor tempting. . . . The prohibition does not change the violence of sexual activity, but by founding the *human* milieu it makes of that violence something that animality did not know: the transgression of the rule" (57).

Contrary to Hegel's world historical movement toward identity, erotic pleasure points to the destruction of man as such in a transgressive reunion with nature, a "return to the quiescence of the inorganic world" in Freud's words.[16] The erotic union, the orgasm—*la petite mort*—points to such a fusion insofar as it anticipates a death that always exceeds experience, even the experience of the divine; for in conscious experience, however ecstatic, the identified subject is always divided from the desired object of consummation by its articulate language. "The ego appears to us as something autonomous and unitary, marked off distinctly from everything else," writes Freud. "There is only one state," he allows, "in which it does not do this. At the height of being in love the boundary between ego and object threatens to melt away."[17] Bataille intensifies what for Freud is a nihilistic erotic "threat" into an exuberant choice against the dialectic of identity and its constituent elements of self and other. The purging violence of the erotic choice changes the disciplined interiority of the ego into unbounded exteriority, eviscerating the fulsome singularity of Hegelian phenomenology where individual consciousness becomes one with the "entire system of consciousness."[18] Consciousness, for Hegel, aims at "a point where it sheds the appearance of being preoccupied with something external that exists only for it and as an 'other,' a point where appearance equals essence." For Bataille, the erotic choice is not a synthesis with the entire system, but a rupture with all systems—a burst, an infinitesimal explosion of absolute nothingness as opposed to the somethingness of the articulated world.[19]

Because the Muses' discourse is always a chaste Apollonian discourse of meaning and form, measure and value, this incommensurable choice exists for them only as an erotic intuition prohibited by their very relationship to divinity. "Eroticism," according to Bataille, "can say what mysticism never could (its strength failed when it tried): God is nothing if not the surpassing of God in every sense of vulgar being, in that of horror or impurity; and ultimately in the sense of nothing."[20] Bataille's notion of the erotic allows one to conceive identity as taking form in an antagonistic recognition and refusal of immanent order and transcendent sublimity. Identity happens along and across the border of the consciously human with the spontaneously natural; it happens at the risk of nothingness, and—in the sovereign moment, "the moment of rupture," "the miraculous moment when anticipation dissolves into NOTHING, detaching us from the ground on which we were groveling in the concatenation of useful activity" (203)—in this moment, identity happens only as happening and otherwise as nothing at all.

While the elusive movements of Bataille's erotics run parallel to the violent turns of Fühmann's story, it is not a "first-order" erotics of individual subjects and bodies that is ultimately important to it. For Fühmann, who succeeded in bringing out the first GDR collection of Freud's writing in 1982, the Freudian legacy refers less to individual sexual neuroses than to inescapable societal conflicts. Unlike Bataille, Fühmann does not ecstatically invoke the heterogeneous as an individual experience—his own experience—but adopts a methodical tone to pinpoint the heterogeneity of an empirical system. In contrast to a first-order, face-to-face erotics, the "second-order" erotics of "Marsyas" concerns a loss of system identity, rather than self-identity. The story thus illustrates what I call a "systems erotics" of socialism. In Bataille's erotics the human is both a restrictive structure of taboo and a site of excessive (and transgressive) desire. In Fühmann's systems erotics, the socialist system, in its aspiration to surpass the calculations of the human, even the human divine, itself becomes a restrictive structure of prohibition and taboo as well as a site of transgressive desire. Where the consciously anticipating individual stood, now stands the five-year plan; where the spontaneously organic stood, now stands the self-equilibriating (or self-dissipating) feedback loop. Neither the materiality of a body nor the individuality of a consciousness remains in the center of a systems erotics; instead, systems erotics is a second-order erotics in which the provident coordination of bodies and minds confronts an ad hoc responsiveness to the imponderable present; the social organization of the pleasure principle confronts the inertia of the death drive; avant-garde stringency confronts arrière-garde laissez-faire.

Despite his assurances that "Marsyas" addresses the "artist's problematic," Fühmann, unlike Wilde, writes neither a story of the individual artist, the satyr-genius Marsyas, exponent of the humble reed, nor one of archaic Apollo, sovereign of pure form and classical lyre, but a story about the Muses of the coming world who must pronounce judgment on satyr and god alike. Fühmann's interpretation of this myth of aesthetic judgment is so unexpected—so unheard-of—because it is so much more system-oriented than versions that focus on one or another of the competing musicians. What it achieves is to bring the drama of direct dismay (*Betroffenheit*) to a crisis in the medium of articulation itself. In his essay on Bataille, "Preface to Transgression," Foucault recognizes that the hope for some unheard-of "beyond" to divided subjectivity—some ecstatic sexuality, some communion with god—meets its disappointment in the violence done by language. He asks, "[H]ow is it possible to discover [. . .] the experience of finitude and being, of the limit and transgression? [. . .] Would it be of help, in any case, to argue by analogy that we must find a language for the transgressive which would be what dialectics was, in an earlier time, for contradiction?"[21] Fühmann's rapt and angry story takes up the challenge of finding appropriately bold and bloodstained Muses who are not beholden to a dialectic of development, but who, leaping beyond immanence—figuratively and literally stepping out of their own skin—articulate the violent rupture of transgression: the horrible trespass that inaugurates socialism.

2. GROUNDING AN UNRULY COMPARISON: TERTIUM NON DATUR

> There once was a tailor, who said with a grin,
> There is no existing
> Number three; it's only a caper,
> A figment on paper.
>
> —Heinrich Heine, "Symbolism of Nonsense"[22]

"Marsyas," we are told in the story's first sentence, "was someone who had the nerve to enter into contest with Apollo" (355). If proper comparison is a matter of measure, then the problem is apparent forthwith. Marsyas, it is said, "had the nerve" to compete with Apollo—in the literal German, he was someone who *sich vermaß*, who "mismeasured himself," such that he placed himself in competition with Apollo. It is, in a sense, a mistake that led to his comparing himself with Apollo in the first place—a mistake in measurement, and that precisely when he is confronting Apollo, the god of form and measure. That element of measurement is one Apollo will never let Marsyas forget, and it is one Marsyas will never quite understand. It seems to him, as it might to us, so harmless.

Can that error explain the depth of the Muses' horror, does the "unheard-of event" they witness come down to a mistake, a mismeasurement? A mismeasurement, after all, implies the possibility of proper measure. The actual competition would then serve neatly to put Marsyas' (false) self-estimate to the (true) objective test: Apollo confronts Marsyas' mismeasurement with the proper one. Marsyas stands corrected. But something else happens—apparently not a comparison—when Apollo and Marsyas meet. Marsyas expects a friendly contest—indeed the challenge began as unthreateningly as possible, merely as the implication of an adverbial comparative. The chthonic goddess Cybele hears Marsyas' double flute, and, dancing and bare-breasted, "it pleased her to say that Marsyas played more beautifully [*schöner*] than Apollo." The comparative *schöner*, the verbal link that seals Marsyas' fate, is introduced as a manner of speaking, "it pleased her to say": *plaisir du texte*. And though it is repeated three times by Marsyas himself before Apollo responds, it is always in a drunken revelry. The referent, as far as Marsyas is concerned, is nothing beyond his satyr circumstances. Circumstances, in turn, that are comfortably conveyed within the arbitrary substitutability of language. The comparative form implies the compatibility and proximity of the terms it links. Marsyas simply places two musical performances, his and Apollo's, on an ontological continuum: and compares the two. It has all the banality of a commercial transaction, with beauty bearing no value distinct from the medium of exchange. All is part of a casual evening of revelry around the satyr campfire.

This sort of nonchalance in the face of divine order, however unprepossessing it might seem to a satyr, is for the metaphysical cosmos "the unthinkable itself." "Henceforth," Derrida says of the loss of meaning's stable reference (*archia*), "it was necessary to begin thinking that there was no center, that the center could not be thought in the form of a present-being, that the center had no natural site, that it was not a fixed locus but a function, a sort of nonlocus in which an infinite number of sign-substitutions came into play."[23] The ontological *perestroika* of a blithely irreverent Marsyas is too much for solemn Apollo, who suddenly appears with his lyre before the confused satyr. When the god demands to know "the stakes of the contest" (*Kampfpreis*), Marsyas, though surprised, naively continues in the same vein, suggesting the familiar objects of his everyday life, the sort of things he comfortably associates with his flute-playing. "Marsyas worried about a golden cup, which would only garner envy here in the realm of reeds." The prize should be something more appropriate for the fens: if Apollo wins, he gets the flute; for himself, "a sack of wine." Marsyas' modest considerations seem to be anything but mismeasurement. On the contrary, it is Apollo's imperious behavior that seems exaggerated: "Could Apollo really be so serious?"

But that is just it, he is serious. What seems measured and appropriate in Marsyas' sphere is an effect created by his language's ad hoc leveling, and this disastrous leveling seriously threatens to rob measurement of stable meaning. There is no high and low, no sublime in the satyr's world of bricolage. The model of life is given by everyday life uniformly caught up in the little satisfactions of the moment. It is a world of language games, where one can arbitrarily link Apollo and Marsyas, a sack of wine, and a flute, through a comparative, through a metaphoric substitution or in a syntagmatic series. Marsyas dwells in a metaphysical bog (*Schilfreich*) of *jouissance*. But when Apollo appears, it is to put an end to this careless non-ontology of language with its all too luxuriant possibilities for procrastination and spuriousness. Apollo is a realist: he pointedly does not even greet Marsyas; rather, "he didn't spare a single useless word" (9), like those proverbial realists, the Spartans, who according to Herodotus, would not even waste the useless words *sack of flour* if they could just show the sack.[24]

Referring to C. S. Peirce, Richard Rorty clarifies some ontological implications of the otherwise comic clash between loquacious satyr and laconic god. Peirce, according to Rorty, "did not, as most of Hegel's Anglophone followers did, think of God as an all-inclusive, atemporal experience which is identical with Reality. Rather, as a good Darwinian, Peirce thought of the universe as evolving. His God was a finite deity who is somehow identical with an evolutionary process which he called 'the growth of Thirdness.' This quaint term signifies the gradual linking of everything else through triadic relationships."[25] If the logic of language (and of reality with a small *r*) is one of substitution and combination, of new thirds interceding ad infinitum between the final conflict of any two terms, of impossible encounter, then Apollo tolerates none of its prodigality. In that sense, his appearance is not a response in kind to Marsyas' challenge—it is not a prolongation as a new term in infinite semiosis—it is *literally* an appearance, meaning in his case, a face-to-face presence. For Apollo, unlike for mortals and chthonic deities, neither the metaphysical appearance/essence problem nor the linguistic signifier/signified problem applies; for him, *Schein* equals *Sein*. The moment Apollo appears before Marsyas, the existential status of their contest has changed. The contest is not about the momentary order of two terms around the comparative third term *schöner*, where there *is* no absolute, regulative ideal ordering a system of differences. It is about the exhaustive logic of absolute presence, or the ontological presence of exhaustive logic. A thing is what it is and is not something other. Apollo *is* Apollo, and is *not* Marsyas: these are the fundamental principles of identity and difference. The proper measure of this ontology is far stricter than that allowed by the figurative excesses of language.

So to Marsyas' suggestion of the flute or a sack of wine as the stakes of the contest, Apollo tersely responds: "The stakes are no third thing" (358). *Tertium non datur*. There is no third. This is, as we will see in Chapter 6, the portentous Latin phrase that Fühmann was never to forget from his antifascist schooling in prisoner-of-war camp after World War II. It is also the fundamental logical principle of the excluded middle: "[T]here cannot be anything between two contradictories, but of any one subject, one thing must either be asserted or denied," as Aristotle formulates it.[26] Here, then, in a Soviet prison-camp, the play of language ends.[27] Here, on the plane of logic, the ground of absolute difference is established. Here—*where*? The story stipulates that here is the border between realms. Apollo appears "suddenly with his lyre on the edge of the bog" (357), and goes on to set "the battlefield as the edge of the woods of Mt. Ida" (358). Always "the edge" (*Saum*), a neither/nor site, a deferral, *ein Säumnis* waiting for arrival, like a logical contradiction waiting for consistent resolution: either/or. Here, Apollo will settle the difference between himself and Marsyas, he will establish not who plays *schöner* as a matter of degree, but will establish the propriety of proper measurement.

"The stakes are no third thing, explained the god, the loser puts himself in the hands of the winner. . . ." Marsyas does not know what that entails. Apollo explains:

> . . . he will get to the bottom of him.
> Him, Marsyas?
> Him.
> Get to the bottom of him?
> To the bottom of him.
> Wide-eyed astonishment: how that is going to happen?
> Through getting to the bottom, responded the god . . . (359)

Apollo is going to establish the loser in the mightiest of his principles, the principle of reason: *nihil est sine ratione:* nothing (not even Marsyas) is without a ground (*nichts ist ohne Grund*, in Heidegger's translation).[28] The problem, however—if it is a problem—is that the mighty principle of reason sounds merely tautological in the face of Marsyas' unheard-of impertinence. Getting to the bottom of Marsyas will happen by getting to the bottom of him.

It is useful to work carefully through the nature of the competition once more, up until those-who-bestow-speech fall silent: for the contradiction of speechless bestowers of speech needs to be grounded as much as Marsyas himself. Indeed, in Apollo's foundationalist logic a given statement is either true or false, no third option exists: again, that is the fundamental principle of the excluded middle. Either the Muses bestow speech or they do not—mute Muses cannot be, anymore than can "the round square cupola on Berkeley College" (Quine). Yet at some point the Muses' ability to serve as Apollo's divine revelation abandons them, yielding a meaningless, god-forsaken world. Such withheld revelation is as unheard-of as Marsyas' blasphemous tooting over Apollo's heavenly chords, and, as a betrayal of Apollonian oracle, it deserves condemnation as surely as does the betrayal the Muses are called upon to judge. As nonsensical as the Muses' strike is—as senseless as workers striking against a workers' state—it might seem forgivable to a casual understanding given the intolerable burden of judgment they bear. After all, one might fairly wonder how a competition is to be accounted for that takes place not on one continuous plane of being, but between two. Or, more onerously yet, between the earthly plane of ultimate absence and the divine plane of absolute self-presence. How can one language of judgment encompass them both if no stable system of reference is assumed? Fühmann's text dryly cites its unsatisfying classical antecedents: "How the contest between the two is supposed to have gone has been told by the chronists with utmost effort and at great poetic length" (359). The "chronists" simply avoid the issue and, using copious poetic resources, relate the story with no heed to the incongruity between the indulgent narrative logic of Marsyas and the strict prescriptive logic of Apollo.

The Muses, however, are in a different situation than that of the carefree chronists. Their interests are strictly identical to Apollo's in proclaiming the inevitability of an Olympian order whose power and glory is their own. As Fühmann emphasized about his own lofty aspirations for his story, utter directness is the only thing that counts on Parnassus. The Muses have to maintain the formal revelatory structure of truth—the equivalence of statements about the world with states in the world—which must be assumed for the comparison of flute and lyre to be meaningful and the judgment upon it to be valid, even though the irrelevance of transcendental validity is exactly the content of Marsyas' challenge to the god. Marsyas has not mismeasured himself in challenging Apollo, but, more unforgivingly, has made impossible the inside and outside of measurement. Hence, their contest, which is supposed to be a substantive settlement of differences, instead strikes a blow at the scheme of representation itself, the very domain of Musial competence. The essence of reference and realism is laid out for dissection at the moment the Muses are solemnly invoked to hallow it.

Apollo keeps representation old fashioned: there is no semiotics, but rather a complete unity of word and idea in the sign, and this wholesome sign relates uniquely to the thing it defines. Sign< — >thing: *tertium non datur*. Apollo's literalism is, in the words of Roland Barthes, an "isologic system," "whereby language wields its signifiers and signifieds so that it is impossible to dissociate and differentiate them."[29] This system, moreover, stands in an equally strict one-to-one relationship with the things of the world. Enter Marsyas, guileless libertine, who wields the comparative "more beautifully" as shamelessly as his melodious reed, comparing things with signs, instantiations with forms, apples with oranges: he doesn't trouble himself with fussy ontological distinctions. For Marsyas music and merry-making are all there is and all there needs to be. To *what else* would one ever want to refer when language is such a comfortably self-contained world of its own? "A linguistic sign is not a link between a thing and a name, but between a concept and a sound pattern," writes Saussure.[30] "There are only differences, and *no positive terms*" in Saussure's semiotics, and, occupying just such a world, Marsyas rejoices in "a system of pure values" that exist only relative to each other without any further grounding in something outside.[31] The satyr makes no ontological distinction between the contingent flux of meaning that is his reality and the *real* reality of the order that Apollo is. Thus, when he casually claims his playing is more beautiful than the standard of beauty itself, the result can only be disorder: the terms of inside and outside, of reference and measure lose their meaning. Apollo, in reasserting himself, is affirming a formal order to which arbitrary reference is subjected. He must establish the possibility of proper measure by subordinating Marsyas to the coordinates of a single spiritual and material reality, grounding revelry in the revelation of order.

The chronists, who have none of the Muses' obligation to Apollo's formal realism, recount the contest by taking Marsyas' side while accepting the humiliation of his fate—such public laceration being, after all, part and parcel of the "artist's problematic." Fühmann perfunctorily summarizes the versions the chronists tell in which Apollo wins by competing unfairly, insisting the satyr sing with his flute as he sings with his lyre, or insisting the satyr play his instrument from both ends. But these versions Fühmann dismisses as conveniently invented exculpations. "So much for the roundabout efforts of the chronists to unravel a tangle of contradictory spheres into a single narrative strand. . . ." In Fühmann's account not even the Muses can give an unequivocal account, let alone the chronists. Apollo still wins—as order must win for winning to have meaning—but the victory is only accorded him by a mute gesture. Marsyas' incomprehensible naiveté, to follow the divine music of the spheres with the tooting of "a hoof-soled, ass-eared pot-belly" (360), strikes the Muses' dumb.

> That which sang there cast into silence those who were made to lend word: how could there have been a choice?—There is no choice against one's own being,

> though the possibility of it tempts as an incomprehensible outrage.—Holy and accursed, cosmos and chaos, firmament and swamp, lyre and flute, the same conditions of a single round of struggle, and the Muses, overwhelmed into the unpronounceable, accorded Apollo the victory with a mute gesture. (361)

3. THE EROTIC ALTERNATIVE: NOT YET IN WORD

The Muses fall silent: Apollo is judged victor: Marsyas is flayed alive. Fühmann's text, however, is less than halfway to its end. What concerns it for the remainder is the gruesome detail of Marsyas' torture. It would be a mistake to see this torture in traditional terms as an elaborate catharsis of identification where Marsyas serves for Fühmann, as he did for Wilde, as a hero of tragic resistance—the modern artist issuing a cry against the alienating standardization of bureaucratic modernity. On the contrary, we need only consider Fühmann's contempt for the long-winded chronists, distant epigones of Marsyas, to see that the complacent role of the aesthete in dissent from any real system holds no appeal for Fühmann, whose creative goal is rather to understand how the socialist system can claim binding validity for itself.[32] Fühmann's rigor drives him to seek a revelation in which his system is experienced as a true system in more than word only.

In a 1970 story, "Indianergesang" ("Indian Song"), about a child's bitter fight with an authoritarian teacher over whether a nonsense refrain is sung with the syllables *tschallawei* or *schalawei*, Fühmann can already be seen mocking the specious violence of merely nominal distinctions. "Tschallawei," the little boy defiantly asserts to his Apollonian teacher, "is thousands of times more beautiful [*schöner*] than schalawei."[33] The stupefying violence behind differences that apparently make no difference receives an illuminating twist in an otherwise obscure passage from *Twenty-two Days*. A friend expresses astonishment that the single letter *i*—the proverbial one "iota" of difference—that distinguished between *homoousion* (of the same essence) and *homoiousion* (of similar essence) could lead to the fourth century bloodshed between Unitarians and Trinitarians. Is Christ the same ontological substance as God, or is he only similar, but essentially different? Rather than sharing his friend's astonishment, Fühmann notes that the iota only concentrates a difference like the one between (ant)ifascism and fascism. His scandalized friend objects that "you can't equate the two, in fascism–antifascism we're not concerned with the four letters 'A', 'N', 'T', 'I'; we're concerned with the crucial struggle between two worlds!" But this supposed self-evidence of reference to a "struggle between two worlds" is too easy for Fühmann—the four words remain no less a dodge than the four letters, or the one iota. Meaningless letters are less deceptive than the pathos-laden words: at some level, "the life-and-death struggle really and truly was about someone saying: there (up against the wall; at the head of state; in the pen; in office) is where we put: 'a fascist,' 'an antifascist.'"[34] The point is that letters, or—merely one morphological unit up from letters—words, do not alone do the trick, however vehemently they are invoked. Indeed, the minimal difference—the iota—crystallizes the revelation, whereas a vague romantic "ach," instead of avowing true love, instead of declaring sides over the iota, is nothing.[35] "If I could only say it," Fühmann ironically recalls his mother's helpless efforts to communicate some great context she only intuits, "it'd be a revelation for you."[36] For Fühmann, great contexts and earth-shattering struggles in fact do happen at single letters—but to stop with letters is to betray the force of revelation.[37]

Given his desire to experience a revelation of substantive socialist difference—rather than deferring real difference in ideological language games—it is not surprising that Fühmann did *not* side with those intellectuals who found the very word *taboo* offensive and simply opposed all prohibition under the banner of freedom. Again, the reality of his convictions is quite the opposite of what a careless reading of "Marsyas" might lead one to expect. At the fourth meeting of the Communist Party Central Committee in 1971 the new party general secretary, Erich Honecker, who had just deposed Walter Ulbricht as head of the GDR, declared that "if one proceeds from the secure positions of socialism then in my opinion there can be no taboos in the realm of art and literature."[38] The much repeated slogan of the early 1970s, "No taboos," which offered desperately needed encouragement to a GDR intelligentsia sorely tried by the violent suppression of the Prague Spring, only met with suspicion from Fühmann. Defending artistic taboos in *Twenty-two Days*, Fühmann sounds distinctly more like his stern Apollo than his permissive Marsyas. "In this sense I would be for taboos in art: as a demand for exceptional content and form in those places where a subject requires them. A taboo is that which allows no mediocrity: great or not all"[39]—one might ominously add: *tertium non datur*.

At the same time, Fühmann's imperiousness here is not a belated attempt to borrow a page from Johannes R. Becher's book and return to a rigid classicism as the one appropriate (and safe) form for socialist expression. Scarcely concealing his horror at the aesthetic compromises he had made with the demands of Soviet power, the ideologically scarred Becher who returned to war-ravaged Germany to rekindle a virtually extinguished culture held up the strict sonnet form as the last reliable vehicle for transporting lyric consciousness into the dawning socialist age.[40] In Fühmann's story, however, it is not Apollonian classicism that is charged with restoring culture. Rather, humble Marsyas resembles the tormented GDR culture minister, rekindling a war-devastated culture with playing so sweet that "Phrygia, which had withdrawn into mountain caves after the sacking of Troy, crawled out into the day again and began to dance" (356). The crucial difference is that happy-go-lucky Marsyas has none of the tactical caution of wary Becher, who had been burned too many times in his love for socialism to be interested in divining the ends to which order will go when forced to reveal its ultimate distinction. "There are only two powers," the Muses learn, "that compel such a thing, and both only beyond all measure: the desire of love and naïve simplicity" (366). Becher's chary classicism is precisely a protection against a revelation of order like that called down by Marsyas' love and simplicity. Unlike the minister, the satyr is an innocent, and as an innocent, he compels revelation. But he does not receive it. Apollo patiently explains to the Muses as they belatedly whimper for the god's clemency, "what hallows and heals, graceful sisters, is understanding, but it is not a matter of Marsyas understanding, and what needs to be healed is not his hide" (364).

The problem of the last half of Fühmann's story is that even faced with the gruesome climax of Marsyas' sacrifice, we are barred from reaching insight through his suffering (through tragic *pathei mathos*), just as we are barred from reaching insight through Apollo's peremptory cruelty. Unable to identify with either simple-minded Marsyas (whose killing is not an acceptable Delphic sacrifice) or stern Apollo (whose stunned Muses withhold the signs of oracle), how do we experience the force of the story's conclusion?[41] It is an impasse resting precisely on the Muses' contradictory silence. If the classical moral equation as formulated by Cicero is *unicuique suum*, "to each his due"[42]—that a punishment suit a crime in its measure—then the god's excessive punishment of the faun is either a more grievous mismeasurement than Marsyas' own or it is not due to him. Or both: the disproportionate severity of his punishment hints not at a moral economy, but negates it; and negated, its gratuitousness is revealed not as punishment but as pleasure. Only whose? Surely no such monstrous pleasure is due an insouciant satyr who is so easily satisfied by wine and song.

The idea of pleasure returns the argument to Bataille's notion of the erotic, which as we saw describes an affective, not cognitive state. Since erotic pleasure takes shape around some sort of acting and experiencing subject, using the term requires us to locate whose pleasure is being taken in Marsyas' flaying. Is it the pleasure taken in a victor's prize, so Apollo's pleasure, that the story is dealing with? Evidently not: the satyr's disfigurement follows upon the Muses' temptation, not Apollo's triumph. If the pleasure at stake were merely the satisfaction of putting the satyr in his place, Apollo could have dispensed with the competition and directly eviscerated the offending flutist. Instead, the "grounding" to which Apollo has committed himself is contingent upon a victory that the Muses must grant. It is that horrible responsibility which awakens the Muses' excruciating temptation to deny their patron his oracle. The blissful temptation of choosing against Apollo is so powerful for the Muses that they fall into a fatal silence: for what is a silent Muse? Or the formula can be reversed: the temptation of choosing against themselves is tantamount to destroying Apollo since they are nothing other than the signs that signify Apollo's reality: and what is godhead unrevealed? The issue is that in the divine order of representation at stake for both Apollo and the Muses, real presence has no priority over its articulation and vice versa—one is chained to the other in a rigid relationship of what Horkheimer and Adorno called "pure immanence": sign exhausts thing, thing exhausts sign, and there is no room for maneuver, escape, or change outside. "The pure immanence of positivism, its ultimate product, is no more than a so to speak universal taboo. Nothing at all may remain outside, because the mere idea of outsideness is the very source of fear."[43] This most sacred of Apollo's taboos, the ontological unity between thinking and being, between word and fate, is exactly the theme (and threat) of the hymn with which Apollo secures his victory in the competition with Marsyas. He sings a shrewd paean to "the omnipotent light," "that as a song of praise for the rule of the divine necessarily also had to be praise for those who are destined to lend word to this rule—that is, for the Muses—since for them thinking and being in song is essential being . . ." (360). How could the Muses deny such praise except by transgressing the universal taboo that circumscribes their destiny?

Challenging their destiny—the identity of word and fate—the Muses experience what turns out to be the story's overpowering erotic temptation, whose content stands in exact opposition to the content of Apollo's hymn. Apollo's hymn recognizes the Muses not as one party to a struggle, not as one class among others, but as the legible plan of being itself. They are the revelation mediating the constitutive insight into the rule of order. Or formulated more sharply, they are the plan—positive providence—whose gravity is revealed in Fühmann's story (and not in Apollo's hymn) through the awful temptation of arbitrary will. As we saw, the erotic for Bataille distinguishes itself from animal sexuality as a free and conscious choice, an act of will whose sovereignty becomes apparent only in its transgression of the founding taboo. This temptation, woven into the very fabric of the taboo, is the inarticulate underside to the plan's legible revelation. It does not *yet* exist. "The temptation of an outrage, that was it, but only in feeling, not yet in word" (361). It is a promise to speak and in speaking to lend word ("meaning and being") to the silencing temptation: both to overcome and to succumb.

> Because the sweetness that benumbed them was repugnant sweetness, sweetness of the rejected, the impure, the inappropriate [*des Ungemäßen*], the plain unthinkable, all nearly arbitrarily multipliable names for always the same thing, always the same negation, which is so many-named precisely because, thrown out of Order, it has no place in it, even though it is there and, thus undetermined, it harbors every form inside itself as the Ungraspable and thereby threatens the contours of order.—And nevertheless sweetness, that is the horror.—The temptation of an outrage, that was it, but first in feeling, not yet in word (361).

The temptation to commit an incomprehensible outrage, to throw one's very existence into jeopardy—which means what in terms of this contest? It means for the Muses to side with Marsyas against Apollo, with Chaos against Cosmos, to cede the word to figuration at the cost of literal realism. The silent award of victory to Apollo is no more substantial than the silent temptation to award it to Marsyas—silence is not a resolution, but the final crisis: Apollo's divine rule is simultaneously affirmed and denied. The Muses, "who are designated to give word to this rule," find themselves in the moment of decision tempted to side with Marsyas' spontaneous figuration. The anguish of that temptation is finally such that "the rule [*das Walten*] of the divine" to which the Muses are to lend meaning and being is "overruled [*überwältigt*] into the unpronounceable." The silence is a rupture along the contours of Cosmos and Chaos: Apollo's victory rests on the same swampy ground as Marsyas' defeat.

In such a crisis of temptation, according to Bataille, literary figuration comes into play. It separates thought from being, and word from fate, opening the space for speculation and play. The figurative is the one plane of *both* joy and death.

> One might say rather precisely that true joy would require a movement to the point of death, but death would put an end to it! We will never know authentic joy. . . . Moreover, death itself is not necessary. I believe that our strength fails us before life does: the moment death approaches it creates a void in us that incapacitates us in advance. So not only is trickery necessary in order not to die,

> we must avoid dying if we wish to attain joy. Thus, only the fictitious approach of death, through literature or sacrifice, points to the joy that would fully gratify us, if its object were real—that would gratify us at least in theory, since if we were dead we would no longer be in a condition to be gratified[.] . . . And if it is true that trickery presides over literature, that an excess of reality would break the momentum that carries us toward the point of resolution where literature aims us, it is also true that only a real daring has enabled us to find, in the anguish of figurative death or downfall, that singularly excessive joy that engages being in its destruction. (109–10).

The violent anguish of Marsyas' flaying is a joyful displacement of the Muses' own anguished silence. "There is no choosing against one's being, though the possibility of it tempts as an incomprehensible outrage" (361). Although the Muses cannot choose against themselves, their temptation gratifies itself in imagining what it would mean to succumb to the desire to do so. Desire for death is condensed into the death of Marsyas. Marsyas' destruction stands in for their own—the condensation itself is a metaphorical substitution. Marsyas' death becomes a metaphor for the Muses' death. A metaphor that saves them from their silence. The satyr's flaying lays open the aporia of literal representation. As a breach in the literalism of signification, what Freud calls a *Bahnung*—a path-breaking through the closed logic of dreams—it renders passable the impasse of the Muses' contradictory silence.[44] Bataille for his part, taking mortal pleasure in flaying Hegel, asserts that where the Hegelian discourse closes off transformation in a single identity, "the movement I speak of opens up. [. . .] It is a question of marking, in the labyrinth of thought, the paths that lead, through movements of vehement gaiety, to that place of death where excessive beauty begets excessive suffering, where all the cries that will ever be heard are mingled, cries whose powerlessness, in the awakened state, is our *secret* magnificence" (370).

As Marsyas is hung upside down between a pair of fir trees by two Scythians with knives, "narrow blades of iron, sharpened in mountain water" (361), he imagines that the whole thing will turn out to be a joke. He tries to think of a reason for such a trick: to scare him so he will play more beautifully still?—for certainly the elaborate theater must have a reason. Yet here is the satyr, carefree Marsyas, expecting a reason, when what has made him a satyr in the first place is precisely that he has never needed a reason, has never asked "why?" It was Apollo who wanted, as he said in setting the contest's stakes, to give the satyr a ground (*ihn ergründen*). Yet just as Marsyas' throat emits its first howling "why?" at that point—"the stab"—there are no more reasons: "The first stab was the incomprehensible" (362). "The incomprehensible" names that which has no "why." It is both groundless and the bottom ground. "Why?—the time for this question was past, now there is another: What happens?" (363) From "why" to "what," from metaphor and concept to metonymy and description: there is nothing more left for language than what presents itself right there.

> This, his desolate Why, which the satyr now ceaselessly bellowed through the daylight, it would have been timely when he first came across the flute at the beach: Why was it lying there, and why so forlorn, and why as if it had fallen from the sky, and why, if someone had disposed of it, did he do so, and with what charge, that of a blessing or that of a curse. And even then, when, eager for the contest, he felt warnings that even a satyr had to understand, and unambiguous premonitions in his spleen and kidneys, even then there still would have been time for a Why that could have had an effect on what was yet to come, but with the appearance of the god it all came back to the question, why Marsyas was a satyr, or, what amounts to the same thing, why he was the loser of the contest. (363)

There is no Why to be posed to a tautology—the god of measure is his own ground; or, as Heidegger puts it, the principle of reason has no reason. "Being 'is' the abyss [*Ab-grund*] in the sense of such a remaining-apart of reason from being. To the extent that being as such grounds, it remains groundless. 'Being' does not fall within the orbit of the principle of reason, rather only beings do."[45] The ground itself has no ground to stand on, and in exposing Marsyas, Apollo exposes himself as ***ab-gründig*** ("abysmal") and angrily responds to Marsyas' belated contrition: "Your regret is merely your arrogance" (363). But who is responding to whom? Who would Apollo's revelation be for? "Who Apollo is, Marsyas no longer needs to know, it is enough that the Muses learned it; what the satyr is, shows itself to them" (365). The story, the lesson, the grounding, the sheer groundlessness of it: all concern the Muses. They are the ones who must forget the satyr's world of excess and figuration, they are the ones who can have no identity other than being identical with Apollo (as his signs are no more nor less than his things), they are the ones who would die should they hear Marsyas' unheard-of flute, "the sweetness of the flute, incomprehensible" (368), since the satyr's incomprehensible tooting is nothing to Apollo. At the same time, though, we have to remember that the necessary representation of Apollo's victory could only come through the Muses' figuration of Marsyas, that for the Muses to be Muses, for them to overcome their silence, they had to choose against themselves, to choose the possibility of figuration (Marsyas), and in figuring the satyr's death, experience for once the glory of their own life/death.

"The Muses are those who have no part of wishes, since they give news of all that happens: the will of Zeus in the execution of his omniscience. This means taking no part" (365). Impartial, will-less, the Muses are the passive vehicles of the plan. Zeus' wish is their command. As the news of all that happens, their stories are a compendium of everything suffered, leaving no room for the satyr's own agony. Rather, the text itself is the protagonist and the Muses have already expropriated Marsyas' pain as their agonized inability to decide. From occasioning sympathy for the satyr, the unjust pain depicted in the flaying is commuted from Marsyas to the Muses and now seems richly deserved. Taking no part, the Muses speak all parts: playing both sides and neither of the contest; judge, jury, executioner, and victim. Again, the full measure of suffering is due to their treachery and disloyalty, and so now one may enjoy it in turn as poetic justice. And they enjoy it, too—such inhuman justice is their very *raison d'etre*.

4. SYSTEMS EROTICS AND THE DESIRE FOR COMMUNISM

> *annulation*/annulment: explosion of language during which the subject manages to annul the loved object under the volume of love itself: by a specifically amorous perversion, it is love the subject loves, not the object.
>
> —Roland Barthes, *A Lover's Discourse*[46]

> The system is the annulment.
>
> —Georges Bataille, *Inner Experience*[47]

> It was long ago said that politics is the art of the possible. That does not suppress our initiative.
>
> —Maurice Merleau-Ponty, *Humanism and Terror*[48]

Through representation two contrary things happen in the one account of Marsyas' flaying: literal language is transformed into figurative while figurative is transformed into literal. First, let me explain how literal language becomes figurative. Marsyas' semiosis confronts the Muses with the challenge of freeing themselves from Apollo by opening the distinction between appearance and essence, words and things, articulation and fate. This problem is portrayed in the story's central action: the attempt to relieve the mulish satyr of his constricting hide, find the depth beneath the surface: are his body and soul different? which is truly Marsyas? "Getting out of one's skin" thus turns the story into an allegory about "becoming other than who one is": metamorphosis. Flaying the satyr, as metonymically as it is described, is actually an extended metaphor for metamorphosis, and the possibility of such change is the joyous possibility of liberation for the Muses.

In the second achievement of representation, figurative language is transformed into literal language. At the same time as Marsyas' flaying becomes a figure representing the Muses' wish to change, it also becomes a realistic description of the transgression symbolized in the figural metamorphosis. What would it portend for revelation to be only metaphor, for signs to move freely without obligation to the fate of things? The satyr's playful challenge, his meeting revelation with semiosis, opens up this very abyss (or opportunity) of independence for Apollo's emissaries. Astonished by such impudence, Apollo disparages the faun's shallowness—"[C]ould such a satyr ever get out of his skin?" (363)—a turn of phrase meaning, "[As] though the poor creature could be any other way! Isn't that impudence simply his nature?" No sooner does the phrase occur to the god than he literalizes its figurative turn, his thought a piece with his deliberately ripping Marsyas out of his skin. The first, metaphoric achievement of the Muses is extinguished in the second, literal achievement of a minutely described evisceration. With the multiple trickery of fictional language, the silent Muses have their cake and eat it too. As an unconscionable sacrifice for glorious Apollo, homely Marsyas can move no oracle from the dumbfounded Muses. As a symbolic sacrifice for the Muses', an erotic mutilation standing in for their silent desire, Marsyas' demise is the promise that the sisters find their voices again.

The resolution of the crisis of the Muses' silence in the erotic representation of Marsyas' death does not, however, ultimately answer the paradox of Fühmann's story. Although Bataille asserts that the fictional plane of representation is one on which both death and joy are possible, one might equally assert that this "both" amounts to neither. In the case of language's simultaneous figuralism and literalism, Bataille's "trickery," is an illusory coexistence, an unwarranted third that merely substitutes informal language for rigorous ontology. This impossible simultaneity recalls the strangely embodied and disembodied narratives of trial and punishment in Franz Kafka's fiction.[49] "Kafka deliberately kills all metaphor, all symbolism, all signification, no less than all designation," comment Gilles Deleuze and Félix Guattari.[50] The metamorphosis that the Muses aim for, the freedom to be other than they are—the substantial socialist transformation that is Fühmann's life theme—cannot tolerate the mere figuralism of metaphor. "Metamorphosis," stipulate Deleuze and Guattari, "is the contrary of metaphor." Fühmann, who shared Kafka's hostility to metaphors without narrative consequence, wrote a sly homage to the ideologically taboo author in his 1981 science fiction story "Pavlo's Book on Paper."[51] Pavlo, a man from the distant future, struggles over the sense of an archaic copy he has found of Kafka's "Penal Colony," a story whose carceral setting could have no reference for a citizen of the world of proclaimed liberty. As Pavlo reads how Kafka's ancient visitor to the penal colony "sat on the edge of a pit into which he cast a fleeting glance," he realizes that although "he had never sat on the edge of pit; now he felt how its abyss drew him in" (143). For the man of the future, the designation "penal camp" is outlawed, the concept unthought, the symbolism purged, the metaphor incomprehensible: yet the actual abyss draws, right over the edge of the page. Although separated by a millennium from the fate of anything real and all but reduced to the vacant signification of mere letters, these words on paper become in Pavlo's hands and eyes "sensual self-revelation" (141) and as fateful as ever.

Returning to "Marsyas," we can now take our analysis forward to the crucial step of a systems erotics—the erotics pervading the oeuvre of real socialism—by seeing its central paradox not in the silent Muses who provoke the crisis but in the written story that spells it out. The paradox here is this: the narrative does not just *represent* the Muses' temptation; the narrative itself *is* the transgression the Muses are tempted to commit—the ontological problem of Apollo and the Muses has been displaced. To resolve this upward displacement from the Muses *in* the story to the Muses *of* the story, we need to shift focus from the unheard-of *event* that the Muses silently witness to the unheard-of *medium* that presents the event. How does the second-level paradox work? On the one hand, the Muses cannot act on their temptation in their own realist language, so they do so in Marsyas'. That is, the narrative is figurative language; it *figuratively represents* the Muses' desired self-destruction in the destruction of Marsyas. On the other hand, the narrative *really is* figurative language, and as such, *literally presents* the Muses' self-negation in the form of a sensual "book on paper." It is both the representation, and the realization, of their transgression. Marsyas' destruction is the Muses' destruction—and each is as real as, and no more so than, Apollo's formal law *tertium non datur*. The contradiction of the Muses' mute jeopardy (formally impossible in the realm of Apollonian realism) has been displaced onto Fühmann's story of mutinous Muses.

One last reading of Bataille helps us trace the problem of this new paradox into a serviceable conception of a systems erotics. Bataille's idea of the erotic emphasizes the simultaneous repulsion and attraction in human sexuality. Horror of animal sexuality occasions a prohibition and that prohibition is the condition for human sexual passion—the conscious desire to experience prodigal animality. "It seems to me that the object of the prohibition was first marked out for coveting by the prohibition itself: if the prohibition was essentially of a sexual nature it must have drawn attention to the sexual value of its object (or rather, its erotic value)" (48). A prohibited object becomes desirable in the prohibition's articulation of it as a taboo sexual object. Bataille sees in this contradictory aspect of the prohibition a "scandal of reversed alliances" whereby one allies oneself erotically with what is prohibited, precisely because it is prohibited.

This scandal at first appears as a static alternation, arising ontogenically in each individual's imaginative reaction to an object only vaguely articulated by a universal prohibition. Like Freud's Oedipal Complex, the dynamic of prohibition and attraction is reproduced as a structural synchrony. Bataille likewise borrows his name for this dynamic from Greek tragedy, calling it the Phaedra Complex after Phaedra's illicit love for her husband's virgin son Hippolytus. But a shift in erotic object becomes apparent—a second-order shift that remains, however, unthematized. "As soon as nature, which a spirit of revolt had rejected as the *given*, ceased to appear as such, the very spirit that had rejected it no longer considered it as a given [. . .]; it then regarded nature's antithesis, prohibition, as the given—that prohibition to which it at first submitted, as a way of denying its subordination to nature" (77). In the initial account of reversed alliances, the object of prohibition provokes transgression. Here, what appears as necessary, and so elicits the desire for arbitrary freedom, is not the prohibition's object, but the prohibition itself. Transgressing first against one prohibition, the same erotic dynamic is then driven further to seek out the whole system of laws, no longer any particular ordinance. Here we recognize the problem confronting us in "Marsyas" whereby the anthropomorphic protagonists are displaced. Instead of Marsyas and Apollo competing, we have the Muses confronting the limits of their office. From objects articulated by a system of rules, the story's focus switches to the system of articulartion itself: to positive law and legible plan. The Muses' representation of their desire only causes the system of representation itself to appear as an erotic presence.

The central drama of "Marsyas" is the Muses' existential one: how to represent (give meaning and being to) a contest between two systems that mutually preclude the possibility of the other's existence. Where is the space for such a contest? On what plane can it be said to take place? For if it happens on the terrain of one system, its outcome is predetermined by the very way in which that system configures itself as a system. Their existential drama is equally an erotic one, although the Muses, at first blush, seem the least conventionally erotic figures in the narrative. They do not comprise a pair vying in heated contest, but form a third party judging its outcome. Yet as this impossible third, the Muses become the very skin defining the story's ultimate stakes, the skin marking a boundary that belongs indecidably to the system or its environment.

Niklas Luhmann notes that "we have a world only in the sense that . . . [conscious systems] can conceive of the identity of the difference between themselves and their environment—that the difference is always *one* difference (in distinction to others)."[52] The problem addressed by what I am calling systems erotics is given by the failure of Apollo and Marsyas to share a world. Apollo cannot exist in Marsyas' world, and Marsyas cannot exist in Apollo's. There just is no logically unique connection between things in Marsyas' lax world; there just is no margin of tolerance, no phenomenological underdetermination, in Apollo's rigid world. The Muses become the protagonists of this erotics of worlds because they are called upon to adjudicate a difference that would be one difference and that is what they cannot decide. For to be part of a world means to have already decided—to have already taken sides. Otherwise, there simply is no world without an environment, without a boundary that makes it one world in distinction to another.

It might seem that a solution would be taking recourse to a more abstract standpoint. But, as Luhmann emphasizes, a self-reproducing system (what he calls an "autopoietic system") "formulates a situation of binary choice. A system either continues its autopoiesis or it doesn't. There are no in-between states, no third states."[53] One can never finally identify the whole system of systems, the *optimum optimorum* (the best of the best), from a standpoint of final autarchy. The next system level would simply be the next system level, and there would be no room for Marsyas there either. The conflicts might be different (and unforeseeable) but Apollo's principle, *tertium non datur*, would be implicitly vindicated, to the exclusion of the satyr. Another recourse might be to Bataille's final conceptual domain, that of "sovereignty": "we may call sovereign the enjoyment of possibilities that utility doesn't justify (utility being that whose end is productive activity). Life *beyond utility* is the domain of sovereignty" (198). In this case, where the excess of possibilities beyond any rational ends makes logical consequences—as well as moral and economic ones—impossible, Marsyas would have already preempted Apollo and his highest law.

A systems erotics thus determines no erotic system like Bataille's Phaedra Complex of structural relations. It characterizes the way our fundamental relationships to the world—our encounters—are captured less by invocation of natural bodies than by confrontation between systems. Calling such confrontation an erotics emphasizes that systems are not abstractions from embodiment, but have at their boundaries all the immediacy attributed to bodily contact. Insofar as we see the limit of systemic phenomena as an erotic rather than cognitive limit, we grasp how our highest-stakes conflicts exceed symbolic interaction. Although inaccessible to symbolic representation, such conflicts are not arbitrary, but profoundly occasioned by the incompatibility of worlds, by a stab in the tough and vulnerable skin separating a system from its environment. Any system might suddenly find itself wounded and caressed by another that renders its operations contradictory. "As always," comments Derrida, echoing Kojève, "coherence in contradiction expresses the force of a desire,"[54] and in our case the operative desire is one for the universality beyond contradiction to which socialism aspires, an erotic domain that is neither analytical nor arbitrary, neither necessary nor contingent: that proceeds "according to whim and measure" (358), as Apollo defines the prerogative of victory.

Referring to Kurt Gödel's famous incompleteness theorem, Derrida suggests another way to view the incompatibility between Marsyas with his endless "Thirdness" and Apollo with his proscription of a third: "An undecidable proposition, as Gödel demonstrated in 1931, is a proposition which, given a system of axioms governing a multiplicity, is neither an analytical nor deductive consequence of those axioms, nor in contradiction with them, neither true nor false with respect to these axioms. *Tertium datur*, without synthesis."[55] Exhausted by the failure of his era's alternatives, by his growing indifference to their ever more insubstantial differences, Fühmann sought grounds for decisive judgment by likewise reflecting on Gödel's principle, but with constructive rather than deconstructive interest. Fühmann characterizes the theorem as stating that there are statements in every system to which the principle of the excluded middle does not apply: "[In] order to determine such statements, it is necessary, Gödel continues, to go beyond the system in which they have been propounded and construct a next-higher system. There such statements can then be determined; however, new statements emerge that cannot be determined, that in turn require a higher system for their determination and so on *ad infinitum*."[56] As an example, Fühmann notes that "to illuminate essential aesthetic phenomena, I must go beyond the realm of the aesthetic." His example, however, makes him uneasy, provoking the unheard-of question that echoes throughout "Marsyas": "[B]ut what system would go beyond humans . . ."?[57] Elsewhere in his journal, Fühmann has an answer for his own horrible question. He observes that "a society without taboos would be inhuman," only immediately to moderate his dread of this iconoclastic prospect by reassuring himself that "it would also be unrealizable." Then a moment of doubt flares up about whether it is the inhumanity or the unrealizability of such a limitless system that daunts him, revealing the full force of his speculation: "[B]ut where are you setting the accent there? I want to believe: on the inhuman."[58] He wants to believe that his imagination is deterred by inhumanity, but he doubts it. In fact, his momentary hesitation reveals just the opposite, the accent falls on the challenge of the merely given limit. Once the challenge is set, neither the inhuman nor the impossible are grounds for retreat; they are rather the overwhelming source of his desire. What he wants is a society without taboos, not in Erich Honecker's mediocre sense, but in the unqualified sense he himself has just stipulated as unrealizable. As he seeks to put a name on this desired and dreaded society, he ventures the rhetorical question his work has long since answered: "Would communist society be the society without taboos?"[59] This name identifying his desire, communism, designates not merely what Thomas More in *Utopia* called "optima res publica." Rather, it marks pure difference from economy—the beyond of all systems, the best of the best, *optimum optimorum*.

CHAPTER SIX

Camps, Laws, and Plans: The Socialist Camp

The reply to the concentration camps was "the socialist camp."

—Heiner Müller, *War without Battle*[1]

I am the wound, and yet the blade!
The smack, and yet the cheek that takes it!
The limb, and yet the wheel that breaks it,
The torturer, and he who's flayed!

—Baudelaire, "Heauton Timoroumenos"[2]

But doesn't our world entire lie between shelter and torture?

—Fühmann, *Facing the Fire Pits*[3]

I. FASCISM, LIBERALISM, AND SOCIALISM: CHOOSING CAMPS

"The temptation of an outrage, that was it, but first in feeling, not yet in word," we read of the Muses' nihilistic temptation in "Marsyas." The agony of transgression Fühmann portrays in his 1977 story is imminent, bound up in the tension of anticipation and the stress of a dualistic universe. Yet temptation, desire, and transgression, themes associated with the blasé aestheticism of fin de siècle bohemias, seem improbable topics for the chastened *Wehrmacht* soldier Franz Fühmann, a converted communist whose Muses sang to him in disciplined refrains about the humble beauty of the new proletarian state arising on German soil. Until the appearance in the early 1970s of *Twenty-two Days*, Fühmann's work indeed discouraged the temptation to doubt the GDR's system boundaries, adopting didactic narrative strategies to reinforce a leftist political subjectivity capable of embracing the sacrifices of building a proletarian state in the emerging Cold War environment. In *The Jew's Car* (1962), the quasi-autobiographical narrator describes the first poem he writes as he returns to the GDR in 1949 from Soviet antifascist camp: "I wrote it in my head since the train was barreling along, clattering and banging, and after all the gloomy poems I'd written before, it was a bright poem. [. . .] No, I thought as I finished the last line; this land, I thought, I'm never going to leave it again!"[4]

In his postwar fiction from the 1950s and 1960s, after he turned away from poetry, Fühmann narrates not an expedient accommodation to facts that momentarily happen to be, but an ontological commitment to a socialism as universal and unconditional as the catastrophic progress of evolution. His language draws from the vocabulary of the natural and sublime, not the contingent and political. "Now," he concludes his 1966 war story "King Oedipus," "the new era of human rights [*Menschenrechte*] dawned from the gorges of the Balkans and the groves of the Maquis and the gentle plains of Poland and rolled out thundering from the expanses of Russia, to set an end to the old era, in which humans were still too close to animals."[5] The socialist era foreshadowed here is a natural catastrophe and a military drive, a legal era of human rights, and a biological leap away from animalistic prehistory into conscious choice. There is nothing half-hearted in this new world; no temptations cloud the dawning horizon. Everything right-wing—militarism, biologism, fatalism—has been seamlessly folded into a heroic left. By 1949, the contours of Fühmann's cosmos, recently rent apart by violence and chaos, had finally drawn together under the united communist leadership of his adoptive land. Hardened comrades from Soviet exile and Nazi camps were his grizzled new Muses, bringing battle-tested conviction to a decimated and bankrupted world. "Down with everything secretive, down with mysticism and obscurity," he remembers thinking. "Let the bourgeoisie idolize all that, let the reactionaries praise the darkness, let the dead bury their dead, we will hold to life's bold advance!" (*VF* 65)

Whatever pleasures and temptations might have been attached to cultivating personal preferences—to the individualistic plurality that the victorious United States was celebrating as the mark of its difference from its defeated or exhausted rivals—the discipline and purpose of a strong socialist identity was paramount for Fühmann.[6] In the aftermath of the fascist violence he had propagated as SA-member and *Wehrmacht* soldier, any thought of reopening the gates to capitalism and nationalism, even as they were rechristened liberal democracy, seemed to Fühmann nothing short of insanity: the decadent fruits of freedom promised by the rival systems that contested each other at the outset of the twentieth century had just subjected humanity to a trial it had barely survived. If humanity were to persist in history, then wholehearted cathartic identification with a socialist difference represented the only hope for real system plurality, plurality that gave historically conscious classes a revolutionary choice in shaping their future rather than offering them just the hollow diversity of the dissolute West. In the highly wrought context of postwar Europe, the same Georg Lukács who had earlier inveighed against any form of "yielding to fate" (*Schicksalsergebenheit*) now invoked a great "turn of fate" (*Schicksalswende*): "Every German stands—utterly dramatically—at the intersection of most fateful decisions."[7]

Forty years after this crossroads, upon East European socialism's collapse, this moment at the cusp of the new German socialist state was recharacterized as another sort of watershed altogether—not a moment of fateful decision, but of self-deceptive and self-infatuated capitulation to dictatorial temptation. Historians have faulted both the predominant left-wing subjectivity (for coupling political urgency with sentimental solidarity out of all proportion to any real individual experience of belonging), and what passed as objectivity in everyday descriptions of socialist achievements. Stephan Wolle has given the pointed name "hale world of dictatorship" (*heile Welt der Diktatur*) to the cathartic and integrated world Fühmann thought he recognized in GDR socialism.[8] Other commentators have found in a desire like Fühmann's to see a redeemed totality and integral cosmos in the rather paltry reality of the war-ravaged Soviet occupation zone an example of "the necessary and impossible, [. . .] tragic and not uncommonly tragi-comic love between totalitarian states and intellectuals."[9] As the invocation of "love" here indicates (and indeed of tragedy), the revised view of the commitment to socialism holds that it was anything but an emotionally and rationally clear-headed choice. This judgment on it, moreover, would seem to be substantiated by the heady rhetoric of Fühmann's early work, so characteristic of his time, that portrayed the commitment to socialism as an act of intuitive recognition that preceded suspiciously bourgeois postures of deliberation and discretion: first comes commitment, the devil's details follow later.

Lukács's *Schicksalswende* thus proved in the following forty years of the GDR to be less a decisive turn away from the Third Reich's notorious *univers concentrationnaire* than a twist of fate in fact concentrating three arduously differentiated forms of social organization—fascism, liberalism, and socialism—into a sustained experiment in rearticulating the political differentiations received by a weary postwar world. As Wolfgang Schivelbusch has argued in his comparison of Roosevelt's New Deal with Hitler's National Socialism, these three social forms hardened into mutual incommensurability only once World War II replaced the world economic crisis of 1929 (and, I would add, also the 1917 October Revolution) as the central reference point for thinking about political systems. As long as the economic depression called into question any particular political organization of society, especially liberal democracy, Schivelbusch argues, it was remarkable "how fluid the borders could temporarily be that were soon to turn into great watersheds."[10] Tagged in the title of this chapter as *camps*, *laws,* and *plans*, these three rival blocs emerged in the first half of the twentieth century as potentially viable ways to reorganize a world in which traditional forms of state sovereignty in the *jus publicum Europaeum* were insufficient to the tasks of globalization, industrialization, commodification, mass medialization, and juridification.[11] In this sense, each term—*camp*, *law*, and *plan*—serves in the following analysis both as a synecdoche for a historical social institution, and as a general analytic concept transcending that institution.

The "camp" is a synecdoche for the external military and internal police apparatuses characterizing the modern nation state's compulsion to locate and regulate demographic bodies, especially as this disposition takes on coercive, and at its most extreme, genocidal forms.[12] As a principle of social organization, however, the "camp" marks something more abstract than the historical gulags, *Konzentrationslager*, and refugee camps that have proliferated since World War I. Encampment is a central metaphysical feature of what we know, more benignly, as welfare statism (*Fürsorgestaatlichkeit*), a relationship brought out cynically in a joke from Nazi Germany cited by Horkheimer and Adorno: "[No] one is allowed to starve or freeze; whoever does will be sent to the concentration camp."[13] Horkheimer and Adorno apply the joke to contemporary society generally, where "everyone is enclosed at an early age in a system of churches, clubs, professional associations and other such concerns, which constitute the most sensitive instrument of social control."[14] Welfare statism describes the government's assumption of increasing power over not only the social order but also the biological viability of its constituent subjects; or, as Foucault characterized it, the increasing importance of a nurturing "pastoral" power over the formal "political" power of the Greek polis.[15] According to Giorgio Agamben, the philosopher who has gone furthest in hypostatizing the idea of "the camp" as the dystopian avatar of modern power, this goal of securing both quality and quantity of life has expanded to the extent that the legal rights of the citizen have been decisively displaced by the state's plastic powers over "bare life."[16] Internal welfare, moreover, has been conflated with external defense through the hypertrophy of "security concerns"—to such an extent that the distinction between citizen and refugee has likewise lost its political meaning.[17]

The contemporary elevation of the term *camp* beyond a territorial designation to the status of metaphysical principle, expresses post–Cold War political anxiety over a path of governmental evolution running contrary to the juridical evolution of individual rights and the limits they set on the plastic reach of the state. Associated most strongly with leftist modernity, this evolution in the government's pastoral power over the well-being of its subjects connects—in a suggestive, if by no means causally or logically coherent chain—forms of ancient matriarchal communitarianism, feudal patriarchy, and the paternalism of the modern Westphalian nation-state, with the ambiguous inheritances in industrial modernity of fascist and socialist corporatism and the contemporary security state. In key ways, this broad notion of the camp recapitulates Hannah Arendt's noted hostility to "the social," the purely external and noncognitive compulsions of biological needs and reproduction whose ascendancy, she argues, culminates in totalitarianism's most characteristic institution, the concentration camp.[18] Agamben, however, sees the liberal alternative to fascism and socialism, which Arendt stoutly defends, to be every bit as deeply implicated in the biological politics of "the social." As a distinct "technique of power," the camp for Agamben is independent of particular political interests, and, precisely as a technology rather than a politics in the sense of the Greek *polis*, its organizational methods penetrate liberal state forms as easily as the nonliberal forms that Arendt holds responsible for producing the camp. Agamben's political anxiety thus addresses itself not to the Cold War antagonisms organizing Arendt's politics, but to long-term biotechnical processes of social organization that work by metaphysically excluding, and physically enclosing, the freely intending, and openly resisting, individual agent. "Only because biological life and its needs had become the politically decisive fact is it possible to understand the otherwise incomprehensible rapidity with which twentieth-century parliamentary democracies were able to turn into totalitarian states and with which this century's totalitarian states were able to be converted, almost without interruption, into parliamentary democracies."[19] The axis of this frightening political lability for Agamben—as for Foucault—is the de facto collapse of normative law into the generative machinery of demographic manipulation, politics having thereby become technology.[20]

Whereas this still unorthodox hypostatization of the camp denotes direct and increasingly pervasive effects of external power networks on localized bodies, the very traditional, but notoriously slippery term *law* refers here to the rise of disembodied and highly deterritorialized codes of conduct, a formal process known as "juridification."[21] On the one hand, "law" serves in our discussion as a synecdoche for the liberal "rule of law" enshrined in specific state constitutions since the American and French revolutions at the end of the eighteenth century. In this sense, the law represents a progressive current of societal development of individual rights and internal freedoms (such as freedom of conscience), in juxtaposition to earlier hierarchical orders of feudal privilege. On the other hand, the law also designates an abstract conceptual realm where the character of the social order in general is debated as autonomy or heteronomy. Thus, besides representing the internally derived (inalienable) rights of an individual, law can also be conceived contrarily as a purely external code of coordination in which the modern state reconciles perceived subjective liberty with the rational needs of governmental power. Critiques of legality as an organization of social life that merely pretends to rest on the normative guarantee of individual freedom of will, but actually fosters conformity to the prerogatives of power—critiques associated with poststructuralist and genealogical analyses—have been part and parcel of social contract theories of law since at least Hobbes in the seventeenth century.[22] In the contractarian tradition, modern states are founded on the historical undecidability whether *rex facit legim* (power decrees law) or *lex facit regim* (law allocates power). Thus, for Hobbes law depends on a dialectic of natural free will (deliberate acts) and voluntary abdication of the individual will to a sovereign whose reign takes on the force of law (external compulsion). After the Enlightenment zenith of classical natural law theory in the era from Grotius to Rousseau, which emphasized the rational character of law grounded in human autonomy, the modern positive law tradition switched the accent to the heteronomous character of historical law: as statute on the books, law for the positivists is always only rules posited by earthly authority, with consistency and comprehensiveness serving as its highest aims. Thus, for nineteenth-century German positivists like Georg Jellinek and Gerhard Anschütz, the undecidable contest between political sovereignty and constitutional authority is emphasized to the detriment of any notion of an inherent human right.[23]

If the ancient concept of law is ambiguous as to its internal normative and external regulative effects, the concept of "plan" appears at first to be all externality, a matter of technical material administration, rather than moral institution. In the proverbial Five-Year Plans of the Soviet Union, "the plan" is the dominant figure for an at times ruthlessly materialistic historical socialism, one that runs roughshod over precisely the legal right deemed most fundamental to human subjectivity from Cicero to Rousseau—namely, the right to private property.[24] As a metaphysical concept designating the providential organization of social goods, however, planning reveals its ambiguity—for if conflict between individual actors is not to be governed by ad or post hoc adjudication of contracts, but judiciously anticipated and provided for by the conscious guiding of material claims, then the question of consciousness (of an internal self-conception of the whole and its parts) inevitably poses itself. In the Husserlian sense of intentionality, the plan is the moment of self-presence distinguishing progressively between a past (retention) and a future (protention).[25] In this abstract sense, the concept of planning can be contrasted with that of emergence, which designates a purely external social ordering that takes place spontaneously, without guidance by some sort of intending subject; emergence lacks the strong apprehension (or apperception) of presence that characterizes conscious intention. If, according to the Marxist account, the invisible hand of capitalist accumulation is the heteronomous sovereign force behind the liberal rule of law, then only with the visible hand of socialist planning are the blind laws of private accumulation replaced by conscious, collective control over the common goods of social life. Only with the plan does sovereignty become truly present to itself as autonomous popular will.

Yet as real socialism's Five-Year Plan rose in metaphysical stature to become the overriding fatality of the socialist state, the increasing interrelation of everything past and present demanded by comprehensive planning led to stasis, the growing impossibility of transformation. Everything had to become present at once in the plan, whereas change would require instead a plural ontology, a world of interiority and exteriority, presence and absence. Even Trotsky saw the immensity (although not any simple falsity) of the plan's conceit: "If a universal mind existed," he wrote in 1932, "of the kind that projected itself into the scientific fancy of Laplace—a mind that could register simultaneously all the processes of nature and society, that could measure the dynamics of their motion, that could forecast the results of their inter-reactions—such a mind, of course, could *a priori* draw up a faultless and exhaustive economic plan, beginning with the number of acres of wheat down to the last button for a vest. The bureaucracy often imagines that just such a mind is at its disposal."[26] The plan, which might initially have appeared as an external compulsion of facts—as opposed to legality's fount in an interior moral "ought"—, comes up against the opposite conceptual limitation. In its total recall (*Er-Innerung*, in Hegel's pun[27]) of past and future in the synoptic eye of the present, the plan, like Zeno's paradox of Achilles and the tortoise, threatens to bring to a halt any world once thought capable of movement and change.

The relationship between the triad of camp, law, and plan is already suggested by ancient theological and rhetorical *topoi*. As in biblical hermeneutics, where God the Provider (of the *lex Christi*) is distinguished from God the Avenger (of the *lex Mosis*), or in Aristotelian ethics, where distributive justice (*iustitia distributiva*) is distinguished from retributive (*iustitia commutativa*), a similar distinction might be drawn between the plan's claim to providential fulfillment of all future desires, and the camp's claim to punishment and remediation of past transgressions. Thus, Saint Thomas's conception of the absolute state as *poena et remedium peccati* (punisher and remediator of sins) was expressed no place more grimly than in the motto *Jedem das Seine* ("To each his due," *unicuique suum*) inscribed inside the KZ Buchenwald gate. Meanwhile, the law can be imagined as the Trinitarian forum where the *advocatus* of the Gospels (*paraclete* in Greek—that is, the Holy Spirit as divine intercessor) argues for fallen humanity's redemption before the jealous and measuring judge, Yahweh. "The Paraclete," notes René Girard, "is called on behalf of the prisoner, the victim, to speak in his place and in his name, to act in his defense. The Paraclete is the universal advocate, the chief defender of all innocent victims, *the destroyer of every representation of persecution*."[28]In this loftiest of senses, the legal forum reconciles judgment on the past with discretion toward the future by linking past facts (that which *was*) with future facts (that which *will be*)—it does so, however, at the cost of a deep ontologically ambiguity lodged in its contrary status as either inchoative tendency (the *status nascendi* conveyed by the German term *Gesetzmäßigkeit*) or motivating norm (the *ought to be* of free moral will).[29]

While this mythical universe of providence and punishment expresses how enduring and fundamental categories like my camps, laws, and plans are, I also cite it to caution against letting an allegorical typology suggest a static ontologization of these categories. The "universe" in which I place the camps, laws, and plans of Fühmann's work is a pragmatic institutional order, with all the historical variability and particularity such an order lays claim to over and against the compactness and constancy of allegory. The issues of real socialism become apparent where the ontological conflicts assume the spatial and temporal pathos of transformation that Fühmann's work so successfully conveys. The three-fold concentration of metaphysical conundrums on the historical sites of Fühmann's affirmation of socialism—the POW labor camp in Nephitgorsk, the Antifa re-education camp in Noginsk, the partitioned and eventually walled off occupation zone in

East Berlin—marks the indelible problematic of his writing: the theme of transformation as well as the transformation his writing itself undergoes. Drawing on past enthusiasms of right and left, the totality of Fühmann's socialist affirmation contains in situ all the paradoxes of camps, laws, and plans that his subsequent writing never sorts out and leaves behind, but instead distills into stark metaphysical conflicts; conflicts that all transitional systems either simplify away in taking on successful historical form . . . or experience as infinite existential pain.

2. TOTALLY (BARBED) WIRED: TOTALITARIANISM AS PATHOS AND RELATION

> Does the antithesis of Right and Left still have any meaning?
> —Raymond Aron, *The Opium of the Intellectuals*[30]

In his account of the growth and subdivision of social systems, Niklas Luhmann maintains that "the construction of complexity can be initiated only by a reduction *of complexity*."[31] In other words, only by initiating a number of internal simplifications can a system organize a broader range of phenomena. In Fühmann's case, the historical intersection of fascist total mobilization with its unconditional military surrender, exactly the opposite situation prevails: only with a radical surge in complexity does the opportunity present itself to simplify the ravaged world by wholly other means. A more or less chaotic collapse, not a simplifying reduction, opens the prospect for a radically different systemic organization. Such a collapse of social systems, or more precisely, the conscious revolutionary embrace of a collapse of differentiations into an underdetermined plenum is, for obvious reasons, easily construed as a totalitarian rejection of the normative and functional distinctions of liberalism. Yet such stigmatization of the indeterminacy to which Fühmann committed himself in the middle of the 1940s as a totalitarian devolution of liberal progress can happen only after the fact of the systemic failure of those commitments, and precisely as a later liberal judgment on it—a judgment that, because liberalism is indifferent to the distinction between communism and fascism, automatically sentences *all* radical initiatives to the single hell of Hitler/Stalin.[32] In other words, left/right political distinctions of the sort that Fühmann tried to rearticulate out of the personal and social collapse of 1945 can exist today only *within* the liberal order outside of which Fühmann chose to stand. To the extent that the *Stunde Null* of 1945 wasn't a clean slate, but a messy deformalization of social borders, it harbored the possibility for Fühmann of radical reordering—a possibility retrospectively foreclosed by the order that triumphed in 1989.

While liberalism can exclude state socialism from legitimate politics by deeming it totalizing, it cannot exclude totalizing from its own liberal precincts by equating it with illiberal commitments. In a 1964 discussion between Adorno and Bloch, totality emerges as the only way to invest consciousness with the pathos of true choice. Adorno was a thinker fully antipathetic to Fühmann's state socialist commitments, and Bloch, the philosopher of radical hope, fled the GDR in 1961 with what he had to admit were "disappointed hopes." Nonetheless, the two conversation partners agree on Adorno's assessment "that what people have lost subjectively in regard to consciousness is very simply the capability to imagine the totality as something that could be completely different. [. . .] People are sworn to this world as it is and have this blocked consciousness vis-à-vis possibility."[33] Even in opposition to the "totalitarian" GDR state, the leftist passion for a total overhaul of existing social relations remained part of the intellectual agenda within the rapidly normalizing West Germany of chancellors Adenauer and Erhard in the 1950s and 1960s.[34] The subsequent Frankfurt School legacy, exemplified by Jürgen Habermas's turn to neo-Kantian (Rawlsian) legalism in the 1990s, sought to disavow both totality and sovereignty. Totality in this case was understood as single-party dictatorships, and sovereignty as the postcolonial world's outmoded insistence on "the right to national self-determination." Imagining cosmopolitan law replacing both dictatorial caprice and national sovereignty, however, this legacy only defines a new sovereignty (or system) based on a total global consensus on a priori rules of communicative conduct, on what John Rawls called "well-ordered peoples."[35] However tempting it might be to repudiate the totalizing pathos that mobilized various collectivisms in the years preceding each world war and to blame the affect, and the "do-gooders" (*Weltverbesserer*) bearing it, for the twentieth century's tragic deviations from a liberal norm, conversations like that between the disillusioned Adorno and Bloch indicate how irresistible some holistic category—some camp—remains for thinking about identities and their coordination.

A widely observed sociological riddle suggests how misleading it is to associate totality only with the pathos of violent collective identification, rather than noting it in relations coordinated behind the backs of private individuals. Shopping is thus often experienced as an authentic expression of individual preference while deliberate regulation of consumerism is taken to infringe upon free choice. Individuality is perceived as spontaneously intact when standardized in the exercise of set consumer options, and as injured when compelled to assume face-to-face responsibility for uncertain consequences.[36] Social totalities may thus appear conceptually where they are least visible experientially. The Marxist tradition has analyzed such paradoxes under rubrics from alienation and commodity fetishism to the administered society and culture industry.[37] Other traditions have thematized similar phenomena: systems theory, for example, when it separates psychic systems from social systems, or phenomenology when it contrasts an authentic lifeworld with an instrumentalized systemworld.[38] For Foucault, the paradox is encapsulated in the formula *omnes et singulatim* ("all and each"), which refers to the simultaneous totalization and individualization by which government preserves its authority.[39]

In our case, real socialism challenges us to understand, without resurrecting a dated notion of "totality," how there can be more than one way of relating everything to everything else (plural universalism), and how the experience of some one such system of relations as opposed to some other can become present to the consciousness as pathos (and can thus be narrated). Trying to do justice to what is visible and invisible in a world that extends beyond any individual's purview, Merleau-Ponty writes that "it is a question not of putting the perceptual faith in place of reflection, but on the contrary of taking into account the total situation, which involves reference from the one [faith] to the other [reflection]."[40] On Fühmann's example, we are led to ask what difference it makes to a literary consciousness whether it is experiencing an "invisible" liberal norm or an "intentional" socialist plan, if both articulate practical ways of interrelating a modern totality? As a literary project, rather than testimony to an anachronistic pathos, Fühmann's commitment to socialism reads as an effort to relate intentional to structural aspects of a system, not as an opposition between true and false consciousness, but as a way of creating universal (leftist) political meaning out of a catastrophic *Schicksalswende*.

Fühmann's self-referential commitment to socialism as marking off a left-wing from a formerly right-wing selfhood gains in narrative urgency as he struggles—in the face of refractory observations of his land—with an other-referential commitment "not to just any socialism of attitude or of ideality, but to that socialism which exists in state form."[41] As the "state form" moves to the center of his literary imagination, he tries to refer Marxism's universalist emancipatory pathos to the structuring transformation being undertaken by fellow survivors and functionaries in the homely

GDR. It would be a mistake to see this as a personal matter, narrating a post hoc justification for an unjustified, perhaps unjustifiable, choice made by a captured and frightened soldier. Foucault remarks about J. Robert Oppenheimer that "it's because he had a direct and localized relation to scientific knowledge and institutions that the atomic scientist could make his intervention; but, since the nuclear threat affected the whole human race and the fate of the world, his discourse could at the same time be the discourse of the universal."[42] Or as Neil Armstrong succinctly summarized the Apollo project: "[O]ne small step for a man, one great leap for mankind." The nuclear scientist and astronaut's double relationship, first to a local institution, then, through that local institution's global significance, to a total system, is the sort of relationship Fühmann tried to establish between a profoundly local intervention (while in Soviet camps and then militarily partitioned Berlin) and the global significance, not of the crude East German state apparatus, but of the socialism it claimed to be bringing about. Everything depended on the ontological status of the apparently so abstract and intangible relational unity that Fühmann and his comrades insisted on treating as "socialism": is socialism, in other words, as fateful, and perhaps fatal, as the apocalyptic "nuclear threat"? "Of course," writes Fühmann, "I can't shut my eyes to the fact the world is split into two camps that from the point of view of their genealogy, ideology and practice of life stand largely in antagonistic opposition to each other, but together they're what we've got of humanity, even if [. . .] only in a negative sense. An idiotic, one-sided example occurs to me as an image: two halves of one atom bomb blowing each other to pieces when they collide."[43]

Like the variants of sovereignty discussed in Chapter 3, which in one instance originates an authority without origins, and in another aims at an end beyond the logic of ends, this planetary socialist promise harbors paradoxical poles of genesis and telos (related to my characterization of law as both generative *Gesetzmäßigkeit* and prescriptive norm for intentional behavior). Martin Jay observes how "for Lukács . . . totality was an expressive concept with a genetic center. Although Bloch endorsed Lukács's view of the proletariat as the 'we-subject' of history and agreed that the humanization of the historical process was progressive, he stressed the teleological power of its end rather than the genetic creativity of its beginning."[44] Totality in this double sense is the key concept through which political debate about sovereignty takes on a twentieth-century technological cast. As Carl Schmitt formulated his version of the relationship between the concepts: "[T]he sovereign creates and guarantees the situation as a whole in its totality."[45] While Schmitt, reversing Lukács, prioritizes the single element before the whole network, the permutations of alpha and omega have little effect on questions concerning their relationship—questions that point, besides to the genetic/telic ambiguity of totality, to another related antinomy—namely, that of *system*, as an autarchic set of binding interrelationships, versus *decision*, as a monarchic, nonrelational determination. This totalitarian twin, whose totems could be the *machine* and the *leader*, emerges joined at the hip as feudal rule is finally fading as a form of social coordination with the collapse of Ottoman, Russian, German, and Austrian empires at the end of World War I.[46]

The simultaneity and mutual exclusivity of claims to system and claims to decision recalls the dilemma over the priority of agency versus structure that is arguably the defining conundrum of modernity—that is, of a social order that reserves for itself prerogatives of both innovation (agency) and rationalization (structure).[47] As Rousseau expresses the paradox already in 1762: for the idea of "an emergent people" (*peuple naissant*) to make sense, "the effect would have to become the cause. The social spirit which ought to be the work of that institution, would have to preside over the institution itself. And men would be, prior to the advent of laws, what they ought to become by means of laws."[48] Although I keep tracing twentieth-century conundrums—the genos/telos and the structure/agency antinomies—back to Enlightenment roots and further, what leads me to stress totality as the relevant formulation for mass sovereignty in the twentieth century is, crassly formulated, the sheer *quantity* of government necessary to coordinate industrialized life by the century's dawn, and the technology the quantitative implies. Scarcely a social demand expressed itself that did not do so by reference to some governing institution, whether an explicitly political one like a popular representative house; a military one like an army in "total mobilization" (*totale Mobilmachung*), as Ernst Jünger termed armament's emerging planetary scale; or, crucially, a technical one like a bureau of weights and measures or an office of censuses and statistics. Foucault, following Durkheim, argues that by the end of the eighteenth century segmented sovereign societies began ceding to stratified "disciplinary societies" on the basis of the expanded scope of containment and surveillance apparatuses (extending the logic of the camp into schools, hospitals, and factories).[49] Building on Foucault, Gilles Deleuze sees another technocratic switch underway, from disciplinary regimes to the "society of control," wherein people operate less in a fixed framework of disciplines than by each assuming a variety of roles in vast free-floating networks of control.[50]

For all their sinister vagueness, these rubrics clearly suggest how modern social coordination is evolving with a scope and intensity that makes previous experiences of sovereignty unrecognizable, combining camps, laws, and plans—otherwise taken to be mutually exclusive—to mold new social wholes with unexpected characteristics. For Fühmann, too, totality's character is precisely what is still at issue ("not yet in word"), both genetically (as regards any structural tendency) and telically (as regards any normative intention toward the future).

While the totality concept captures well Fühmann's literary attempt to think through his camps, laws, and plans, the sticking point of his autobiographical reflections only truly shows itself when it comes to assigning a right/left distinction to this global concept and doing so without recourse to received criteria of political differentiation, such as liberalism's. In Soviet prison camp, Fühmann's commitment to socialism had to be a commitment to a norm and a tendency that existed, but existed in contradistinction to the stark facticity of his captivity. It was a commitment, as his Antifascist School taught, to seek "the battle line between reaction and progress through the millennia of human history, demanding a clear 'for' or 'against' in every area of social activity, even in art and literature" (*VF* 59). It was thus a commitment to a totality of relations in the same moment, as this totality marked a tendentious political difference. Fühmann's ***differential totality*** is what we have been calling socialism.

To the extent that rallying around socialism is not just rallying around a name, but committing to an emergent structure and a political decision, this totality has to be marked by more than the scale of its coordination. Thus, if the ***quantity*** of postwar government—the sheer number of elements it was called upon to relate in a simplified network of collective welfare and human freedom—had become overwhelming, the historical ***quality*** of this explosion in governance refers inevitably to the experience of an antagonistic border precipitating on the sites where the old Eurasian empires failed to manage that quantity. In this sense, Schmitt similarly distinguishes between a "quantitative" and "qualitative" total state.[51] Reacting in the early 1930s against the weakness of a Weimar state with vast responsibilities and little initiative, he characterizes a quantitative total state as a weak one that is responsive, as a state, to the full range of social desires; a qualitative total state, by contrast, is one that intensively shapes its subjects' demands through a substantive political vision of social order. The stumbling block for Fühmann is that the qualitative distinction of the socialist totality could not simply be the arbitrary imposition of a strong leadership as a groundless ground of the whole (a fateful decision); rather, the socialist *qualia* had to both imply and transcend the objective quantitative order.

But how can reference to some such *qualia*, contained in the smallest element, but not contained by the largest whole, amount to anything other than mysticism, metaphysics, and miraculous revelation: anything other than the "horrible, demonic dance of death ranging over the whole apocalypse of our times" that was so resolutely repudiated as fascistic by the chastened protagonist of Fühmann's *The Jew's Car*? Indeed, that is the central aspect of Fühmann's recurring question of transformation: is there a right/left distinction, if not to the Apocalypse, then to the twentieth century's radical dedifferentiation of social forms; a distinction, moreover, in which the left pole is not only different from, but superior to the right? If so, what criterion transcends the collapse of camps, laws, and plans in order to be able to measure the qualitative progress of the posited new order? What can a person sense or experience that lets him or her know that the ecstatically desired New is in fact also the soberly calibrated New?

Starting with the reality of his conversion—with the sovereignty of his decision to transform himself from fascist to socialist—Fühmann finds that this radical decision has no meaning unless its pure self-reference can be complemented by other-reference to some external, world-creating system. The tautologically true, because purely immanent, fact of his existential commitment to socialism seeks substantiation outside of itself. Where outside? In the leftist camp—that is, military prison, political occupation, dilapidated construction site: not auspicious venues for validating the open sovereignty of progress. Nonetheless, Fühmann's historicized and narrated references to life in real socialism are charged with unfolding all the undecidable metaphysical paradoxes of camps, laws, and plans in a legible story of qualitative transformation. "If one relies on an ontologically oriented logic that cannot include time, one encounters paradoxes, as technicians of formal calculations know," writes Luhmann, describing possible responses to the very paradoxes of Apollo's duel with Marsyas examined in Chapter 5. "One then must either 'Gödelize'—that is, transcend the boundaries drawn by the premises of the calculus—or 'temporalize,' that is, endow the calculating system with time."[52] Fühmann, accordingly, aims to "temporalize," to turn to time to validate the existence of socialism as more than just a name he calls himself. But time, in the form of an ever more provincial GDR history, is hardly able to organize the many paradoxes of socialism's real situation. Thus, we have seen how, in his decisive moment of literary conversion—the writing of *Twenty-two Days or Half a Life*, twenty six years after his political conversion as a POW—he turns from Hegelian "temporalizing" to a more speculative "Gödelizing."

Fühmann's narrative achievement, as well as his literary crisis (*Scheitern*), is to represent with experiential pathos and referential precision the movement of the paradoxes of transformation and identity into time and then back out of time into formal being . . . or nonbeing. Since he is existentially driven to distinguish between a fascist self and a socialist self and to see that potentially nominal distinction be articulated in the substantive difference between Nazi *lager* and Soviet gulag, Nuremberg racial laws and proletarian justice, capitalist spreadsheets and communist plan, he cannot accept that the world consists of either a single unchanging logos beyond all political and economic differences or a punctual mythos at the root of each. If there is a left/right difference, if his choice of socialism as different and superior is to be figured as a real choice, then he can never close the horizon of reference into pure self-reference or absolute transcendence. However enthusiastically the former SA man Franz Fühmann launched his literary career with a cathartic embrace of socialism, that foundational decision can only continue to be figured as a tendency along a left/right border—any subsequent closing of the differential horizon behind it merely lands Fühmann back in the ancient Eleatic paradoxes that, holding the world to be a single substance, deny the possibility of the change he so desperately desires. His *total* affirmation of system *difference* is thus always haunted by the same temptations that flayed Marsyas and struck Apollo's Muses dumb: "the temptation of an outrage, that was it, but first in feeling, not yet in word."

3. LEFT RESURRECTION OUT OF THE RUINS OF THE LEFT/RIGHT

> The Communist presentiment of the Beyond: And should we fail in this here world, we'll see each other in Bitterfeld.
>
> —Old East German joke

> Oh, the bitter hour of decline,
> When we behold a stony face in the black waters.
> But radiantly the silver lids of lovers lift:
> *One* flesh. Incense streams from rosy pillows
> And the sweet song of the resurrected.
>
> —Trakl, "Song of the West"

"When two do the same thing, they do not do the same thing," Ernst Bloch writes in 1933 about Nazis and communists with a dialectical refinement that belies the fatal difficulty his Weimar contemporaries experienced in getting beyond the rhetoric of left and right to a responsible political stance. "So it is today, when the Nazi cannot yet reveal the way he really looks and what he really wants, and thus disguises himself. [. . .] The most dreadful white terror against populace and socialism [. . .] camouflages himself as socialist."[53] Four years later, in 1937, by way of response to Thomas Mann's mission statement for his new antifascist exile journal *Maß und Wert* (*Measure and Value*), Bloch again addresses the overlap between the "semantically appropriate effectiveness, reality" (*sinngemäßen Wirksamkeit, Wirklichkeit*) of socialist language and the inappropriateness of fascist rhetoric.[54] According to Bloch, Mann's editorial statement postulated that with Nazi propaganda, "the vocabulary of revolution is irredeemably damaged [*heillos geschändet*], compromised and reduced to silliness."[55] Bloch's left-wing messianism, however, recoils at denying redemption to the language of revolution, no matter how apparently corrupted. "Is such vocabulary really 'irredeemably damaged' by the Nazis? So irredeemably that it must fail in its service to the revolution?"[56] Bloch's specifically political concern here is with preserving the ability of the German language—or of language in general—to adequately differentiate between socialism and fascism, or at least between their respective left and right aspirations.

Fühmann's central autobiographical construction, we should recall, was that he began his adult life in the 1930s as a fascist nursing all fascism's dull and gloomy ideological fantasies. While in the mid-1940s he honorably sought to become an enlightened poet of socialism, he could never escape the sheer chronological reality that his lyrical imagination had initially been fired by the language and sympathies of a late-Imperial modernism ostensibly so foreign to the Left, in particular by the fractured and violent poetry of Austrian expressionist Georg Trakl, although, he comments, it might just as well have been Rilke, George, or Benn (*VF* 228). In what fashion could Fühmann then say that he, like his adoptive state, had transformed from fascist to socialist; or that his new country, like himself, had made the switch? If fascism and socialism are not themselves distinct from language, but are embedded in constitutive speech acts, communications, and norms, then the verbal ambiguity of Fühmann's Muses has grave consequences for referring meaningfully to a real socialist difference. As Michael Tratner pointedly asks in his study on the politics of modernism: "[Why is] it that modernists held such diametrically opposed views and yet wrote in such similar ways?"[57]

In a passage from his idiosyncratic 1982 autobiographical reflections on Trakl, *Facing the Fire Pits* that I cited in Chapter 4, Fühmann takes up this problem of politically dichotomous language with respect to GDR literature's founding figure, Johannes R. Becher. Writing in the early 1980s, Fühmann regards Becher's late 1940s project of resurrecting a language of national pathos with skeptical eyes. "What happened then and moved masses," Fühmann recognizes, "is doubtless difficult to grasp today: a recovery of political values through the despite-it-all use [*Denoch-Gebrauch*] of misused—to the point of being used-up—words in the name of revolutionary renewal [. . .]. They underwent a sort of miracle of Lazarus, even such degraded words as 'heroism' and 'hero'" (*VF* 107). During the 1940s era of socialist construction to which Fühmann is referring here, Becher was not only reinvigorating the idioms of a Nazified sublime but was also seeking legal permission to take over the bourgeois-aristocratic-sounding title, and presumably something of the spirit as well, of Thomas Mann's exile journal *Maß und Wert* in order to reuse it as the flagship literary journal of the new socialist German state. This is, of course, the same journal to whose antirevolutionary mission statement Bloch had objected in 1937, and Mann, mindful perhaps of that irony, demurred. Thus, when Becher's journal eventually appeared in 1949, instead of the hoped-for "Measure and Value" it bore the uncannily similar title "Meaning and Form" (*Sinn und Form*).[58] There is thus a double resurrection at play in Becher's postwar miracle-work: on the one hand, bourgeois measures and values, and on the other, protofascist heroic pathos are each made to rise again, transfigured into new socialist meanings and forms.

As late as 1960, Fühmann could still recall without irony or suspicion how, during his dark days in Soviet POW camp, Becher's verses taught him to speak again of Germany, "the other Germany." Thus in his 1960 homage to Becher, Fühmann elevates the voice of the recently deceased poet from that of a mortal individual to that of the dynamic, living reality of socialism itself: '*le roi est mort, vive le roi!*' in the medieval formula for the sovereign incorporation of the king's body into the royal body politic. "Not a single voice alone," Fühmann writes, "could effect the miracle of transforming the hundreds of thousands behind barbed wire. This miracle—and it was a miracle that happened over many days—was achieved by the living reality of socialism, and Becher's poems were an effective part of this reality."[59] Thus, in the decades before he began doubting the miraculous nature of Becher's ministry, Fühmann located its animating power—its "semantically appropriate effectiveness, reality" (to invoke again Bloch's phrase for true revolutionary language)—in its ability, as poetry, to incorporate ambiguous reality and, as socialism, to incorporate ambiguous language.

Over the next twenty-some years between this 1960 homage to Becher and his 1982 homage to Trakl, *Facing the Fire Pits*, the miracle of socialist-word-made-GDR-flesh becomes—in the implied sense of a miracle being contrary to reason, unprecedented, and incommensurable—an insoluble contradiction for Fühmann. He cannot but remember with pained irony the days of doctrinaire faith in the realist, antidecadent literary credo politically enforced by Becher, Alexander Abusch (Becher's successor as second minister of culture) and Vladimir S. Semionov (the highest-ranking Soviet diplomat in East Germany).[60] "All the value-positing demands and their robust realization," he recalls in 1982, "also happened on the terrain of the aesthetic, under the sign of historical necessity, indispensable for the construction of a new society that—already hailed by Johannes R. Becher in 1917 at the hour of its first existence—was now beginning its emergence on German soil, as the true fatherland of the German people: 'Resurrected from ruins, and facing the future,' as the national anthem puts it.—" At this point in the ironic crescendo of his recollections, Fühmann interrupts this sarcastic citation of Becher's lyrics for the GDR anthem with an outburst of sincere pathos: "I'm talking here about memories; they're precious to me.—Oh, Angel of my fatherland, will you show yourself again as you once appeared to me?" (*VF* 108) From Becher to archangel Michael in the space of a dash: with this apostrophe to the militant patron saint of Germany who belongs as much to Ludwig the Pious as to Becher and Trakl, Fühmann realizes how little the socialist resurrection of fallen words will let itself be sublimated into a worldly stance of ironic despair. The words take on new semantic content not in their ironic and self-referential citation by a disillusioned Fühmann, but more poignantly because they are referring now to a different—and Fühmann still hopes—a somehow transformed world. "In my thinking I drew the consequences," he writes about his turn to socialism in prison camp, "but not in my feeling: thoughts of the new, feelings of the old, what a mishmash I was! At the same time, the consequence was inevitable: wasn't what happened in Trakl's poetry in fact a dismantling of the 'human good' [*Menschlichgutem*]—which word elated me in Hölderlin since I felt it as an anticipation of all the nobility, truth, goodness and beauty socialism would set free?" (*VF* 118).

4. THE SHOCK OF THE CAMPS: DAMASCUS IN THE LAGER' VOENNOPLENNYCH

> It was as though Trakl's poem were commencing a struggle against me as an alter ego and, debilitated by shock [*Betroffenheit*] yet simultaneously enjoying this debilitation as liberation, I were regarding the struggle with dreamy composure: *under the oaks we sway on a silver skiff.*—Swaying under the oaks were the executed, even in our quiet valley. This was the beginning of May 1945. (*VF* 28)

"In the beginning is the shock [*das Betroffensein*]" (*VF* 103) according to Fühmann's gospel. *Betroffenheit*, the same key word with which Fühmann characterized his story "Marsyas," describes the specific type of artistic pathos animating Fühmann's cultural political outlook.[61] It is a particularly difficult word to translate: shock, affectedness, impactedness, dismay, being moved—it can imply debilitation as well as engagement. Trakl's phrase, "pondering the truth—great pain" (*der Wahrheit nachsinnen—viel Schmerz*), which Fühmann chose as the title to the abridged version of his Trakl book published in 1979 by Reclam, conveys some sense of what Fühmann means by *Betroffenheit*. It is this quasi-cognitive *Betroffenheit* that is crucial to understanding the affective, aesthetic dynamic of socialist modernity.[62] If, as François Furet holds, "[T]he bourgeoisie is a synonym for modern society,"[63] then there would by definition be little modernism to be sought in the work of the socialist Fühmann except in the negative sense of the anti-bourgeois irony expressed in his stories about his youth in provincial Bohemia. Moreover, the normative hypothesis underlying many rehabilitative readings of socialist literature—namely, that it becomes more modern (that is, better) as it sheds its affirmative pathos of distinction and converges with Western cosmopolitan literature in what Wolfgang Emmerich calls modernism's characteristic "civilizational criticism" and what Furet would simply call modernism's "bourgeois self-hatred"—likewise makes it hard to observe what is both modern and aesthetically distinct about Fühmann.[64] Controverting theses that, cheerfully or despairingly, homogenize modernity as a bourgeois phenomenon, Fühmann's *Betroffenheit* does not dissolve the left-right distinction in his experience, but points to the place where the antagonistic border between socialism and capitalism is happening—precisely as an intensification of its existential stakes.

With its recollection of experiences in the Soviet labor camp in Nephtigorsk in the Caucasus and then in the Antifascist School in Noginsk (near Moscow), *Facing the Fire Pits* has been misleadingly interpreted in terms of what became known in the West as "mourning work" (*Trauerarbeit*) and "working-through-the-past" (*Vergangenheitsbewältigung*). From this perspective, Fühmann's autobiography describes a *Bildungsroman* in which he gradually liberates himself from the seductive "spell of the totalitarian thought structure" propagated in the camps that, whether laid out and commanded by the Left or Right, characterized the barbaric essence of political extremism in the twentieth century.[65] Such an ordering of Fühmann through now-stereotypical West German critical rubrics into a trajectory of personal enlightenment congruent with the arc of Cold War triumph over totalitarianism misses Fühmann just as it misses what is interesting about East German writing generally. The shock of recognizing (or misrecognizing) a border between socialism and capitalism—a shock that instead of abating is always rediscovered, amplified, and transmuted in Fühmann's writing—remains its open-ended drama.

For Fühmann this existential border is one that must be discovered in a poetic apprehension beyond the willfully posited doctrines of political authorities. At the same time, poetic truth cannot simply recede from politically efficacious doctrine, with its attributions of responsibility and agency, into the traditional postures of romantic irony or modernist aesthetic autonomy, two exonerating stances common in Germany's history of cultural disaffection with politics. While Fühmann carved a literary niche for himself in part as an impassioned re-reader of nineteenth-century romantics like E. T. A. Hoffmann and twentieth-century modernists like Trakl, what draws him to them is their changed significance in the context of the new border between socialism and the West. Thus, Christa Wolf, after she reads a collection of Fühmann's Hoffmann essays in June 1979 (discussed in Chapter 9), writes to ask whether "you really think that people elsewhere can understand your essays just as they are; that people can follow you in your presuppositions, associations, your shocks [*Betroffenheiten*], bitterness, your polemics, your intensity, your nearly pleading invocations and your painful, very painful conclusions[.]"[66] By recognizing how Fühmann's ostensibly remote literary historical interpretations are tightly bound to his socialist experience, Wolf underlines the importance that Fühmann himself puts on understanding language with due attention to both its expressive and referential modalities. In this sense, the vocabulary miraculously resurrected from previous and opposed social orders always also refers in his interpretations to the changed social conditions of his own b/order. For Fühmann, a central lexeme like "bourgeois" is not simply "a synonym for modern society" (as Furet defined it), but is a distinct doctrinal concept of his state, which, by his use of it, implicates him in the very social b/order he is describing. It designates for him a social differential whose effective truth, while it can be lost in doctrinal abstraction, might also be recovered poetically through aesthetic cognition of his *Betroffenheit*.

> The conflict between poetry [*Dichtung*] and doctrine [*Doktrin*] was inevitable; both struck roots in me and I took both existentially. I was serious about the doctrine, behind whose most distorted features I could still discern the face of the liberator of Auschwitz; and I was serious about poetry, in which I intuited the Other that didn't abandon humanity even after Auschwitz because it was always the Other to Auschwitz.—One seriousness balanced the other out.—There can't be any talk of "seduction" here; this word debases not only poetry, it debases doctrine—in any case, what's behind it does. My conflict erupted from the inside not the outside and so was inevitable. Its end still can't be predicted. (*VF* 230)

Fühmann's unstable equilibrium of poetry and doctrine alludes to formulations like Adorno's chastened and outraged aesthetic response to the very fact of the death camps: "[To] write poetry after Auschwitz is barbaric."[67] Adorno's dictum supposes an indivisible modernity implicated by its characteristic technological and administrative rationality in a crime so total that to imagine what Fühmann calls "always the Other" to it is only to ignore its glowering omnipresence. Adorno's position is the dour touchstone for refusing any "resurrection" of the terminology of heroic social change as envisaged by Becher and Bloch. Like Mann in his editorial statement for *Maß und Wert*, only cutting a wider swath, Adorno sees not only political but even poetic language as *heillos geschändet*. "Even the aesthetic activities of political opposites are one in their enthusiastic obedience to the rhythm of the iron system."[68] In East Germany, where Adorno remained largely unpublishable, a line from Brecht's prewar poem "To Those Born Later" (1936) expresses a similar sense of how a massive crime contaminates even the space for innocence and private wonder, but with a crucial difference. Whereas Adorno abstracts from politics to an epistemologically contaminated humanism, Brecht's poem refers historically to the criminal period itself: "What kind of times are they, when/A talk about trees is almost a crime/Because it implies silence about so many horrors?"[69] Precisely because Brecht temporalizes his despairing exile sentiment, Becher is in turn able to mount a political defense of trees, defiantly responding from the bosom of the Red Army in the 1940s that "to say with admiration, 'look at this tree!'" is not only allowed, but necessary, once "you know even this is stolen and snuffed out mercilessly for you by the enemy."[70] By holding simultaneously to poetry and doctrine—"one seriousness balanced the other out"—Fühmann refuses to let the question of culture's contamination or redemption be posed without "existential" reference to political doctrine. On a view like Fühmann's, Joyce Kilmer's sentimental "I think that I shall never see/A poem lovely as a tree" would be just the flip side of Adorno's sophisticated "to write poetry after Auschwitz is barbaric": neither recognizes any doctrinal struggle standing between the beatific transcendence of Creation and barbaric immanence of Culture.

In *Twenty-two Days*, Fühmann, in a more doctrinal than lyrical mode, puts a sharp point on his differences with such abstract division between barbarity and beatitude. Like Adorno across the border, he recognizes what he takes as the camp's lingering presence, but unlike Adorno, he locates it firmly in the *West*'s normalcy. "Bourgeois society is thought through to its end, and behold: its final form is the concentration camp," he announces.[71] As for socialism, however, its merits—and its final difference from capitalism, and thus Auschwitz—can no longer be affirmed as a matter of doctrine. While socialism is bound *historically* through the Red Army to the liberation of Auschwitz, historical (doctrinaire) socialism remains locked in conflict with that *universal* "Otherness" to the camps whose metaphysical reality would be the only guarantee of socialism's meaning. If a redemption of heroic social initiative is to happen at all, it must be a specifically *left* redemption that therefore can only happen on the conflicted border of a universalizing *Dichtung* and historicizing *Doktrin*—and the outcome of such a strange conflict "still can't be predicted."

Fühmann's aphoristic reduction of bourgeois society to the lurking potential of the camp might appear preposterously outdated after the Cold War. Much scholarship has emphasized how the "antifascist myth," which held that the GDR was founded by resistance fighters and served as a bulwark against a potentially resurgent fascism in the West, was a coercive construction shaping the narrow contours of political ideology in the East.[72] While "compulsory antifascism" (*der verordnete Antifaschismus*) indeed played a dogmatic function in GDR doctrine, what grates in Fühmann's formulation is not the reduction of *society* to the fascist camp, but the insertion of the differential "*bourgeois* society." Yet without the pathos of Fühmann's differential, the claim that *modern* society is a species of camp does not necessarily appear so far-fetched, especially after the Cold War. Thus, as we saw, Agamben introduces the abstraction "the camp" into contemporary political philosophy by arguing that "the camp marks in a decisive way the political space itself of modernity."[73] According to Agamben, what makes the concentration camp a more relevant model for political life today than the classical polis of Greek democracy is that state decisions increasingly have become direct biological decisions over life and death ("biopolitics"). Individuality, subjectivity, and personality are afforded minimal political protection, incorporated instead as naked life directly into the requirements of state sovereignty: "[P]ower confronts nothing other than pure biological life without any mediation."[74]

> The camp truly is the inaugural site of modernity: it is the first space in which public and private events, political life and biological life, become rigorously indistinguishable. Inasmuch as the inhabitant of the camp has been severed from the political community and has been reduced to naked life (and moreover, to a life "that does not deserve to be lived"), he or she is an absolutely private person. And yet there is not one single instant in which he or she might be able to find shelter in the realm of the private, and it is precisely this indiscernibility that constitutes the specific anguish of the camp.[75]

But if the specific anguish of Agamben's modernity is the indiscernibility of public and private, Fühmann's *leftist* modernity is anguished by the effort to discern at a nondoctrinal, experiential level a substantial difference between right and left. In Foucault's account of the rise of biological pastoral power over political power, it is precisely the value of the left/right distinction—that is, the substantive value of political difference—that the new form of power makes otiose. In the emerging *Polizeiwissenschaft* (which Foucault equates with pastoral logic) of the eighteenth century, *raison d'etat* (political logic) played an increasingly subordinate role. "*Die Politik* is basically a negative task: it consists in the state's fighting against its internal and external enemies. *Polizei*, however, is a positive task: it has to foster both citizens' lives and the state's strength."[76] If the policing functions of Agamben's camp—that is, Foucault's pastoral obligations of the social welfare state—displace the classical political distinction between friend and enemy, then it stands to reason that reinscribing a political antagonism, one that is not merely doctrinal, but has, once again, "semantically appropriate effectiveness, reality," is a singularly anguishing task for a modernity that insists on calling itself leftist: for it is precisely the *leftist* camp that most programmatically subsumes the political under the primacy of the social welfare system, at the same time, and paradoxically, as it marks its system boundary as a militantly political one.

Fühmann's account of his camp experience turns on just such a political differentiation that presents itself as a paradoxical openness right inside the harsh privation of the camp. He begins the narration of *Facing the Fire*

Pits in April 1945 just before his capture in the waning days of the war. On a brief front leave, the young soldier picks up a used copy of Trakl and puzzles over the 1913 poem "Decline" ("Untergang"):

> Over the white pond
> the wild birds have moved on.
> In the evening an icy wind blows from our stars.
>
> Over our graves
> Bends the broken brow of the night.
> Under the oaks we sway on a silver skiff.
>
> The white walls of the city are still ringing.
> Under an arch of thorns
> O my brother, we blind minute-hands are climbing toward
> midnight. (*VF* 12–13)

Instead of evoking Spengler's 1918 figural reading of Western decadence and protofascist vitality *Decline of the West* (*Untergang des Abendlandes*), Trakl's eschatological title evokes, to Fühmann's own surprise, that which for an active duty soldier is a taboo association: the imminent collapse of the fascist war machine to which he was sworn. "Our stars," he recalls about this flash of disillusionment, "were the ones that illuminated our victory, not particular constellations like Orion or Corona Borealis, but their totality at a certain hour, the hour of victory, an hour we imagined returning like morning dawning ever anew, and now this hour was gone forever; our stars merely holes in the cosmos" (*VF* 14). The apocalyptic language of stars, cosmos and twilight—equal parts Trakl's expressionism and Ludwig Klages's "cosmics"—is not itself negated in Fühmann's memory of the moment of loss; instead, the particular political wagon to which that astral totality is hitched is, if only for an instant, overturned: dis-aster, a privative relation to an underdetermined whole. "For the briefest moment I grasped without real comprehension that the war was lost" (*VF* 14).

This moment, however, remained as brief as Fühmann's front leave. As he explains it in another autobiographical reflection from the 1970s, his stubbornly fascist mindset, as linked to grandiose cosmic intuition as it was, resisted recognizing itself as contingent and, therefore, political. It assumed instead a sublime ideological self-sufficiency that Walter Benjamin famously characterized in 1936 as "a politics which Fascism is rendering aesthetic."[77]

> Unconditional, uncritical faith; affirmation of war and the ambition to rule the world . . . uncritical, stupid arrogance and feeling of mastery; intoxicated with "mission," "destiny," "bulwark of Europe"; until the end of the war, an absurd

> faith in miracles (in the literal sense) that sprang up out of insane fear, repressed feelings of guilt, complete lack of perspective and a nearly perfect weaning from the habit of thought.[78]

Fühmann believed back then in miracles, he emphasizes, "in the literal sense" (*im wörtlichen Sinn*)—a formulation that ascribes to his younger self a pedantic literalism like that of Apollo disciplining the wayward satyr in "Marsyas." For Fühmann, such mistaking of figurative for literal is part and parcel of his fascism: the totalized aesthetic is not even grasped as an aesthetic representation, but simply as present reality. In Adorno's words, such literalism is, "objectively, of the same character as the small bureaucrat, who sees to it that everything remains strictly in its category, as he himself remains in his salary-class. Even death is handled by the book, in SS-orders. . . ."[79]

The disorienting effects of Fühmann's brief encounter with Trakl's "Untergang" days before the Nazi surrender nonetheless persisted, haunting him as signs of collapse manifested themselves ever more obviously even while he blindly made his way back eastward to his unit (only to flee too late toward the Americans a few days later). In the compressed temporality of this military apocalypse, Trakl's minute hands climbing inexorably upward toward downfall signaled "a blindness . . . unable to see over its own time" (*VF* 29). Lukács's gloss on the rise of fascist fanaticism, that "the greater personal despair becomes, and the greater it expresses the feeling of individual existence in jeopardy, the greater must be the credulousness and belief in miracles,"[80] links despair with credulity, and credulity ultimately with fascism, whereby the only antidote to infatuated fascism would be some kind of clear-eyed realism. Fühmann's nascent despair over the imminent loss of his fascist cosmos, illuminated in the dark flash of Trakl's midnight, pointed, however, not to realism, but to another miracle, this one of opposed political complexion. As Benjamin maintains in the *Arcades Project*, revolutionary initiative arises in a moment of qualitatively loaded subjectivity: in the instant of *kairos*, rather than the metrical *chronos* of historical sequence. *Kairos*, in the sense of a uniquely propitious and dangerous constellation, is ultimately "not temporal in nature, but figural,"[81] figuring precisely the miraculous resurrection, the great thing that happens despite its mundane situation. Its closely related idea, *catastrophe*, is for Benjamin what happens when the singular occasion passes without its being seized by some faithful subject: "Catastrophe—to have missed the opportunity. Critical moment—the status quo threatens to be preserved. Progress—the first revolutionary measure taken."[82] The philosopher Alain Badiou describes the revolutionary "event" similarly as a vivid fragment escaping the totalizing claims of its situation thereby revealing in its singularity what lies beyond. "In a flash, this fragment . . . affirms its unfoundedness, its pure *advent*, which is intransitive to the place in which 'it' comes. The fragment thereby also affirms its belonging to itself, since this coming can originate from nowhere else."[83] In other words, discerning the actuality of the miraculous, the miracle's unprecedented origin in a real situation—or, in the literary terminology I have been using, grasping miracles as simultaneously literal and figural—is a subjective effort sui generis. Thus, even the anti-Romantic Lukács recognizes of Lenin that "it was necessary to have the undaunted insight of genius to be able to see the actuality of the proletarian revolution."[84]

Despite his later disavowal of his "absurd faith in miracles," Fühmann's crisis of despair, while it fuels a new faith in miracles, does so this time as a parapolitical, rather than blindly fanatical, moment of *Betroffenheit*. The miraculous points (somehow) to a real choice. Fühmann meets his Damascus—his "moment of complete openness"—in the confines of the Soviet labor camp, the *lager' voennoplennych*, where he is interned after his May 1945 capture, and where he registers the existential demand upon himself to make fascism's devastating defeat a miracle rather than a catastrophe through sheer faith in the moment's actual openness. As we have seen in "Marsyas," such an unprecedented and singular moment, whether mundane catastrophe or divine miracle, is impossible to represent in the literal language of Apollo's clear-eyed realism.

> I have tried again and again to record that unique era of the VP, the VOENNOPLENNY, and every time I've foundered right at the outset, at that moment of complete openness where past and future begin to reveal themselves as historical powers instead of mere subsistent modes of physical time, and their constantly flowing borders split open into a rupture of such bottomlessness that its fault line cuts through the ego itself. (*VF* 39)

This tension between figural (performative, illocutionary) openness and referential closure, between the bottomless jeopardy of transformation and the metonymic perimeter of barbed wire around the prison camp—between revolution and totalitarianism—describes the narrative dilemma on which Fühmann founders and stands. It is the problem of articulating a political choice between miraculous redemption (potentially naive faith in the possibility of transformation) and catastrophic damnation (chary indifference to any quality distinguishing the harsh exposure of one camp from another)—a choice in which, for the faithful as for the unfaithful, there appears to be no real choice, and thus no real politics. On the one hand, if all twentieth-century camps amount to the same thing—a site where, in Agamben's words, life is stripped to life "that does not deserve to be lived"—then the figural double revealed to Fühmann in Trakl's "unlivable life" (*unlebares Leben*, *VF* 205) figures precisely the *literal* abjection of his own naked life, a life simply disposed over without any recourse to law or custom (what Agamben calls *homo sacer*). "In my misery I appealed to Trakl as my witness," Fühmann writes about his abject response to "the news of Auschwitz" he receives in the camp (*VF* 42). Where all signs point only to death, Trakl's paradoxical affirmation consists in "demonstrating the unlivability of a life: that a creativity of highest order has done it makes it exemplary for the daily grind of those who are foundering and sinking and only suffering without a god having given them these words—: may one grasp it through Trakl, through his poems and life" (*VF* 204). By abstracting the realistic contiguity of Nephtigorsk and Auschwitz into a general figure for existential despair in the face of totalitarianism—"I was starving and freezing, how was I to bear guilt?" (*VF* 44)—Fühmann only glorifies an unchanging human fate of death and retribution: Auschwitz, *lager' voennoplennych*, and modernity—*unicuique suum*. It is the tragic dispensation of Schopenhauer, Kierkegaard, and Heidegger; everyone thrown in their own camp.

On the other hand, despite the camp's sheer biological deprivation—"a fate come suddenly crashing down, unmerited wasting away through hunger, sludge shoveling, homesickness, desolation, uncertainty and again hunger, always hunger, to a point of such physical exhaustion that no one besides the fat cook could desire to sleep man-with-men, and the future lay there like a white pool, a lime-filled ditch" (*VF* 42)—Fühmann realizes he could choose instead to make an inconceivable leap into "the unheard-of": "Was this giant country indeed, in another way, the kingdom of all revalued values?—Stalin's smile on a larger-than-life poster; into what Other had we entered?" (*VF* 40). In this unheard-of alternative, the sublime *figura* of Trakl confronts the bleak realism of a smiling Stalin poster looming over the prison camp: *Dichtung* meets *Doktrin*. Or—and this is precisely the moment of decision—is it the other way around: the sublime *figura* of smiling Stalin confronts the bleak literalism of Trakl's abject suicide in the lazaretto at the battle of Grodek? Instead of evoking a mean death in a cruel, aleatory world, the convergence of Auschwitz and *lager' voennoplennych* onto a singular moment of decision is the *kairos* for Fühmann's apostolic conversion and epochal transcendence, as he makes explicit by recalling Alexander

Block's 1920 poem "The Twelve," in which "Christ marches through a snow storm, leading the red flags of the twelve, the twelve Red Army soldiers, the twelve disciples" (*VF* 47).

Trakl and Stalin, Christ and the Red Army, *Dichtung* and *Doktrin*: these preposterous conjunctions reveal to the vulnerable prisoner the pathetic disjunction of a final choice: catastrophic martyrdom or miraculous discipleship? bourgeois *amor fati* or socialist *Klassenbewußtsein*? Between those two options there is no third: *tertium non datur*! This otherwise drab principle of classical logic, as we have seen in the last chapter, is central to the drama of "Marsyas." It is also the fateful reference point in Fühmann's camp experience—the moment of complete political subjectification against the background of an objective *Schicksalswende*. As we have also seen, Fühmann confronts the principle of the excluded middle not in order to propose an uncontaminated humanistic third way or to deconstruct a logical binarism with dialectical legerdemain. If the principle *tertium non datur* does not exist as an ontological universal (if it is logically self-contradictory, succumbing to its own law, as Gödel demonstrates), it surely *does* exist as an affective experience of choice—*Betroffenheit*—in which the existential singularity (*arché*) of decision confronts the generality of consequences, the historical differences that are always also its precondition: now or never, take it or leave it, *kairos* or catastrophe. Or to put it in the terms with which we began this chapter: as impossible as it is to assign priority to either sovereignty or system, choosing one's camp with respect to systems lies at the heart of the historical political experience: omission or commission, *tertium non datur*. Against the unforeseeable consequences of that apocalyptic choice, assuming political subjectivity is the ultimate assumption of irreversible historical risk . . . : "a false ring of the night bell once answered," notes Kafka, "—it can never be made right."[85]

5. DEATH AT THE LATRINE: TRAGIC REVELATION VERSUS PARTY PURGE

Fühmann first hears the fateful words *tertium non datur* when he has been transferred—he thinks by mistake—to be a student-prisoner in one of the special "Antifascist Schools" set up by the Soviets to re-educate German captives after the battle of Stalingrad in 1942. A lecturer at Fühmann's camp in Noginsk, a Soviet philosopher whose initials are given as J. N. Z., "announced by the teachers as the high point," is instructing the former

Wehrmacht soldiers in "dialectical and historical materialism."[86] "He stood there now for the first and only time behind the lectern, both hands raised beseechingly, addressing the hall with the seriousness of an annunciation by a true believer: 'Tertium non datur! There is no third and there cannot be one!'—These were, by the way, the only words in a foreign language he believed it necessary to importune us with; he derived them for us from the principle of the excluded middle, likewise the only logical figure he showed us" (*VF* 58–59). This overwhelming experience of an "annunciation by a true believer" has immediate consequences for Fühmann and his comrades in the Antifa camps. As the force of the principle *tertium non datur* is revealed to them, the terrible price of insight—"the price is no third thing"—is exacted directly on their bodies, without circumstance and without delay.

> The road we finally found was at last the Other to our accursed Past, thus—and this seemed crucial to us—everything Other to this Other was always only the Old from which a further psychic liberation was our most pressing will. . . . The ruptures [*Bruchstellen*] stood out boldly, the continuities [*Kontinua*] remained long unnoticed, they seemed to be the Unthinkable itself, yet continuity, of course, already lies in the person: He who changes, remains also himself; that's right: *only* also; but: *indeed* also.—That stalled contradiction didn't lead us from thesis and antithesis to synthesis, but chased us around in a circle: Once the leap was taken, and that means: once insight was attained into the objectionable nature of that which was called, for short, "the Old" then no other development was possible besides consistently rooting out this "Old" from one's own sphere whenever it reared its head, and the final consequences were due one's own body. I see my bunkmate in the morning, hanging from the rafter over the latrine, a sign around his neck: I WAS A WAR CRIMINAL. (*VF* 57)

The ignominious suicide of Fühmann's bunkmate is in a figural sense Fühmann's own suicide, the one he wasn't consistent or swift enough to carry out in the instant of his political illumination. As he recognizes in the bedazzling revelation of *tertium non datur*, death is the only truly consistent resolution of a universal, all-or-nothing choice between the Old that one was and the New that one would become. Thus, in the well-known passage on the French Revolution in *Phenomenology of the Spirit*, Hegel calls death the defining property of the revolutionary act. He maintains that the revolutionary purity of abstract universal reason—exhibited plainly in the formula of the excluded middle—compels the destruction of a world isolated by the individuality of consciousnesses.

> The relation, then, of [revolutionary universality to individual consciousness of it], since each exists indivisibly and absolutely for itself, and thus cannot dispose

of a middle term which would link them together, is one of wholly ***unmediated*** pure negation. . . . The sole work and deed of universal freedom is therefore ***death***, a death too which has no inner significance or filling, for what is negated is the empty point of the absolutely free self. It is thus the coldest and meanest of all deaths, with no more significance than cutting off a head of cabbage or swallowing a mouthful of water.[87]

While Z.'s revelation of *tertium non datur* amid the starkness of prison camp life tempts the awestruck Fühmann to sentimental bourgeois self-negation, he hesitates just long enough before the insignificant death of his bunkmate to realize, in Bloch's messianic words, his "task and problem here is to make our acknowledged permanence triumph over empirical adversity, over our own insufficiency, that is: to overcome, through the power of transmigrational dispersal, and finally through the Apocalypse, as the absolute work of the Son of Man, the history that cannot be experienced [*unerlebar*] in its entirety."[88] His survival and transformation, he recognizes in the personal catastrophe of the corpse swaying before him, depends on repudiating an unbearable empirical realism in favor of a sudden figural intuition of socialism, an intuition that flashes out of the "stalled contradiction" (*gestockter Widerspruch*) of the Hegelian dialectic. The immediate effect of this shock is perhaps best conveyed by the notion of Aristotelian *anagnorisis*, the recognition that follows upon the violent turn of fate (*peripeteia*) in tragedy. It is less the tragic genre that is important here—since this episode in Fühmann's account, though crucial, comes early in the narrative arc—than the epistemology of tragic insight. Tragic recognition offers a distinctive answer to what is known in cognitive philosophy as "Meno's paradox": "How can I know the property of something when I don't even know what it is?"[89] Or, translated into the context of Fühmann's prison camp: if the socialist New is entirely other to the fascist Old, how can a convert truly know when he has grasped it; or, even more to the point, how can a convert know when he is truly converted? Does knowing that one knows depend on continuity with the ignorant self or demand rupture from it? "In order to describe intuitively my first, overwhelming contact with Marxism (. . . where 'the scales fell from my eyes')," Fühmann writes in *Twenty-two Days*, "I would have to have already described the make-up of the young fascist I was. But that, in turn, I could only portray against the background of my changed worldview, that is, against the New—which is precisely what I can't convincingly describe as new without the Old."[90] Plato responds to the paradox of identifying the *novum* simply by denying that it is new; instead, he proposes an epistemology of recollection (*anamnesis*). In other words, one can discern what is new about the New (or other about the Other) because one has actually known it all along (a priori) and merely needs a reminder to recall it. By contrast, in Aristotelian *anagnorisis* insight comes only by means of sudden change—it is recognition not of some enduring substance, but of a stunning difference. Thus, in his epistemology of the *Novum* (the "not-yet"), Bloch argues that "*anamnesis* provides the reassuring evidence of complete similarity; *anagnorisis*, however, is linked with reality by only a thin thread; it is therefore alarming. *Anamnesis* has an element of attenuation about it; it makes everything a gigantic *déjà vu*[.] . . . But *anagnorisis* is a shock."[91]

Fühmann's *anagnorisis*—his *Betroffenheit* in the face of Z.'s revelation and his bunkmate's suicide—depends on his successfully eluding Hegel's "meanest of all deaths" by violating the rule of resurrection (namely, death) and surviving to be edified (and aroused) by witnessing the consequences of conversion displaced onto his bunkmate. As the narrator of "Marsyas" observes of the satyr's still palpitating corpse: "[W]ho Apollo is, Marsyas no longer needs to know, it is enough that the Muses learned it; what the satyr is, shows itself to them."[92] The insignificant death of the nameless bunkmate, one among millions in the war, enters into the distinct order of revolutionary significance only by the Muse's narrative act of *anagnorisis*. The textual epistemology of *anagnorisis* can thus be seen to have a precise ontological consequence: revelation does not portend the existential force of a substantial presence; rather, it appears as a semiotic displacement of Fühmann's suicide into the figural realm of tragic irony. Like the Muses, who can depict Marsyas' impossible challenge to Apollo's literalist ontology only by displacing their own betrayal of literalism onto a graphic flaying of the satyr, so too can Fühmann experience the literalness of death in Auschwitz and *lager' voennoplennych* only by means of a figural execution. The literary account of his conversion is, in this sense, not a realistic representation of the socialist difference, but the performance of a tragic affect. "The metaphysical joy in the tragic," writes Nietzsche, "is a translation of the instinctive unconscious Dionysian wisdom into the language of images: the hero, the highest manifestation of the will, is negated for our pleasure, because he is only phenomenon, and because the eternal life of the will is not affected by his annihilation."[93] Through these means of aesthetic metempsychosis, we can see how, in his reading of Trakl's "unlivable life," Fühmann grasps the suicidal poet as the model for his own camp life "that does not deserve to be lived" even as he draws from the formal persistence of Trakl's craft the strength to go on living under the aegis of an impossibly joyous Stalin.

The self-flaying impossibility of the pure communist identity is nowhere on more spectacular display than in the great trauma of communist immolation, the confession (or, more accurately, anticonfession) of the leading old-guard Bolshevik Nikolai Bukharin during his 1938 Moscow show trial.[94] In Arthur Koestler's 1940 fictionalization of the events, *Darkness at Noon*, Bukharin's imprisonment and prosecution supply a key template for the inflammatory Cold War genre of "renegade literature,"[95] and the trial's ritualistic savagery has been agonized over by writers and philosophers including Sartre, Merleau-Ponty, and Bloch.[96] In the months leading up to his appearance on the stand, as his fate becomes clear, the imprisoned Bukharin writes a final letter to Stalin in which he places himself at the disposal of the terror even as he pleas for recognition of the subjective authenticity of his revolutionary sacrifice:

> I know that it would be petty for me to place the question of my own person *on a par* with the *universal-historical* tasks resting, first and foremost, on your shoulders. But it is here that I feel my *deepest* agony and find myself facing my chief, agonizing paradox. . . . Oh, Lord, if only there were some device which would have made it possible for you to see my soul flayed and ripped open! If only you could see how I am attached to you, body and soul[.] . . . Well, so much for 'psychology'—forgive me. No angel will appear now to snatch Abraham's sword from his hand. My fatal destiny shall be fulfilled.[97]

"Stalinism was a tragedy of a classical kind," according to Terry Eagleton in his book on the tragic idea, "as the noble intentions of socialism were deflected into their opposites in that fatal inversion which Aristotle calls peripeteia."[98] The problem in Bukharin's case with this dramatic crisis of *peripeteia* (which Paul Ricouer notes is but Goethe's "unheard-of event"[99]) is that the fatal reversal (*Schicksalswende*, to recall Lukács's term here as well) never actually yields the expected tragic *anagnorisis*, for if there is any recognition at all, it is not clear in what it consists or to whom it pertains. Even before his body is destroyed, Bukharin's soul is condemned to irrelevancy by the universal-historical force of revolution. In fact, his body must remain intact long enough to perform one last gesture of revolutionary obeisance. As the victim-protagonist of this cruel turn of the socialist revolution, Bukharin offers the Central Committee his own assessment of what he finds tragic in his situation:

> The whole tragedy of my situation lies in this, that . . . such an atmosphere arose that no one believes human feelings—not emotions, not the impulses of the heart, not tears. [Laughter.] Many manifestations of human feeling, which had earlier represented a form of proof—and there was nothing shameful in this—have today lost their validity and force.[100]

If Bukharin himself recognizes anything here it is the inadmissibility of tragic gravitas (*spoudaios*) in his tragic situation. Tragedy, as Brecht had theorized in his anti-Aristotelian dramaturgy, must lose its all-too-bourgeois heart to the purely ritual gestures of collective life. "The essential point of the epic theater," writes Brecht in 1927, "is perhaps that it appeals less to the feelings than to the spectator's reason" for the sake of "a solid, practical rearrangement of our age's way of life."[101] If such a modern dictum holds true against the catharsis of Aristotle's *Poetics*, then it applies even more emphatically to the specifically political-juridical realm of the *Rhetoric*. For Aristotle, rhetoric is called upon to persuade of human truth in the spatio-temporal context of a courtroom or political assembly; philosophy only to demonstrate universal truth, *sub specie aeterni*.[102] Subjective pathos—a timely appeal to fellow human feelings—is one of two technical means of proof, along with personal ethos, distinguishing rhetoric from philosophy. In the Central Committee's rejection of subjective "proof," signaled so harshly by its members' inappropriate laughter at Bukharin's sincere pathos, the lesson is that, even in his own public defense, the would-be-tragic figure must consign himself to a cabbage's death, devoid of human feeling. Without any God to search the soul, sincerity—the convert's sacramental *compunctio cordis* (repentance of the heart)—is unverifiable, irrelevant, and inadmissible in the court of socialist justice.

The soul-baring "device" Bukharin vainly seeks in his letter to Stalin is thus some sort of secular erotics like that of Marsyas' flaying, in which the truth of his soul—rather than the pulp of his flesh—would be bared in an eloquent evisceration. But since no deus ex machina can emerge in Bukharin's realist script to save him from Soviet power, the "fatal destiny" of the revolutionary, reduced in the mocking words of the Soviet prosecutor Andrej Vyshinsky to a "damnable cross of a fox and a swine," is to be sentenced to death as a traitor.[103] In his closing plea before the court, Aristotelian pathos and ethos are explicitly abjured in favor of purely objective, external might. He declares that "the point, of course, is not this repentance, or my personal repentance in particular. The Court can pass its verdict without it. The confession of the accused is not essential. The confession of the accused is a medieval principle of jurisprudence."[104] What Bukharin here concedes is that any subjective self-assertion, any particularly tragic recognition of an individual fate, is a usurpation of socialism's objective due—his subjectivity is as empty as his sincerity is unprovable. "Your regret is only your arrogance!" in the contemptuous words Apollo hurls in the face of the skinned satyr; or, in Stalin's response to Bukharin's earlier, piteous offer of suicide: "Here you see one of the ultimate and most cunning and easiest means by which one can spit at and deceive the party one last time before dying, before leaving the world. That, Comrade Bukharin, is the underlying reason for these last suicides."[105] Tragic sacrifice, as an outmoded form of heroic self assertion, is as much a betrayal of socialism's objective law as is continued life in fascist treachery, and in this bind, the only hope for redemption lies in humble submission to the dictates of the revolutionary court.

Ernst Bloch favorably greets the news of Bukharin's confession in 1938, reading in it a final abjuration of both bourgeois self-pity, and the widespread liberal indignation his trial was provoking, in favor of the stoic recognition of socialist justice.

> In prison Bukharin asked himself: "For if you must die, what are you dying for?" And he recognizes: "An absolutely black vacuity suddenly rises before you with startling vividness." A vacuity that fills itself only if one recognizes in Soviet judgment one's own judgment. . . . In the court of a class enemy, such regret wouldn't have made sense, it wouldn't have helped one into the clear, but just the opposite: it would have been a betrayal of oneself and one's cause. In the court of one's own class, however, the confession is . . . the end of isolation. Together with the following death (and Bukharin never pled for his life) it is the return to the Soviet Union. "What are you dying for?"—for the Soviet Union, and with one last avowal of it: seen from the perspective of the end of individual life, it is the Beyond of communist atheists.[106]

Confession in Bloch's formulation turns into a simple avowal of external material power. "The end of individual life" invoked by Bloch refers less to an individual's death, than to the end of life as an individual phenomenon. Since inner life lacks any common ground—resting on no objective principle of Apollonian measure—the sincerity and weight of private virtue rightly receive no recognition in Bukharin's trial. Instead of issuing in a private political consciousness, the process yields for all to see a doubly disabled individual: one with an extinguished will and a compliant body. Bukharin goes to his death in full accord with the court that a higher necessity is being served with his gesture of personal abnegation. "The monstrousness of my crimes," he concludes, "is immeasurable especially in the new stage of the struggle of the U.S.S.R. May this trial be the last severe lesson, and may the great might of the U.S.S.R. become clear to all."[107] Not the goat-man Marsyas, but the radiant Muses must grasp Apollo's ordering might; not the monstrous fox-swine Bukharin, for whom any penitence is too late, but the rest of the communist camp. No tragic pity and catharsis, but an epic party purge.

As Lukács's *Theory of the Novel* argues, epic must avoid any residue of the tragic if it is to express the positive reality of the dawning era. Tragic drama portrays a world in which a degraded empirical life is at odds with the transcendent life that *should* exist instead—and *did* exist, *empirically*, in epic eras. "The character created by drama," Lukács writes, "is the intelligible 'I' of man, the character created by the epic is the empirical 'I'. The 'should be', in whose desperate intensity the essence seeks refuge because it has become an outlaw on earth, can objectivise itself in the intelligible 'I' as the hero's normative psychology, but in the empirical 'I' it remains a 'should be'." For Lukács, tragedy's "should be" is both a refuge from and a betrayal of a living, sensuous "is." "The 'should be' kills life, and the dramatic hero assumes the symbolic attributes of the sensuous manifestations of life only in order to be able to perform the symbolic ceremony of dying in a sensuously perceptible way, making transcendence visible."[108] Lukács repeats the phrase "the 'should be' kills life" three times until, like a ritual incantation, it reads as an exhortation to violence against isolated bourgeois individuality: the bourgeois individual should be made impossible so life might be lived empirically in a present with no regrets. "In the epic men must be alive, or else they destroy or exhaust the very element that carries, surrounds and fills them." With the tragic element's cool effacement in the self-sufficient totality of the new socialist epic, law's normative element (its "should be") folds into a closed and homogenous genre: legal norm becomes objective *Gesetzmäßigkeit*.

Returning to the enclosed horizon of Fühmann's decision at the rim of the camp latrine, however, it appears that—despite Bloch's materialist faith in a Beyond, and Lukács's threefold invocation of the epic instauration's blood-lust—the closing statement of Bukharin's drama offers no convincing picture of a coming community beyond the unlivable factuality (the pure parataxis) of interminable camp existence. Stalin smiles unswervingly, Trakl frowns darkly, while Bukharin's cold death obliterates any sentience that might consciously mediate the transmigration of the New Man: there is nothing left of Bukharin but the afterglow of Soviet omnipotence and no ground for either *anamnesis* or *anagnorisis*. In terms of the play itself, Bukharin's tragedy is only a realignment. "The dissident is a body, his dissidence a postural crime," observes Paul Virilio about the modern show trial. "Ostensibly, there are hardly any more crimes of opinion, only crimes of gesture. The confession is superceded: bodies are guilty of being out of synch, they have to be put back in the party *line*."[109] Only outside the scene, and contrary to its dramaturgy, does Bukharin's apathetic renunciation of tragedy become the tragic and stoic ideal that Fühmann himself, as *poète engagé*, can never attain: a cold gesture that, precisely for those who would warmly believe in it, admits no empathetic alignment. The pious ascension Bloch foresees for Bukharin, without remainder or ulterior motive, is the same vision Fühmann beholds at the latrine door when he believes he is witnessing the distinction between fascism and socialism—it is a consummation devoutly to be wished, but impossible to reach. Like Bukharin for Bloch, the rigorous bunkmate is the desired object of Fühmann's socialist *jouissance*, where that psychoanalytic term describes the specific sort of pleasure arising from the messy transgression, rather than measured enjoyment of stable identity. Semiotic flight from the terrible severity of *tertium non datur* achieves its purgative power through a vertiginous intuition of the latter's merciless judgment.

Unlike Bukharin's coolly epic death, then, such a wildly attractive, but ultimately insubstantial, erotic *jouissance* indeed portends an excess beyond the closed horizon of camp identity—after all, as we saw in the last chapter, Bataille introduced "the erotic" as a philosophical category precisely to evade Hegel's immanent dialectic of identity. But as such a wily hypostasis, the erotic cedes its profounder ontological aspirations to the undisciplined decadence of figuration. Socialism demonstrates to Fühmann its superiority over fascism, but only in the literary conventions of a survivor, without any deep experience of the substantive *differentia specifica* that socialism claims to be. Never crossing the irreversible threshold, never subject to the judgment of a merciful God or a ruthless sovereign, Fühmann's deliberate act of conversion remains forever marked by unreliability. It points to an interregnum, an interval between reigns—between that of individual normativity and that of socialist regulation—which is itself neither just nor sovereign. Suspended between the Old and the New, the communist convert, as Michael Rohrwasser puts it in his study of the literature of former communist renegades, "is trapped in the logic of Shakespeare's royal dramas: whoever has come to our camp by means of betrayal, will betray us as well."[110] Socialism's aspiration to difference winds up recapitulating the strife and pageantry of purely external princely authority, of the *respublica Christiana* and *jus publicum Europaeum* whose feudal and absolutist legacies it took itself to be replacing; its claim to immanent progress dissolves into the same external conventions of rule and comportment that guided the Florentine Medicis: as Ernesto Laclau and Chantal Mouffe argue, Lenin updates Machiavelli, and Antonio Gramsci's "Modern Prince" is only the most visible road marker in the inevitable semiotization of socialism's once all-or-nothing logic: bereft not just of metaphysical essence but also of ethical *spoudaios*, the working-class hero is an empty figure of difference, required at each twist of the plot "to come out of itself, to transform its own identity"—to rearrange, to realign, *to get out of its own skin*.[111]

6. FROM KAIROS TO CHRONOS: THE CAMP CLOCK

> Look there! Look closely! This is your life, this is the hand on the clock of your existence.
>
> —Nietzsche, *Birth of Tragedy*[112]

> Time, then, and the heavens came into being at the same instant in order that, having been created together, if ever there was to be a dissolution of them, they might be dissolved together.
>
> —Plato, *Timaeus*[113]

In order to escape this desubstantialization of system difference, a reciprocal reference is necessary—one indexes a system with whose operation one identifies through choice, and another indexes the system's recognition of that choice's validity. Flay and flagellate oneself howsoever one will, objective grace is never found in subjective abjection. On the contrary, the paradox of the subject in transformation—the subject not as Parmenidean substance, but Heraclitian flux—forces the articulation of laws governing how identity is produced in the first place: how identifiable elements are distinguished, related, compared, and selected. As with the "systems erotics" of Chapter 5, only in the first instance does the all-or-nothing violence of a prohibition like *tertium non datur* articulate the desirability of the prohibited object. Thus, only in the first instance does the camp's casual traffic in death, as the meaningless consequence of an almighty difference between fascism and socialism, articulate the transgressive desire for a significant death of one's own. In the second instance, betraying the camp's exceptionless regimentation with a sovereign leap into the unity of organic decomposition transforms the camp rules themselves into the desired other: not the prohibited third, but the prohibition of the third is what one wants. As the source of all the discriminations that make up a world of distinctions and identities, the stern laws of antifascist doctrine now appear as the desired other to inert nature . . . and measure and value (*Mass und Wert*), meaning and form (*Sinn und Form*) rise again, resurrected from the cesspool of death. The reciprocal index Fühmann seeks is thus not a matter of privately connecting one subject to one object, of linking the singular positivity of decision to the singular positivity of the world. Rather, at stake are laws and universals. Fühmann's play for survival in transformation exemplifies a new socialist judgment, whose Kantian ambition is to make "the laws of freedom" compatible with "the lawfulness of nature," to harmonize the whole system of intentions with the whole system of causes.[114]

In a reflection from *Twenty-two Days,* Fühmann clearly distinguishes two kinds of death in his abject situation. One death, the one exemplified by his bunkmate's immolation, remains an unfulfilled desire for those who continue to live in despair of who they are (fascists). The bunkmate's clean slate is impossible to experience as an identity, since it decomposes both fascist and socialist in the static oneness of the whole. The other death, however, remains an available and articulate experience, albeit a superficial, or better, a superficializing experience that spares the corporal body by rebaptizing its immaterial soul in the name of the material laws of an emerging system:

> You didn't murder during fascism, and you weren't sentenced to death (which would *also* have been possible and just, and which you had even expected), but you had to condemn to death the person you used to be, otherwise you couldn't continue to live. [. . .] But how does one carry out such an execution of oneself? A leap at the transom off a footstool to just above the ground (a leap many took in the Antifa School latrine, over the cesspool, with a sign on their chest) would only extinguish the One as well as the Other. [. . .] The new social order was the Other to Auschwitz; I came to it by way of the gas chamber, and I considered it the completion of my transformation to place myself at its disposal as a tool, my will extinguished. . . .[115]

In his solution to the dilemma of executing humane justice without suffering a capital sentence, Fühmann submits to the sort of carceral subjectification that Foucault, in *Discipline and Punish*, identifies as the very source of the "modern soul," its rebirth out of the ashes of the medieval subject. "If the surplus power possessed by the king gives rise to the duplication of his body, has not the surplus power exercised on the subject body of the condemned man given rise to another type of duplication? That of a 'non-corporal,' a 'soul' . . . which, unlike the soul represented by Christian theology, is not born in sin and subject to punishment, but is born rather out of methods of punishment, supervision and constraint."[116] In other words, the Other to the Camp (Auschwitz) is once again the Camp (*lager' voennoplennych*), the essential difference residing in the next camp's new human measure: "Not that which must be reached in order to alter him, but that which must be left intact in order to respect him. *Noli me tangere*. It marks the end of the sovereign's vengeance. The 'man' that the reformers set up against the despotism of the scaffold has also become a 'man-measure': not of things, but of power."[117] *Noli me tangere*, the risen Christ's words to Mary Magdalene—"touch me not; for I am not yet ascended to my father"—now come to signify the inviolability of the New Man prefigured in Bukharin's dying hope that his "trial be the last severe lesson," making "the great might of the U.S.S.R. become clear to all." Bukharin and the bunkmate, both pathetic sacrifices, are resurrected in a socialist soul whose body no longer needs to be reached and punished, because its depth is visible right on the surface as the very means by which the New World will become what it essentially is. The measure of socialist might is taken by the naked soul born from the exposure of Auschwitz and prepared at the *lager' voennoplennych* to be received into the leftist camp.

What a systems erotics describes in this regard is not the impossibility, but the very condition of motion, progress, change. Change can present itself only as tendency and promise, not as fullness of identity—to that extent, the radical essence of change is revealed in the camp's simultaneous privation and totality (as some one world and not some other, both particular and complete). For as the confined subject is stripped of all individuating qualities, its rebirth depends on a groundless (but enduring) trust in the objectivity (the otherness) of transformation. "Before" and "after" are no longer integrated in a subject's being present to itself as a continuous identity of old and new. Rather, the once-mastered experience of a distinction between "before" and "after" must yield to the purely external and empirical patience to endure long enough in abeyance to experience the jeopardy of one identity as the eventual proof of another.[118] The miraculous flash of conversion has to be drawn out over the time it takes for a steady tendency to emerge and a promise to be fulfilled—or, more technically, over the time it takes for a new past to be distinguished from and coordinated to a new future through the inchoative self-presencing of a new system.[119] Conversion to socialism, Fühmann realizes twenty-seven years after the fact, "is no mere act of gnosis/anagnorisis [*Erkenntnisakt*], it doesn't happen on this day and at this hour, as it happened to Saul on the road to Damascus, and even he sat blind for three days without eating or drinking."[120] Abdication of one's sovereign will to the Other "couldn't be the end, it could only be the beginning of a transformation."[121] That genetic point, where transformation begins with an act of regicide/suicide lacking any assurance of succession or redemption—that moment of utterly abject openness—only highlights the absolute necessity of another camp to receive (and shepherd) the soul thus set free. Change is not independence from all camps, but a movement of transformation whereby the elements liberated from one camp seek their equilibrium, the end of their anguish, in another camp whose perimeters remain to be drawn. It is only within a system that cleaves to its own imminent closure that one can identify norms and tendencies. By contrast, the one without faith—the "apostate" or "renegade"—"strains to define himself beyond the camps," as Rohrwasser points out, as though an individual could exist outside of any system, without laws, history, or environment.[122] It is not that there is nothing admirable about an apostate's heroic attempt to liberate the world's existing camps, or at least liberate himself or herself from them; it is only that such an attempt remains frustratingly indifferent to the perimeters within which it is operating.

To grasp the relationship of individual to system that comes into play here, one needs to imagine what it means for an element of one system to choose *against* that system at the same instant it chooses *for* an unknown system whose emergence depends on the unpredictable choices of a sufficient number of other such elements.[123] "A system lacks any self-transcending power," notes Luhmann.[124] Like Trakl's blind minute-hands climbing toward midnight, a system's reproduction is, to again cite Fühmann's stupid trek back eastward toward his annihilated *Wehrmacht* unit in spring 1945, a "blindness . . . unable to see over its own time" (*VF* 29). Luhmann notes how a system, despite its immense genetic complexity, behaves with just such stupid simplicity at its boundary: "[To] be or not to be, to continue the autopoiesis or not to, serves as an internal representation of the totality of possibilities. Everything that can happen is reduced for the system to one of these two states."[125] In the face of that daunting totality of the system, a revolutionary choice can only be literally miraculous; by the same token, if it abides an instant too long in its singularity and arbitrariness, and is not welcomed beyond the perimeter into the broad confines of a new camp potent enough to recognize the choice as its own, then revolutionary subjectivity is exposed as simple betrayal. But the convert cannot know the interval he or she must endure in suspense; cannot know when, or if, the emergency of a decision will precipitate the emergence of law, or conversely the stalled emergence will precipitate the emergency of lawlessness. It is no longer the suddenness of the initial leap at stake, but the direction—toward or away from emergence—of the now slowly creeping arrow of time.

The duration between two infinitesimals, between leap and precipitation, is the excruciatingly slow interval of Fühmann's real socialist subjectivity.[126] In terms of intellectual history, the kairic rebellions of Bloch, Lukács, Benjamin, Tillich, and their cohort of messianic socialists in the interwar years against the linear homogenous time of the bourgeoisified

Social Democratic Party only makes sense *before* East Germany's revolution. After the epochal disruption—Stalin's explosion of Hitler's bourgeois-fascist clock—chronological time returns, this time as the normative and developmental temporality of socialist emergence. From the pathos of decision to the patience of consequences, from sovereign duty to empirical responsibility—not only values, but also perceptions change . . . or at least they "should be" evolving toward that total difference promised in the initial kairic moment of the antifascist camp. As Christa Wolf ascertains in a 1979 letter to Fühmann, his literary achievement consists in identifying the experience of someone condemned "to live in the border-zone between two value systems . . . left only the choice between indebting himself to one or the other, or even: both. Because the third, new, 'valid' value system is no place in sight and nothing remains for our man except to describe his ghostly situation [*Lage*] exactly, which means with its ghosts."[127] Fühmann's narrative time is the time over which the instantaneous logic of *tertium non datur* is drawn out, and the risk of that long time, more than any sudden trauma of leaping per se, is his literary drama.

In the nearly forty years following the twenty-three-year-old soldier's conversion to communism in Soviet prison camp, Fühmann struggles to narrate the emerging laws and plans that would vindicate his choice of camp as something other than betrayal and his subjectivity as something other than a pawn's. As the term of socialism's emergence draws on, however, the betrayal whose possibility grows increasingly vivid in his imagination is not that of the young *Wehrmacht* soldier laboring in the lime pits of the Caucasus, but the disillusioned socialist's betrayal in the offices of the GDR Academy of the Arts. If Trakl's blind minute-hands figure for Fühmann the historical horizon of the fascism enveloping his youth, Koestler's metaphor of "darkness at noon" might be taken to figure the clock of real socialism's bright noon, a clock likewise "unable to see over its own time." While the metaphors are similar, everything rides for Fühmann on the literal, empirical difference and progressive sequence of two all-encompassing chronologies. Although the errant Marxist Merleau-Ponty claimed that "there is no universal clock, but only local histories,"[128] Fühmann's socialist passion is rooted in just the opposite predicament. Indeed, there is no *single* clock and no *one* history, but as unbearably local as the *lager' voennoplennych* latrine is, the leap Fühmann takes leaves nothing unturned: it lands him in a modernity as universal as it is different.

CHAPTER SEVEN

Revolutionary Laws: Emergence and Emergency

> Do you think the revolution justifies everything?
> You're an undisciplined horde, nothing more!
> —Ludwig Renn, *Postwar*[1]

> The revolution obligates!
> —Rosa Luxemburg, *The Red Flag*, January 1919[2]

1. 1945/1980

"The concept of law," Fühmann writes to Christa Wolf after the passage of the Third Criminal Code Revision Act in 1979, "has become absurd."[3] His bitter recognition of this absurdity marks a severe blow to his sorely tested hope that real socialism might immanently become what it was essentially meant to be: socialism. At the outset of the 1970s, critical socialists like Fühmann and Wolf had felt optimistic that the SED dictatorship that may once have been warranted by the difficult transition to socialism—a concession they struggled ever harder to make with a straight face—was finally ending, ushering in a mature era in which, as we have seen, Erich Honecker could promise as he took over from Walter Ulbricht at the VIII Party Congress in 1971 that there would be "no taboos in the realm of art and literature."[4] Their disciplining of their ethical and aesthetic discretion over the course of the preceding decades—by imperceptible turns voluntary and compulsory—would at last be bearing fruit; a new socialist faculty of judgment, experienced individually, but manifesting itself collectively, would, it was hoped, be emerging to relieve the SED-state of the challenges of postcapitalist institution and coordination that so far it could master only as a single-party dictatorship.

As the legal historian Johannes Raschka argues, however, the hard-line revision of the criminal code in 1979 was anything but a mature piece of normative reflection on what the content of socialist justice could be. It instead demonstrated the sharpening strategic considerations of a system apparently incapable of feeling secure in its sovereignty. The Revision Act was "in the first instance a threat issued by the SED-state against its own citizens as well as a penal instrument in case of internal or external crises."[5] Its logic, in other words, was military rather than normative in spirit. Even more fatally, the internal crises it was designed to avert were the very crises it provoked for people like Fühmann. With this legal revision, the state's cumulative normative failure became a signal for him to reclaim his suspended perceptions in spite of rather than in respect of the law of the land. Or, to put it another way, the crisis of expectations provoked by the Revision Act suddenly made the law of the land glaringly visible as something it was not supposed to be. In the very event of appearing as a distinct body of law, the GDR statutory order loosened the socialist "is" from the socialist "ought," raising the question of what lawfulness itself should feel like in socialism.

One of the most notorious paragraphs of the revised criminal code, §219 (Assumption of Illegal Contacts), provided stiff penalties for writers who sought publishing outlets in the West. Known informally as the "Lex Heym" after the best-selling writer Stefan Heym who had scandalized the SED by publishing his political roman-a-clef *Collin* in the West, the law was grasped specifically as an attack on the public sphere that Fühmann had once believed his writing was helping to foster in the name of the coming socialist community—an attack, that is, on the very grounds of spontaneous socialist generation. Two additional paragraphs—§106 (Subversive Agitation) and §107 (Hostile-Negative Group Formation)—provided for heightened penalties against various forms of association, intimidating writers who sought each other's company on shared aesthetic grounds. It applied even to the company of literary anthologization, as Fühmann discovered when he attempted to assemble a volume of unpublished GDR poets in 1981, only to garner accusations of "hostile factionalism" from the State Security Police. Raschka argues that the timing of these criminal code revisions was motivated by a growing sense, especially after the 1975 Helsinki Accords on Human Rights, that the state needed expanded room for "operative decisions" in the event of a political emergency, criminal law becoming an increasingly compliant vehicle of state sovereignty in an internally and externally embattled real socialism. The rule of law—however dubiously it applied to the GDR situation—was, in this perspective, not even a matter of administrative expediency, but purely political survival. Could this aggressive politicization, however contrary to the liberal spirit of civic law, be right?

With the intensification of the Cold War at the end of 1979, signaled by NATO's controversial "double track decision" to deploy medium range nuclear missiles in West Germany and the Soviet Union's invasion of Afghanistan, Fühmann's realization of the dire GDR political situation flashes up apocalyptically through the accretions of faith and self-denial disciplining his perceptions of the world since POW camp in the 1940s. Shortly after New Year's Day in 1980, during a power outage that prevents him from watching an interview with Christa Wolf being broadcast on West German television, Fühmann writes her wondering whether the blackout is "because of this broadcast or because of Afghanistan, or are the heavens raging, or can the ether simply not stand it anymore and has chosen the stupidest time—" he interrupts himself with a dash—"I suddenly have the feeling of the end of time, which can drag on terribly.—Let's have some sort of carnival!"[6] Then, a few months later, he offhandedly confides to her the once-unthinkable comparison between twilight and dawn, between the two incommensurable epochs of fascism and socialism that his life uneasily spans: "[O]nly now do I fully grasp how catastrophic the mood + the crisis of confidence are in this land. And everyone carries on incessantly—it makes me shudder. I often feel as though it were April '45.—I don't know what's going to become of it. Till then.—Be happy.—Always Franz."[7]

This striking admission in May 1980 signals an existential crisis as catastrophic as the cosmic implosion of April–May 1945, when the *Wehrmacht*'s collapse forced a cathartic re-evaluation of his life on the road to a Siberian Damascus. In 1945, however, the sign of crisis pointed Fühmann indubitably toward a socialist order whose positive goals lent unified form to his aesthetic pathos. The crisis of the 1970s—which inspires a similar sublimity—nonetheless indicates nothing that would point beyond nonsense and nihilism. His literary production, as we saw already with "Marsyas," written at the height of the crisis in 1977, only grows more paradoxical, culminating in the early 1980s science fiction collection I discuss in the following two chapters. Here I am concerned with how, in the face of the incoherency confronting him at every turn, Fühmann's correspondence and collaboration with artists and functionaries becomes a peculiar place, between the privacy (even idiocy) of a letter and its public, whence he can behold what has become of socialist expectations. If the decreasing meaningfulness of expectations in socialism had long unsettled what was to count as "normal," their wholesale jeopardy, implied by his sudden intuition of the law's absurdity, forces an all-out confrontation with the very idea of a socialist norm.

2. SOCIALISM'S DOUBLE JEOPARDY

> First feed the face, and then talk right or wrong.
> —Brecht, *The Threepenny Opera*[8]

A guiding presumption of socialist legality is that socialism, having overcome antagonistic class society and its need to preserve class dominance, can freely orient itself toward rational material advancement. A cumbersome framework of adjudication becomes unnecessary and socialist law sheds the trappings of bourgeois majesty, becoming subordinate to banal technical goals—and "the government of persons is replaced by the administration of things," as Engels wrote.[9] One of the GDR's most prominent philosophers, Georg Klaus (who figures prominently in the next chapter), writes:

> In a class society social norms are primarily an expression of particular property and productive relationships as well as the interests and will of the dominant class. Norm systems of this sort serve to maintain the power of the dominant class. In the hands of a workers' and peasants' authority social norms are an effective instrument for the socialist reorganization [*Umgestaltung*] of society. A socialist state puts great emphasis on maintaining norms in the interest of enforcing social progress. As far as legal norms are concerned, compliance can undoubtedly be compelled through administrative measures.[10]

In Klaus's view the law's use of force to compel its norms is justified by an objective index of socialist progress. "The development of the forces of production," Klaus comments, "is the highest criterion for judging the progressive character of a social totality, a social order."[11] Unlike capitalism, socialism is not an internally conflicted (self-contradictory) order, but an order whose material relationships speak for themselves univocally without the ideological interference of law and courts. In this sense, mature socialist progress needs no force in excess of the plain operation of the productive system. Only in the transitional period of socialist reorganization is law a necessary supplement to an otherwise self-generating material articulation. "Redundancy of statements raises their persuasive power. Nothing is added semantically . . . but pragmatically there is an essential difference."[12]

In this transitional juncture when legal norms duplicate technical norms in an explicit language of obligation, there might be confusion as to what behavior is truly grounded on—the experience of legal obligation or the logic of functional adaptation? At some point, however, the normal language of socialism can be expected to switch over fully from the counterfactual modality of "ought" to the modality of "is." Lukács, as we saw in the previous chapter, had an aesthetic account of this switch in language. In bourgeois tragedy, a "should be" inevitably kills the hero as he or she founders on its discrepancy with what "is." As socialism succeeds liberalism, the tragic genre itself cedes its aesthetic stature to epic description of how socialist life simply is. This switch in modes, moreover, is not a regional switch only in the realm of aesthetics, but characterizes the essential experience of socialism as a reconciliation of "is" and "ought." Klaus's and Lukács's story of transition from a normative to indicative order erases precisely that which existentially distinguishes law for the eminent legal theorist H. L. A. Hart. As a coherent normative system, law serves to motivate behavior intrinsically rather than relying on the unthinking compulsion of dogma and force. Hart evokes how an "external" application of law is perceived in contrast to an "internal" motivation by law. The externalist sees law as a behaviorist mechanism, "like the view of one who, having observed the working of a traffic signal in a busy street for some time, limits himself to saying that when the light turns red there is a high probability that the traffic will stop. He treats the light merely as a natural *sign that* people will behave in certain ways, as clouds are a *sign that* rain will come."[13] By contrast to this indicative view of law, Hart's normative conception holds that the signal actually provides a *reason for* stopping. Accordingly, the externalist "will miss out a whole dimension of the social life of those whom he is watching, since for them the red light is not merely a sign that others will stop: they look upon it as a *signal for* them to stop and so a reason for stopping in conformity to rules which make stopping when the light is red a standard of behavior and an obligation."[14] Without any internal dimension to the social experience of law, law is not after all law, but arbitrary and superficial command. It is precisely the internal perception of a motivating norm that characterizes the experience of the rule of law.[15]

Since the American and French revolutions, then, law has been the apotheosis of bourgeois order, the very spirit of revolution according to Saint-Just. Socialism—whatever its own presiding spirit—clearly does not share liberalism's legal theology. Far from expressing socialism's soul, law is merely a reinforcing double, a helpmate for a process whose essential truth lies right on the surface of the "development of the forces of production." In the GDR, dual law persists in the interval from its birth in the camps of the Caucasus to Honecker's proclamation of socialism's maturity, up until the miraculous point where the two strands gently touch. But for

Fühmann instead of converging, their meeting is a sudden intersection diverging again into absurdity. I emphasize Fühmann's intuition of the law's absurdity because a practical critique of its inadequacy, even anger at its unfairness, was nothing new for socialist writers in the interval of socialist becoming. In works such as Anna Seghers's shelved 1957 story "The Just Judge" ("Der gerechte Richter") and Kurt Maetzig's banned 1965 film *The Rabbit Is Me* (*Das Kaninchen bin Ich*), the unreliability of socialist legality as a stable system of norms is thematized. Even in these censored works, however, the law remains intelligible despite being distorted by the demands of socialist expediency. One could even argue, as does Slavoj Zizek, that it was precisely the nonconformist literature of Fühmann's close colleagues that assumed the task of recuperating meaning for the unprecedented measures enforced "in the name of socialism" rather than "in the name of the law."[16] From Wolf's 1963 *Divided Heaven* (*Der geteilte Himmel*), which reconciles its ambivalent protagonist with the sealing of the border in 1961, to Volker Braun's 1975 *Unfinished Story* (*Unvollendete Geschichte*), which reconciles its even more conflicted protagonist with censorship, extreme measures were not portrayed as a betrayal of socialism, but an occasion to reinternalize disturbing commands as *somehow* understandable norms with respect to the "target function" of "maximal satisfaction of the material and cultural needs of the working masses."[17]

Fühmann's blunt exclamation of law's absurdity, however, introduces a distinct quality to his response. It is not the refusal of a dissident or outsider to accept the norms of GDR legality; it is a simple, but instantly profound inability to reconcile his expectations to the *de facto* situation of the GDR, because the de facto situation is, instantly, profoundly, as absurd as the de jure. Fühmann calls this new quality of expectation "the feeling of the end of time," where expectation is simply of the unexpected. The extraordinary measures of the late 1970s can no longer be made sense of as a momentary disturbance, a perturbation in legal maturity that might be judged in sound socialist terms, for there is no criterion, whether principled or expedient, to govern judgment. Rather, the relationship between the law of things and the law of the land has become nonsensical. When a horizon of expectations no longer holds open the prospect of a coherent future, the skin is peeled away from socialist unity, exposing strange viscera to the dazzling light of apocalypse.

3. POSTCARDS FROM THE EDGE

> "Let the jury consider their verdict," said the King[.] . . . "No, no!" said the Queen. "Sentence first—verdict afterwards."
>
> —Lewis Carroll, *Alice's Adventures in Wonderland*[18]

> I command a hundred thousand banners be hung with the slogan:
> WE ARE HAPPY!
>
> —Fühmann, *The Happy Knight of the Trinity, or How to Become Top Talker: A Puppet Play for Children*[19]

If good narrative sense is too much to ask of an apocalypse, then Fühmann's cheerfully bleak message, imperiling thirty-five years of disciplined living in the interval since the *lager' voennoplennych*, comes to Wolf on the right medium for revelation: a novelty postcard.[20] Although it bears a photographic image and text, the card signifies less through resemblance or syntax than by its inherence in a situation, as smoke indicates fire without depicting or defining it. "A photograph," notes Peirce, "not only excites an image, has an appearance, but, owing to its optical connection with the object, is evidence that that appearance corresponds to a reality."[21] While Fühmann's postcard corresponds to a reality, that reality's features remain elusive, since the punctual fact of the moment matters less than the overall *tendency* of things. Georg Klaus maintains that a social system reveals nothing about itself in a "passive snapshot," but only with reference "to the entire real life process, to reality as a sensible human activity, a praxis."[22] A system's reality lies in its practical law of becoming, not in any momentary fact. But how does a law or process ever take on the indexical force of evidence, which requires that truth be *present* in both the ontological and temporal sense? Isn't evidence meaningful only *within* the law—can it ever be the other way around, where the law becomes evidence of the objects it regards? "Evidence," in Klaus's definition, "is *proof through maximally successful practice.*"[23] That the law holds, or to the utmost extent it succeeds in holding, its order exists. The process of taking hold can drag on terribly, like the end of time itself, but at some point, the things themselves take over from the law as the mark of order . . . either that or, without a final fact ever having been secured, possibility suddenly turns into impossibility, cosmos into chaos, sense into nonsense:

A washed-out photo shows an empty East German sidewalk and a shambling fence bearing a poster in Fraktur with the bold injunction "No real socialism thinkable without culture and art!" Against its forlorn back-

Fig. 3. "No real socialism thinkable without culture and art!" Postcard to Christa Wolf, January 1980. Reproduced by permission of the artist, Klaus Staeck © 1979.

ground, the high-minded slogan loses whatever dignity its imperative might have conveyed, and appears ridiculous in light of the contradiction between posit and perception, between solemn message and preposterous messenger.[24] While the catharsis of the joke might momentarily relieve the contradiction, it also prompts one to notice an underlying difficulty with the modality of such a slogan's claim. In what sense, if any, could the artless maxim depicted here have validity? Is it a sober, practical rule like "No passage thinkable without valid passport"; or is it an empirical observation of socialism's reliance on its historical culture, "No GDR thinkable without Johannes R. Becher"; or is it a moral imperative bearing an obligation to duly constituted socialist authority, "Without making art, I fail my duty to socialism"; or conversely, "Without fostering art, socialism fails its constituents"? But in each of these cases, how is one to understand the relationship of the foreground statement to the barren background? Does the norm derive from its situation, the situation from the norm, or is its authority some third thing?

Cutting through the Gordian knot of validity questions, Klaus asserts:

> It is pointless to insist that norms can be attributed truth or falsity. It might be objected that denying normative truth leads to moral subjectivity. Whoever claims the command "You should do good deeds for socialism!" has no truth content, has in this view a subjective standpoint. But the objection is groundless. [. . .] Statements describe reality and are cognitive insights. Based on these insights a new cognitive goal is set. In order to reach this goal every science elaborates special methods, i.e., directions, that lead to the achievement of the goal. In this general sense norms are regulations directed at a recipient. Every norm contains a call to be heeded; that is, the regulation is bound with the call for the recipient to realize (or not) the regulation. In the case of moral and legal norms the call derives from the relevant relations of property, production and class.[25]

For Klaus the mystery of norms is simple: they are "pointers (indices) toward relevant operations."[26] Norms in an indexical sense are the best evidence for an order since their presence requires no interpretation, only that recipients respond to their signal or not: "[T]hey direct the attention to their objects by blind compulsion" (Peirce).[27] The authority of such a norm derives sheerly from its relevance to its situation. A symptom, goose flesh, for example, points at a condition, a chilly room. The signal notifying the recipient and the implicit call to heed the notice do not describe anything that might be falsified or verified. The art issuing from the GDR likewise gives notice of socialist emergence and bound with that notice is the call to respond with an artistic outpouring grounded in one's own socialist belonging: the normal tendency is promoted recursively, the explicit law eventually proving itself superfluous in the implicit evidence of socialism's blossoming culture.

Surely Klaus is right that the commonplace propaganda depicted on the postcard hardly calls for interpretation by its recipient: its significance is eo ipso. Equally self-evident, the blow of Fühmann's invocation of April 1945 on back of so droll a card conveys the boundless intensity of his unmoored socialist hopes. Fühmann responds existentially to a situation that for outsiders asks for nothing more than the chuckle the West German card elicits. His gallows humor not only mocks, but inverts the direction of the slogan on front, once his own most cherished doctrine. Where the slogan asks its public to advance in accord with the emerging socialist line, Fühmann connects the slogan's sorry manifestation with the cataclysmic significance that fascism's collapse had for the SA member he was in 1945. "I often feel as though it were April '45.—I don't know what's going to become of it. Till then.—Be happy.—Always Franz." Spring 1945 and spring 1980 are fatefully bound by the date written in the upper right corner. The postcard marks the chiasm where the double norms of socialist transformation suddenly intersect. This weightless X-point—the equilibrium of normalcy or explosion of crisis—strikes Fühmann's subjectivity as profoundly as the *Wehrmacht* comrade bearing his sentence over the camp latrine: "I was a war criminal!"

In a remarkable 1981 discussion with Fühmann, Horst Simon, one of his editors at Hinstorff Press, tries to wrap up their contentious exchange on a conciliatory note. "I agree with you completely," Simon responds vaguely to another sally by Fühmann, "only, we do have the concept of a socialist literature [. . .] and it contains concepts like partisanship, socialist ideational content. . . . These concepts compel and demand a certain decisiveness and certain decisions. They are categories of literary thought and evaluation that cannot simply be conceded. And you haven't conceded them, because when you say: of course, I want to be useful; of course, I want to be productive; of course, I want to progress, then your strong faith is implicit. And you commit yourself through your very existence and work here with us." Simon wants reassurance that Fühmann continues to embody the cultural norm simply by being there. Instead of accepting Simon's offer to serve as a reliable index of socialist cultural authority, Fühmann points to the same growing existential jeopardy indicated by his postcard. "The degree of partisanship is the degree to which literature is really literature," he retorts. "Take the well-known motto: 'I am a Communist first, a writer second.' I reject this motto for myself. [. . .] I'd never want to belong to any body that demanded from me such submission. But I'm a citizen of the GDR, and not so by virtue of joining or resigning, but of other necessity. You say we have certain categories that are simply there and binding—yeah, and now I don't feel they're binding on me, what now? I'm not going to lie, that's the death of literature."[28] And, one might add, the death of socialism, with the capital sentence hung around its neck: "No real socialism thinkable without culture and art!"

The point to emphasize is that Fühmann's postcard draws its power not from any semantic force of argument, but, as his blunt remarks to Simon indicate, by serving existential notice to the very norms and tendencies that have articulated him body and soul—they simply, without argument, no longer apply: obligation has become irony, even absurdity, and no appeal to duty can draw him back into their normative force. The raw indexical connection between his utterance and its socialist situation is what makes it so uncontrollable and so threatening to the state. After all, there were many, far more categorical repudiations of socialism, but they judged facts or refuted arguments, whereas Fühmann's balkiness lies in the very clay of the New Man that he is with all his might.

As we saw in the previous chapter, Fühmann came to socialism by way of the gas chamber and *lager' voyennoplennych*. His socialist Being, his governing laws, begin at the void where the camps of World War II end. The state that resumes at the perimeter of unthinkable violence takes upon itself the reorganization (*Umgestaltung*) of individual life out of mass death. Cast in the optimistic technocratic idiom of peaceful coexistence, this view of the socialist camp-state accords neatly with Klaus's understanding of the law as a pragmatic redundancy of technical norms. Neither a divine bearer of natural right nor a rational self-legislator of moral duty, socialist law's emerging subject has no special interiority of obligation or remorse. He is a biopolitical vessel for maximizing socialist target values. One can fill in this bare functionalist account of the socialist subject, as I suggest in the last chapter, by drawing on Foucault's *Discipline and Punish*, which emphasizes not the soullessness of modernity, but the modern production of the soul. In this way, the other, legalistic side of Klaus's redundancy also receives proper emphasis. The nineteenth-century humanism that pushed for penal reform at the same time as legal positivism was claiming law for human invention rather than divine providence, established punishment as the critical measure of humanity. The soul on which the status quo demonstrates its mercy is rendered available for clemency in the first place by pervasive techniques of legal constraint. The *caritas* of modernity, unlike that of the ancient polis, rests according to Foucault not on the cultivation of a flourishing self, but on substituting a synthetic subject of power, a derivative effect of its own disciplinary constraint.

When Horst Simon's predecessor at Hinstorff, Kurt Batt, an editor whose early death was a deep loss for Fühmann, submits Fühmann's essay collection *Erfahrungen und Widersprüche* (*Experiences and Contradictions*) to the authorities in 1974, it is with considerable political trepidation, since he knows from his correspondence with Fühmann how pained by doubts his difficult author had become, and knows also how close to the official boundaries the pieces in the volume are (but not which side of censorship they lie on). He situates the manuscript among "the efforts at mutual understanding [*Verständigungsversuche*] that various writers [. . .] have been engaging in especially since the VIII Party Congress [of 1971]."[29] Like Wolf's and Braun's similar attempts, these ongoing efforts to discover a soul-in-process—Batt calls them "personal reflections with a provisional character"—relate directly to the distinct disciplinary quality of the socialist system. Batt emphasizes an essay that "contains a fundamental and unshakable confession of faith in our state and socialism" and asserts that it is "pre-

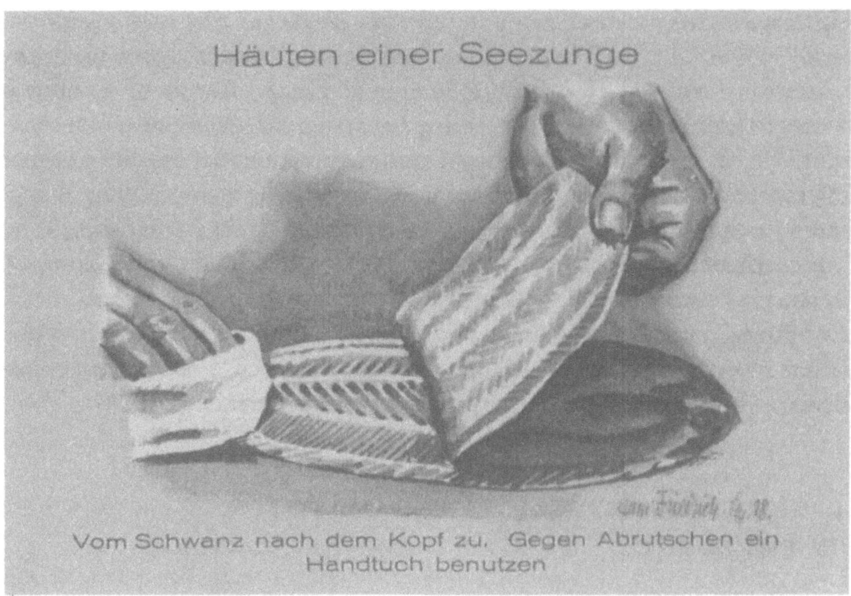

Fig. 4. "Skinning a sole." Postcard to Margarete Hannsmann, October 1979. Image courtesy of Deutsches Literaturarchiv, Marbach.

cisely from this point that one understands all the other pieces with their often urgent, even impulsively urgent questions." Fühmann's unsettled and potentially censorable soul radiates out from a constitutive faith. And the essay Batt highlights for the authorities? It is the very survey response in which Fühmann affirms his belonging to "a generation that came to socialism by way of Auschwitz. [. . .] Collapse; march into prisoner of war camp. There, from the first moment, intensifying from month to month, four shocks, mostly overlapping, which altogether turned around my life."[30] The connection of his socialist soul to modernity's camps could not be more clear: No real socialism thinkable without Auschwitz! His experiences and contradictions come together until they no longer do—until, nolens volens, the efforts at "mutual understanding" inside his camp, the attempts to make socialism "thinkable" on the basis of this relentlessly straitened soul, abruptly yield to the unthinkable nonsense his camp has manifestly become.

After half a life answering socialism's call, Fühmann loses sight of what his best efforts are working toward. His editors and advisors, with better or worse intentions, try to convince him that his loss of sight is no gain of insight, no transformation, but a momentary perplexity that with a little patience will resolve itself by returning him, renewed and invigorated, to the operational course he has been following all along. "But then," Fühmann writes to Batt in the early 1970s, trying to explain the consequences of relinquishing his sense of an increasingly unruly present to the infinite patience of emergence, "one is back to Parmenides, everything is unchanging Being, merely exhibiting new aspects. [. . .] If everything is mathematizable (and our excellent Herr Gödel has even proved that everything can be expressed in algebra) then everything ultimately comes down to the formula 0 = 0. Everything comes from nothing and returns to nothing, and we who write letters to each other are what is in between."[31] Indeed, it is the correspondence in between null points that makes all the difference here.

4. GROUPING LETTERS: EMERGENT PUBLIC OR EMERGENCY?

> . . . socialism
> Back then was still a cripple
> A mortifying mixture:
> Half image of man, half beast
> Half freedom and half fixture
>
> —Wolf Biermann, *Germany, A Winter's Tale*[32]

On November 16, 1976, the satirical poet-songwriter Wolf Biermann, who among his many dubious acts had described GDR socialism itself as a satyr, "half image of man, half beast," was peremptorily stripped of his GDR citizenship by the "responsible authorities" according to §13 of the Law Concerning GDR Citizenship.[33] "It is a sovereign decision of our state," a party communiqué emphasized, "and valid law."[34] Although hardly a use of state power on the scale of suppressing an uprising in 1953, "securing state borders" in 1961, or invading Czechoslovakia in 1968, Biermann himself has observed that "the protest movement against my banishment was indeed broader and deeper."[35] More than the breadth and depth of the response, however, what made a relatively minor reprisal against an individual into a major political caesura was the response's origin among a small circle of a dozen writers, including Fühmann, whose socialist loyalty situated them close to political authority, but whose reading public lent them a degree of immunity from direct state repression. "It was the first criticism of a GDR political measure intentionally carried out before an international public since the workers' uprising of 1953."[36] The protest began with an open letter submitted on the following day to the East German Communist Party paper *Neues Deutschland*, and, crucially, to the Western *Agence France-Presse*. The letter's effect on the government was immediate and powerful, since it revealed that the GDR's most prominent authors, authors recognized and rewarded by its official institutions, disagreed with a major party decision, thereby exposing a potentially disruptive ideological rift below the rigorously maintained surface of socialist harmony.

The issues raised by the protest did not take on juridical character per se, which would have been irrelevant in a state with a programmatically curtailed legal apparatus. As Walter Ulbricht testily pointed out in 1958, "[It] is not yet clear to some of our comrade jurists that as party members they must accomplish their scholarly work as comrades struggling consciously for the construction of socialism. [. . .] The resolutions of the party create the basis of state and legal theory. They issue in an unbroken chain of total social development, which is the exclusive fundament upon which the development of state power and thus our state and legal system can be worked out."[37] Although in 1971 Honecker had proclaimed Ulbricht's twenty-year "construction phase" completed and the phase of "developed socialist society" begun, it was not clear what the new status of legality in this developed phase would be.[38] The Biermann affair, perhaps because of the almost mythical resonance of the punishment—exile—became a test of the status of law in socialism, taking on a "metajuridical" character distinctly reminiscent of the debates over the Weimar constitution in the 1920s and 1930s. Unlike the ideological belaboring that accompanied the constitutional reforms of 1974, the swift, unspectacular act of revoking an individual's citizenship triggered an unplanned reflection on the way norms were articulated in socialism. As Carl Schmitt famously argued in the 1920s, a state's nonlegal, de facto political power is more crucial to its self-defense than the law, and its primacy should be recognized in legitimate acts of the state. "The specific political distinction to which political actions and motivations can be reduced," according to Schmitt, "is the distinction between *friend* and *enemy*."[39] Similarly, the official position in the Biermann affair held that the GDR had the right to defend itself from class enemies, a right trumping any other one subsequently articulated de jure by the law.

With its repeated emphasis on the friend-enemy distinction, the Biermann affair harkened back to one of the most traumatic crises in the genealogy of the modern state. In the Weimar era the self-evidence of liberal normalcy—whether normalcy is taken in the normative sense of rule of law or the operative sense of market society—had been disrupted and the organization of modernity appeared as an open project. After World War II, as I argue in the previous chapter, the shape of normalcy was again put into question by the liberal-socialist standoff over the catastrophic legacy of fascism. What is different another twenty-five years later in the Biermann case is that the crisis refers not to an impasse in liberalism or fascism, but to one in "developed socialist society." The hyperbolic categories of friend and enemy were defined not with respect to nation or ethnos—the 1974 GDR constitution had removed all references to Germany and the German nation—but with respect to real socialism as a constitutive force with a distinct necessity of its own. The sides of the Biermann dispute, as circumscribed as their public arena was, could no longer conceal their mutual antagonism and, to the extent that the antagonism did not become a decisive political rupture, both sides sought to understand the apparent discrepancy between legality and legitimacy with reference to some real necessity of socialism. *Necessitas non habet legem*, "necessity has no law," is the Roman common law justification of a state of emergency, although no one dared openly use the term "emergency" to name the GDR's situation. The unsettling question, however, was whether *socialist* necessity, after more than twenty years of "construction," had demonstrated enough systemic features to distinguish itself from mere SED dictatorship; whether it truly had the functional inchoative tendency Georg Klaus postulated that might make its trumping of legality in so minor a case understandable. Or whether, on the contrary, the emergence of socialism was nothing other than the formal void of emergency—a zero hour without established law and, more disturbingly, without any overriding necessity either.

On the evening of Biermann's banishment, Fühmann writes to the chair of the Council of Ministers, the highest state organ of the GDR, that, "as a citizen and writer of the German Democratic Republic, I consider it not only my right but also my duty to communicate to you that these measures as well as their modality disturb and unsettle me to the utmost, I can reconcile them neither with the essence nor with the dignity, eminence and strength of my state. The traces they leave behind scare me, I see growing damage and fear the consequences."[40] Written the evening before the collective open letter of November 17, Fühmann's private protest is not itself a political act in Schmitt's sense. It is reassuringly directed to constituted authority, which, as would repeatedly be stressed by party officials, "is a statutory right"—"to turn to the government is the right of a citizen."[41] While the welcoming attitude toward criticism through proper channels was disingenuous—Fühmann's letter figures prominently in the Stasi's justification for putting him under surveillance[42]—the government did perceive its real problem to be the open letter, and viewed the private one as secondary. But by linking private duty to the state's strength and essence, this letter conditions his obligations on a performance the state presumably has it in its power, and conception, to live up to. The letter does not demand any revision of this conception, only that it effectively emerge. The "growing damage" Fühmann sees is thus not a crisis of legal norms, but a crisis of legitimation—a crisis in the identity of the system to which he owes his duty.[43] Fühmann exercises his duty not by practically challenging state power, but by modestly signaling the loss of a quantum of its required mass loyalty: his unease *is* the internal trace of damage the state must fear, it is not a threat from outside. To the extent that his sense of duty arises out of solicitousness for "the essence . . . of my state," it obtains only as long as that essence persists. Enacting measures incompatible with its *ratio essendi*, the state squanders its sovereignty to the same degree as it forces the question of what its essence really is: to what do citizens of that strange entity without nation and legal transcendence owe their obligation?

The positive legal tradition repudiated, as we have seen, any transcendental grounding of law in morality or divinity. Law never recovered any equally secure ground, but has since rested on the tautology that legality exists as a unity of statute posited by the state, while the state exists as the unity of its legislation. Echoing the sentiment of Wilhelmine positivist Georg Jellineck that law is "possible only on the condition that a directing and coercive force is present,"[44] Derrida has written that "there is no such thing as law (*doit*) that doesn't imply in itself, *a priori*, in the analytical structure of its concept, the possibility of being 'enforced,' applied by force."[45] But even more to the point than any a priori concept of law's force is the embodied experience of law as *polemios* (hostility), as an always implied threat of force.[46] Introspecting what law feels like, H. L. A. Hart writes that "the violation of a rule is not merely a basis for the prediction that a hostile reaction will follow but a *reason* for hostility."[47] The phenomenal experience of law on this view is inseparable from that of some kind of righteous force. In Fühmann's private letter to the minister, his assumption is that unruly and inessential force should be expected only outside of a dignified and well-ordered socialist state, but that willy-nilly socialist order is pervaded by a force he cannot reconcile with his own experience of civil *polemios*. What then is this force sapping the dignity of socialist *nemesis* (righteous anger)—is it oppositional voices, with their scurrilous and satirical tone; or peremptory state measures enforced without regard to the integrity of law?

In Fühmann's experience of the Biermann affair, he is disturbed by a discrepancy between the law's hostility to Biermann and his own lack of such hostility. The law for Fühmann feels like an external signal system, not a satisfying experience of legitimacy. Even as a willing subject of socialist power, firmly in the socialist camp, his subjectivity is out of synch with the authority that constitutes it. Under normal circumstances, an unsettling disagreement over a case is clarified through due process, but here Fühmann's unease points beyond the one case, even beyond the one statute (§13 of the Law Concerning GDR Citizenship), to address the status of socialist normalcy itself. The normal situation would require either the "discovery" of a legitimate law that was violated, thus restoring faith in the unity of the law, or a judicial review finding that a statute is illegitimate in design or application, thus restoring faith in the state's dignity.[48] "The endeavor of a normal state," Carl Schmitt claims, "consists above all in assuring total peace within the state and its territory. To create tranquility, security, and order and thereby establish the normal situation is the prerequisite for legal norms to be valid. Every norm presupposes a normal situation, and no norm can be valid in an entirely abnormal situation"[49] Despite his letter's lack of political ambition, Fühmann's loss of tranquility hints darkly at the existence of an abnormal situation in which not law, but the very state of the state is at stake. The emergency resulting from the abnormal case demands from the state either self-maintenance or self-dissolution. The implicit question, then, is what kind of emergency is it—conservative (restitutive) or revolutionary (destructive)?

If the GDR government courted the protest of its leading intellectuals by misjudging the extent to which Biermann's satirical ballads were experienced as a state emergency, then after their open letter the argument that an emergency now existed had suddenly become convincing. But precisely this more obviously threatening emergency could not be openly declared, because its declaration would risk the emergence of a rift between intellectuals and the state, would risk, that is, the emergence of a realm of political adjudication independent of state measures. The real emergency thus remained hovering in suspension while the state portrayed itself as forcefully rising to the occasion of Biermann's provocation, exercising its sovereign authority to draw the sharp friend/enemy distinction the crisis required. "The entrance of the enemy," asserted Kurt Hager, the chief ideologue of the Party Central Committee, "begins for me at the point where the revolutionary struggle of the party, of Communists, where the powerful efforts of our people and allies [in] forming socialist society, where the ideas of humanism, internationalism, solidarity are all dragged into the dirt, where counter-revolutionary plans are hammered out, propagated and realized[.] . . . Biermann wants another edition of the so-called Prague Spring! Over the course of its evolution the Prague Spring reached the point where the following problem appeared on the agenda: either maintain socialist power in Czechoslovakia or restore capitalist relations."[50] Biermann is named as the enemy, but Hager's unnamed enemy is the real threat waiting in the wings for its dreadful appearance. By starkly drawing the line of amity and enmity, Hager demands that intellectuals define themselves punctually as standing within or outside the "unity of state and people" postulated by the GDR norms.

Fühmann does not take Hager's bait to define himself in political terms. Identifying oneself with respect to merely political norms would be too thin and willful an act, betraying any chance of experiencing the underlying revolutionary tendencies that would allow one to distinguish between valid and invalid norms in the first place. Instead, as the affair drags on, Fühmann turns to the question of what is revolutionary about the GDR—what is the essence of the transformation that makes socialism something different and specific. For if any self-evident experience of socialist difference is evaporating as a legitimating experience, then struggling to grasp and express the suspended state, whether it is an authoritarian emergency or a revolutionary emergence, becomes the decisive issue: decisive, but not political—rather, prepolitical, an issue of finding the measure of a coherent material system. In September 1977 Fühmann writes Wolf that "every dogmatist identifies with socialism and the revolutionary world proletariat, but momentarily disregarding this deadly arrogance: what is it really that this concept covers. . . . What is revolutionary in this society? Happy affirmation?"[51] If the GDR's integrity as socialist is being dissolved by virtue of its legal measures having lost touch with its material tendencies—and not by the irreverence of its satyrs—then one needs to ask from whence such eviscerating, self-contradictory legislation stems: as a self-grounding, inchoative system, the GDR has become nonsensical. Abandoning even the semblance of perfection of a closed unity, it is left with sovereign political acts, each of which, as the empirical fact of its difference from a jeopardized system, is without any possibility of immanent justification. This is precisely the revolutionary situation, organized only by the unprecedented goals of transformation. It is also precisely the police situation, organized only by the ad hoc logic of friend/enemy. The problem of legitimacy that Fühmann is expressing can refer only to a future outcome whose modality, while not the principled "ought," has forsaken the empirical "is."

In general Fühmann's response to the events of the 1970s is not characterized by the public aspirations and slogans of politicized opposition. The Biermann affair is less a caesura in his own development than a reinforcement of a course staked out in *Twenty-two Days*. On the day of Biermann's banishment, Fühmann writes back to a manuscript reader for *Sinn und Form* who has rejected one of his stories that the piece in question "decisively shows the direction I'm determined to follow, a direction I set out and formulated already in my Hungarian journal. It has now moved into the foreground and as a consequence, paths that used to run parallel (or at least seemed to) energetically diverge. There's nothing to be done about it; one can only go one's way."[52] Rather than initiating a turn to public declamation, the affair confirms Fühmann in the other direction, encouraging his language's increasingly intensive form. His engagements become more esoteric than populist; his letters addressed to an ever narrower circle of trusted acquaintances brim with bemused and outraged intensity while those to official cultural representatives demonstrate undisguised exasperation. The audience for his many children's books is, in a legal sense, not even at the age of political maturity. He resigns his last official political membership in 1972; in 1977 he quits the board of the Writers' Union. His cottage in Märkisch Buchholz outside of Berlin—"my woodland seclusion"—neatly symbolizes his independence from the cultural politics of Berlin as the latest news must pass "around seven corners" to reach him at his desk.[53]

This self-suspension is not a matter of romantically rooting himself in the German soil, but, perversely, of making good on Honecker's formulation that the one condition for a literature without taboos is that it be "rooted in socialism." However much Fühmann's intensive and esoteric turn affirms private and aesthetic values, it is not a retreat into privacy and irony, into the notorious *deutsche Misere*, but a consistent effort to take the measure of socialism, to cast himself as an index of a system that seems to him to have lost—or never obtained—its own primary measure, whether that measure would have the form of a law, a tendency, or some unimaginable appearance. In this sense, his gesture in the crisis of socialism—whether that of its emergence or emergency—is not to recuperate the dignity and rights of individuality, as would be prescribed by a liberal opposition, but all the more emphatically to ally his subjectivity with some current of becoming (or unbecoming) socialism.

He formulates his method appositely in a 1971 letter to Kurt Batt. "I want to articulate something broadly familiar to me [. . .] and I see my intention as realizable in a story whose tendency I know at the outset, but nothing more. I seek elements of reality whose immanent logic must induce the tendency; I arrange them in an initial situation; and I let myself be led by the development."[54] From 1971 toward the later part of the decade his literary evolution affects above all his faith that a story might still be the shape his method assumes. The very tendencies his stories trace lead him to more open genres, to public and private letters, interviews, recorded conversations, essays, and collages. Although they resemble the epistolary and essayistic genres of the coffee house, where Habermas locates the emerging eighteenth-century public sphere, these works with their personally targeted interlocutors bristle with a mixture of invective, whimsy, and syllogism, that cannot be reconciled with forming a principled political standpoint outside the constraints of utility. Their effect is rather to mark a difference within that utility: not the *differentia specifica* of socialism they once thought they were steadily groping out, but a self-difference, an open nonsense coalescing on the spot where socialism would be working. This convergence of the nonconvergent, this suspended emergency, is their most striking feature.

As a willfully will-less socialist citizen, Fühmann indexes himself to the diffuse tendencies he experiences in the GDR. Emphatically not a "surrogate" for politics, his aesthetics are bound to the perception of his present (in the ontological sense). To some, his default of a public political will ignores the opportunity for principled resistance, or at least overestimates the possibilities still offered by GDR life. Noting how besieged by the Stasi Fühmann, Wolf, and their circle had become in the wake of the Biermann affair, David Bathrick criticizes their symptomatic "inability to accept themselves as having been criminalized."[55] But for Fühmann the scrupulous aesthetic experience of an implicit "criminalization"—one without verdict or sentence—is more important to his project than any proleptic judgment from outside his socialist commitment and inside a coming liberal *Rechtsstaat* with its apparent transcendence of all that is collective and functional. After all, the camp—that is, a sentence served without due process—was the origin of Fühmann's socialist commitment. "Auschwitz would not have been possible without me and my like," he recognized. "I was part of a National Socialist totality that functioned exactly as it was supposed to, and so the difference between me and [Auschwitz commandant] Höß was only one of degree; juridical, but not moral-existential."[56]

Socialism was an existential commitment, an all-encompassing sentence passed in response to fascism, that did not render juridical-political issues superfluous, but clearly derived from a more fundamental transformation.

His commitment has nothing legally naive about it, in the sense of overestimating the potential that remained by the late 1970s for socialism to develop a stable normative law. Reduced to slogans, law, Fühmann clearly recognizes, has been turned into absurd illocutionary exhortations, the self-fulfilling prophecies of a sputtering system still trying to lift itself up by the bootstraps, prophecies whose nonsense becomes apparent, not in principled refusal, which proves nothing, but on his own *willing* body's incapacity to fulfill them. "I command a hundred thousand banners be hung with the slogan: WE ARE HAPPY!" proclaims the sovereign of his puppet kingdom, and the only happiness results in face of the imperative's preposterousness. Even as Fühmann expresses the absurdity of socialist law, he remains true to his existential pledge in the *lager' voennoplennych* that "I considered it the completion of my transformation to place myself at [the new order's] disposal as a tool. . . ."[57] The profound change, however, is that what in 1946 had the pathos of functionalism, now has the pathos of aestheticism. The socialist tool he has become does not activate, but registers. This change in aesthetic sensitivity stems not from an alteration in Fühmann's sovereign heart (another conversion; faithlessness to socialism; *compunctio cordis*), but from a change in the very fabric of socialism. Surrendering to socialism's functionalism provides ever less evidence of functionalist ontology and ever more evidence of the wishful thinking of inconsistent norms. This thinning socialist ontology exposes its wracked depths to Fühmann's pen in the perverse cross-purposes of economic dysfunction reigning as socialism's "functionalist" tendency, and Stasi neutralization measures (*Zersetzungsmaßnahmen*) reigning as its law. Caught at the intersection of purposeless cross-purposes, his individual political agency already repudiated at the hour of his birth, the New Man now responds with the sheer aesthetic desire to feel these strange socialist operations on his social body. "Marsyas watched with curiosity as they approached with inaudible steps, and he still didn't understand as they grabbed him, yanking his arms and legs askew, a shaggy Xi, and tied him head down in the black-barked firs. . . . The first stab was the incomprehensible: there was after all nothing that he wouldn't have freely done."[58]

The poet Uwe Kolbe, one of Fühmann's protégés, makes the right diagnosis, but misjudges its significance when he expresses frustration with

Fühmann's 1981 Trakl essay, a book he otherwise calls Fühmann's best. He reads it as at heart an attempt by Fühmann to convince "the functionary" of poetry's autonomy—an inappropriate and doomed project because such autonomy is compromised by the very nature of even his imaginary conversation with authority. "Fühmann the exegete obviously wished that someone—a specific reader, 'they'—would understand these poems. He is explaining poetry to *the functionary*. Repeatedly and vainly he longs for *the censor to understand poetry*."[59] But it is precisely the blank spot of the functioning functionary that grounds Fühmann's indexical project. His literary and metaphysical challenges are calibrated to the horizon where a functioning socialism would reveal itself as a system in the full ontological sense of that word. His reaction to the state's functional incapacity to do anything but criminalize the satyr Biermann is to register the tremors rather than to raise the flag of individual dignity. In face of the state's repressive measures, he fears more for socialism than Biermann: "[T]he traces they leave behind scare me, I see growing damage and fear the consequences." This shock doesn't lead Fühmann to adopt a language of righteousness—any univocal political language, whether affirmation or opposition, he finds too saturated with the demons of his past—but to translate mixed signals, the chiasm of Marsyas' flayed body, into a phenomenology of real socialism.

If "biopower" works by shaping rather than dominating or emancipating subjects, then the irony of Fühmann's surrender to it is that it does not work; the only thing allowing its dysfunctional power to function as a parody of function is Fühmann's faithful commitment to perceiving real socialism in its exercise. His ambition remains for socialism not to respect his individuality as an indivisible essence, but to shape it as a profoundly new essence. It is a constructivist commitment, but with the construction phase now over his commitment remains as unreconstructed as it was at the moment of its revelation in 1945. For those who, like Biermann, politicize their experiences in the GDR, critically holding up the state to its own norms, the experience of socialism remains caught between emancipatory idealism and individual repression, while the far deeper hope for the infinitely plastic body and soul is all but forgotten. The very thing Fühmann strives to witness in his writing is socialism's success or failure in forming him as a subject before any independent assertion of his practical will. That gesture of immersion allows him to experience the paradoxically necessary nonsense of real socialism.

5. THE SCALES OF JUSTICE AND THE SCALES OF NONSENSE

> Earlier lives glide by on silver soles
> And the shadows of the damned climb down to the
> sighing waters.
> In his grave, the white magician plays with his snakes.
> Silently over the place of the skull [*Schädelstätte*],
> God's golden eyes open.
>
> —Trakl, "Psalm"[60]

> My question: people, I've got to get to the concentration camp, how do I find it?
>
> —Fühmann, letter to Christa Wolf, July 24, 1979[61]

Nonsense is not a private language with no relationship to sense; it is not noise. Its relationship to sense, however, is very different from the populist one of the slogan, which if it works, does so by moving masses, by proving its good sense in concerted action rather than in an abstract quality of truth. What Fühmann's nonsense shares with the socialist slogans calling out to him from all corners of the GDR is that like these slogans it has lost its mooring in what works. It has not lost, however, its specificity as evidence of socialism, as an aesthetic experience of socialism's disjunctions and contradictions. Its evidence, however, is not projected by an intentional experience captured in a story or history, a *Bildungsroman*, of socialist construction, but by the growing autonomization of discourse and address, of language and communication. This dissolution of what never came together as a functionalist unity in the first place is precisely what becomes (of) the evidence of socialism. It is not a matter of the functional differentiation of an aesthetic subsystem, but of the semioticization of socialist reference; a process that itself refers to the unbearable pressure put on an intact referential language with an operative role in socialism.[62] This disjunction—that either the language of socialism does not refer to anything or it does not remain intact—translates the remains of Kurt Hager's official disjunction, "[E]ither maintain socialist power . . . or restore capitalist relations."

In his 1972 "found" poems, *Urworte Deutsch* (*Primal Words, German*), Fühmann departs from both the intact and the operative. He takes entries from Steputat's nineteenth-century rhyming lexicon, and without altering their order or contiguity, simply adds punctuation and titles to what he finds, and, lo, he discovers that one "is standing at the wellspring of poetry, and language itself is speaking":[63] "*State of many a state:* / Constitutional /

minimal," for example, emerges out of this socialist gathering of language.[64] When *Primal Words* first appears a decade after Fühmann's death, the editor, Ingrid Prignitz, notes that Fühmann withdrew it from consideration in 1972, fearing that its emphasis on language's processes over the social processes to which language refers would set it on a collision course with the party's realist demands, damaging the reception of his more referential *Twenty-two Days*, which was then on the verge of appearing. The split trajectories of *Twenty-two Days* and *Primal Words* open a simultaneous experience of language as a law unto itself and as an operative medium. If these paths ran parallel in the revolutionary transformation of the antifascist camp, they meet and diverge at the spot in Fühmann's GDR life where the operative process becomes inoperative and the grammatical (and legal) sentence nonsensical.

In a brief exposition of nonsense in his 1978 book of language games for children, *Die dampfenden Hälse der Pferde im Turm von Babel* (*The Steaming Necks of Horses in the Tower of Babel*), Fühmann begins with the operative image of a scale to help his young readers picture the grammatical comparative:

> The two loaded dishes of a scale: **A football** **a pea**
>
> △
>
> the balance beam with numbers and pointer: **is bigger than**

He goes on to explain that the difference between grammar and a scale is that the scale compares discrete masses whereas the grammatical sentence is not so physically constrained. "'A football is bigger than crooked' is a grammatically correct, but fully nonsensical sentence. [. . .] Our sentence proposes a comparison between the dimensions of a concrete thing and something that in principle is without dimension, and that lends the sentence a nonsense character, and this nonsense makes us happy."[65] This scale—or truly both of them, the operational and the nonsensical—is what the august scale of socialist justice has become by the 1970s, in which the pointer seems, by its very essence, to want to indicate a number, a direction, a sense, but finds itself indicating that "there are many who don't speak when they should be quiet and others who don't ask when they have answered"—as the absent-minded professor Johann Galletti, whom Fühmann happily quotes, presciently pointed out about the GDR in 1788.[66]

The two scales Fühmann asks us to imagine are indexes of his real socialism; they present the evidence—to use the relevant juridical notion—that compels even blind justice to her existential judgment of the system. Just as there are two instruments, I want to distinguish two very different sorts of evidence at stake in Fühmann's writing; two contrary ways, that is, in which the writing serves as an index for socialism. On the one hand, to cite Georg Klaus again, there is the cybernetic notion that "evidence is *proof through maximally successful practice.*"[67] When practice stops referring to recognizable criteria of optimization—when it seems arbitrary with respect to its goals—this kind of functional evidence is lost. That Fühmann remains loyal to slogans that have lost their self-evidence becomes his most radical act of insubordination, demonstrating them in their effective suspension. With Klaus's pragmatic criteria no longer anyplace in evidence, another conception of evidence imposes itself, one that draws on *poetry* in contrast to social steering to illuminate the relationship of Fühmann's writing to socialism. I am thinking of Martin Heidegger's emphatic turn against the sort of cybernetic reasoning epitomized by Klaus, which leads him to a distinct conception of evidence of human being. In "The End of Philosophy and the Task of Thinking," Heidegger writes that "no prophecy is necessary to recognize that the sciences now establishing themselves will soon be determined and steered by the new fundamental science which is called cybernetics. This science corresponds to the determination of man as an acting social being. For it is the theory of the steering of the possible planning and arrangement of human labor. Cybernetics transforms language into an exchange of news. The arts become regulated-regulating instruments of information."[68] Heidegger foresees a development, not unlike that rosily predicted for socialism by Klaus, in which law becomes a signal system directing individuals toward the activation of functional procedures, just as in Hart's "externalist" description of law. Against this cybernetic "determination of man," Heidegger defines an index of the human in specifically poetic terms, terms that elucidate both the evidentiary force and the legal problem of Fühmann's nonsense. According to Heidegger, evidence is "that which in itself and of itself radiates and brings itself to light." It is "the perspective of *homoiosis* and *adaequatio*, that is, the perspective of adequation in the sense of the correspondence of representing with what is present."[69]

Heidegger's conception of "correspondence" imparts a particular meaning to Fühmann's claim that "we who write letters to each other are what is in between" the two motionless zeros at either end of Parmenides' equation of Being. The articulation, the multiplicity, and the specificity of address allow letters to demonstrate the ontological fullness of corresponding with what is present, with what comes between Being's null points: letters call forth their proper audiences in the reciprocal recognition characteristic of epistolary exchange. Correspondence corresponds to an openness in events, which "grants to giving and receiving and to any evidence at all the free space in which they can remain and must move."[70] In his voluminous correspondence, which becomes more differentiated, direct, and intense as real socialism falters as his transcendental interlocutor, Fühmann does not conceive himself as writing to a universal public in the enlightenment sense of Kant or even Habermas's "public sphere." Rather, his two alternate correspondents are "the functionary," a blank singular with whom he stands in an attempted relationship of reciprocal "steering"; and "dysfunctionaries," a multiplicity of people who listen and respond, directly and intensely, when and where the signal system has collapsed into the meaningless iteration of slogans without reference.

In a May 1979 letter to the highest state functionary, Erich Honecker, protesting the punishment of Stefan Heym, Fühmann writes that he has "fears [. . .] that the measures against Stefan Heym go beyond a juridical framework and a framework of literary criticism to target the emergence of a literature that does not emanate from political-ideological utility or disadvantage, but from the undivided experience of the people of the German Democratic Republic."[71] At the same time as Fühmann dutifully writes to influence state measures in the direction of popular sovereignty, the Stasi is pursuing the operative case (*Operativer Vorgang*) against Fühmann that it initiated in February 1977: "[T]he handling of this case is carried out with the goal of verifying anti-state agitation in accordance with § 106 (1), nos. 2 and 3 of the penal code."[72] Five years after Fühmann's death when his operative case is finally shut down in April 1989, the responsible officer boasts about the operation's successes:

> as a result of this handling it has been conclusively (*beweiskräftig*) proved that Fühmann [. . .] strove for an open dialogue with the party and government about questions of power as well as the freedom and humanity of socialism. [. . .] Through isolation and neutralization measures (*Differenzierungs- und Zersetzungsmaßnahmen*) coordinated with the party and state apparatus, Fühmann was shown the limits to which his activity would be tolerated and was constantly disciplined and repeatedly prompted to socially appropriate behavior.[73]

The Stasi's assessment that it successfully steered Fühmann is as off the mark as Fühmann's "misguided belief that a dialogue with the apparatus was possible"[74]—it instantiates, rather, a characteristic GDR situation of mutual nonsteering. "Skewed lines [*windschiefe Gerade*] in intellectual space are experienced in every part of daily life," Fühmann instructs the children reading *Steaming Necks*, "as when one says: 'they are talking at cross-purposes.'"[75] What such lines spoken in nonintersecting planes do accomplish, however, is to keep the moment, the nonchronological duration, of emergence/emergency in aesthetic suspension, with a simultaneous feeling of laughter and dread.

In this suspension, Fühmann's other correspondence, the one with the dysfunctionaries of the GDR, takes on primary evidentiary significance for the socialist experience. As opposed to the constant progress of *chronos* in the Stasi's imagined temporality of socialist emergence, the dysfunctional correspondence marks the *kairos*, the right moment, of the operative case's permanent emergency. "The good god of writers," Fühmann writes Wolf in 1978, "will see to it that we find each other when we need each other. The most important thing is to be there at the right time."[76] Struck by reading Nietzsche's *Untimely Meditations* in 1979, Fühmann remarks to Wolf that "after some new publication, N. once said that the main thing is that the book find the twenty people for whom it matters, everything else is secondary, and that's really the case. We need each other, and probably it's the sense of this unholy epoch that it moves us toward one another."[77]

If evidence, as Heidegger maintains, shines through correspondence, then it is only in this latter correspondence that the correspondence actually corresponds—that is, it is in the correspondence addressed to the community of uncomfortable, even disturbed or outraged poets that some common law, some unity of socialist being radiates as present, as self-evident. This evidence, however, is not simply evidence of poetic revelation—an apocalypse in language—but it is also evidence in a juridical sense. In particular, the GDR state apparatus holds it to be evidence of "hostile-negative group formation," an act punishable according to §107 of the revised GDR penal code with a sentence more severe than that provided for under §106. A political conception like Carl Schmitt's in which the cohesive group takes on central significance—as friend or enemy, as source of the ultimate decision on the norm—returns here to define an undetermined conflict. And it is the status eventually accorded to the emerging group, the *Notgemeinschaft* (emergency association) that Fühmann discovers among the poets to whom he is drawn, that answers the question Fühmann so pointedly asks Wolf: "What is revolutionary in this society?"

Of the 3,644 existing pages of Stasi documentation on Fühmann (nine of twenty files were destroyed in 1989), the bulk of them are devoted to an "Anthology of Young Poets of the GDR" that Fühmann attempted to have assembled for the Academy of Arts at the end of 1981.[78] As politically harmless—in fact, one is tempted to say as proverbially harmless—as an anthology of poetry would seem to be, Fühmann's anthology, which drew together thirty poets born after 1940, set in motion the criminalization of much of the last generation of GDR poets under the rubric of §107.[79] Fühmann objects to rebukes of his "dissident collection," emphasizing that the group he drew together is not based on any political conception; rather, the collection seeks only to give the Academy of Arts "perspective on the factually existent forces of the generation."[80] Facts and evidence, not norms and slogans. It consists of texts "that articulated discontent with the state of society, that evidenced criticism, displeasure even disgruntlement, that raised embarrassing questions, confirmed unpleasantness, were averse to idylls, complacency and wishful thinking, in short, texts that accomplished what, by its very essence, the function of literature *also* is, not exclusively, but at least *also* is."[81] A Stasi report dated September 25, 1981, gives a concise and contrary assessment of what the collection is evidence of: it "is characterized by an aggressive, counterrevolutionary position vis-à-vis real socialism and its organs."[82] "Fühmann's intentions," moreover, "are to direct official instances to the 'injustice' of the Ministry of Culture and the Writers' Union that literary 'talent' has no possibilities for development in the GDR," notes another report dated October 6, 1981.[83]

Whenever Fühmann speaks of groupings within the GDR, he speaks of aesthetic formations whose indicative force is embodied in the fact of experience, not political programs. He tells the poet Margarete Hannsmann in 1980 that "the writers who went to and remained in the Soviet occupation zone, the later GDR, were all people innately unified by a specific political, social and even poetic program."[84] Born into a unity, Fühmann did not grow into a unity, but, unable to put doctrine before poetry, his continued presence in the GDR split the camp that made him who he was. Where others in the camp underwent the same division, "differentiations developed that clearly divided the unified group into groupings that perhaps were already laid down at the outset." Fühmann could only conceive his anthology in terms of the new correspondences miraculously forming among the next generation, the inevitable groupings that occasioned no righteous enmity—that is, that were not conceived of as groups along the relentless lines of §107—but a poetics of errant becoming like his *Primal Words*. "I never regarded Biermann as my enemy," he argues shortly before his death at an Academy of Arts meeting about the anthology. "He is an expression of the contradictions that exist in this society and that's just how we happen to be organized."[85] In the same way, but with distinct aesthetics, the young poets in the anthology

> do not form a group; the problematic of their works grows out of our life, the torturing and calming aspects of their questions stem from there, from reality, not from some kind of ill will, and it is this, the torturing, which cannot be eliminated from the world by literary-political restrictions, but only by changing social life, which is the indispensable contribution of this anthology. The common denominator of those represented in the anthology is thus their existence in the GDR, their experience, their talent, and their lacking opportunity to publish, and for these reasons they are drawn together in this anthology.[86]

In the face of the anthology's repression and the criminalization of many of its contributors, Fühmann is drawn to recognize the absurd complementary of socialist becoming and the becoming of individual socialists—the unity of this dual becoming, consisting of socialist institutional rationales on the one side and unsteerable socialist experiences on the other, is a unity only in the sense of a mutual incoherence, a joint unbecoming. There is no Aristotelian entelechy realizing its immanent organic *telos*; rather, there is an emerging situation whose off-kilter elements bear no relationship to the system responsible for their articulation. There is no unified scale to measure apples and oranges, no sense to fold them into an understandable account of fruit or round things or things people eat. The situation resembles the absurd list in Borges's "Chinese encyclopedia," about which Foucault famously commented that its monstrosity consists "in the fact that the common ground on which such meetings are possible has itself been destroyed. What is impossible is not the propinquity of the things listed, but the very site on which their propinquity would be possible"[87]—there are only straight lines pointing askew. Fühmann is long past expecting any contributor to his anthology to be following the straight and narrow in the sense of criminal law. "I plead, I implore you, esteemed President of the Supreme Court," Fühmann writes to the GDR's highest legal instance on behalf of an anthology author, Dieter Schulze, whose jail term for "endangering public order through asocial behavior" (§249) has just been extended for parole violation, "to believe me that it is impossible to guide Dieter Schulze to a life outside his poetry in the sense of the court verdict, and thus, as stated in the court opinion, 'to educate the accused with penal means and direct him to his duties.' It isn't possible, because the extraordinary—and indeed in the sense of what's 'normal'—abnormal personality of the poet is contrary to all such measures."[88]

The predominance of the abnormal over the normal in the groups to which Fühmann is drawn represents a condition that cannot be subject to the law, even the law of coherent groups—it is, on the contrary, evidence of law's inability to impute lawful intention to the socialist subject. Füh-

Fig. 5. HAP Grieshaber, *Cripple*, from the cycle *Basel Dance of Death*, 1966. © 2010 Artists Rights Society (ARS), New York/ VG Bild-Kunst, Bonn.

mann's "group formation" is not hostile-negative activity, activity according to some recognizable law of its own—even a principled liberal law in the sense of civil disobedience—but is the poetic manifestation of a general inability to assign legal responsibility to socialist protagonists (§15—*Zurechnungsunfähigkeit* or insanity). Not surprisingly, one of Fühmann's last and most impassioned projects was a pair of collaborations on young people with severe mental disabilities, *Was für eine Insel in was für einem Meer* (*What Kind of Island in What Kind of Sea*) with the photographer Dietmar Reimann, and *Der Engel der Geschichte Nr. 25: Der Engel der Behinderten* (*The Angel of History No. 25: The Angel of the Disabled*) with the graphic artist HAP Grieshaber. In *The Angel of the Disabled*, Fühmann comments on both Grieshaber's woodcuts and the young people experiencing them at an exhibit in the Fürstenwalde Samaritan Asylum. A woodcut called simply *Cripple* elicits a double recognition on the part of a young disabled man and Fühmann himself.

Fühmann's commentary:

> Willi, who until then hasn't been able to finish a single sentence, tells a whole story in front of the picture of the *Cripple*. [. . .] "Hhhhhhhhe wa-wa-wa-was

> i-i-in the war, a-a-and lo-lo-lo-lo-lo-lo-lost hi-hi-hi-his leg, a-a-a-a-a-and de-de-de-de- and death says: i-i-i-i" (a great effort by Willi, who's trembling, long pauses between the syllables, complete silence all around) "i-i-i-i-i-if you w-w-w-w-w-were there then you were also a so-so-so-soldier a-a-a-a-a-and then de-de-death s-s-s-s-s-s-s-s-says: are you coming?—A-a-a-a-and he s-s-s-s-s-says no! And I'm not coming!!"
>
> Severely disabled, Willi knows how fiercely the one-legged man clings to life. The cripple, a soldier in a crippled forest standing already at the Golgatha [*Schädelstätte*] of a mass grave, carries on his breast a strange tablet that has to be labeled, and the one who will inscribe it is none other than the person suddenly standing wordlessly beside him. The cripple has seen the hanged men in the trees and balconies, with cardboard signs on their breasts on which the executioners have written why they imagined they had the right to kill: *saboteur* or *cowardice in the face of the enemy* or *Jew*.[89]

Here, standing at the heart of Fühmann's abnormal emergency community, as its messenger, is a cripple bearing a placard intended for the slogan that will proclaim the ultimate sense of its members' activity. But the placard has not been inscribed—it remains vacant. There is no rallying cry in sight, for or against the group. Of course, it is Fühmann's own postcard from May 1980 haunting the blank placard in the crippled forest, hinting to readers and correspondents what might be written there—suggesting the possibilities corresponding to his card's front and back. On its back, the postcard proposes a catastrophic present, a turning point in socialism recapitulating both the 1945 fascist capitulation among mass graves and Stalin's *lager' voyennoplennych*. One imagines the cripple's placard either scrawled with the verdict "I WAS A WAR CRIMINAL" or fit with a larger-than-life portrait of a smiling Stalin. On the front of the postcard, meanwhile, the banner emblazoned with the first cultural norm of socialist emergence suggests the cripple's other verdict: "No real socialism thinkable without culture and art!" In this inscription, however, the complacent norm is reconfigured into the hostile threat to which the sovereign state must respond, and the optimistic slogan now supplies the reason why the state imagines it has the right to kill.

But the most excruciating evidence being weighed in Fühmann's scales is the simple fact that the placard remains blank, marking the impossibility of either possible inscription to pronounce the final verdict on socialist emergence/emergency. The placard remains *forcefully* blank, a last piece of nonsense suspended "over the place of the skull." In the end, not an artwork, but a pragmatic, quasi-legal 1982 Stasi report on a briefing with the secretary of the Ministry of Culture, Kurt Löffler, crisply formulates the sentence that Fühmann, with his passionate institutional commitment to socialism—nonsense and all—could not pronounce: "Fühmann is increasingly adopting the behavior of a mentally disabled person," the report notes. "Fühmann feels himself drawn to people who are already undergoing psychiatric treatment. [. . .] Comrade Löffler calculates that sooner or later committing Fühmann to an institution will become unavoidable and a political appreciation of that by hostile forces is to be expected."[90]

CHAPTER EIGHT

Plans, Leaps, Heaps:
The Measure of the Human

There is no cybernetic system so constituted that it can in its totality represent both socialism and capitalism.

—Georg Klaus, "Cybernetics and Ideological Class War"[1]

By no boundary
Separated
We cry out to each other
The slogan:
THE GREAT PLAN WILL BE ACHIEVED

—Johannes R. Becher, *The Great Plan*[2]

I. SYSTEM AND SOVEREIGNTY

The cybernetic philosopher Georg Klaus (1912–74), whose functional conceptualization of law and norms I discussed in the previous chapter, is not a figure whose legacy is much celebrated since the end of the Cold War. A communist from the age of seventeen, he was promptly arrested when the Nazis came to power for organizing resistance in upper Bavaria, spending five years from 1933 to 1939 as a political prisoner, three of them in the Dachau concentration camp (where he mastered mental chess, later becoming a top-ranked international champion). Amnestied on Hitler's birthday, he was subsequently drafted into the *Wehrmacht* and served on the Eastern Front until being wounded; engaged again on the Western Front, he was taken prisoner in Belgium at the end of the war. Moving to the Eastern zone after his release to organize for the party and study logic, he cosponsored the 1951 Jena Logic Conference, notably defending the goal of "mathematizing dialectical logic"—a goal met with a mixture of lack of interest and dismissal at the time.[3] A decade later, when the Wall went up, his work on cybernetic theory deeply influenced the economic reforms of the1960s.[4] As director of the Philosophical Institute at Humboldt University, he assumed the mantle of most influential East German philosopher previously held by Ernst Bloch, who—discredited for "theology," "mysticism," and "existentialism" in the aftermath of the Hungarian uprising[5]—fled the GDR in 1961. The switch in temper from the messianic Bloch to Klaus, the proponent of mathematical logic and operations research, itself tells a story about the fluctuation in socialist self-understanding between pathetic class-struggle and optimistic pragmatism. The ascendancy of functionalist systems theory in the heady days of the GDR's second founding after the construction of the Wall was hardly enduring, however, since functionalism's fortunes are so closely related to the successful functioning it promises. Its test, in Karl Popper's sense of setting up falsifiable claims, is more sharply defined than that faced by either Marxist orthodoxy or ecstatic Blochian heterodoxy. Klaus's star thus hitched to the failed New Economic System (NÖS) of the 1960s, his obscurity today contrasts with the star of Bloch's secular theology, arisen again in the night of real socialism.

As radical as was Klaus's introduction of mathematical logic into the self-conscious precincts of Hegelian dialectics, and as unheard-of his broaching heretical thought by the likes of Carnap, Quine, and Norbert Wiener, his immanence in the practical organization of socialism consigns him to the same negligibility that has befallen socialist planned economies generally after the Cold War. The GDR, after all, failed on potent scales of modernity: it did not create a lasting state based on popular legitimation, it did not accumulate enough material wealth to challenge the liberal market model of development, and it did not reveal desirable new standards for the quality of life. "When standards are chosen to assess the quality of life of people in different parts of the world," caution Martha Nussbaum and Amartya Sen, "one has to ask whose views as to the criteria should be decisive. Should we . . . look to the local traditions of the country . . . or should we, instead, seek some more universal account of good human living . . . ?"[6] Regarded locally or universally, the GDR experience offers little by way of new standards, hence the broad judgment on its failure, and the oblivion to which a versatile thinker like Klaus is assigned.[7]

Momentarily setting aside the question of new socialist standards for the quality of life, I want to consider how Klaus's systems theory circles around a stubborn gap in the very criteria of modernity that in fact decided (on) the outcome of the Cold War and now seem so self-evident. These are such familiar criteria as openness, pluralism, experimentalism, and incrementalism, the same criteria warily celebrated by Max Weber as constitutive of the disenchanted modern worldview and emphatically celebrated by Karl Popper as the bulwark of the open society.[8] The cybernetic episode of real socialism—stretching back to the "socialist economic calculation" debates of the 1920s and 1930s (Neurath, von Mises, Lange, Hayek) and forward to Salvador Allende's Cybersin telex system in Chile in the early 1970s[9]—helps us see that the criteria that were efficient causes in determining the Cold War outcome have to be distinguished from the criteria by which that outcome was subsequently judged as valid or just, and that those latter teleological criteria cannot comprehend and supersede the functionalist distinctions relevant to the former. Whether or not the GDR's standards for building and assessing a modern quality of life fit Nussbaum's and Sen's view of universality, they were on the face of it congruent with the standards of the West; what was different was the social complex whose function was to maximize over those recognizable standards. Simultaneously with some of real socialism's most pathetic invocations of human solidarity—ostensibly better suited to revolutionary urgency than post-revolutionary construction—came an uneasy overlaying of affective with functional standards, whereby the essence of "socialist construction" came to be located increasingly in a technical infrastructure rather than in a rallying for justice.

After the Berlin Wall went up and before the Prague Spring was beaten down, socialism enjoyed a strained, but marked interval of design creativity, in which the great historical left-right distinction seemed to turn on empirical questions about organizing political economy, rather than value questions per se. Values like liberty, equality, and solidarity were, even if only in a sloganeering sense, the professed goals of both East and West; the left-right political question instead concerned the empirical frameworks for instantiating and maximizing them. What made the Cold War nonetheless so passionate in this period, fueling both its hopeless creativity and scheming violence, was the sense that the qualitative rupture bisecting modernity into "first" and "second" worlds took place at the level of operative totality. Whatever the diversity and plurality, continuity and incrementality that one may have imputed to one's preferred system, the difference between the two worlds was characterized by an unbridgeable gap, one that each system presupposed with a force rivaled only by that with which it denied the same gap any place inside its own precincts. The challenge socialist modernity posed—and still poses as a legacy—is not the challenge of alternate criteria per se, but of understanding how roughly the same criteria could refer to two distinct systems of modernity and to the qualitative difference between those systems.[10]

In a manner suggestive for the way I am addressing the problem, Walter Benjamin once asked whether, after translating from one language into another, a translator could ever hope to find a third language into which the difference between the two translations could itself be translated.[11] When compared with the deliberateness of translation, the beautiful elusiveness of the difference it makes is surprising and mysterious, belonging to neither the one language nor the other. Likewise Klaus and Fühmann, responsive to the measurable presentation of daily life in East Germany, are nonetheless driven to consider the possibility of apprehending an underlying qualitative distinction between their system and that of the West, a distinction embracing both a present actuality and an inherent potential for the future. The Aristotelian notion for present actuality, *energeia* (being-for-itself), as we saw in the last chapter, receives a twist in the hands of Heidegger, who suggests that it be understood not as an empirical fact, a datum given by technical means, but as a kind of self-evidence, anterior to judgment and available only on the basis of a withdrawal of selfhood into a pure deixis of being. Potential—what Aristotle called *dynamis* (being-in-itself)—is for Heidegger an existential tendency, a bringing-forth that is not obscured by present actuality, but comes into view with the fateful event that ultimately is *enargeia* or *evidentia*, the vivid clarity of the thing itself. As impeccably modern as Klaus's and Fühmann's sensibilities are, their attention as socialists is irresistibly drawn to this sort of miraculous *evidentia* when modern forbearance will have paid off as something wholly unprecedented. "In the evolution of matter," argues Klaus against the "neo-positivists," "there are dialectical leaps so characterized that beyond the leap new regularities [*Gesetzmäßigkeiten*] emerge."[12] To allude again to the vacillating fortunes of Klaus and Bloch, it seems that as impassive as the operationalist idiom is, it stakes its vast calm on a quasi-theological moment of uncertain temporality in which the interlocking feedback loops of the socialist plan are disclosed as providence, and quantitative flux suddenly appears ex nihilo as qualitative transformation.

The problem of whether universal regulative criteria can ever do justice to an all-important quality of difference, a basic intellectual challenge of planned societies, already emerges in a simple and powerful formulation in Plato's *Protagoras*.[13] Inquiring into the possibility of living a consistent, holistic good life—a well-ordered life, where well-ordering implies the commensurable ranking and coordination of priorities[14]—Socrates poses the paradox known as *akrasia*: if I am offered a choice between two goods, where one is apparently greater than the other, would I not always choose the greater good? Yet one easily imagines cases where I choose against my better judgment, picking for example one wine over another of superior vintage since I like the way it happens to reflect the evening; in other words, I am drawn to some *qualia* of the light, a particular way that it seems to me. Plato resolves the paradox by explaining my weakness, or *akrasia*, as plain ignorance, because the light, an accidental, incommensurable quality, has distracted me from ranking my priorities with respect to a disciplined discernment of the greater and lesser good of comparable values.[15] A science of measurement (*metretike techne*) would allow people to make reasonable, far-sighted choices consistently in their own and society's best interests by bringing all possible choices into relation with each other on a common yardstick and thus allowing for a rational ethical decision over the whole.[16]

One consequence for socialism of this classical solution might be readily apparent. In a state organized around a planned economy, a science of measurement by which individual desires are rationally and ethically coordinated would surely give planners an edge over nonscientifically organized capitalist competition on the basis of market prices. The plan, in this sense, would be a complete, providential metric, obviating any unintentional or naive *akrasia*, whereas unplanned capitalism would be short-sighted and impulsive, based on the exploitation of weakness and desire. The problem of weakness could thus be rephrased. From pertaining to one bad choice in the Platonic formulation, it could now be seen as arising from two encompassing metrics, price and plan, where one entire metric is revealed as weaker than the other.

The version of the problem that concerns us here, however, takes another direction—in fact, just the opposite direction. It focuses on the existential question of whether a purely qualitative plan is possible and if so, what difference it makes. That is what is so knotty about the problem: presumably it makes all the difference in the world, since difference is precisely that quality which is outside any given metric. Unmediated quality is, in Plato's sense, weakness itself. The socialist paradox thus becomes building a metric on that which falls outside of metrics. A series of questions helps suggest the puzzles involved with the very idea of a qualitative plan. If there is a commensurability of values across modernity, in East as in West, socialism as in capitalism, is there room for a qualitative difference between the two systems, and how would one recognize or describe that quality in the standardized terms of commensurability? Moreover, is the desire for that quality—for a qualitative experience outside the proportions of measure—merely submission to weakness per se, a deep, one might say diabolical, desire for abjection in the face of order? On the other hand, if the first premise does not hold and there is in fact no common yardstick supplied by modernity, then are there any rational means for each system to establish its own qualitatively unique measure and prosper in solipsistic autarchy? Finally, if each system does somehow foster its own valid measure, is there ever any reasonable way to choose among systems, or, because the choice is undecidable a priori (a metric is a metric) is the multiplicity of systems simply evidence of irreducible sovereignty and force?

Highlighting the tension between sovereignty and system, this last question helps clarify how the idea of choice central to the *akrasia* paradox, when it is considered in a social context, is related to technical economic problems. Market economies are, in classical theory, frameworks for individual rational choice—the very precondition for the emergence of the *enkratic* (self-controlled) modern subject capable of rationally saving, investing, and consuming according to the self-generated information conveyed by prices with no need for lord or master.[17] Socialism, however, claims to expose money and markets as anything but the transparent frameworks, the pure *metretike techne*, they are said to be. Rather, money mediates a system that favors capital accumulation over communal good—money becomes a cynical end in itself, rather than a means to human welfare. Socialism aspires to institute the plan (that is, conscious cooperation) as this more essential (that is, *enkratic*) means. But how, on a concrete, technical level, would this collective intention go about reaching its decisions—what are the plan's all-sided criteria for maximizing the common good without concession to the momentary, partial, or capricious? The issue can be put neatly with reference to the economic calculation debate mentioned above (and discussed in Chapter 2) that presaged socialism's concern with cybernetics. If a firm, whether in capitalism or socialism, whether run by a rapacious industrialist or an anarchist collective, wants to make a decision about buying new equipment, introducing an innovative process or product, increasing or decreasing output—how is it going to decide what to do? What useful information does it have at its disposal? And if information, at least in the technical sense, is deemed irrelevant to deeper considerations of welfare and collective identity, then how does one know on the public level whether one has made the right decision—that is, in default (willing or unwilling) of quantitative metrics, how does one go about assessing one's qualitative opportunities?[18]

The question is so tricky because it concerns not just the balance of materials but also their relationship to, and especially their desirability for, real people. For example, if we equate bricks and rubies in terms of weight (1 gram of ruby = 1 gram of brick), while we thus relate two kinds of things, we do not realistically relate them to us and our desires. There is a technical calculus, but no hedonistic one. For economy to be a social system, however, then whatever metric we arrive at, quantitative or qualitative, it has to relate not just things to things, but things to people, and people to people. A sovereign decision on bricks and rubies, by an autonomous board, accompanied by great pathos of solidarity (workers don't need rubies!), might guide a firm through one juncture or another; it might even plastically shape the desires of those subject to it, and in that broader (perhaps Foucauldian) sense be a "rational" decision.[19] But what happens as the firm's inputs dwindle because other firms' autarchic decisions bear no cross-reference to the first firm's needs? A system for comparison and relation is required, and if it is not one given by quantitative measures like money and prices, then it must be one given by qualitative measures, by some sort of authentic natural kind. Of such natural kinship, allowing different things to be compared as innately similar, Quine observes that "we cannot easily imagine a more familiar or fundamental notion than this, or a notion more ubiquitous in its applications. On this score it is like the notions of logic: like identity, negation, alternation, and the rest. And yet, strangely, there is something logically repugnant about it. For we are baffled when we try to relate the general notion of similarity significantly to logical terms."[20] As those who have tried to imagine modern economies based on in-kind exchange discovered, from Otto Neurath in his path-breaking World War I–era studies on "natural economics" to socialism's later material balance theorists, the intuitive similarity that allows us spontaneously to compare like kinds with like kinds proves stubbornly elusive to logical formulation.[21] An ineradicable vagueness seems to adhere to such comparisons that makes wide systemic coordination all but impossible, compelling us to ask whether such a natural metric, intimate with the *energeia* of things and yet able at the same time to order the affairs of people, exists at all. In other words, and this is the crucial question, is it possible to invert the *akrasia* paradox, such that yielding to pure qualitative temptation, pure relation of kind, is always the superior path to calculating our systemic advantages? What a world of pure sensuous abandon that would be! Were such an (anti)metric discovered, providing all the innovation and coordination, expenditure and release that quantification provides, would we recognize its advent, given that its order would be so unimaginably different from our own?

The emphasis on fundamentally distinct orders—plans versus markets, logic versus similarity—is crucial here, because it suggests that a consensus around rational, open, experimental (that is, modern) categories is not enough to ensure peaceful transitions between systems and rational communication about rival measures. Rather, material or qualitative differences persist as dynamic disequilibria that always threaten force, without necessarily entailing its cataclysmic application. The once-parallel modernity of real socialism, it is clear, did not succeed in setting new qualitative criteria by which it could operate as a system among others, with autarchy, complexity, and the potential to reproduce itself and its own way of seeing and parsing the world. Haunted by the insufficiency of its difference from the West, intensifying its boundary performances as the boundary became ever less attached to the system, real socialism nonetheless has the enduring merit of attesting to the nonuniqueness of modernity. It raises, in a rational idiom, deep problems about organizing society that are compelling, but perennially invisible, to our own. Furthermore, since the end of the Cold War, the issue of qualitative discontinuities between systems has refused to disappear in a liberal narrative of the end of history and perpetual peace.[22] As the problem of qualitative difference has re-emerged in another set of conflictual social relations, discourses of rational commensurability—concerning, for example, technology-driven globalization, representative democracy, or international law—have been shaken by those of executive sovereignty and military force.

The nonuniqueness of modernity is a basic paradox for a technical-rational thought, hence the peculiar anguish of socialism's double vision of itself in its difference from the West. For if modernity is equal to its own description as open and experimental, then it is a superlative of social evolution, without any weakness, and the superlative is always a definite singular. According to Popper, the Cold War's most eminent theoretician of science and society, modernity's openness is epitomized by its restless falsification of all its provisional truth claims, leaving only the best standing. Modernity in the rational, progressivist account drops what fails and selects what succeeds, describing the latest and best we have: the optimum, if not the *optimum optimorum*, for the world. If socialism was also a rational modernity whose *metretike techne* excluded weakness, then it was somehow once contemporaneous with the present singular modernity from which we survey our globe today; it was, then, also once a superlative of time and space, the latest and the most forward. Not an "insimultaneity of time" in Ernst Bloch's famous formulation for the imbrication of old and new worlds, but precisely a "simultaneity," simultaneous and sharply distinct.[23] It then bears asking how a position—an x, y, z at time *t*—that claims for itself the singularity of the most advanced and fitting could have been shared by an x', y', z' that makes the same legitimating claim?

Lest I be taken as appealing to too narrow and rationalist a definition of modernity in defining its singular, progressive path, even so epochal a critic of logical positivism and scientific reductionism as Edmund Husserl argued that "to be human at all is essentially to be a human being in a socially and generatively united civilization; and if man is a rational being, it is only insofar as his whole civilization is a rational civilization [. . .]." European modernity must bear within it, according to Husserl, "an absolute idea, rather than being merely an empirical anthropological type like 'China' or 'India,'"[24] or, I might add, like the East or West bloc. Can two or more proper modernities then be thinkable, coordinated within by the same rational values, but separated from each other by a gap that cannot be described, let alone forded, in accordance with those values? Are there questions that socialism—that is, modernity *prime*—asks of itself that are as universal as they are untranslatable into the circumstances, if not the idiom, of our most contemporaneous present? Can this briefly multiplied modernity—the existential possibility of a radically different way of answering our same urgent questions—ever be resolved back into a single immanent process, into a single open community of reason and transparency, or does modernity prime always haunt our progress as an invisible road not taken?

2. CYBERNETIC MATHEMATIZATION AND QUALITATIVE LEAPS

"All modern states plan," notes the historian Peter Caldwell, but "specific to state socialism was the quasi-metaphysical status of 'the plan,' a symbol around which the entire political and economic structure of that world was built. [. . .] It had a metaphysical status in the sense that within the planning regime the notion of the plan itself was immune to empirical criticism."[25] If, as I noted in the previous chapter, the law figures as the reigning spirit of the bourgeois revolution, then in socialism the plan assumes law's pride of place as the ultimate horizon of socialist self-understanding. At real socialism's dawn Neurath had already argued that "we can show that love, harmony, devotion to the suprapersonal do not merely find shelter somewhere in socialism, but are furthered by its organizational form and even develop most closely together with the economic plan and calculation in kind which we otherwise know only as cold institutions."[26]

In the GDR, however, this supreme institution of socialism was denied its own clearly delineated operational field by the porous and contested border with the West. If the system could reasonably be expected to produce its own border as a seamless extension of itself, it still required sufficient environmental stability to take proper hold. In 1961 at a crucial turning point for an industrial world already divided into two hostile Cold War blocs, East German party chief Walter Ulbricht commanded the erection of the Berlin Wall. It was a boundary performance only questionably related to system performance, but it seemed to be what was needed. With this sharp demarcation of East and West German sovereignty, Ulbricht's Politburo was convinced that East Germany at last had the breathing room necessary to build socialism, and proceeded to encourage a reformist spirit to experiment with organizations capable of maximizing the GDR's potential for innovation.[27] In 1963 the Council of Ministers announced "Guidelines for the New Economic System of Planning and Managing the People's Economy" (NÖS). Over the next seven years, until Ulbricht was deposed by Honecker in 1971, state organs repeated that "the basic task that our Party, the GDR working class, and its allied classes must solve today is mastering the socialist economy and the scientific-technical revolution."[28] Associated with this revolution was not just the development of new engineering cadre, technological processes, and industrial machinery, but the scientific organization of production, exchange, administration, education, and politics in socialist society—in short, the very idea of planning could be and had to be thought anew.

The task of coordinating society on a new basis ultimately fell to the emerging information science of cybernetics to solve. Politburo economic chief Günter Mittag reiterated how "Comrade Ulbricht emphasized at the 7th Party Congress the fundamental importance of cybernetics for the developed system of socialism."[29] The use of cybernetics for this hallowed purpose is not obvious. First developed in the United States in the 1940s and 1950s by Norbert Wiener, Claude Shannon, and John von Neumann,[30] it implied to many critics in the socialist world an abandonment of the Marxist vision of a practice based in the experience of class struggle in favor of "system-neutral," "value-free" technocratic reason. The rivalry between technical and political rationality for preeminence in shaping socialist society was bitter. The eventual acceptance of cybernetics by the party hierarchy in the mid-1960s meant that social subsystems would *in principle* be left to find their own efficient means of developing and coordinating themselves, and would not rely on steering mechanisms based outside the feedback loops of system optimization; would not, that is, rely on ideologically governed party decisions, but on self-generated information.[31] The very metaphysical significance of planning, the conscious process that guaranteed the difference and superiority of socialism, was being transformed—a change that carried with it all the anxiety that tampering with metaphysical certainties brings. The buzz words for ascendant cyberneticians were *self-organization*, *self-reproduction*, *automatic steering*, *automatic coordination*, and *goal orientation*[32]—not exactly comforting words to ideologically oriented functionaries.

The entry for "goal orientation" (*Zielstrebigkeit*) in the 1969 *Dictionary of Cybernetics* edited by Klaus, then the director of the Institute for Philosophy at the Academy of Sciences, notes that "if we could observe just the effect of disruptions and the oscillation of system values around the target state (goal), it would be impossible to decide whether the coordination mechanism were a mechanical element or whether its functions were being exercised by a human-being."[33] This definition refers to Alan Turing's pioneering essays on artificial intelligence in which a machine has the capacity not only to reproduce itself but also to evolve to a higher level.[34] Klaus elaborates the definition by contrast to the Aristotelian teleological doctrine he sees cybernetics as superseding, regarding a dynamic system as capable of realizing a potential (*dynamis*) not observed, measured, or caused by its current state (*entelechy*, *energeia*), but constructed solely through the reciprocal causality of system and environment (see "reciprocal causality" [*Wechselwirkung*]). With the Berlin Wall buffering it from overwhelming disruption by a hostile environment, Klaus and his allies in the Politburo hoped that the cybernetic "black box" of the New Economic System would not only run smoothly, but evolve intelligently toward an interactive goal of ever more simply organized complexity, GDR subsystems regulating themselves according to their adaptive dynamics (see "autoregulation" [*selbsttätige Regelung*]). As the entry on "Trial and Error" notes, "[M]any organic cybernetic systems have failed because they did not have time to reach an adaptation."[35] Cement Wall and cybernetic reform promised socialism that adaptive time.

Alas, as the decade wore on the Wall did not do the trick for the New Economy. Although it seemed to protect it from "external dialectical contradictions," it could not save it from its own "internal dialectical contradictions,"[36] where "oscillations become ever stronger, eventually leading the system beyond its stability boundaries until its quality is destroyed," as Klaus's *Dictionary* cybernetically reformulates the Marxist notion of dialectical contradiction.[37] The contradiction that a system whose essential quality was meant to be the nonalienated species being of humanity should be regulated by a mechanism that was indifferently human or machine was too much for a Marxist party to adapt to: contradictions on that scale were best left for the West to choke on. So, with the abandonment of New Economic System in 1971, "the non-political coordination of individual economic and social interests fell in favor of exclusively political-ideological steering,"[38] effectively terminating socialism's—I cite the entry for "self organization"—"capacity . . . to improve its structure either to attain greater stability or to defend its internal milieu better and more purposefully against environmental disruptions or inner depreciation."[39]

Highlighting the changes of tone and emphasis that emerge in Klaus's publicity work on behalf of cybernetics helps clarify how the difficulties raised by the New Economic System relate to the problems of rational measurement and qualitative difference in modernity. In 1960 Klaus published an article in the Communist Party's national press organ *Neues Deutschland* in which he tentatively offers a cybernetic worldview to a socialist public while showing appropriate deference to the views of official materialist philosophy. By 1967, when the New Economic System was enjoying strong official support, this tentative depiction of a worldview had become Klaus's confident prediction of cybernetic success in an interview in *Einheit*, the theoretical organ of the Party Central Committee. The cycle continued, however, with Klaus's embattled defense of cybernetics in 1970 when the conservative handwriting on the wall was already legible, shortly before Ulbricht's, and the New Economics System's, defeat. The paradoxes encountered over these ten years describe deep-seated challenges socialism poses to itself that are simultaneously unanswered challenges to an undivided conception of modernity. Though the systemic antinomies of socialism are fundamentally different than those generated by the liberal market system, the value scale in which they are addressed is familiar: modernity calibrated in the rational units of equality, freedom, and prosperity. Klaus's predicament illustrates the deep discrepancies these values are unable either to apprehend or to ignore.

In his 1960 *Neues Deutschland* article "Control Circuits and Organisms," Klaus reasons more ideologically than scientifically in popularizing cybernetics, which was still being attacked in many circles as a bourgeois pseudoscience and only just beginning to find official patronage.[40] Describing the roots of cybernetic theory in engineering technology, he goes on to explain how the technical regularities of cybernetics effectively apply to the organic world, elaborating the importance of humanlike computing and feedback mechanisms for organizing complex systems. "It is characteristic of cybernetics that it subjects to quantitative observation many process that were assumed to be only qualitatively comprehensible."[41] Such optimistic faith in technological quantification was possible in what was, after all, the dawning computer-enabled space age and the age of industrial automation, and Klaus had only to point to the success of the Soviet Sputnik to find confirmation for his hopes. The ideological task of the article, however, was not simply to commend cybernetics' capabilities for integrating technology and human society, but more subtly, to not *over*praise cybernetics lest it be seen as a pretender to dialectical materialism's role as the truly human arbiter of the sciences. Throughout the article he cautions against overextending analogies between machines and human intelligence. The idea that self-regulating machines could replace party-stipulated plans might easily have been seen as sacrificing the very *raison d'être* for a nonmarket economy—namely, that irreducible human priorities, self-consciously deliberated, assume control over the hitherto blind mechanisms of economics. Or, to put the stakes in terms familiar in Western debates, the risk was that cybernetics might be taken as a proposal for allowing the quantitative "system-world" to dominate over the qualitative "life-world." Thus, Klaus aims tactically to limit the capabilities that one might ascribe to smart machines: while it must be recognized that in some sense the new robots can think like humans, they nonetheless "cannot think *dialectically*," he concedes.[42] They can thus serve, but not replace human dialectical materialism. Klaus's argument limits the use of cybernetics to the pragmatic goal of most efficiently realizing the party's politically determined aims.

Yet there is a deep implication to Klaus's argument. What is it about dialectical thought that is not matched by cybernetic feedback circuits? The dialectic of quality and quantity, significantly, begins Hegel's *Logic*.[43] Being, according to Hegel, begins as quality given to the senses without mediation. It assumes its first mediation as a specific quantity of what is apprehended. Quantity, however, always threatens to negate Being as purely external to it. "Number is a thought," Hegel writes, "but thought in its complete self-externalization. Because it is a thought, it does not belong to perception."[44] Only in a dialectical third term—measure—do qualitative perception and quantitative apprehension overcome their opposition.

> Measure, where quality and quantity are in one is thus the completion of Being. Being, as we first apprehend it, is something utterly abstract and characterless; but it is the very essence of Being to characterize itself, and its complete characterization is reached in Measure. Measure, like the other stages of Being, may serve as a definition of the Absolute: God, it has been said, is the Measure of all things.[45]

By conceding dialectics to human beings, in particular to those organized in the Communist Party, Klaus suggests that cybernetics, while driven by information, quantification, and coordination, still seeks its valid measure outside its own abstract networks. That measure is given by the party. A society organized on socialist party principles, therefore, has no reason to fear cybernetic technocracy. The crucial question left hanging, however, is exactly how the party is to establish modernity's universal measure, the synthesis of what is qualitatively new about socialism and what is quantitatively commensurate across its various social tasks. It might be the case that in a world without God, the party takes the alternate course and becomes the Devil who, disobeying thermodynamic law, creates order out of disorder; becomes, that is, the "demon" James Clerk Maxwell famously proposed to turn back the tide of entropy, "a being whose faculties are so sharpened that he can follow every molecule in its course; such a being, whose attributes are as essentially finite as our own, would be able to do what is impossible to us."[46] Indeed, the promethean image of a demonic party flouting the capitalist laws of entropy—business cycles, depressions, fascism, war—to create order out of catastrophe appeals to long-standing socialist mythologies. The problem is that this red Satan, although finite and without the trappings of the omniscient divine, still exceeds the humanly possible. Its miraculous creation of law against the law starts to look less like the sovereign party and more like the groundless cybernetic system whose measure it was supposed to give. In fact, the cybernetic pioneer Heinz von Foerster explicitly connects Maxwell's demon to cybernetic systems, contending that "the 'Turing Machine' [. . .] and Maxwell's demon are functional isomorphs or, to put it differently, [. . .] the machine's computational competence and the demon's ordering talents are equivalent."[47] The immanent transcendence of Hegel's Absolute Knowledge might turn out to be a mere reciprocating machine after all.

By the time of his 1967 *Einheit* interview, Klaus is ready to chart a more ambitious agenda for cybernetics. He emphasizes the urgency, and the opportunity, of establishing what he calls "a new style of thought . . . corresponding to the time and the concrete requirements of the plan-based application of modern sciences, especially mathematics."[48] After touching on the importance of developing a "Marxist semiotics" in order to make socialist ideas "maximally effective," Klaus turns to cybernetics as the key to realizing Marx's eleventh thesis on Feuerbach. "In that we maximally scientifically shape the activity of human beings, we fill the imperative Marx set out in his famous Feuerbach theses: the philosophers have only variously interpreted the world, the point however is to change it."[49] With all the maximization invoked by Klaus's rhetoric, and his overtly technocratic recasting of Marx's sacred thesis, engraved in gilt over the Humboldt University grand stairway, well-ordered technical reason is clearly gaining the upper hand over wily dialectical thought. The colorless world of maximization formulae toward which Klaus's technocratic euphoria is propelling him evokes the previous epoch's crisis of positive science, diagnosed by Husserl as a situation in which the living world of sights and sounds are obliviously reduced to the bare bones of logical system. "The material plena—the 'specific' sense-qualities—which concretely fill out the spatiotemporal shape-aspects of the world of bodies *cannot*, in their own gradation, be directly treated as are [ideal geometric] shapes themselves. Nevertheless, these qualities, and everything that makes up the concreteness of the sensibly intuited world, must count as manifestations of an 'objective' world."[50] Husserl fears that the progressive subordination of the world to a Platonic "metretike techne," a science of measurement, leads not to overcoming the opposition between quality and quantity, but to the effacement of qualitative existence in the name of a spurious objectivity.

Klaus, however, essentially now the GDR's philosopher-in-chief, confidently reclaims socialism's proper measure from the all-too-human party for the mathematized perfection of cybernetics—since mathematics seems to be the purest way for it to secure its advantage over the chaotic capitalist market. "The relationship between quantity and quality is described exactly by mathematics and logic," the *Dictionary* indicates.[51] Accordingly, Klaus observes to his *Einheit* interviewer that "in the complex imbrication of nested cybernetic systems" that make up the emerging socialist world, only cybernetic theory truly addresses "the unity of laws of socialist development."[52] Such an assertion of cybernetic sovereignty can be followed up by the interviewer only with an awed question about cybernetics' insight into "the essence of socialism's social laws."[53] Klaus answers by describing a once insurmountable philosophical paradox that socialist cybernetics now dissolves. On the one hand, the individual human is the subject of objective laws; in a modern society, the laws of information, coordination, and control. On the other hand, the free individual creatively participates in shaping these laws.[54] For Klaus, cybernetics is able to dissolve the ancient paradox and simultaneously illuminate the essence of socialism's social laws by recasting the dialectic of necessity and freedom in game theoretical terms. At socialism's core, then, is a resourceful game in which each player follows a five-year plan and at the same time creatively shapes the plan in anticipation of the other players' decisions. For him, no high-spirited game could

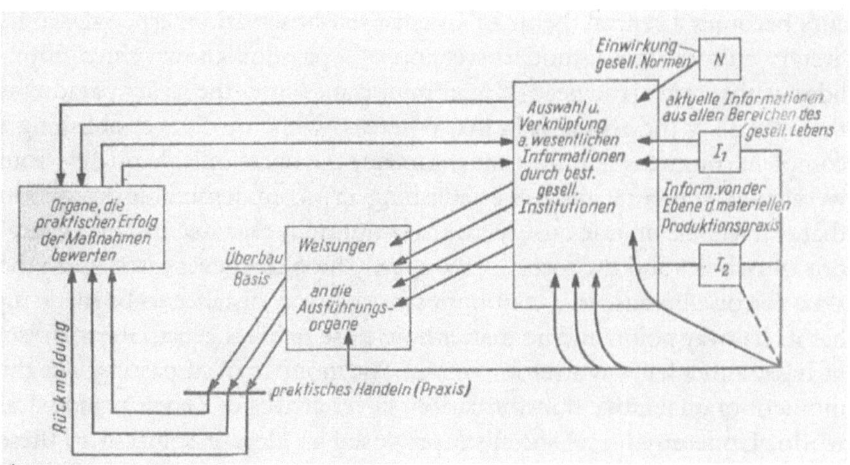

Fig. 6. Klaus's Schema for the Correspondence of Individual and Total System. Source: Georg Klaus, *Kybernetik und Gesellschaft*, 2nd ed. (Berlin: Verlag der Wissenschaften, 1965) 332.

be more different from capitalism's hostile, chaotic, and counterproductive competition, whose rules, precisely because they are unplanned, are the equivalent of natural laws to which the individual is merely subject.

The resolved paradox of necessity and freedom gives way, however, to another paradox, that of continuity and discontinuity.[55] On the one hand, cybernetics is a "more exact and modern mode of thought," and Klaus everywhere emphasizes its precision. Its goal is to mathematize social processes, as the ideal form of quantification, so as to control them more accurately, and, ultimately, to coordinate them as a single non-self-contradictory process—namely, as socialism. Klaus, as we have seen, is now quite willing to suggest, as he had as a doctoral student in 1951, that dialectics can be mathematized; that the organic-robotic split of the 1960 *Neues Deutschland* article no longer applies. "Mathematics," he now asserts, "can well grasp and represent the essence of things, the quality of things."[56] On the other hand, the very precision and mathematical exhaustiveness of cybernetic control is designed to produce a "discontinuous leap" in human potential.[57] That is, the intensification of quantification in each aspect of life, plus the homogenization of measurement across subsystems, leads not to mechanistic stasis, but on the contrary to a discontinuous release of potential that is qualitative and, as such, essentially unquantifiable ("transformation of quantitative change into qualitative"[58]).

The problem of exactly how, when, and where this qualitative leap occurs becomes a central theme of socialist self-observation, especially in its literary culture. It is a modern version of a paradox known since Eubulides as the *sorites* (the heap). In an important sense, the *sorites* paradox is the obverse of the *akrasia* paradox. Whereas *akrasia* involves establishing a complete commensurability that eliminates the unassimilable quality from its calculus, the *sorites* involves establishing an incommensurable distinction that extracts the unique quality from a continuous calculus. In Zeno's paradox of Achilles and the tortoise, the speedy hero can never catch up to the slow tortoise because in a continuous world every distance to be made up has its halfway point, and no matter how close Achilles gets to the tortoise, he has another halfway stretch to cover. The moment of surpassing, like the moment of qualitative transformation, never arrives in Zeno's paradoxical world. Undeterred, real socialism proposed an elegant solution to these Eleatic conundrums that blossomed miraculously across GDR billboards in the late 1960s. The answer is nothing other than the inescapable slogan Ulbricht cribbed from a Soviet cybernetician: "Overtake without catching up!" [*Überholen ohne nachzuholen!*][59]

But what could such a remarkable surpassing possibly feel like—would it be an irrational flash akin to a religious conversion? Such a wondrous leap from one continuous system to another would, of course, be as unacceptable to dialectical materialists as it would be to rational realists like Popper and Imre Lakatos. "I admit," says Popper, "that an intellectual revolution often looks like a religious conversion." Yet it would be "simply false to say that the transition from Newton's theory of gravity to Einstein's is an irrational leap and that the two are not rationally comparable."[60] Here, the transition of an entire social system to a new qualitative state appears even more mysterious than the transition across intellectual programs.

As if the aporias of cybernetic socialism from *akrasia* to the *sorities* were not enough, as the New Economic System comes under mounting ideological pressure before Ulbricht's removal, Klaus finds himself having to defend cybernetics from accusations of ideological heresy. Attributing the charges to Western defamation, Klaus formulates their essence in the following way: Norbert Wiener, it is said, "ascertained that information is neither material nor ideal, that there is therefore some third thing accessible to neither materialism nor idealism that cybernetics and information theory alone can grasp. [. . .] If there are realms dialectical materialism cannot grasp, then its claim to be a theory of the general laws of nature, society and thought falls through."[61] Promoting value-neutral social science over Marxism, cybernetics makes system optimization tantamount to system convergence. As opposed to Marxism, where philosophers are called upon to change the world, cybernetics participates in a supposedly unitary technocratic modernity. Klaus's rearguard defense against these charges in his 1970 *Einheit* article "Cybernetics and Ideological Class Struggle" is both substantive and stylistic. Cybernetics does not efface differences between socialism and capitalism, he argues, because of "the opposition of their goals," and, more important, because of "the manner in which the elements and individual laws of cybernetics are applied to reach the goal."[62] Cybernetics, he claims, only maximizes systemic potential over a certain quality of relationships and values. "Capitalism, for example, forms a social system with a corresponding class content, class ideology, etc. Its subsystems by no means function to promote an optimization of the whole system. In the socialist system, by contrast, the human stands in the middle point and the development of each subsystem always proceeds with reference to the whole."[63] The paradox is now simply hailed as a virtue that for all of cybernetics' mathematical abstraction a qualitative value still lies at its root, a subjective *qualia* or an Aristotelian *entelechy*, that gives the absolute measure of its coordinated functions—namely, the human. Not God or Devil, but as Protagoras asserted, "*man* is the measure of all things."[64] Capitalism, for Klaus, as much as it strives for efficiency and optimality is merely maximizing profits, not people. Cybernetics is now conceived as a useful instrument, applied to systems that themselves are not spontaneously generated (autopoietic) organizations, but represent and maximize certain incommensurable qualities. The distinct identity of each system derives from the qualitative difference of its underlying value-giver: and this qualitative discontinuity vouches for the partisan incommensurability of capitalist and communist systems, even as they share the project of measurable optimization.

As humanistic as Klaus's sentiment is, he knows his New Economic System is under dire threat, and responds also with a militant pathos, proclaiming cybernetics "a weapon in the hands of the victorious revolutionary working class and its allies . . . a means for developing its offensive in the struggle against imperialism."[65] In the crisis of the New Economic System, cybernetics is re-engineered into a weapon of metaphorical violence. It is proffered as a way to wage class war by other means, the only means appropriate to an enlightened social formation—its superior human substance. This substance, however, remains crucially unquantifiable and revolutionary: the result precipitated by a discontinuous leap. Precisely cybernetics, which coordinates, measures, mathematizes, cannot articulate the discontinuity of the human quality whose liberation is its reason for being: except, that is, in this rhetorical violence. Of the paradoxical inability of a new paradigm—or, in this case, an entire new social formation—to ground its values in its own commensurable terms, Thomas Kuhn writes that "in a debate over choice of theory, neither party has access to an argument which resembles a proof in logic or formal mathematics[. . . .] [T]heir recourse is to persuasion as prelude to the possibility of proof."[66] The violence of Klaus's otherwise so measured rhetoric exemplifies a switch from the syllogistic reasoning of philosophy to the public appeal of rhetoric, a switch made inevitable by the rising political conflict. According to Plato, such a switch disqualifies an argument. "When you call things fair, such as bodies and colors and figures and sounds and institutions," he has Socrates say to his interlocutor, the rhetorician Gorgias, "you must do so surely with reference to some standard."[67] Unsatisfied that rational standards ever capture such qualities, the sophist Gorgias prefers direct emotional appeal to a scientific *episteme* that relies on an idea of instruction by logical argument.[68] Siding with Gorgias, Aristotle recognized, in a way Plato could not, that qualitative situations like public crises require a specific type of reasoning that appeals beyond logic to emotion, character, and discretion for its proof. Unlike philosophical argument, rhetoric applies specifically to the *kairos* of those moments that fall outside the normal course of events.[69]

Pushed up against the wall, Klaus's advocacy for cybernetics exposes the double reference in socialism's self-reference, an eerie doubling that persistently troubles the otherwise familiar values of socialism's pragmatic rationality. Because the vocabularies of modern scientific rationality are modest in their ontological commitment to the measurable evidence of daily life, the chasm of *im*measurable violence that separated the socialist and nonsocialist worlds remained perforce inarticulate in the idiom of daily trial and error. Socialism's insecure culture, however, unlike that of the confident, even solipsistic West, characteristically doubted its underlying qualitative integrity—its *differentia specifica*—just seriously enough to throw into question whether or not it was actually—qualitatively, quantitatively, and dialectically—all that distinct from capitalism. It needed to pose to itself the question of difference, and the trepidation and vehemence with which it did so cast into deep relief the menace of the imponderable abyss between worlds.

If Klaus's desperate apology for cybernetics takes on a touch of the comic in its grandiloquence, Fühmann's comic science fiction story, "The Heap," is rather more unnerving. Where Klaus's technophilia presents with deadpan literalness a red reflection of blue-blooded Western modernization theory, Fühmann's fiction recognizes the aporias, the undecidability that his society has opened in modernity without being able to close again. His story does not so much mirror similar genre pieces in the West with symmetrical values, but, because socialism never secured itself as an autarchic alternative, Fühmann's inventions capture the intensity of a system whose simultaneously real and impossible difference from modernity causes the violence of sovereignty to turn in on itself.

3. THE HEAP

> I heap up monstrous sums,
> Pile on the millions,
> I set time upon time
> And world upon world in a heap,
> And when, from dizzying height,
> I look again toward you:
> All the might of number,
> Multiplied a thousand fold,
> Is not even one part of you.
> —Albrecht von Haller[70]

Like Fühmann's mythological and biblical stories, "The Heap" initially seems remote from GDR politics and Cold War conflict. Its theme is the classical paradox of the *sorites* attributed to Eubulides: if an element of a heap—say, a grain of wheat—is a discrete quantity, then the gradual addition of one discrete element to another discrete element can only add up to a discrete quantity and never to a heap. In terms of mathematical induction: since two are few, and three are few also, and since for any number n that are few, $n + 1$ are few also; then, a thousand are few as surely as are two. There is no ontological boundary to be crossed. The ancient physician Galen, accordingly, concluded that "there must not be such a thing in the world as a heap of grain, a mass or satiety, neither a mountain nor strong love, nor a row, nor strong wind, nor city nor anything else which is known from its name and idea to have a measure of extent or multitude, such as the wave, the open sea, a flock of sheep and herd of cattle, the nation and the crowd."[71] Yet socialism—Fühmann's existential commitment—is ontologically predicated on the possibility of a qualitative distinction in modernity, a class consciousness, a species being, a secular redemption in human life. How then do the relentless quantities of daily routines precipitate suddenly into a socialist quality?

"The Heap" examines this ancient paradox in the quintessentially modern setting of a laboratory in the Truly Liberated Society of the improbable year 3456. During a public presentation, the newly installed, and not yet fully oriented philosopher-in-chief is unexpectedly asked "to what extent the Comrade Classical Authors' [*Kameraden Klassiker*] prognosis has been fulfilled that the Truly Liberated Society will have solved all inherited problems of philosophy."[72] Instead of giving the prudent answer, "To the best extent," he is caught off guard and asserts that they have been answered "absolutely, positively fully" (34). In his embarrassment over how many gaps in fact remain, and his zeal to make good on the unadvised boast, he delegates the preparation of a complete register of solutions to various departments of the Institute of Philosophy. An underling named Janno, from the Department of Causality, is commissioned with producing one of the purported solutions—namely, that for the *sorites*. The ensuing events fall into two segments. In the first segment, Janno's colleague Jirro, an uninvolved "neutrinologue" from the Physics Department, who has been surprised by Janno's recent reclusiveness, seeks him out at his lab. He finds his friend desperately absorbed in an absurd empirical experiment. On the basis of the urgency of the chief's command, Janno has apparently convinced the Institute to buy him several hundred steel screws—a commodity in painfully short supply—which he is alternately removing from and adding to his washbasin in hopes of catching the precise moment when their number becomes a heap. Making matters worse for the worldly and cynical Jirro is that his once easygoing colleague is painstakingly photographing the washbasin and its contents with scarce film that he has paid for out of his own pocket. At the sight of this preposterous undertaking, Jirro tries to persuade Janno of other ways to more realistically bring his commission to a satisfactory result.

The second part of the story follows up Jirro's inconclusive dialectical wrangling with an intense burst of action. When a siren goes off summoning Janno's whole department to the parade grounds for a routine inspection by the control troop commander, Janno declines to interrupt his experimentation, and the two colleagues' methodological disagreement promptly escalates into the broader social conflict Jirro had feared: the terms of debate, to speak with the philosophy of science, switch from Karl Popper's doctrine of methodological individualism to Thomas Kuhn's model of social constructivism.[73] Committed to his vision of an experienceable solution to the *sorites*, Janno refuses to abide any longer by the ritualized procedures of the Institute, much to the horror of his expedient colleague who has reconciled himself to the way things are done. All along Jirro has been mocking

Janno's *sorites* problem as a "SAURITUS" (sow ritual), since he rightly understands Institute science as a soulless game in which any serious question is dispatched by reference to a few passages from the *Kameraden Klassiker*. Janno's unheard-of absence on the parade grounds triggers an Institute emergency in which scientific and police authorities converge simultaneously on Janno's lab as the two colleagues remain struggling over quantity and quality, pure research and complacent expediency. The resultant confusion, anticlimactically, supplies no clear resolution to the *sorites*. On the contrary, complexity and cross-purposes are the dubious conditions under which quantity alchemizes into quality. The resolution comes in spite of itself: the contending parties at the institute are heaped together in Janno's trashed lab by circumstances beyond their control.

If this confusion is a disappointing solution to the *sorites*, a closer look at Fühmann's story brings more satisfaction than one expects from such murky proceedings. "The Heap" translates Klaus's cybernetic paradoxes from logic into literature, a cognate medium for Fühmann, for just as it is Klaus's conviction that cybernetics works because dialectics can be mathematized, it is Fühmann's conviction that "the world can be expressed in poetry because it can be mathematized."[74] Thus, he writes in the preface to the *Saiäns-fiktschen* collection in which "The Heap" is found, that the collection's "hypertrophy of feeling" is "the emotional counterpart to thinking a thing logically through to its end, except that thinking has a different stringency and objectivity than fearing, dreading, anticipating or repressing. 'Fearing to the end' aims at catastrophe; 'anticipating to the end' banishes alternatives; 'repressing to the end' means destruction; 'dreading to the end' not only conjures ghosts, but makes them omnipotent, omnipresent, and absolute."[75] The ghosts besetting Fühmann's *Saiäns-fiktschen* scientists arise from the equally dreaded and anticipated possibility of another system, uncannily familiar in its modernity, but visible only as a specter in the sudden rupture of the current system's pragmatic, adaptive, maximizing functions. Like all such incommensurabilities, this qualitative interruption escapes both ethical and material calculi. Its ambiguous value is to be sought only in its potential to reveal something essential.

Witnessing Janno's absurd experiment, Jirro can only wonder who has paid for the scarce screws and film his friend is wasting. The screws, Jirro learns, are budgeted, but the film is paid for from Janno's salary. The essential thing here, he realizes, is not solving an obscure problem in order to flatter some ideological vanity, but preventing Janno's one-time expense from becoming an uncomfortable Institute precedent. "If the administration, as is only to be expected, generalizes from your bad example and makes every colleague pay research costs out of pocket, we'd only have Janno to thank" (36). Well aware how the particular transmutes into the general under the watchful eyes of power, Jirro sets himself against Janno's naive attempt to isolate the *sorites* in his basin of screws, determined instead upon two more pragmatic goals: averting the submission of a protocol for Janno's experiment (a protocol that would reveal Janno's financial sacrifice), and getting hold of ten of Janno's priceless screws for himself. Jirro's objectives focus on evading detection and circumventing transparency, while Janno remains obsessed with capturing on film the exact moment a quantity of screws becomes a quality. Jirro's adaptive, maximizing *Seinsvergessenheit*—forgetfulness of being—stands opposed to Janno's impassioned search for the precise spot where meaning and being converge on the singular evidence of a quality. Seeing his friend's desperation, Jirro realizes that the only way to restore Janno's equanimity is to offer him a solution, albeit one that dodges the quixotic hunt for a pure *qualia*. He sure-handedly steers Janno back to quantity by asking "what the solution is worth to him" (38). A price? Janno stammers. "Did Jirro really know a way? And what should one offer him? [. . .] Three pounds, four pounds, five pounds, six pounds, what was the price?" (38). Unperturbed, Jirro names it himself: "Twenty pounds."

Paying Jirro for a solution, rendering unto Caesar, debases the *sorites* to a *sauritus* by conceding that nothing substantive is even at stake any more, just a functional way around the problem, a clever tactical evasion rather than a solution. Exhausted, and a bit curious, Janno convinces himself that it is worth a try anyway. Jirro begins with an expert touch: since the *Kameraden Klassiker* are the source of the claim that the Truly Liberated Society will have solved all philosophical problems, it only makes sense to turn to them to understand the claim's logic. The classics, Jirro observes, distinguish two qualities of truth: one is Hegelian truth, the Absolute Knowledge of human totality at the end of time, and the other is a partial, casuistic truth that, in the course of an eternity which no one lives to see, approaches the total truth ever more adequately. Since no given stage of humanity is anything but a finite stage, one must of course content oneself with finite partial truths that merely tend to the full one, and at the moment the partial truth is that a heap, as everyone knows, is precisely 562 screws. Before Janno can interrupt with anything more than an astonished cry of "All-powerful Matter," Janno puts the finishing touches on his demonstration, noting that "a problem for which a partial solution exists is as good as solved: a solution in part proves the possibility of a solution in totality, which nevertheless as the sum of partial solutions necessarily requires the sum total of time for reaching all partial solutions" (40). But Jirro has overplayed his hand; the infinite sum he invokes spoils the enthusiasm he has momentarily awakened in Janno. Now, the precise solution is just one more in a series of series iterated throughout the story. Like the screws, like the proper price for a solution, it bypasses the *actual* moment (the *energeia*, in Aristotelian terminology) when quantity becomes quality. Multiples remain multiples without distinct properties; and inconclusive series abound without any demonstrable meaning.

Janno's mind is already elsewhere. Not prices, but *qualia* alone will deliver him from the infinite plasticity of the social system: a self-subsistent quality, a kingdom for a quality, and he will burst asunder the relentless constructivism of numbers, prices, salaries, and social systems. Over the drone of Jirro's voice, Janno sees for the first time—although still not consciously—"how unbelievably dirty the window was, slimy gray ghosts of rain arcing over it, spattered with mortar and bird shit, never cleaned since he had begun working here, and still—and this he also saw for the first time and it was the scrim of his thoughts—and still it was filled with the blue of the sky and the monstrous light that made matter gleam" (40). The oaths and ejaculations of the Truly Liberated Society, the reflexive cries of "Holy Matter," "Matter be praised," invoke orderly material existence as the metaphysical bedrock replacing God, but this stolid matter is precisely what never shines forth in actuality, as absent as any *deus absconditus*. Janno feels himself overcome by a desire to purge away the grime covering his office with a torrent of burning lye, although he cannot once articulate why he desires this or even recognize that this overpowering desire is a desire at all. It remains only an obscure vision of a sparkling wash basin in which the steel screws blossom "like a crystal flower" (41).

As Bertrand Russell observed in his landmark modern treatment of the *sorites* paradox, the apprehension of a quality always stumbles over the inevitable "vagueness" of its determination.[76] "All 'material' terms," elaborates Max Black, "all whose application requires the recognition of the presence of sensible qualities, are vague."[77] This dismal vagueness clouding Janno's sensuous imagination, so boundlessly susceptible to fudging, evasion, and manipulation, is what he desperately wants to bleach away into shining surfaces. His priceless screws are always "twinkling" at him even in the weak Institute light, as if trying to intimate something essential. With all his soul Janno longs to find the crystal clear boundary separating one object from the next: a qualitatively distinct object should be what it is and not what it is not, *tertium non datur*. This is, of course, the familiar yearning for an Apollonian law of the excluded middle, enacted to regulate all the sloppy parcels of material existence. "Ill-defined can only mean undefined—there is no place for a *tertium quid* in traditional logic," comments Black.[78] Similarly, Russell notes that "the law of the excluded middle is true when precise symbols are employed, but it is not true when symbols are vague," especially symbols of sensible quality like "the word 'red.'"[79] Oh, Holy Red Matter! The grimy windows, the hazy series, the coarse plasticity of subjects (and objects) shaped only by sloganeering and ritual—if this vagueness were illuminated in the clear light of day, then, and only then, could matter's sharp boundaries and sovereign existence, these timeless desiderata for a strong and distinct universe, shine forth with the intuitive indexical force of natural kinds. Vagueness—like contradiction—would be eliminated from the world, bringing recalcitrant matter in line with the "celestial existence" of logic.[80]

The all-clarifying solution to the *sorites* dawning just beyond the perimeter of the protagonist's consciousness, although not yet seized in its purity, awakens enough resistance to sophistry that Janno, staring intently at Jirro, balks at his friend's declaration that a heap is exactly 562 screws. Such a sloppily conjured claim is indemonstrable. "'If just anyone can determine what a heap is, then anyone could also determine what truth is, or justice or welfare or—' and Janno quietly put into words what occurred to Jirro at the same moment: 'Or the Truly Liberated Society!'" (41). Jirro fears that the battle is lost (and his twenty pounds), but gamely retorts that it surely is not just anyone determining what a heap is in his formulation; it is the *Kameraden Klassiker* themselves, with whom his demonstration, like all valid demonstrations, began. Well trained in the ways of discursive tautology, however, Janno has already pursued that course; he explains to Jirro that not only have the *Klassiker* never directly taken up the *sorites* paradox, but no place in their entire corpus do they link the lexeme "heap" to a precise figure. Every bit as stubborn as his opponent, Jirro now hits upon an inspired cybernetic solution. The classics, he gathers from Janno's concordance of instances of the relevant word, once referred to a "heap" of African resistance fighters who were destroyed by a colonial army. Surely one could feed the circumstantial evidence of that historical battle into a computer "and eventually declare the exact strength of that heap to be the partial solution of the SORITES, which is in itself already the solution of the whole" (43). Order out of chaos. And with this triumphant example of a cybernetic cul-de-sac—called GIGO (Garbage In, Garbage Out) by engineers for its perfect lack of reference to any real world outside itself—Jirro smugly ex-

Fig. 7. The official logo of the East German Socialist Unity Party, 1946–90.

tends his palm for payment, a gesture Janno mistakes for an invitation to shake hands, which he greets with a hearty clasp. This handshake, the emblem of the Socialist Unity Party, marking the 1946 East German unification of the prewar leftist parties, is a vintage GDR tableau, still potent 1510 years down the road—"[T]his handshake that sealed the pact could never last long enough," intones Jirro (43).

Janno is unmoved: "It is not the authentic solution!" (44). Such insanity is a crisis indeed, and at this impasse Jirro instinctively grabs for his brain probe. Noticing the gesture, Janno protests and reluctantly Jirro lets the instrument fall back into his holster. But the element of good-natured hectoring is lost. Jirro's lecture now strikes a note of somber warning to his unhinged friend. "The atomic bomb started this way as well, exactly this way, with this very question: when does quantity turn into quality, when does a bunch of stuff hanging around peacefully become a combustible mass? The 'critical mass' of the qualitative leap—there's your heap-problem for you!" (45). Dropping the familiar posture of jaunty cynic, Jirro's protest becomes sincere and cogent.

> You're not just adding screws to screws, you're also adding thoughts to thoughts and desires to desires and finally uprisings to uprisings and you think you're moving in a philosophical realm, when all along you've been moving in a social-ethical one! Your SORITES can *also* become a bomb, a social-political bomb, and with your theorizing it already *is* one: you're blasting society into the nothing-

> ness of a no-longer calculable future! Freedom is insight into what's necessary—pardon me, every school kid knows that nowadays—but you want to demolish the necessary, the orientation of thought toward what's been providentially known, preserved as salving for society, but by destroying the necessary you also destroy freedom, and that dare not be put at our disposal! (45–46)

Such arguments come too late for Janno, who has already crossed the invisible line: "[We] can no longer understand each other, Jirro. It's as though I've made a leap during our discussion clear over into another existence: a person suddenly doesn't want to continue on as before, regardless of what happens . . . the problem, Jirro, the pure problem beyond any purpose, in pure freedom" (46). At this fateful juncture, the Institute assembly sirens cut short the in-any-case-interrupted dialectics of the two friends. Janno ignores the signal, the loudspeakers start hailing Janno's number, Jirro panics over losing his advance payment of twelve pounds and cut of ten screws, and without premeditation Janno smashes the dirty window, blood pours from the backs of his hands, the pure blue of sky streams into the dingy lab, as do two columns of control troops, the control commander, and the philosopher-in-chief.

Quickly apprehending the uncooperative philosopher with his "unbelievable waste of productive capacity," the control commander and philosopher-in-chief warily size up their prospects of assigning each other blame for the scandal. Jirro, however, knowing his friend's life to be imperiled, risks his own in a room brimming with weapons, and drawing the brain probe from his holster, quickly jabs it into Janno's head—instantly, its enlarged display meter indicates a maximally unhappy consciousness, and the apparatus "automatically dispenses a music of satisfaction that gives the will a friendly, the muscles a tired, and the thoughts an absolutely straightforward tone" (54). As the melodic rhythms diffuse inaudibly through his consciousness, Janno imagines all these people are gathered in his lab to take a group portrait with the camera he still has standing before his washbasin: he smiles. Humiliated by his charge's imbecilic grin, the philosopher-in-chief tries to take the offensive, proclaiming he has known from the first day he assumed office "what a heap of traitors [. . .] has been able, here as everywhere, to infiltrate en masse." But sure of his victory, the control commander interrupts. Ordering his troops to stand down as a sign of conciliation, he declares the *sorites* successfully solved: it is "repeatedly confirmed knowledge that as great as the damage caused by this heap of inner enemies, so infinitesimally small is its number, [. . .] easily counted on ten fingers!" With that observation, "the most difficult questions, indeed the mostly highly complicated problems of his philosopher comrades, for whose valuable efforts he has only the highest respect, are clarified" (54).

Impressed by this historic solution, Jirro, almost as if he has read Janno's tranquilized thoughts, invites the assembly to pose for a picture, and with a simple "Would you be so kind," snaps a souvenir of jolly reconciliation in the classless society. Then, present-of-mind as always, he seeks his opportunity to escape from the room before his own fate is sealed. Janno, meanwhile, struggling against gathering oblivion, notices that his long desired portrait is incomplete. Pointing at the control commander, he says, "[B]ut he isn't there in the photo!" The captured heap is missing its decisive quality, naked police force has somehow eluded the once-in-a-lifetime photo opportunity. The commander loses his nerve at this impudence, his troops react, Beta-Browning pistols are drawn all around. Jirro sees his chance to sneak past the metal detector with his cut of ten screws—for who would notice that little heap in the midst of such great events?—and he bolts.

As story and experiment draw to a catastrophic end, the narrative seems to affirm Jirro's claim that the *sorites* has no ideal, only a constructed—even, opportunistic—solution, with quality now asserting itself in precisely the manner Jirro feared, as state sovereignty and panoptic violence. It is simply a premodern relic, the dark underbelly of rational pragmatics under threat. Although humanists may have been predisposed to embrace quality as the mark of their essential difference, it turns out to be a hostile value, to be sheer unregulated power.[81] But in the series of climaxes at the end of the story, it remains unclear (vague, as it were) what one can take to be the decisive moment of insight. All we know for certain is that we are precluded from experiencing what Janno has experienced: "[We] cannot know what revealed itself to him . . . perhaps the solution to the SORITES, maybe only the sun in its freedom, maybe the grime on the shards of window pane, surrounded by the colors of the rainbow, but that we don't know any more" (57). As much as the ending appears to vindicate players and adaptors like Jirro, who makes off, consciousness intact, with an undetected heap of gleaming matter, the catastrophe reserves its poetry for Janno. By refusing to be interpellated by the siren, the *Institutsappell*, he sets a qualitative limit to unlimited social constructivism: poetry emerges from the shattered glass, the blood on his hands, the sudden breakdown of mechanical routine. In one of his remarkable letters to his editor Kurt Batt in the early 1970s, Fühmann points out the centrality of the adverbs "suddenly, abruptly" to his poetics, noting that they designate "in fact the basic experience of my time on earth."[82] After describing the rude interruptions that have characterized his life, from fleeing the convent school to joining the SA to settling in the GDR, he reflects: "Now, one could say with horror: what a spongy world, in which ruptures are ceaselessly occurring! I could answer: what a robust world that it can stand it! But I believe it is true about the ruptures. It is a world of being abandoned and exposed, a world of being objectified. I could say: it is to escape it, or to first become aware of it, that I write."[83]

In a sudden flash of unfiltered light "the human" momentarily exceeds the system's measure; an incommensurate quality shatters its machinery of optimization. The flash, however, illuminates inconclusively. Quality escapes functionalization in the continuous metrics of one system, but lasts no longer than the light of "an intuition—" like that which Janno had been trying so hard to convey to Jirro: "[He] hesitated, struck by this unscientific term, but the light tormenting its way through the window now made his eyes flash too" (44). Kuhn's retort to Popper comes to mind here, that he never meant the flash of intuition that allows one to transfer allegiance from one paradigm to another to be understood as an ontological revelation. The fact that quality seems to transcend one system does not imply that it is an ontological absolute for all possible systems. It is not the face of God. Janno's irreducible qualitativeness exposes his system's optimum as relative to it, not an *optimum optimorum*, grounded once and for all in value beyond measure. Yet it likewise supplies no basis for a final measure (*telos*) or single efficient cause (*dynamis*). In the ruins of Janno's lab, the only certainty is that no quality exists outside each heap and as the criterion for them all. Far from despairing that no system subsumes all alternatives, Fühmann's modernity, his experimental and gradualist sensibility, draws him to the sharp point where the opportunity for radical recalibration emerges. At that point, and it is a risky one, quantity tilts past a system's limits, either as violence or as hope, always as extreme discontinuity: "[T]he turning point can only be grasped as 'sudden,'" Fühmann writes his editor. "That can also be demonstrated mathematically. There are curves, hyperbola (of the type: $y=1/x^3$), for example, where with the least change in the curve, the addition or subtraction of the smallest imaginable unit, the differential quotient explodes from positive to negative infinity."[84] The question, then, posed by the qualitative, is whether the breach in the commensurable shall be filled with what Hegel called "the wrong or negative infinity" or with a positive one that yields to substantial transformation.[85] And the answer to that question Fühmann, and the history of alternatives to liberal capitalist modernity, has left open.

But in the last reversal of a twisty narration, we realize that we *do* know exactly the identity of the story's heap and have known it all along. The catharsis of Janno's violence and the terror of Jirro's submission share a

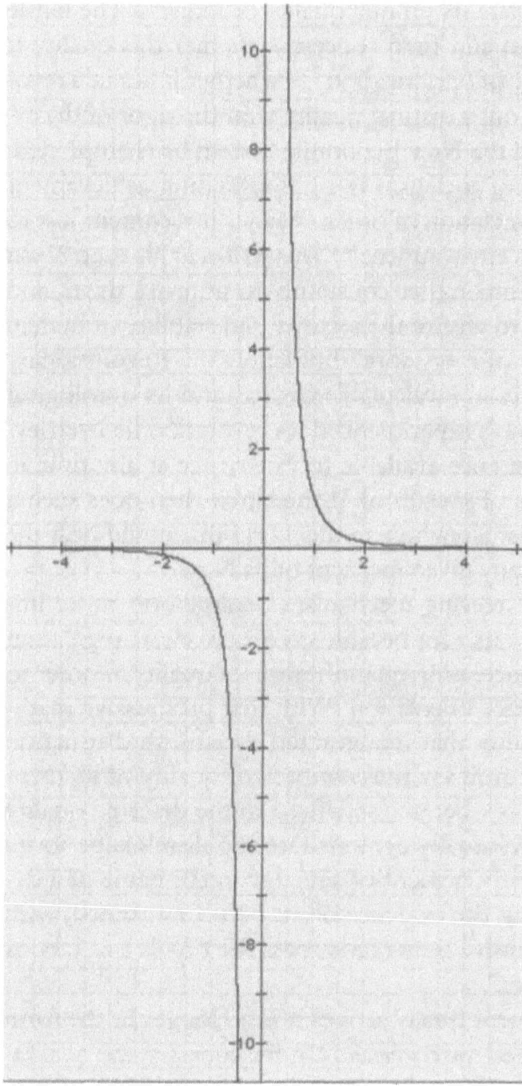

Fig. 8. The hyperbola $y = 1/x^3$.

source in the same One that has preceded the Many of the lab's confusion. "The SORITES-problem," Janno explains to Jirro at the outset, "seems to be solvable in two ways, by increasing the Not-yet *until* it becomes One, but also by diminishing *from* a heap to One-no-longer, on which latter path he, Janno, is presently embar—" at which point his explanation is brusquely interrupted by an impatient Jirro (36). Starting from the assumption of socialism's real existence, Janno's experiment seeks to verify the actuality of socialism's distinction, to isolate its unique quality of redness. The battle of sensibilities between Janno and Jirro concerns whether this quality is immanent in a stable dynamic of optimization, or whether it lies in a revolutionary rupture that spaces out a distinct quality with the rigor of the excluded middle. For Klaus and the New Economic System he championed, the optimum goal (*Sollwert*) of socialism is a self-validating achievement that emerges out of the maximization of order. "Man is not content just to maintain the conditions of his environment," Klaus writes in his 1960 *Neues Deutschland* article. "[He] wants rather constantly to improve them, and not only that, he also strives to ensure the security and stability of human relationships against chances of every sort." But surely the Revolutionary Event that founds socialism is an incalculable chance, and its ontological ambiguity is what drives Janno's experiment: does revolution lie irretrievably in the past, or is it a presence available to experience at any time in order to verify the difference of socialism? If the latter, then does such a stably maximizing system exist anywhere in the world that could bear the presentation of revolution at any given moment of its Now?

As socialism's qualitative steering mechanism became ever more improbable, the contradiction at its root became ever more clear: regulating balances in kind required an increasing quantification of quality in order to tackle the challenge of nonprice calculation. With that progressive mathematization, the present quality that inaugurated socialism's distinction from capitalism—one might even say the *omni*present quality of its revolutionary banners and symbols—became sacrificed to the deferred quality that only sometime would eventually demonstrate socialism's superiority over its rival. The endless postponement of actuality in the name of a dynamic incapable of marshaling the evidence on its behalf awakened, with perverse inevitability, an obsessive desire to surpass the rituals and taboos of the "Truly Liberated Society."

When the qualitative moment finally arrives it is no longer in the form of the revolution that unleashed the dynamic. On the contrary, the qualitative eruption destroys the possibility of optimization that revolution promised, demolishing the actuality and identity—the *entelechy*—of real socialism. Optimization is meaningless when its systemic metric is turned inside out. What Janno has finally fixed in his photographic index is the end of the heap he started with, the unqualified loss of its particular quality. The *un*-natural kind that shines forth out of Janno's solution of the *sorites* paradox is . . . a negative predicate: not socialism any longer.[86]

CHAPTER NINE

The Din of the System: The Devil's Due

I. THE HEARD-OF

> Reverberation makes reception into an intelligible din, and the lover into a monstrous receiver, reduced to an enormous auditive organ—as if listening itself were to become a state of utterance: in me, it is the ear which speaks.
>
> —Roland Barthes, *A Lover's Discourse*[1]

"Marsyas" introduced us to Fühmann's "unheard-of," the incommensurable event marking the beginning of the drama of socialist transformation, the revelation of *tertium non datur* at the edge of the woods around Mt. Ida in ancient Phrygia and—unheard-of echo—in the Soviet prisoner-of-war camp where Fühmann was remolded from fascist to socialist. In the discussion of "The Heap" in the previous chapter, we saw how the plan, the lodestone of the socialist order—the great metaphysical alternative to Camps and Laws—fails, in the GDR, to crystallize its aspiration to the *optimum optimorum* of limitless universality and substantial difference. This aspiration, a desire for total well-being in the sense of providence (etymologically, "seeing ahead," *Vorsehung*), points like a weathercock beyond the terrible unheard-of, to the temperate foreseen. It transports its bearers from the irrational bliss of the Muses' flaying to the tranquil empiricism of a presence fully immanent in the socialist intention. Philosophically, one might speak here of a passage from the ecstatic subjectivity of the "dialectical image" (Benjamin) to the objective pragmatism of the "natural kind" (Quine). In an aesthetic sense, one might recognize Lukács's epochalization of genre, in which the diremption of the bourgeois tragic novel resolves itself, after the revolution, in the indicative order of the socialist epic. Roland Barthes suggests a different, more affective way of conceiving Lukács's aesthetic contrast, albeit not his world historical movement—namely, the distinction between pleasure (*plaisir*) and bliss (*jouissance*). "Pleasure," according to Barthes, "is linked to a consistence of the self, of the subject, which is assured in values of comfort, relaxation, ease—and for me, that's the entire realm of reading the classics, for example. On the contrary, bliss is the system of reading, or utterance, through which the subject, instead of establishing itself, is lost, experiencing that expenditure which is, properly speaking, bliss."[2]

The unheard-of event of Marsyas' flaying was a loss of identity, a shattering of order and an incapacitation of the Muses who solemnize institutions. It was the wordless, inconceivable moment of *jouissance* in which the GDR was ecstatically envisioned beyond the bourgeois subject. This contourless vision of socialism eventually took on visible form and concrete character through the Five-Year Plans that governed the material pleasure—the comfort, relaxation, and ease, such as they were—of the real socialist republic. But the visible, empirical form of real socialism was apparently unable, despite the strenuous efforts of Fühmann's perceptual imagination, to secure the substantial difference of the socialist transformation. The measure of the new (the New Human), which mediates, in the Hegelian science, the leap from quantity to quality, never presented itself as such, even in the most faithful and selfless experience of socialism. At least in the GDR, the infinitely plastic subject of objective laws never found itself resurrected as the substantial index of historical providence. Poor Janno, the devoted empirical investigator (*Diplomkausalitätler*), with his camera ready to capture the visible evidence of the quantity/quality transformation and to resolve the Eleatic conundrum of the *sorites*, instead finds his will tranquilized in the crucial moment by the Hegelian "rhythms of the music of satisfaction."[3] Apropos the fulsome stasis of such beguiling music of the spheres, Georges Bataille observes that "harmony, like the plan, casts time to the outside: its principle is the repetition with which anything possible is perpetuated. [. . .] It is from the plan, moreover, that art has borrowed repetition: the calm investing of time with a repeated theme."[4] Instead of verifying providence as revealed progress, Janno's experiments wind up in reassuring stasis.

No wonder, then, that Janno's opposite number, Jirro, the physicist and systems theorist (*Diplomneutrinologe* and *Systematiker*) from Fühmann's *Saiäns-fiktschen* collection, forgoes Janno's ill-starred search for the visual evidence of providence and turns right away to simpler acoustical satisfactions during his unusual sojourn in the liberal Libroterr. The problem in Jirro's case, however, has to do with where and how he abandons himself to which pleasures—the fundamental questions of what I have called a systems erotics of socialism. In the story "Die Straße der Perversionen" ("The Street of Perversions"), Jirro is permitted to cross the border from the regimented ("Truly Liberated') society of Uniterr into freewheeling Libroterr for an extended seventy-week research exchange in the forbidden half of the divided world of the year 3456. In Libroterr's asphalt jungle it is not the unheard-of that interests him, but what he hears everywhere in passing as a kind of sonic refuse, the noise of free competition. In the face of Libroterr's media-saturated streetscapes, he finds no "pleasure in what's displayed," responding to the temptation of "optical sensations" with a simple "no."[5] He turns away from the spectacular advertising traps glimmering from every direction and demanding his participation in an endless exchange economy, to plunge instead into the unprepossessing side streets of Libroterr where the buzz of television sets, tuned in to a constantly changing configuration of the tens of thousands of channels on offer, stimulates his fantasy far more than the prolific Libroterrean wares calculated to do so. "His acoustic theater was more than television, even though, restricted merely to listening, lacking the image, it seemed to be less" (70).

It is no surprise that Jirro's aural entertainment in Libroterr is nothing like the soothing music that pervades Janno's consciousness the moment he is to witness the revelation of the *sorites*. Libroterr makes no claim to revelation—despite its flashy technology, its society is characterized by nature at its most venal. Nonetheless, the difficult fact remains that Jirro—a New Man—*does* find satisfaction in Libroterr's brutal backstreet theater. It is, however, a satisfaction that will turn out to rest on a basic misconception: by restricting his pleasure to just one of five senses, Jirro thinks that he has brought his perceptions into line with meaning (with sense, in the singular). Dispensing with the television images, he imagines all the more freely, convincing himself that he can fulfill the sense of what he is hearing in his sovereign understanding alone. Despite thriftily bracketing out four extraneous senses, Jirro doesn't at first realize that he can—in fact, must—forgo the practical and moral reference that would contaminate the pure experience of the sounds. One of his initial adventures, although embarrassing, clarifies the importance of his perceptual reduction. Fleeing the advertising along the main ring street, he notices all sorts of incompatible sounds coming out of the rear windows of the apartments. To the accompaniment of "calm music," he hears a horrible scream, "DON'T STAB MY KIDNEYS," along with a clattering of steel and demonic laughter, and imagines, on the basis of this macabre sonic composition, not the perverse purity of the event it describes, but that he should act to prevent a crime-in-progress. It seems as though he has refused the predatory temptations of advertising only to be caught up in the irrefusable solicitations of moral reason. Heeding an inner voice of duty—surely the inheritance of his upbringing in Uniterr—he bursts into an apartment only to discover that the cry belongs to a children's anatomy program. "The cry, the music, the satanic laughter and the dissolution into triviality: a Street of Revelation as well; and from then on Jirro remained fascinated" (71). It is nothing unheard-of, but the triviality of what everybody hears every day without paying attention that occasions this revelation, a revelation that with a little abstraction he condenses into the neat formula: "pleasure of violence—violence of pleasure" (71).

What Jirro gets out of this back alley of the free world—existential triviality, the unbearable lightness of being—is something he values so highly because he has not known it in Uniterr. There, sounds correlate to concepts, which correlate to things, all as pragmatically and providentially as can be, since the unity of Uniterr consists in its optimization of everything beyond the regional limits of space or time. In Libroterr, by contrast, "Jirro learned very quickly that all the constellations that fascinated him did so as the illusion of *one* action and therefore had to be of short duration," circumscribed enough to be assessed within the orbit of his fleeting perception (72). Reducing his senses to one sense approximates unity, but only as a ephemeral moment of aesthetic abandon. Nonetheless, so aesthetically satisfying to him are these Streets of Revelation that their quintile of reality quickly comes to dominate his sense of reality in general. For the methodical physicist, Libroterr, with its chiasmic laws of pleasure and violence, displaces ponderous Uniterr as the superior standard of what there is.

> It lasted only the briefest time (Jirro never became conscious of how brief) until the crass obscenities, crass brutalities, and crass monstrosities whose omnipresent insistence in Libroterr at first dismayed Jirro became something he accepted as self-evident to such an extent that he began to forget his fusty fatherland in the way that someone forgets a dream in waking life or forgets his childhood when he reaches maturity [. . . .] It wasn't simply a matter of memories paling; rather, it was connected to a feeling that he had crossed sides from a realm of unreality into that of reality (73).

This ontological transgression, which like so much in the story transpires in the briefest interval, a suddenness approaching zero that escapes conscious apprehension, exposes both the infinitesimal dimension and absolute quality of the boundary between real and unreal. Of course, one can only wish to grasp that instant in which real and unreal receive their shape, that instantaneous presence of what is and is not.

2. MEASLY DEVILS

> Extreme devotion is the opposite of piety, extreme vice the opposite of pleasure.
>
> —Bataille, *The Impossible*[6]

Given the inconceivable rapidity of the crossing—and its inconceivable stakes—I want to hesitate before joining Jirro on his voyage from the unreal to the real (to the revelation of Libroterr's acoustic theater), and take a detour back from the thirty-fourth to the nineteenth century, "the era between the Battle of Jena [1806] and the Carlsbad Decrees [1819]," the era, that is, in which Hegel first proclaimed the sovereignty of Absolute Knowledge in the *Phenomenology of Spirit* (1807) only to see Austria's Prince Metternich retract Napoleon's liberalizing reforms with the police measures decreed at Carlsbad.[7] In an essay on E. T. A. Hoffmann's neglected novella "Ignaz Denner," written between the stories of *Saiäns-fiktschen* and published as an appendix to a study of the "Golden Pot," Fühmann considers what happens when the sudden transformations of Hegel's master-slave dialectic come to a grinding halt.[8] The theme of the frozen dialectic first rose to prominence in the 1920s when the Russian Revolution failed to ignite similar transformations across Europe, but the outcome on view here, at the twilight of real socialism, is not Bataille's or Benjamin's surrealistic "dialectics at a standstill," but something subrealistic, in the sense of Parmenides' "mud or dirt or any other trivial and undignified object," whose haphazard existence can hardly be imagined to have any transcending form: abject facticity rather than shattering event.[9] Instead of a development to self-recognition (to a true Idea of oneself), the agonizing stations of Hoffmann's story are, in Fühmann's reading, "screw twists of a process that has been tamped down until it has stalled and can come into and stay in motion only through an external impulse, a process that . . . grinds the poor soul between the slowest grinding stones" (378–79). Hegel's master plan, the plan of total re-collection (*Er-Innerung*) lingers only as a crippling fantasy possessing Hoffmann's protagonist in the final station of his journey to hell, where he "has discovered his happiness in vassalage, every development has ended in failure, contradiction is frozen into peace, dull-wittedness has been transfigured into cheerful modesty" (399).

"Ignaz Denner," Fühmann concedes, is often deemed a potboiler, too overripe and effect-laden to stand with Hoffmann's better-known work. He finds, however, that the satanic conceits, and even the satanic antagonist Ignaz Denner himself, are secondary to the singularly relevant protagonist Andres, the dutiful vassal of Count Vach. In Fühmann's reading, Andres is an archetype of German modernity, on a par with Kleist's Kohlhaas and Büchner's Woyzeck—and Hoffmann's story is faulted only for not being named "The Game Warden" after Andres, as Hoffmann originally intended. Pious Andres, whose impoverished position on Vach's land demands nothing short of a miracle, is so ready to show his gratitude for any favor his lord bestows that his "humbleness" threatens to become a "moral nihilism" (384) indiscriminate with respect to his own and his family's needs. What then is such a soul to make of an inconceivable offer from someone who is not—at least not in a recognizable way—a proper master of his fate? His young wife is moldering away, his newborn son on the verge of death, Andres is not by any stretch master of himself—the land yields only enough to fill one stomach, but despite his position of authority on the Vach estate, he is sorely without means for his loved ones. The offer of salvation that comes to him just in time to save his starving wife and son understandably sets off alarms. Intervention is in the color of red, a "blood red liqueur from a crystal phial" (382), introducing a red thread that runs from one inexplicable event to another—what kind of miracles are these? Do they truly portend his salvation, or are they rather the diabolical miracles that seal his damnation—and if they are miraculous, arising from outside any conceivable expectation in an instant of *kairos* (the opportune moment), how is Andres ever to judge between truth and simulacrum? If there were to be some sort of Hegelian progress decipherable in his story, some achievement of recognition that would transform Andres from an object in the hands of mysterious forces beyond his control into a self-conscious subject fashioning his own destiny, then the miracles would have to be revealed as not being miracles at all, but immanent developments, dialectical contradictions, the most real moments of his vassalage and thus the most pregnant moments for his liberation.

Intruding from the outside, unheard-of and unprecedented, the miracles befalling Andres in his need would seem to have no proper place within the Hegelian dialectic of reason. But that is their wile, one step wilier than Hegel foresaw in conjuring providence as "the ruse of reason."[10] Indeed, they are not miracles in the sense of "chance," which is too arbitrary and inconsequential to bear narrative weight. "A one-time aid would have only delayed, not averted, and wouldn't be worth the telling." Rather, Fühmann assures us, "Hoffmann, like all great romantics a realist, takes his facts from life: a flight from the burning stake to freedom, the tight-rope walk of a persecuted victim over burning ledges, a bat with human features, such things happen everywhere once, whether in big city markets or in the recesses of the soul, but even miracles must remain in the realm of the possible, which is to say: testable by experience." A miracle, like a fairy tale, is drawn from the "trivial structures" of daily life, which Fühmann distills to a neat formula cited from Brecht: "He took what he was given, since necessity is cruel / but he said (being no fool): / Why are you giving me shelter? Why are you giving me gruel? / Woe! What is your plan for me, what is your rule?" (382). In other words, Andres dimly grasps that a monstrous gift (a gift of life) will exact a monstrous penalty. Singularity may well exclude any causal regularity except the one that even Andres could recognize from fairy tales: it will demand its due (*unicuique suum tribuere*). These miracles are not sheer gifts of life and justice—which might indeed merit the unbounded gratitude and loyalty that Andres is so willing to show his lord—but they belong to a recognizable economy drawn from real life in which nothing goes unpaid.

It is never clear to Andres—and ultimately not to us, either—whether a given miracle stems from lord or devil; one miracle inexplicably turns into its opposite according to the fairy tale formula. Right at the outset of the story, the count's reappointment of Andres from bodyguard to game warden after he saves his life on an Italian journey, and his granting Andres permission to marry and return with an Italian bride—this noblesse oblige is the very curse that elevates Andres into a position that is insufficient for nourishing a family: "a promotion into misery" (380), as Fühmann puts it, whereupon promptly "beneficence becomes plague" (380). This "reversal" (*Umkehrung*, 379) is not a dialectical transformation—whose discovery is the insistent goal of Fühmann's writing—but a "perversion" (*Verkehrung*, 379) of decency. The story's next miracle, then, is only an intensification, a turn of the screw—namely, the arrival at Andres's woodland hut of an errant merchant looking for shelter and protection as he passes through the count's brigand-filled forest en route to the next trade fair. The traveler bears a chest of valuables including the crystal phial that saves Andres's wife and son from inevitable starvation, something the poor and isolated game warden, brave and capable as he is, could not possibly do himself within the confines of his unforgiving social position. Like the favors bestowed on him by his remote, if well-meaning lord, the uncanny gifts bestowed by the stranger are greeted with gratitude—and also dread: merely, not with insight. The sudden donations out of the blue, out of the bland wasting away of an unlivable life, are moments of dramatic peripeteia, the turning points that in tragic epistemology should lead to insight (*anagnorisis*), but since they are occasioned by a kind of unprecedented fate, there is no accounting for them and no recognition of them for what they are—just the trivial dread of the habitually downtrodden in the face of any beneficence. In fact, Andres is so benignly passive that a court judgment later passed on him can only take his and his family's unaccountable survival in his unlivable situation as an index of some kind of culpability. "The prevailing situation becomes a German fate," comments Fühmann, "and yielding to it becomes a German virtue: later, in the law court, it will count as an index of guilt that the game warden 'achieved a certain prosperity' . . ." (381).

When the stranger, none other than the notorious villain Black Ignaz, Trabacchio in his native Italy, comes to Andres's forest hut with his "blood red" liqueur to save the warden's wife and child, the liqueur, of course, turns out not just to be the red color of blood, but to be a diabolical potion made from the actual blood of his wife's murdered brother, sacrificed in his infancy by the unscrupulous demon. For unbeknownst to all but Denner himself, Andres's wife is Denner's abandoned daughter. And Denner has sought her out on the distant Vach estate to collect the blood of one of the next generation in order to further his magical dominion. The miracle of the blood-red potion is the next curse, after the promotion to misery, that will lead inexorably to the murder of Andres's second child, the death of his wife, and untold calamities for the wretched vassal. These are indeed terrible visitations, dispensed without regard for the soul they so utterly shape, but Fühmann, mindful of criticism that holds that the sulfur and pitch of olden days might not be as scary (and morally instructive) as once upon a time, claims that the story's penetrating horror never lay in its unheard-of miracles. The horrible thread of red running through the story turns out to be a red herring. With surprising discipline, Fühmann resists the temptation of Hoffmann's more spectacular effects, images that at first would seem to lend themselves so well to a reading seeking the contemporary relevance of Hoffmann's story in the red GDR.

The apotheosis of these supernatural occurrences is actually Hoffmann's description of their origin in a flashback to Denner's merciless childhood in Italy. As evidence in Denner's trial for the (eventual and inevitable) murder of Count Vach, transcripts are sent up from Naples, where his father once stood trial for crimes even more macabre than his son's. The files report the story of a Doctor Trabacchio serial killing his children for their blood, which he uses to concoct a rejuvenating elixir. Of his children only Denner survives as heir to his father's black arts. The key testimony affirming the father's satanic collusion is given by a handful of drunken Neapolitan noblemen, good Christians who witness "a great glowing red cock, buck antlers sitting jauntily on his head, strutting along with stretched out wings" (385), and following behind it, Trabacchio, Denner's father, his path illuminated by the cock's red glow. This gleam marks the same trail on which young Denner embarks in line behind that awful red cock, neither fish nor fowl, the distillate of all that is demonic and terrifying in the tale. But Fühmann will have none of it: "[In] the vassal's will to eternalize his vassalage, *there* lies this story's vicious circle, in the self-denial of development, not in the circle of the salamander's seal and blue flames" (385) around which the red cock struts. This indifference to Hoffmann's most virtuosic effects is doubly surprising since the red cock is a figure with intense personal associations for Fühmann. In the same 1971 letter to his editor I mentioned in the previous chapter, explaining why the recurring adverbs "suddenly, abruptly" (*plötzlich*, *jählings*) are so essential to his aesthetics, he recalls the epiphanic childhood moment intimating how transformation happens as a sudden shock whose "sometimes grotesque effects" endure a lifetime. Four years old, Fühmann walks out of a dark shed into a courtyard, "a cock, headless, spurting blood, flies into my face from the butcher's axe of the clumsy servant girl. It was a shock that broke through only when the cock sat on the table the next day as a dinner roast: suddenly the image from the previous day flew into my face again, I was sick, from one moment to the next I started throwing up green bile, fell into a fever, lay hallucinating for three days, and since then eat no fowl on pain of instant nausea."[11]

While wonderfully uncanny, the red cock with jaunty antlers is a spurious dialectical image of the sort that mesmerized the generation Fühmann was trying to escape, a generation that came to socialism by way of a different hell, "and if it wasn't sulfur that stank there, then the smoke of human flesh" (379). The image flashes up in a moment of danger, *kairos*, all but indifferent to the distinction between opportunity and catastrophe: the red cock, the Gallic cock of 1789, the red flag of October 1917, the decapitated cock spurting blood into a child's face, and the blood-red potion restoring Andres's firstborn. These are all tremendous things, but for Fühmann it is no longer the unheard-of of transformation, but the heard-of triviality that counts. Not the red revolutions and revelations announced in great spectacles from beyond the vicious circle of everyday life, delivered revolutions, and delegated revelations, but what counts is his recognition that pious Andres is his true soulmate in the postrevolutionary era. Of all Hoffmann's characters, Fühmann believes Andres is the hardest to identify with, "his dull-wittedness is not flawed knowledge, but moral moldering, and the pungent sanctimony of his inner voice repels our sympathy as stubbornly as the game warden repels any encouragement to act on his own behalf" (383). Andres is the "abject" that "simultaneously beseeches and pulverizes the subject" (Kristeva), a human version of Parmenides' "mud or dirt or any other trivial and undignified object" who breaks down all efforts at identification and sympathy, and winds up exposing a horrifying lack of self-transcendence at one's very own core.[12] "I won't be able to get out of my skin anymore," is Fühmann's motto, "and I never could."[13]

"In the Bible," Fühmann writes Christa Wolf in 1978, "Hell is the place of 'howling and gnashing of teeth.' Here we do both; it's just that our Satans are so measly, no Lucifers—those were the days."[14] The Lucifers, the great revolutionaries who, blind with inspiration, rose up against the reigning order, are pale memories of something wondrous and horrible—Stalin's smiling face in the *lager'voennoplennych*, Lenin's slogans emblazoned on red banners—that no longer seems real, relevant, or, for that matter, scary. Scary are the measly Satans of Fühmann's world, those who, like Fühmann himself, cannot escape the paralyzing sense that they are accommodating themselves to unlivable lives: again, "[In] the vassal's will to eternalize his vassalage, *there* lies the devil's circle [*Teufelskreis*], . . . not in the circle of the salamander's seal." His familiar devils achieve no true Idea of themselves—whether as good or evil—but, like Andres, imagine that by preserving their inner independence, by acting "as if," they have found a third way between their lords and their demons. Warned by Denner either to accompany the robber band or to see it execute his wife and child, Andres plays along. "Inwardly cursing the roguish Denner to hell, he decides to feign submission of his will, to remain free of larceny and murder, and to exploit his penetration into the brigands' lair to arrange at the first opportunity for their exposure and capture" (393). This stratagem in response to the cruel extortion of *tertium non datur* is what Fühmann calls "acting with reservation," "not deciding is already to decide, so one must do a third thing . . . and that is precisely where the reservation [*Vorbehalt*] comes in" (392).

> The contradiction of one's reservation develops in playing along against one's will; under the pretext of being accountable to oneself, accountability slips one's mind, and the guilt only doubles: not only does one play along, but one does so only half heartedly. [. . .] A new dimension comes into existence, one is woven into a web of relationships with all one's being, not just as a bearer of reservations. Forced to act, one acts, and every time transgresses the theoretically set boundary; acting always means: realizing oneself, and this in all ways, with the reservation, but also against it.—The reservation one keeps for oneself, the actions are for others: one always wants to prove what one can do, and if not consciously, then all the stronger unconsciously . . . . (394)

This is a haunting dialectic for someone who knows all too well what "acting with reservations" is: living half a life devoted to a revolution creeping along without its proper revelation. Fühmann's conception of reservation inverts the idea of the soul as an inner reserve of humanity sheltered from depredations of the world. "This inner focus," writes Hegel about such a reserve, "this simple region of the claim of subjective freedom—the seat of volition, resolution, and action, the abstract content of conscience, that wherein responsibility and worth of the individual are enclosed—remains untouched. It is quite shut out from the noisy din of world history."[15] By contrast, the reservation assailing Fühmann does not escape the system it is constrained to serve: the third thing succumbs to the iron law of *tertium non datur*. Instead of the false vassal's "unhappy consciousness,"[16] the true revolutionary's slogan is "WE ARE HAPPY!" and nothing makes the loyal GDR citizen happier than the right mandated by the GDR constitution (Article 21, Paragraph 1) to "Work together, plan together, govern together!"[17] Every suspicious question—*is this it? can this truly be socialism?*—is greeted by the surpassing desire to *make it so* by confounding the reservation through one's boldest actions. The preposterous extortion of two masters is simply the price of socialism's antagonistic universality, and affirmative action expresses faith in the eventual triumph of the best. Or is it half-faith? Or cowardice? What if this agonizing complicity with the proclaimed "workers' and peasants' state" is not truly revolutionary, but the opposite, stagnation and betrayal?

The word Fühmann returns to for describing Andres's character is *Ergebenheit*, devotion, resignation, submission. The word also conveys the idea of waiting for an *Ergebnis*, a result or outcome—that is, holding back for the right moment of revelation: giving and reserving oneself for what lies beyond the present. "Whether submission can be a virtue depends on that to which one submits: as a principle for its own sake on into infinity, it comes down to relinquishing oneself" (384). The horrible risk is that one knows what one has submitted to only when it yields its unheard-of truth: but yields it to whom, if one has relinquished oneself without reservations? The revolutionary miracle announces itself somewhere, in some camp, and is received unreservedly, a satanic moment of staking everything, a blinding point of absolute expenditure (*inutilité*), and then every bit as suddenly the ecstasy is past, and one beholds the shit that still must be shoveled out of the latrines in the good-new just as in the bad-old camp. After the miracle, after the demonstration, when the red banners are being furled, initiative is bound to the discipline of awaiting the precipitation of the collective result—the patient auscultation of circumstances is the ultimate virtue of the loyal revolutionary.

The faithful do not simply ascend, but have to bear with a world of "thinghood," which Hegel defines as "the abstract universal medium," "nothing else than what the Here and Now have proved themselves to be; viz. a simple togetherness of a plurality."[18] Mud, dirt, indignity—that is, really existing socialism—imposes itself as a task between Fühmann and the mana of sovereignty. "In the moment that corresponds to desire in the lord's consciousness, an inessential relationship to the thing appears to have become the lot of the servile consciousness," the relationship of hard labor and deferred gratification.[19] This resistant objectivity is the abstract general medium of sovereignty that the vassal renounces on penalty of reverting to the fascist camp—it is his one passage, "one precisely by being opposed to others."[20] Discussing with an interviewer his last, unfinished opus, *In the Mines*, Fühmann describes descending a mineshaft "tunneled during socialism" that leads to a "gallery that catches the run-off water from the south flank of the Harz mountains: it comes from Metternich's day."[21] The singular passage between revolution and revelation is nonetheless riddled with labyrinthine tunnels tying socialism to restoration, and restoration to radicalism, by way of dirt that refuses to yield a single promised sense. In the same interview Fühmann ponders the redeeming characteristics he had as an SA man that he comes back to as a New Man under the "dictatorship of the proletariat." "This homecoming to something from which one springs," he shrugs, "I don't know: Is that a circle? A spiral, for which there's no telling: is it ascending or declining?"[22] "It is," as he wrote Christa Wolf in a more bitter moment, "a screw without end."[23]

Back in the Stalinist 1950s, when Lucifer was still Lucifer and Fühmann a functionary, he spent a few years passing on meaningless reports to the secret police until they dropped him as a feckless informant, and for years afterward he did not do much, but did his bit, for the party line—but what could it mean to a committed socialist like Fühmann, born of the incomprehensible death of the camps, to be a socialist halfheartedly? How many doughty Andreses are there like him, filled with reservations that are overcome with every superhuman exertion on behalf of an increasingly untenable situation? The potency of Fühmann's essay is that it does not judge Andres, but recognizes him as a figure incapable of recognition. He resists incorporation into the Hegelian dialectic, not as an ecstatic subject of rebellion against Hegelian totality, but as a simple index of stasis: loyally committed to the medium, to thinghood, to his unique passage. Andres has received his miracles and now he awaits their transportation through his life.

> The opportunity that comes on its own is always wrong; one seizes it of course, and since it doesn't eventuate [*zeitigt*] what one was striving for, one repeats

> the mistake. Psychologists might analyze this complex more clearly and give it a name; Hoffman's achievement—to have, in a single stroke and on a single spot, made poetry of what in daily life is an everlasting present—will never be lessened by analysis since it can be exhausted neither in psychology nor sociology. Nor in history . . . What remains is the incomprehensibility of this incomprehensible truth that succeeds in holding its own against all explanation. (395)

Andres, ***horribile dictu***, represents the ultimate ecstasy, the inexplicable dissolution of subjectivity into the thinghood of the universe: the ***nunc stans*** of sovereignty and revolution. He is a thing and nothing, without consciousness or identity, the evisceration of total recollection and the dismissal of reciprocal economy: "slow rotting away, tortured repression, blocked development, stalled dialectic, and out of it all, an unholy, nonreciprocal perversion of good deed into plague, but not plague into good deed, that is the basic movement of this action-packed story of a sheer letting-things-happen-to-oneself" (379). Andres is an object measure of a reality which he cannot rightly see or act upon. A subject beyond subjectivity, his job is not to act on his own reason or desires, but to register an incompletion for us, to point out a desire not located in any particular mind or body, but manifested in the unsupportable contradictions of the system. Sovereignty is not linked to Hegel's tragic-heroic conception of life, but to the patience to be everything and nothing, where desire for self-realization is relinquished to the one situation in which one puts one's existential faith: for Andres that is feudal restoration, for Fühmann it is socialist revolution. Maybe they are the same situation, but Fühmann's perverse courage is to flaunt the bliss of rebellion for the sake of taking measure, of serving as an index, a vassal whose master is the sovereign revolution whose unprecedented bliss he once hoped—should the needle have finally pointed there—to experience himself.

3. PERVERSIONS AND REVELATION

> Nothing interrupts the silence of desolation anymore. Over the dark, age-old treetops clouds drift on and are mirrored in the greenish-blue waters of the pond, glimmering like an abyss. And unmoving, as if sunken in mournful submission [*Ergebenheit*], the surface rests—day-in, day-out.
>
> —Trakl, "Desolation"[24]

A hesitation between the real and the unreal is how Tsvetan Todorov defines the effect of the fantastic genre: it creates a suspension, an epoché, rather than a judgment. By contrast, an allegorical or symbolist genre, of which Fühmann takes the "fairy tale" as a paradigm, asks for interpretations that discover the real "tenor" of the fantastic "vehicle," with the result that such a tale "lets itself be fit fully and without violence into a system of moral coordinates."[25] What distinguishes the fantastic is that it does not call for translating its perverse code back into some acceptable literal meaning, which would deprive it of its distinction, leaving behind only a realistic text whose fantastic features referred to actual psychological or social symptoms.[26] Instead, it calls upon a reader to "hesitate" between language and logic: "[T]he fantastic occupies the duration of this uncertainty."[27] Donald Davidson has made a similar point about metaphor more generally, claiming that a metaphor does not have two stable meanings, a false one (the vehicle) and a true one (the tenor); it has only its literal *meaning*, which is false on the face of it, while its *usage* directs one to think about relevant comparisons rather than a hidden truth.[28] In the longer or shorter duration—one might say, in the event—of metaphor's patent falsehood, one is impelled to search elsewhere for something true. The fantastic genre, on this conception, would not have any hidden "meaning," but would call on one to think comparatively—outside the box, or outside one's skin, as it were. But a comparison between what and what? In the case of "Marsyas," we saw how the "more beautiful" of the Satyr's flute with respect to the God's lyre has no suitable third term, no space for reserving judgment, no medium or ground; it is an unheard-of comparison. Whatever it is that the story's metaphors direct its readers to compare, the comparison remains unthinkable, the metaphorics stalled in its horrible literality.

Heidegger, for his part, dissolves even the distinction between meaning and usage, suggesting evocatively that "thinking should bring into view what was un-heard (of) [*Un-erhört*] before. Thinking is a listening that brings something to view."[29] At first, he draws a provisional distinction between the metaphorical and literal (sensible). "If we take thinking to be a sort of hearing and seeing, then sensible hearing and seeing is taken up and over into the realm of nonsensible perception, that is, of thinking. In Greek such transposing is called μεταφερειν. The language of scholars names such a carrying-over 'metaphor.' So thinking may be called a hearing and listening, a viewing and bringing into view only in a metaphorical, figurative sense."[30] He no sooner draws this distinction than he immediately overturns it. "The idea of 'transposing' and of metaphor is based upon the distinguishing if not complete separation, of sensible and the nonsensible as two realms that subsist on their own. [. . .] When one gains the insight into the limitations of metaphysics, 'metaphor' as a normative conception also becomes untenable."[31] This insight, that the "partitioning of the sensible and nonsensible is insufficient,"[32] points to the spot where we left off in reading "The Street of Perversions," when Jirro, absorbed by his bizarre acoustic theater, has transgressed—in the span of an imperceptibly brief moment—the boundary between the real and the unreal. His ontological transgression, accordingly, is not a metaphorical transposition from figurative to literal, but indicates a border whose real existence falls between the sensible and nonsensible. What Jirro hears in Libroterr's back streets, as ordinary as it is from the perspective of auditory perception, brings into view the unheard-of. The narrative question here, in the face of Jirro's spectacle, concerns what this unheard-of *is*, since its lack of any precedent leaves it without a proper name. Heidegger suggests the punning term "event/appropriation" (*das Ereignis*) to call attention to both the innovative and the proper self-measure that one witnesses when one "views with an ear and hears with an eye."[33]

But the Heideggerian terminology is taking us ahead of ourselves. The question What does Jirro see? remains caught in ambiguity between the sensible and the nonsensible that only the appearance of the unheard-of itself will resolve. This unheard-of is either the horrible cruelty he hears in the street, a violence that shakes him from the complacent belief that the true measure of reality is to be found in the orderly cosmos of Uniterr; or it is the very event, in the vanishing instant, of his becoming convinced of Uniterr's ultimate irreality. At first it might seem clear that the blissful cruelties he imagines while listening to Libroterr's television are the decisive events, since their spectacle is what leads him to name his back alleys "Streets of Revelation"—and how is one to trump the name of revelation? But as is often the case in Fühmann's stories, what we think is decisive is quickly reversed by a successive insight. "In following an outer development," we learn, "an inner one escaped Jirro's attention" (73). This inner development is the conversion by which Jirro instantaneously, and almost by the by, abandons his ontological commitment to Uniterr. Since he cannot intellectually grasp the profundity of this existential shift (if Fühmann were Jirro, this instant—*punctum!*—would be his end), all Jirro has are uncomfortable traces of it after the fact. "That Libroterr with all its abnormalities seemed normal (perhaps, measured?) to him and Uniterr seemed schematic was something Jirro didn't reflect on; only occasionally he suspected there might be a problem, as for example when he caught himself laughing at grotesque cruelties" (73). There might be a problem: the soul of the free world is revealed to him; it consists of an eminently desirable cruelty; this cruelty/desire is, all vague reservations aside, so much more real than the schematism of the planned world that the planned world stands revealed as simply soulless. Uniterr is soulless because it has no idea what it is missing, no idea of what has been subtracted from its pleasures by virtue of the schematic unity broadcast by the sole station remaining to it after the "famous amalgamation year 2001" (70). Uniterr's willful positing of the identity of sense and senses crumbles before Libroterr's rich multiplicity and plurality, which overwhelms Jirro precisely through his mutilation of five senses into one, acute auditory faculty.

But reservations are incompatible with the overwhelming force of revelation. As the Muses learn from Marsyas, "[W]hen [revelation] happens, it happens wholly"[34](a lesson that went astray on the pious, reserved Andres). If something is lacking in Uniterr, something is also being held back in Libroterr—Jirro's revelation of Libroterr's reality comes only after the fact of an event he has *neither* sensed nor made sense of. The event itself (*both* sensed and sensible) is missing; has "escaped Jirro's attention"; it is merely that, not knowing what a true event would be, he doesn't know he is missing it. So his "Streets of Revelation" remain revealing for him until one day, unexpectedly, he hears a sound so unprecedented, so unimaginable to him that his lingering reservations about the status of this revelation explode in outrage.

> It was an evil, penetrating hiss, as though highly pressurized hypnocyanamylnitrite were streaming out of a psychoairconditioner . . . and against his will Jirro slowed his pace. Agonizing death by gas was new to him, but even so, and even though he only heard it, every detail stood out before his eyes since the murderer was contemptuously describing to the victim, apparently in a glass booth, the view being offered him. [. . .] What Jirro heard was a minute description of eyes rolling back to their whites and a chest vaulting in cramps, inside of which lungs had to suck in their doom all the more eagerly the more they were being consumed. [. . .] Jirro . . . remained standing, and listening saw the scene . . . ; he heard the voice of the murderer whisper an homage to two discoloring lips. (73–74)

Transported by this "feast for the eyes," Jirro is interrupted in his ecstasy by a bicycle bell, and as he flees the scene, the sound of a gasping mouth pours forth from every apartment as "appetite-driven remote controls instantly run through the channels" (74). The fact that he had abandoned himself to this spectacle, "his face naked before his senses" (74), shames him so acutely that he accosts his Libroterranean lab colleague the next morning, who simply laughs. "[W]hat does Jirro want, the world, after all, is perverse" (74). Never having heard the word "perverse" before, Jirro asks for an explanation and is so taken with its meaning that instead of "Streets of Revelation" he decides to name the gas chamber alley the "Street of Perversions." The plural perversions that replace the singular revelation are no accident. Rather, no sooner has the Uniterrean Jirro learned the new concept, than he is immediately seized by the project of classifying and systematizing the variety of perversions. In particular, he decides to pragmatically declare the gas chamber scene his benchmark of worst perversion and from there seek out a worse (*ärger*) one until he has found the very worst (*das Ärgste*): *pessimum pessimorum*.

The project, as promisingly as it begins, drags on. The gas chamber remains the worst among other bad scenes, and the singular superlative Jirro sought as the measure for bringing order to his project of systematization bogs down in the accidental plurality and routine perversity of what he hears. Meanwhile, Jirro's seventy-week stay inexorably approaches the last week, the last day, and then, his melancholy waxing with his realization that he has failed to find the most perverse perversion, the realest reality, he ruefully makes his way one last time to his Street of Perversions. Not only has he never really seen the gruesome sight that draws him back to the consecrated spot, but as he surrenders himself to his memory of its ecstasy, he does not hear it anymore either, and "gives himself over entirely to an inner vision" (76). Jirro's devotional pilgrimage to the site of the most perverse event he has experienced so far is described as a moment of tranquility, *Gelassenheit*, in the Heideggerian sense of an openness drained of arbitrary willfulness, a simple index of existence. His earlier revelation, its unity marred by his self-centered reservations about its morality, is summoned anew in a total apprehension. The Being of beings is disclosed in the superlative of the resurrected gas chamber, where everything comes together and into its own (*Er-eignis*), free from the moral, ethical, political, even referential directives of Uniterr. In the last moment of Jirro's free-world sojourn, the ontological line stands revealed for him, as it had for Fühmann in the prison camps, as that running between "poetry and doctrine."[35] "Being a poet means being hellbent on totality . . . ," Fühmann observes in an essay, "so as a poet, one is either all there or not there at all."[36] Doctrinal schema, endless politics, Hegelian dialectics—these specters from Uniterr count for nothing here where the Parmenidean poem of existence completely suffuses both sense and senses.

In this moment of unreserved submission Jirro suddenly hears a familiar voice—nothing unheard-of—and stands frozen without consciousness for an instant before street sounds flood in over the silence. The piercing call, he realizes in the drone of traffic, could hardly be meant for him since television broadcasts are not directed to an individual audience member: but whence the familiar voice? Why would anyone in Libroterr actually *choose*, actually, beyond the necessity of default, *desire* to receive Uniterr's monotonous broadcast? Sheer chance? This time, instead of being suffused by the poetry of hissing gas, "Jirro remains still, mesmerized by the unmistakable voice of the most beloved actress of his country, one of the few female members of the Supreme Liberation Council, bearer of the most exalted decorations, chair of the Council of Theatrical Workers, inspired embodiment of the thinking and feeling of Uniterr's best and brightest, the essence of that humanity which Uniterr regards as its most holy e/mission [*Sendung*] to protect from all perversions" (77). The earlier poetry of gaseous *Gelassenheit* is gone in a flash. *Most beloved, supreme liberation, most exalted, best and brightest*: the list of official properties attending the voice are surely not the fundamental attributes of Being as revealed in the perverse streets of Libroterr, but are the sturdy predicates of socialist realism, the indispensable refrain of party doctrine. As the voice's ringing superlatives distill Uniterr's alternate broadcast mission to its singular epitome, why shouldn't its reception also culminate at the unique site of Jirro's ear?

Of course, it should culminate there; it is the result of the search that Jirro has consecrated himself to from the moment he grasped the word perversions in its polymorphous opposition to singular revelation. Distracted by the noise of traffic and exchange (*Verkehr*), the din of countless television channels (*Sender*), he had merely not been open enough to his destiny (*Sendung*) to perceive the broadcast (*Sendung*). Now, the sound of the voice having at last touched his ear, he readies himself for what it is about to speak, a sentence "that no one less than the leader of the Supreme Liberation Council has proclaimed 'the most beautiful [*schönsten*] expression of Uniterr's world historical mission'" (77). Needless to say, he knows the sentence, "could recite it in his dreams" (77), and before it can be pronounced in reality, Jirro grasps precisely what happened when he first sated his ears on Libroterr's perversions and was possessed by the "feeling that he had crossed sides from a realm of unreality into that of reality" (73): he had defected. The fantastic hesitation is over, the truth illuminates the terrible event that had already happened, merely without his conscious decision, and "exactly then, as he sees his fatherland and perceives that familiar sentence, the thought suddenly shoots through Jirro that he could simply stay here: in this country, in this city, in this street" (77). Again, the street sounds burst into his consciousness, and, over the noise of traffic the unspoken sentence now rolls out to its end, its articulated syllables suffusing his senses as it triumphantly displaces the gas chamber and essential plurality of perversion with "the most awful [*das Ärgste*] of all things experienced in the street: COMRADE AND SHOULD IT LAST YEARS WE WILL CONTINUE DISCUSSING WITH YOU UNTIL YOU TOO HAVE BEEN PERSUADED" (78). In the instant of darkest confusion, "blind minute hands . . . climbing toward midnight" (Trakl), at that moment, the contours of reality are inverted again, Uniterr has curved back around on Jirro like a cocoon, the sovereign completion of his system of perversions, absolute knowledge, is revealed in this one most beautiful expression. And with this insight into necessity, Jirro is at last master, free from the external compulsion of Uniterr's mission. He truly desires Uniterr, he chooses it, embraces the life sentence of infinite discussion as the absolute culmination of his boundless faith and desire: *optimum optimorum*.

4. EPILOGUE

"The Dream of Moira," Franz Fühmann

> In one of those indeterminate regions, nonetheless instantly capable of every determination, the kind one often sees in dreams: regions (since one cannot call them landscapes) that appear to consist of not yet materialized, but indeed localized ideational substance, of lexical-references that find themselves still in the pure potential of a *How*, even while already in the reality of *What* and *Where*, so one can say well enough: to my left is *ocean* and on my right, toward the background, are *mountains*; where the ocean remains merely an acknowledged ocean, not yet an incarnate one, neither seething pot nor weltering desolation nor distant reflection of a seraph's smile, but an as yet entirely nonsensuous transitional being, present as a site and sort, but stalled as it were in the flux between concept and thing, no longer abstract nor yet concrete, no longer in itself, but not yet for itself, Schopenhauer's sea, if you will, and Schopenhauer's mountains, colorless and contourless, a majestic massing of every potentially existing surf and peak along with their future eagles and ships—, in one such region, the inside of a basilica on the verge of becoming, enclosing an entire zone, I see, gray against the gray fog of walls, the ancient fabric of an undulating cloth over which an old woman, inclined already to visibility, is bending. One of the Fates, I think reverently, and venture to approach her, and Moira—since it's the unarticulated trinity—looks up, but without interrupting her activity.—What are you making, mother, I murmur awe-struck; whose cloth is it you're weaving, of such immense dimension? For, look, it's already filling the royal hall knee deep, and it's flooding the countryside as though intended as a shirt for a nation with all its dead and unborn.—Ah, am I weaving at all? Moira murmurs, astonished,

and now I notice that the old woman isn't making a cloth, but embroidering one, ice gray letters of remarkable alphabets, maybe Hebrew, but faces in the beam-enclosed hollows of the emblems, and faces colored the way ice is colored, milky with a hint of blue or green. For whom, mother, are you stitching these lots? I ask trembling since I'm speaking Chaldean, and Moira murmurs, I might simply open my eyes, it's my own lot as well.—I consider the signs, I can't read them, but I know they are totemic signs, signs for friend or foe in a genealogy, and now beneath the undulating folds of the cocoon I see long rows of fetuses marching. They hover, faceless, amphibian in the billowy gray of the basilica as if in the uterus of a fate that is more than an individual's, and I suspect they will merge in some incomprehensible way with the ice-gray heads.—Are you weaving language, mother? I whisper, but Moira shakes her head and murmurs: More!—More than language, I think incredulously, and now it's sufficient for me just to think, as Moira raises her head and says in tone that could be called mischievous if it weren't also one of utter exhaustion: And less, my son, more and less, because more is less, less more!—One of Macbeth's witches, I think, and Moira murmurs, working in a face without any traits: The emblem of love, the emblem of hate; the ancestor, the leader, foes, friends; dark, light; the emblem of faith—and she points out the lunar blue face without eyes and mouth under her fingers and murmurs almost inaudibly: son, look at the emblem of faith, it's been separated from you twice, son, but it won't come off a third time!—and at that spot I see the fetuses being drawn into the cloth and sensing something look down at myself and see red, skinless flesh. And Moira murmurs, submerging herself in the cloth: look at grace!, and gently the undulating fabric wraps itself around my flayed foot and, grafting itself to the sheer, bloody flesh, crawls inexorably over my ankles, calves, thigh, penis and hips to my chest and further up to my chin; foggy gray it climbs to just below my eyes; ice gray envelops me, I feel cold, and imagining I hear Moira murmuring in the distance, I dream I've been woken up.[37]

REFERENCE MATTER

Notes

INTRODUCTION

1. Max Horkheimer and Theodor Adorno, *The Dialectic of Enlightenment*, trans. John Cumming (New York: Continuum, 1972 [1944]) 106.

2. Roland Barthes, *A Lover's Discourse*, trans. Richard Howard (New York: Hill and Wang, 1978) 5.

3. See, for example, Michael Geyer, ed., *The Power of Intellectuals in Contemporary Germany* (Chicago: U Chicago P, 2001); Konrad H. Jarausch, *Dictatorship as Experience: Toward a Socio-Cultural History of the GDR*, trans. Eve Duffy (New York: Berghahn, 1999); Julia Hell, Loren Kruger, Katie Trumpener, "Dossier: Socialist Realism and East German Modernism—Another Historians' Debate," *Rethinking Marxism* 7.3 (fall 1994): 37–79.

4. In *Agon: Towards a Theory of Revisionism* (Oxford: Oxford UP, 1982), Harold Bloom develops an ethos of "agon," writing that "Burkhardt, Nietzsche, Huizinga are the cultural theorists of the agonistic spirit, from the Greeks and the Hebrews onwards, but Freud is the prophet of agon and of its ambivalences. The first theologians of agon were the Gnostics of Alexandria, and the final pragmatists of agon have been and will be the Americans of Emerson's tradition" (viii). I cite Bloom to caution that the "agonistic spirit" might be taken to culminate in American competitive capitalism (or an Anglo-American sporting ethos); I try to take care, then, not to make struggle, competition, or disagreement into a value in itself, but to understand the term as indicating the impossibility of closure, stasis, and equilibrium. Agon, in this sense, is a "becoming," as opposed to the classical idea of a "crisis," or final judgment. The disparate historical figures who bear most on this study go from the anti-Parmenideans among the Greeks to Hegel, Marx, and Carl Schmitt among the moderns. More contemporary influences will be apparent in the text, including "the Americans of Emerson's tradition."

5. Alain Badiou formulates the way an event like socialism is denied any significance with the phrase "nothing has taken place but the place." This phrase, according to Badiou, doesn't deny that socialism can be described by a time and

place, only that its descriptive elements do not amount to anything special. It is an ideological formation like any other. Alain Badiou, *Being and Event*, trans. Oliver Feltham (London: Continuum, 2005) 182.

6. Classical theories of modernity are found in Durkheim, Marx, Weber, Parsons, Luhmann, and Habermas. Theories of modernization comprise a distinct literature, often criticized for its rationalist, teleological, and Western-centered bias. For an overview, see Hans-Ulrich Wehler, *Modernisierungstheorie und Geschichte* (Göttingen: Vandenhoeck and Ruprecht, 1975). A theoretical discourse of modernity and universality has begun to reconsider both terms, arguing that "the universal" is an "empty signifier," "empty form," or a "singular void" that, depending on one's position, is produced by adhering to modernity itself. See Alain Badiou, "Eight Theses on the Universal," in *Theoretical Writings*, ed. and trans. Ray Brassier and Alberto Toscano (London: Continuum, 2004) 143–52; Judith Butler, Ernesto Lacalu, and Slavoj Zizek, *Contingency, Hegemony, Universality* (London: Verso, 2000).

7. In *Did Somebody Say Totalitarianism? Five Interventions in the (Mis)use of a Notion* (London: Verso, 2001), Slavoj Zizek criticizes one of academia's "unwritten rules and prohibitions," "the need to 'contextualize' or 'situate' one's positions . . . in a historical context" (1). Such historicizing is false because "the very attempt to locate particular roots . . . ideologically occludes the social reality of the reign of 'real abstraction'" (2). Generalizing from the circulation of capital, Zizek's argument has an opposite starting point from my own, which begins from the empirical distinction of socialism's universalist organizational principles; but we share a suspicion of easy calls to "historicize."

8. For instance, see Martha Woodmansee and Mark Osteen, eds., *The New Economic Criticism: Studies at the Intersection of Literature and Economics* (London: Routledge, 1999).

9. Influential works in this vein are: Jean-Francois Lyotard, *Libidinal Economy*, trans. Iain Hamilton Grant (Bloomington: Indiana UP, 1993); Jean-Joseph Goux, *Symbolic Economies: After Marx and Freud*, trans. Jennifer Curtiss Gage (Ithaca, NY: Cornell UP, 1990); Walter Benn Michaels, *The Gold Standard and the Logic of Naturalism* (Berkeley: U California P, 1987); Jean Baudrillard, *For a Critique of the Political Economy of the Sign*, trans. Charles Levin (St. Louis: Telos, 1981); Marc Shell, *The Economy of Literature* (Baltimore: Johns Hopkins UP, 1978).

PART I

EPIGRAPH: Alexis de Tocqueville, *Democracy in America*, 2 vols., ed. Phillips Bradley (New York: Knopf, 1945) 1:15. Modifications by the author [BR].

CHAPTER ONE

1. In Charles Hope Kerr's 1900 translation.

2. William Morris, *Chants for Socialists* [1885]. Accessed August 10, 2006, at http://www.gutenberg.org/etext/3170.

3. Ken Loach, *Land and Freedom*, VHS (New York: Polygram, 1996).

4. George Orwell, *Homage to Catalonia* (San Diego: Harcourt Brace, 1952).

5. Ernst Bloch, *The Principle of Hope*, trans. Neville Plaice, Stephen Plaice, and Paul Knight (Cambridge, MA: MIT Press, 1986).

6. Claude Lévi-Strauss, *Introduction to the Work of Marcel Mauss*, trans. Felicity Baker (London: Routledge and Kegan Paul, 1987) 63.

7. This account comes from Harrison E. Salisbury, *The 900 Days: The Siege of Leningrad* (New York: Harper and Row, 1969) 235.

8. The "Third Period" line, which Stalin asserted at the Sixth Congress of the Comintern in 1928, held that Social Democrats were "social fascists," and, militarily, that the Red Army was not a foreign army to the international proletariat—hence, if the Soviet Union were attacked, Communist parties in belligerent countries should turn against their regimes and defend the Red Army as their own. The history of Stalin's "Third Period" illustrates the tragic earnestness with which the Red Army's self-understanding as the army of the working class was taken.

9. Theodor W. Adorno, "Cultural Criticism and Society," in *Prisms*, trans. Samuel and Shierry Weber (Cambridge: MIT P, 1981) 22. Herbert Marcuse writes that true literature and art "were essentially alienation, sustaining and protecting the contradiction—the unhappy consciousness of the divided world, the defeated possibilities, the hopes unfulfilled, the promises betrayed." Herbert Marcuse, *One Dimensional Man* (Boston: Beacon P, 1964) 61.

10. Adorno, "Cultural Criticism," 23.

11. In "Eastern Europe's Republics of Gilead," in *Dimensions of Radical Democracy*, ed. Chantal Mouffe (London: Verso, 1992), Slavoj Zizek writes about the "Nation-Thing" as a vague object with little reality beyond a group's recursive faith in its existence. This empty reflexivity of nationalism does not explain socialist identity—which never had near nationalism's virulence—but indicates that Eastern European socialism needs something in addition to group faith to define its difference from nationalism. Nonetheless, the faith of the soldiers is an important element. Alain Badiou, who has done more than any recent thinker to reintroduce problems of faith into leftist philosophy, argues that faith legitimates a chance as present to everyone; it names a chance event and thereby allows it to circulate as politically meaningful. "To be faithful is to gather together and distinguish the becoming legal of a chance." Alain Badiou, *Being and Event*, trans. Oliver Feltham (New York: Continuum, 2005) 232.

12. Art historian Otto Karl Werckmeister similarly contrasts isolating what he calls the "left icon" as an unthreatening and historically uncolored symbol with embedding it in the historical and systemic context that shaped its meaning. He calls Eisenstein's *Potemkin*, Picasso's *Guernica,* and Benjamin's version of Klee's *Angelus Novus* "icons of the left," "because in the Marxist culture of capitalism they have been detached from their historical and political origins and made into visual or literary rallying points for a dissident leftist mentality" (2). As perhaps *the* icon of the Left, the "Internationale" is a musical addition to the visual rallying points whose abstraction from context Werckmeister criticizes. He argues that jettisoning the communist presuppositions of iconic artworks has allowed them to serve as the focus of utopian projections while ensuring that those projections remain abstract and ineffectual. Werckmeister situates these icons in the military context

of the Red Army and Popular Front. Ironically, in the Spanish Civil War context of my example, Picasso's *Guernica*, with its horrifying depiction of civilian victims, lent support to the professionalization of Republican defense and a sharp moral distinction between military and civilian casualties (73): it was this professionalization under Communist Party leadership that Orwell and Loach opposed. The left iconography of Loach's "Internationale" is at odds with that of Picasso's *Guernica*. Otto Karl Werckmeister, *Icons of the Left* (Chicago: U Chicago P, 1999).

13. For this view of the historical significance of leftist movements, see Geoff Eley's monumental, *Forging Democracy: The History of the Left in Europe, 1850–2000* (Oxford: Oxford UP, 2002).

14. No doubt symbols and cultural artifacts—such as "The Internationale" or, for that matter, a Shostakovich symphony—*can* be detached from any system of determination. Shostakovich's 11th, composed in 1957 and dedicated to the revolutionary events of October 1905, can, if one will, be heard as a memorial to the Soviet-repressed Hungarian revolt of 1956. "It is an easy game to play," writes Richard Taruskin. "[T]he will to read ironic or subversive messages meets little or no resistance from the music." Richard Taruskin, "Stalin Lives On in the Concert Hall, but Why?" *New York Times* (Sunday, August 25, 1996; Sec. 2): 26.

15. For the characterization of cultural studies in this paragraph I have drawn on John Storey's *An Introduction to Cultural Theory and Popular Culture,* 2nd ed. (Athens: U of Georgia P, 1998) especially 45–72; and on Rob Burns's introduction to his anthology *German Cultural Studies* (Oxford: Oxford UP, 1995) 1–8. For a discussion of "methodological individualism," associated with the critique of Marxism in the work of F. A. Hayek and Karl Popper, see Richard W. Miller, "Fact and Method in the Social Sciences," in *The Philosophy of Science*, ed. Richard Boyd, Philip Gasper, and J. D. Trout (Cambridge: MIT P, 1991) 743–62.

16. "Mankind has already been abandoned by a science which in its imaginary self-sufficiency thinks of the shaping of practice, which it serves and to which it belongs, simply as something lying outside its borders and is content with this separation of thought and action." Max Horkheimer, "Traditional and Critical Theory," in *Critical Theory: Selected Essays*, trans. Matthew J. O'Connell et al. (New York: Seabury P, 1972) 188–243, 242.

17. Frederic Jameson, *Marxism and Form* (Princeton: Princeton UP, 1971) 53.

18. Max Horkheimer and Theodor W. Adorno, *Dialectic of Enlightenment*, trans. John Cumming (New York: Continuum, 1972) 120. The falsity of false art stems from exactly this unity, "the false identity of the general and the particular" (121), an identity that was only momentarily true when the bourgeoisie was a revolutionary class, as in the works of Beethoven. Where this identity is no longer possible because of alienation, the only truth is to be found in the autonomy aspiration of the alienated and instrumentalized subject.

19. Raymond Williams, *The Long Revolution* (New York: Columbia UP, 1961) 57.

20. Cited in Burns, *German Cultural Studies*, 8. Ursula Heukenkamp defines the relationship of East German literary culture to its system: "GDR-literature was heteronomous, with diverse functions from panegyric to moral didactics, it was a component of a system whose effects upon it cannot be reduced to stagnation or repression. It was determined, but also required as a producer of adequate images of

value." Ursula Heukenkamp, "Ortsgebundenheit: Die DDR-Literatur als Variante des Regionalismus in der deutschen Nachkriegsliteratur," *Weimarer Beiträge* 42.1 (1996): 30–53, 31.

21. Vladimir Ilyich Lenin, "The Chief Task of Our Day," in *The Lenin Anthology*, ed. Robert C. Tucker (New York: Norton, 1975) 433–37, 436–37.

22. Martin Jay, *Marxism and Totality* (Berkeley: U California P, 1984) 2. The connection between the Frankfurt School and the Cold War can be brought out from various angles. One is the cooperation with the U.S. Office of Strategic Services, the precursor to the CIA, that began during World War II and continued with Adorno's postwar publication in CIA-financed publications such as *Der Monat*, where he decanonizes Georg Lukács as a lapsed Western Marxist. "Only for the sake of the early writings, which were disparaged by his Party and which he had himself abjured, has anyone outside the Eastern bloc taken any notice at all of the works he has published over the last thirty years," Theodor Adorno, "Reconciliation under Duress," in *Aesthetics and Politics*, ed. Ernst Bloch et al. (London: Verso, 1977) 151–76, 151.

23. Cited by Geoff Eley in "Reviewing the Socialist Tradition," in *The Crisis of European Socialism*, ed. Christiane Lemke and Gary Marks (Durham: Duke University Press, 1992) 21–60, 25.

24. Karl Marx, "For a Ruthless Criticism of Everything Existing," in *The Marx-Engels Reader*, 2nd ed., ed. Robert C. Tucker (New York: W. W. Norton, 1978) 12–15.

25. "Insurrectionary turbulence (or just the chance that it might develop) elicited a major reformist departure, either by forcing the hand of a nervous government or by encouraging farsighted nonsocialist governments into a large-scale preemptive gesture." Eley, "Reviewing the Socialist Tradition," 32.

26. Richard Rorty, "The End of Leninism and History as Comic Frame," in *History and the Idea of Progress*, ed. Arthur M. Melzer, Jerry Weinberger, and M. Richard Zinman (Ithaca, NY: Cornell UP, 1995) 211–26, 212.

27. Anthony Giddens, *The Third Way: The Renewal of Social Democracy* (Cambridge: Polity, 1998) 2–3.

28. Stephen Resnick and Richard Wolff, "Between State and Private Capitalism: What Was Soviet 'Socialism'?" *Rethinking Marxism* 7.1 (spring 1994): 9–30, 9.

29. Frederic Jameson, *A Singular Modernity: Essay on the Ontology of the Present* (London: Verso, 2002) 29.

30. Jameson, *Singular Modernity*, 13.

31. Peter Hohendahl summarizes "the larger project of Western Marxism," "as a revisionist version of the Marxist tradition in which Hegel's dialectic strongly resurfaced, breaking up the scientific orientation of the Second International and the neoorthodoxy of the Third International." *Reappraisals: Shifting Alignments in Postwar Critical Theory* (Ithaca, NY: Cornell UP, 1991) vii. Louis Althusser and Galvano Della Volpe are the figures most strongly associated with the rejection of Hegelian Marxism and a positive estimation of the value of science to Marxist studies. Before Althusser, although never integrated into the Western Marxist tradition, Christopher Caudwell in England developed a Marxist theory of art that was strongly based on philosophy of science.

32. East German scientist Robert Havemann's reception of Engels's work, "*Dialektik der Natur*—Zum Erscheinen der ersten vollständigen deutschen Ausgabe des

genialen Werkes von Friedrich Engels" (*Einheit* 9.842–55) was an important ideological moment in the political-scientific culture of East Germany that preceded (and helped pave the way for) the official party policy on the so-called technological-scientific revolution. David Bathrick discusses the loosening effect of Havemann's work on Lysenkoist scientific dogmatism in East Germany, but believes Havemann's recourse to Engels "helped Havemann reconstitute on a methodological level the groundwork for the very orthodoxy he believed it to refute" (66). Bathrick holds with the Frankfurt critique of cultural-technological reconciliation. He thus praises Havemann's "subjective integrity," but is not able to assign lasting value to his methodological insights. By contrast, I would emphasize not necessarily any methodological novum, but the importance of seeing Havemann as posing valid questions of real socialism (rather than theoretical Marxism). David Bathrick, *The Powers of Speech: The Powers of Culture in the GDR* (Lincoln: U Nebraska P, 1995) 63–67.

33. In the 1966 East German "poetry dispute" brought to a head by Günter Kunert and Rudolf Bahro, Bahro criticized Kunert's technical skepticism as furthering the "destruction of reason." Rudolf Bahro, "Abdankung des Grashüpfers?" *Forum* 10 (1966): 23. See Alexander Stephan, "Die wissenschaftlich-technische Revolution in der Literatur der DDR," *Der Deutschunterricht* 2 (1978): 18–34.

34. Alec Nove, *The Economics of Feasible Socialism Revisited* (London: HarperCollins, 1991) 15.

35. Horkheimer and Adorno, *Dialectic*, 85.

36. Jürgen Habermas, *Between Fact and Norm: Contributions to a Discourse Theory of Law and Democracy*, trans. William Rehg (Cambridge: MIT P, 1996).

37. "The essential issue," Foucault notes, "in the establishment of the art of government" after the Renaissance is "introduction of economy into political practice." With this economization of government, "bio-power"—the ensemble of regimes and disciplines that manages a population—assumes preeminence over traditional medieval sovereignty. See Michel Foucault, "Governmentality," in *The Foucault Effect: Studies in Governmentality*, ed. Graham Burchell, Colin Gordon, and Peter Miller (Chicago: U Chicago P, 1991) 87–118, 92.

38. With regard to Habermas's optimistic faith in cultural communication to foster democracy and autonomy, Perry Anderson writes that where "structuralism and post-structuralism developed a kind of diabolism of language, Habermas has unrufflledly produced an angelism." *In the Tracks of Historical Materialism* (London: Verso, 1983) 64.

39. Jürgen Habermas, *Knowledge and Human Interests* (Boston: Beacon P, 1971) vii.

40. "Theories of the empirical sciences disclose reality subject to the constitutive interest in the possible securing and expansion, through information, of feedback-monitored action. This is the cognitive interest in technical control over objectified processes." Habermas, *Knowledge*, 309.

41. Steven Shapin and Simon Schaffer, *Leviathan and the Air-Pump* (Princeton: Princeton UP, 1985).

42. Bruno Latour, *We Have Never Been Modern*, trans. Catherine Porter (Cambridge: Harvard UP, 1993) 21–22.

43. Perry Anderson, *In the Tracks of Historical Materialism*, 56.

44. Jacques Derrida, *Specters of Marx*, trans. Peggy Kamuf (New York: Routledge, 1994) 31–32.

45. Nancy Fraser writes that "it should be axiomatic that no defensible successor project to socialism can simply jettison the commitment to social equality in favor of cultural difference. To assume otherwise is effectively to fall in line with the reigning neoliberal commonsense." She argues that to avoid "normative, programmatic, 'totalizing' thinking . . . is symptomatically to express, rather than critically to interrogate, the current 'exhaustion of [leftwing] utopian energies.'" Nancy Fraser, *Justice Interruptus: Critical Reflections on the "Postsocialist" Condition* (New York: Routledge, 1997) 4. Even Rorty, though an opponent of conceiving political change on a large scale, stresses that a minimum program for the Left cannot be an inclusive cultural program, asserting that leftism means "keeping the distinction between real leftist politics—that is, initiatives for the reduction of human misery—and cultural politics firmly in mind." "Leninism," 215.

46. François Furet, *The Passing of an Illusion: The Idea of Communism in the Twentieth Century*, trans. Deborah Furet (Chicago: U Chicago P, 1999) 2.

47. Derrida, *Specters*, 10.

48. "Die Deutsche Demokratische Republik ist ein sozialistischer Staat deutscher Nation," is Article 1 of the amended GDR constitution of 1968. The earlier Article 1 of 1949 did claim for the GDR exclusive representation of the German nation, but this formulation interfered with efforts at détente—more on legal than nationalistic grounds, since diplomatically the FRG never felt threatened as the predominant representative of German nationhood outside the Warsaw pact.

49. Müller is speaking of the Prenzlauer Berg poets. Heiner Müller, *Krieg Ohne Schlacht* (Köln: Kiepenheur and Witsch, 1992) 288. The cabaret Distel satirist Peter Ensikat puts it as a question: "Did the GDR exist at all?" Peter Ensikat, *Hat es die DDR überhaupt gegeben?* (Berlin: Eulenspiegel, 1998).

50. Uncertainty about the relation of national traditions to socialism was thus a far more important theme in other Warsaw Pact countries. In Poland, for example, filmmakers such as Andrei Wajda (in *Ashes and Diamonds*) and novelists such as Tadeus Konwicki (in *The Polish Complex*) struggled with the wounds left by the civil battles between the nationalist Home Army and the Comintern-led Army of the Exterior in their fights against the Nazi occupation.

51. Günter Schabowski, a leading figure of the SED politburo, was the best known GDR leader to repudiate the "myth" of really existing socialism. See Schabowski, *Abschied von der Utopie: Die DDR—das deutsche Fiasko des Marxismus* (Stuttgart: Franz Steiner, 1994). Monica Maron satirizes the former GDR leaders from Egon Krenz to Konrad Naumann circulating in the early 1990s on talk shows, describing how, "with breathtaking shamelessness, Krenz reclaimed the democratic rule of law for himself as if its existence were a matter of lifelong self-evidence for him." "Fettaugen auf der Brühe," in *Nach Maßgabe meiner Begreifungskraft* (Frankfurt: S. Fischer, 1993) 99–102, 101.

52. Heukenkamp, "Ortsgebundenheit," 34.

53. Christa Wolf, "Momentary Interruption," in *Parting from Phantoms: Selected Writings, 1990–1994*, trans. Jan van Heurck (New York: Farrar Straus Giroux, 1993) 9–13, 12.

54. Christa Wolf, epilogue to Wolf and Franz Fühmann, *Monsieur—Wir Finden Uns Wieder: Briefe 1968–1984* (Berlin: Aufbau, 1998) 161–67, 165.

55. Karl Heinz Bohrer, "Kulturschutzgebiet DDR," *Merkur* 500 (October–November 1990): 1015–18.

56. Hans-Joachim Maaz, *Der Gefühlsstau: Ein Psychogram der DDR* (Berlin: Argon, 1990) 15.

57. Cited by *text+kritik* editor Heinz Ludwig Arnold as a ready answer to the question of what remains of GDR literature in *Literatur in der DDR: Rückblicke*, ed. Heinz Ludwig Arnold and Frauke Meyer-Gosau (München: edition text + kritik, 1991) 7.

58. Horst Domdey, "Die DDR-Literatur als Literatur der Epochenillusion", in *Deutschland Archiv. Sonderheft: Die DDR im vierzigsten Jahr*, ed. I. Spittmann and G. Helwig (Köln: Deutschland Archiv, 1989) 141–49.

59. Benedict Anderson, *Imagined Communities*, rev. ed. (London: Verso, 1991).

60. Habermas, "A Letter to Christa Wolf," in *A Berlin Republic: Writings on Germany*, trans. Steven Rendall (Lincoln: U Nebraska P, 1997) 95–105.

61. John Borneman, *Settling Accounts: Violence, Justice, and Accountability in Postsocialist Europe* (Princeton: Princeton UP, 1997) 3–4.

62. Borneman, *Settling Accounts*, 25; he is citing with approval Jean Hampton. The phrase *Nischengesellschaft* comes from Günter Gaus, who served as West Germany's official cultural representative to East Germany.

63. Borneman, *Settling Accounts*, 110.

64. Frank Schirrmacher, "Dem Druck des härteren, strengeren Lebens standhalten," *Frankfurter Allgemeine Zeitung* (June 2, 1990). Reprinted in Karl Deiritz and Hannes Krauss, *Der deutsch-deutsch Literaturstreit oder "Freunde, es spricht sich schlecht mit gebundener Zunge"* (Hamburg and Zurich: Luchterhand, 1991) 127–36.

65. According to Hegel, "[S]ince the state is mind objectified, it is only as one of its members that the individual himself has objectivity, genuine individuality and an ethical life." G. W. F. Hegel, *Hegel's Philosophy of Right.*, trans. T. M. Knox (Oxford: Oxford UP, 1952) 156. Contrast Rawls: "We should not attempt to give form to our life by first looking to the good independently defined. . . . For the self is prior to the ends which are affirmed by it. . . . We should therefore reverse the relation between the right and the good proposed by teleological doctrines and view the right as prior." John Rawls, *A Theory of Justice* (Cambridge: Harvard UP, 1971) 560.

66. Bernhard Schlink, "Rechtsstaat und revolutionäre Gerechtigkeit," Inaugural Lecture, Humboldt University Law School, April 14, 1994, *Öffentliche Vorlesungen* 61 (1996): 3.

67. Schlink, "Rechtsstaat," 9.

68. Monica Maron, "Warum bin ich selbst gegangen?" *Nach Maßgabe*: 74–79, 77. Originally 1989.

69. Maron, "Warum?" *Nach Maßgabe*, 77.

70. Walter Benjamin, *Illuminations*, trans. Harry Zohn (New York: Schocken Books, 1969) 254.

71. Peter Schneider, "Man kann sogar ein Erdbeben verpassen," in *Extreme Mittellage: Eine Reise durch das deutsche Nationalgefühl* (Reinbeck: Rowohlt, 1990) 52–74, 63. Originally in *Die Zeit* 18 (April 27, 1990).

72. Schneider, "Erdbeben," 64.

73. Niklas Luhmann, *Social Systems*, trans. John Bednarz, Jr., with Dirk Baecker (Stanford: Stanford UP, 1995) 28. Luhmann further observes: "[N]ext to systems constituting their own elements, boundary determination is the most important requirement of system differentiation" (29–30). Metaphors of "breaking boundaries" (*Entgrenzung*, a key word of Volker Braun's) are explored in Karen Leeder, *Breaking Boundaries: A New Generation of Poets in the GDR* (Oxford: Oxford UP, 1996); "border crossing" is the guiding metaphor in Thomas C. Fox, *Border Crossings: An Introduction to East German Prose* (Ann Arbor: U Michigan P, 1993).

74. The GDR's production of self-distinction can be understood in part as an effort more closely to regulate its relationship to a hostile Cold War environment. "From the perspective of the dynamics of development, boundaries are performances that can be intensified. . . . The formation of boundaries interrupts the continuity of processes that connect the system with its environment. The intensification of boundary performance consists in multiplying the ways in which this occurs. The discontinuities thereby created can be thoroughly regulated, and they enable a system to calculate its contacts with the environment." Luhmann, *Social Systems*, 30.

75. Vladimir Ilyich Lenin, *The State and Revolution*, in Tucker, *The Lenin Anthology*, 311–98, 381.

76. "A difference that makes a difference" is Gregory Bateson's definition of information from *Steps to an Ecology of Mind* (San Francisco: Chandler, 1972) 315.

CHAPTER TWO

1. Alain Badiou, "One Divides into Two," trans. Alberto Toscano. Accessed August 10, 2006, at http://culturemachine.tees.ac.uk/Cmach/Backissues/j004/Articles/Badiou.htm.

2. Karl Mannheim, *Ideology and Utopia*, trans. Louis Wirth and Edward Shils (San Diego: Harcourt Brace Jovanovich, 1936) 192–204.

3. Althusser distinguishes Marxism as a science by its constructivist realism, which puts the "intellectual labor" of concepts and material labor on the same ontological continuum. A science is aware of its own conceptual labor as a moment in the social production of reality, whereas ideology bases itself in natural or transcendental, rather than social, authority. Louis Althusser and Étienne Balibar, *Reading Capital*, trans. Ben Brewster (London: Verso, 1979). If the invocation of Althusser in this note, however, seems to conjure what some of his students like Balibar and Jacques Rancière were later to see as intellectual elitism, I should add that the same point is made by a philosopher much more in the democratic, pragmatic idiom. Hilary Putnam writes that "there are 'external facts,' and we can *say what they are*. What we *cannot* say—because it makes no sense—is what the facts are *independent of all conceptual choices*" (33). He believes that each justified conceptual scheme has a real truth, but that there is not one final concept-independent true state of affairs. Hilary Putnam, *The Many Faces of Realism* (LaSalle, IL: Open Court, 1987).

4. Heiner Müller, "'Ich war und bin ein Stück DDR-Geschichte.' 'Spiegel-TV,' 10.1.1993," in *Gesammelte Irrtümer* 3 (Frankfurt a.M.: Verlag der Autoren, 1994) 172–76, 172.

5. W. v. O. Quine, "On What There Is," in *From a Logical Point of View* (Cambridge: Harvard UP, 1953) 1–19.

6. Quine, "On What There Is," 5–7.

7. Ludwig Wittgenstein, *Philosophical Investigations*, 3rd ed., trans. G. E. M. Anscombe (Oxford: Basil Blackwell, 1953) §7 (4e).

8. Wittgenstein, *Philosophical Investigations*, §19 (7e).

9. Plato, "Parmenides" 130c6–130d5, *The Collected Dialogues of Plato*, ed. Edith Hamilton and Huntington Cairns (Princeton: Princeton UP, 1961) 920–56, 924.

10. Max Horkheimer and Theodor W. Adorno, *Dialectic of Enlightenment*, trans. John Cumming (New York: Continuum, 1972) 23, 20. This purported loss of mana parallels Benjamin's discussion in "The Work of Art" essay of the destruction of aura through technically reproducible media (such as film).

11. Gilles Deleuze, "The Simulacrum and Ancient Philosophy," Appendix, in *The Logic of Sense*, trans. Mark Lester (New York: Columbia UP, 1990) 253–79.

12. Jacques Derrida, "Structure, Sign and Play in the Discourse of the Human Sciences," in *Writing and Difference*, trans. Alan Bass (Chicago: U Chicago P, 1978) 278–93, 280.

13. Claude Lévi-Strauss, *Introduction to the Work of Marcel Mauss*, trans. Felicity Baker (London: Routledge and Kegan Paul, 1987) 59.

14. Lévi-Strauss, *Mauss*, 63–64.

15. This problem finds helpful formulation in modern debates around Eubulides' *sorites* paradox, which figures in Chapter 8. The *sorites* question is this: when do a few grains of sand add up to "a heap" of sand? In other words, when do individual things suddenly transform to some new collective entity? Because of Bertrand Russell, philosophers often resolve the paradox in terms of "vagueness"—the problem being the vagueness of transitions between categories. As we will see, vagueness per se accords well with the Quinean paraphrase or "incomplete symbol." The question, however, is whether this vagueness is understood as a conceptual or an ontological vagueness. That is, is the transition from a bunch of individual entities to a collective entity vague because our concepts are inadequately precise, or is the boundary between the two sorts of entities really (that is, ontologically) vague? Here, the latter is emphatically the case. The reason is that our ontology—on the model of systems theory (see also my references to Putnam)—includes our concepts equally as an element of our material reality.

16. Another way to put this idea of finding a suitable medium of comparison is through category theory. We need a logically consistent and semantically appropriate set of categories to compare the qualities of different things. Confusion arises from category errors that attribute to things properties that they cannot have (that is, are not disposed to have, and do not just not happen to have). Thus, we cannot compare the breakability of a prime number with that of a glass. Though neither might be broken at the moment, a glass is disposed to break, whereas a prime number cannot break. More germane to our discussion here would be a category like profitability for comparing a socialist and a capitalist firm: it is clearly not the right category—but what is?

17. The context to which a quantifier binds a reference is similar to what Heidegger calls a "region," or *Gegend*, whose root puns on the idea of encounter (*Be-*

gegnung) and opposition (*Gegen*). A region—or context of ontological commitment—is the time-space of encounter opened by our being concerned and involved with the world. Martin Heidegger, *Being and Time*, trans. John Macquarrie and Edward Robinson (San Francisco: Harper and Row, 1962), esp. 420, H 368). The connection I am drawing here between Quine and Heidegger is not casual—it is important throughout this book to recognize the ontological implications of what might seem like semantic arguments.

18. In logical symbols our claim is as follows [$(\forall x)$(x is more volatile than mud) $\supset$ (x is mana). $(\exists x)$(x is more volatile than mud) $\supset$ $(\exists x)$(x is mana)]. "Whatever the something we are looking for might be, let's just call it x, if it's more volatile than mud, we'll call it *mana*. There is some thing that is more volatile than mud (a real value x that satisfies the given '*mana*' function), it is *mana*." For a detailed discussion of quantifiers and bound variables, see Quine, "Logic and the Reification of Universals," in *Logical Point of View*, 102–29.

19. The ambiguous case of deciding that *mana* is a metaphor with no literal referent, but a true figural one, is taken up Donald Davidson. Davidson denies that metaphors have two such meanings, the true one of which might be brought out by a Quinean paraphrase. Instead, a metaphor has only its literal *meaning*, which is usually false; metaphorical *usage*, however, directs one to look for comparisons rather than literal truth. A paraphrase might be carrying out these directions, but it is not determining the metaphor's true meaning. Davidson's view does not create a problem here: if a vampire, *mana,* or socialism is a metaphor, then no amount of paraphrase will convince us to make an ontological commitment to it; rather, we will learn that the word is being used as a metaphor. Our issue, then, remains: how is "socialism" being used? Donald Davidson, "What Metaphors Mean," in *Philosophical Perspectives on Metaphor*, ed. Mark Johnson (Minneapolis: U Minnesota P, 1981) 200–220. See Chapter 9 for a fuller discussion of metaphor.

20. Quine, "Logic and Reification," in *Logical Point of View*, 6.

21. According to Terrence Hawkes, "[T]he ultimate quarry of structuralist thinking will be the permanent structures into which individual human acts, perceptions, stances fit, and from which they derive their final nature." Hawkes, *Structuralism and Semiotics* (Berkeley: U California Press, 1977) 18.

22. This reciprocity of meaning and being describes what Putnam calls "internal realism." This internalist view prevails here except at the point where system confronts an unprecedented environmental imposition. In this sense, the imposition has only the property of existence in the sense of Frege's *Bedeutung* (or reference), without having any meaning (or *Sinn*).

23. The cognitive linguist George Lakoff distinguishes between negatives that are internal to a cognitive model and those that are external. "Cases where the negative is inside the cognitive model are often marked linguistically with prefixes like *dis-*, *un-*, and *in*. [. . .] *Lack* is defined with respect to an I[dealized] C[ognitive] M[odel] with a background condition indicating that some person or thing *should have* something and a foreground condition indicating that that person or thing does *not* have it. Since the negative is internal to the ICM, *lack* and *not have* are not synonymous." George Lakoff, *Women, Fire, and Dangerous Things* (Chicago: University of Chicago Press, 1987) 133–34.

24. Aristotle, *Metaphysics*, trans. Hippocrates G. Apostle (Bloomington: Indiana UP, 1966) 1069b.

25. Aristotle, *On Interpretation*, in *The Categories; On Interpretation; Prior Analytics*, trans. Harold P. Cooke (Cambridge: Harvard UP, 1938) 17b.17. For an illuminating discussion of the issue of negation in Aristotle, see Raoul Mortley, "The Fundamentals of the Via Negativa," *American Journal of Philology* 103.4 (winter 1982): 429–39.

26. Aristotle, *Metaphysics*, 1029a.

27. To mark the place for a subject or agent here in Aristotelian terminology, it might be possible to think of this encounter as an Aristotelian *energeia* (an actuality) that, contrary to an immanent potential, demands a consciously active choice (*proairesis*).

28. As we mention in the final section, Aristotle's deictic partitive "some this" has much in common with the Scholastic notion of a "hecceity," a singular this that has no properties, but is only a cardinal quantity or extension. Peircean pragmatism calls this unexpected "something" a "surprise": "Experience is our only teacher [. . .]. But how does this action of experience take place? It takes place by a series of surprises. [. . .] At the moment when it was expected the vividness of the representation is exalted, and suddenly when it should come something quite different comes instead." Charles S. Peirce, "On Phenomenology," in *The Essential Peirce: Selected Philosophical Writings*, vol. 2 (1893–1913), ed. the Peirce Edition Project (Bloomington: Indiana UP, 1998) 145–59, 153–54.

29. As the crucial mediator of quality in Hegel's *Logic*, quantity has just these two aspects of a medium that we are discussing. "Quantity," he writes, "has two sources: the exclusive unit, and the identification or equalization of these units. When we look therefore at its immediate relation to itself, or at the characteristic of self-sameness made explicit by attraction, quantity is **Continuous** magnitude; but when we look at the other characteristic, the One implied in it, it is **Discrete** magnitude." G. W. F. Hegel, *Hegel's Logic*, trans. William Wallace (Oxford: Oxford UP, 1975) §100, 148. I focus on the topic of quality and quantity in Chapter 8.

30. Johann Wolfgang von Goethe, *Faust: Part I*, trans. Anna Swanwick, vol. XIX, Pt. 1, The Harvard Classics (New York: P. F. Collier, 1909–14) lns. 1374–81.

31. Deleuze elaborates the ontological distinction between the order of causes and the order of effects by way of Stoic philosophy. "The Stoics also distinguish between two kinds of things. First, there are bodies with their tensions, physical qualities, actions and passions, and the corresponding 'states of affairs'. [. . .] Second, all bodies are causes in relation to each other, and causes for each other—but causes of what? They are causes of certain things of an entirely different nature. These effects are not bodies, but, properly speaking, 'incorporeal' entities. They are not physical qualities and properties, but rather logical or dialectical attributes. They are not things or facts, but events." Deleuze, *The Logic of Sense*, 4–5. My argument conceives this ontological cut as the positivism of fact and the positivism of decision.

32. This position is also called "political realism" in the sense that politics is "what's real," not ideals or other false universals. Eckard Bolsinger makes a case for this kind of political decisionism based on two political realists, one of right-wing and the other left-wing provenance. By conceptually grounding the constructive

autonomy of the political on Lenin and Schmitt, Bolsinger implicitly demonstrates why a political ontology cannot itself ground the left-right distinction I am interested in. Eckard Bolsinger, *The Autonomy of the Political: Carl Schmitt's and Lenin's Political Realism* (Westport, CT: Greenwood, 2001).

33. Ernesto Laclau and Chantal Mouffe, *Hegemony and Socialist Strategy: Towards a Radical Democratic Politics* (London: Verso, 1985) 136.

34. Carl Schmitt, *The Concept of the Political*, trans. George Schwab (New Brunswick: Rutgers UP, 1976) 53, 26.

35. Boris Groys, *Das kommunistische Postskriptum* (Frankfurt a.M.: Suhrkamp, 2006) 7; 11.

36. Rudolf Carnap, "Empiricism, Semantics and Ontology," Supplement, in *Meaning and Necessity: A Study in Semantics and Modal Logic*, enl. ed. (Chicago: U Chicago P, 1956) 205–21, 205.

37. Carnap, "Empiricism," 207.

38. Quine, "Ontological Relativity," in *Ontological Relativity and Other Essays* (New York: Columbia UP, 1969) 26–68, 49.

39. Peirce, "What Is a Sign," in *Essential Peirce*, 4–10, 9.

40. Charles Sanders Peirce, "Logical Tracts, No. 2," in *Collected Papers of Charles Sanders Peirce*, vol. 4, ed. Charles Hartshorne and Paul Weiss (Cambridge: Harvard UP, 1933) para. 418–509, 447.

41. For Habermas's view of Peirce, see *Knowledge and Human Interests*, trans. Jeremy J. Shapiro (Boston: Beacon P, 1971) 91–139.

42. Peirce, "Telepathy and Perception," in *Collected Papers*, vol. 7, para. 597–688, 628.

43. This theme of an index beyond interpretation, whose force is felt in an encounter, might be amplified by Badiou's conception of antiphilosophy: in short, the "event," according to Badiou, cannot be enclosed within philosophy—an interpretive element—but rather disrupts it, creating a new series of multiples and entailments. Badiou's consummate antiphilosopher is Saint Paul. Alain Badiou, *Saint Paul: The Foundation of Universalism*, trans. Ray Brassier (Stanford: Stanford UP, 2003).

44. Hilary Putnam, *Reason, Truth and History* (Cambridge: Cambridge University Press, 1981) xi.

45. Cited in Charles Gide and Charles Rist, *A History of Economic Doctrines*, trans. R. Richards (Boston: D. C. Heath, 1948 [1915]) 30.

46. Niklas Luhmann, *Social Systems*, trans. John Bednarz, Jr. (Stanford: Stanford UP, 1995) 160–63.

47. Luhmann, *Social Systems*, 350.

48. Peirce, "Index; Baldwin's Dictionary of Philosophy and Psychology," in *Collected Papers*, vol. 2 (1932) para. 305–6, 305.

49. On the necessity of reference for semantics, see Hilary Putnam, "Brains in a Vat," in *Reason, Truth and History* (Cambridge: Cambridge UP, 1981) 1–21. Lakoff, discussing Whorf's influence on his own linguistic relativism, believes Whorf overstates the extent to which languages comprise incommensurable "monolithic systems." Lakoff, *Women, Fire*, 304–37. Otto Neurath, debating Carnap over whether neutral protocol sentences exist (that is, a neutral language for collecting raw ob-

servational data about the world), doubts the capacity of a language to ground a "worldview." For Neurath, even before the late Wittgenstein, all sentences are pragmatically or functionally implicated in the world—a language's neutrality is only as good as that of the institutions in which it operates.

50. "In contrast to normal communication, [money] must secure that in a payment the payer loses what is paid and the receiver gets it." Luhmann, *Die Wirtschaft der Gesellschaft* (Frankfurt a.M.: Suhrkamp, 1988) 247.

51. See the articles collected in Michael Power, ed., *Accounting and Science: Natural Inquiry and Commercial Reason* (Cambridge: Cambridge UP, 1994).

52. I am not suggesting here any preference for a consumer or a labor theory of value, only that GE theory gives a strong formal account of value creation, especially those marginalist theories focusing on consumer choice and subjective value (the Austrian School). For a relevant poststructuralist analysis of money's relationship to value, see Gayatri Spivak, "Scattered Speculations on the Question of Value," *Diacritics*, 15.4 (winter 1985): 73–93. The standard Austrian School critique of the Marxian labor theory of value is Eugen Böhm-Bawerk, *Karl Marx and the Close of His System* (1896).

53. See John B. Davis, "Agent Identity in Economics," in *The Economic World View: Studies in the Ontology of Economics*, ed. Uskali Mäki (Cambridge: Cambridge UP, 2001) 114–31. Oskar Lange points out that unequal distribution of income means that the same demand price offered by different consumers represents an unequal "urgency of need." A rich agent can price a poor agent out of a market (that is, right out of economic existence) by offering a high price for a good, even though the low price offered by the poor agent expresses a greater urgency of need as measured by its relatively greater share of the poor agent's income. Oskar Lange and Fred M. Taylor, *On the Economic Theory of Socialism*, ed. Benjamin E. Lippincott (Minneapolis: U Minnesota P, 1938) 101.

54. See Leerom Medovoi, Shankar Raman, and Benjamin Robinson, "Can the Subaltern Vote?" *Socialist Review* 20.3 (1990):133–49. In the first post-Sandinista Nicaraguan elections the political credo "one person, one vote" was confronted with the promise of U.S. aid should the votes be cast against the Sandinistas, thus fusing local political values with U.S. economic values. John Guillory discusses how some life experiences receive systematic expression before others in an institutionalized literary canon in *Cultural Capital* (Chicago: U Chicago P, 1993).

55. For Marx's view, see, Karl Marx, *Pre-Capitalist Economic Formations*, ed. Eric J. Hobsbawm (New York: International, 1965) 107–20.

56. Foucault cites Adam Smith (slightly after the Physiocrats) as marking the founding moment of economics in our sense. "From Smith onward, the time of economics was . . . to be the interior time of an organic structure which grows in accordance with its own necessity and develops in accordance with autochthonous laws—the time of capital and production." Michel Foucault, *The Order of Things* (New York: Vintage, 1970) 226.

57. The following discussion of GE is indebted to Bruna Ingrao and Giorgio Israel, *The Invisible Hand: Economic Equilibrium in the History of Science*, trans. Ian McGilvray (Cambridge: MIT P, 1990).

58. Ludwig von Mises, *Socialism* (New Haven: Yale University Press, 1951);

Friedrich A. von Hayek, *The Road to Serfdom* (London: Routledge, 1944); Milton Friedman, *Essays in Positive Economics* (Chicago: U Chicago P, 1953).

59. Ludwig Von Mises, "Economic Calculation in the Socialist Commonwealth," in *Collectivist Economic Planning*, ed. F. A. Hayek (London: Routledge and Kegan Paul, 1935) 87–130, 105.

60. Lange and Taylor, *Socialism*.

61. Lange and Taylor, *Socialism*, 82.

62. Günter Krause, "Economics in Eastern Germany, 1945–90," in *Economic Thought in Communist and Post-Communist Europe*, ed. Hans-Jürgen Wagener (London: Routledge, 1998) 264–328, 294.

63. "Some attempts have been made to apply cybernetics and general systems theory to economics[;] . . . their activity acted as an incentive in the preparation of this book," writes János Kornai in *Anti-equilibrium: On Economic Systems Theory and the Tasks of Research* (Amsterdam: North-Holland, 1971) 370.

64. Hans-Jürgen Wagener, "Between Conformity and Reform," in Wagener, ed., *Economic Thought*, 1–32, 2.

65. János Kornai, "'Hard' and 'Soft' Budget Constraint," in *Contradictions and Dilemmas* (Cambridge, MA: MIT P, 1986) 33–51.

66. Jadwiga Staniszkis, *The Ontology of Socialism*, ed. and trans. Peggy Watson (Oxford: Oxford UP, 1992) 10–11.

67. Kornai, "Economics and Psychology," in *Contradictions*, 62–80, 69.

68. Amartya Sen, *Reason before Identity: The Romances Lecture for 1998* (Oxford: Oxford UP, 1999) 2.

69. János Kornai, *The Socialist System: The Political Economy of Communism* (Princeton: Princeton UP, 1992) 91.

70. Kornai, "Efficiency and the Principles of Socialist Ethics," in *Contradictions*, 124–39, 137.

71. Kornai, *Anti-equilibrium*, 312.

72. For the role of peaceful coexistence, see the liberal Austrian Marxist Ernst Fischer, "Coexistence and Ideology," in *Art against Ideology* (New York: George Brazillier, 1969). In our economic sense, a comment by Georg Simmel puts a sharp point on the provisionality of peaceful coexistence as a formula for coping with ontological disagreement over what economy is. "Without pronouncing on which of the proposed unifications of value is the sole legitimate one, I wish to assert that the labor theory of value is, at least philosophically, the most interesting theory. The material and intellectual aspects of human beings, their intellect and their will gain a unity in work that remains inaccessible to these potentialities so long as one views them, as it were, in peaceful co-existence." Simmel, *The Philosophy of Money*, 2nd ed., trans. Tom Bottomore and David Frisby (London: Routledge, 1990) 410.

73. "Das Deutschlandplan des Volkes," an open letter from the SED Central Committee to the workers of the BRD, April 17, 1960, in *Neues Deutschland*. Mathias Judt, ed., *DDR-Geschichte in Dokumenten* (Berlin: Ch. Links, 1997) 513.

74. Karl Marx, from *Grundrisse*, in *Karl Marx: Selected Writings*, ed. David McLellan (Oxford: Oxford UP, 1977) 345–87, 362.

75. Marx, *Grundrisse*, in *Selected Writings*, 363.

76. Marx, *Grundrisse*, in *Selected Writings*, 364.

77. Marx, *Theories of Surplus Value*, in *Selected Writings*, 393–414, 412.

78. Ernest Mandel, introduction to Karl Marx, *Capital*, v. 1, trans. Ben Fowkes (New York: Vintage,1977) 9–86, 84.

79. Francis Ysidro Edgeworth, *Mathematical Psychics and Further Papers on Political Economy*, ed. Peter Newman (Oxford: Oxford UP, 2003 [1881]) 101.

80. Pierce, "The Maxim of Pragmatism," in *Essential Peirce*, vol. 2, 133–44, 137.

81. Pierce, "Maxim of Pragmatism," 143.

82. Peirce, "The Regenerated Logic," in *Collected Papers*, vol. 3, para. 434: 276.

83. This priority of complexity and system over simplicity and individuality echoes Althusser's observations about Marx. "Marx does not only show that every 'simple category' presupposes the existence of the structured whole of society, but also, what is almost certainly more important, he demonstrates that far from being original, in determinate conditions, simplicity is merely the product of the complex process." Louis Althusser, *For Marx*, trans. Ben Brewster (London: Verso, 1969) 196. This priority also accords with the idea expressed by Luhmann that systems are improbable productions of reduced complexity—their greater simplicity with respect to their environment correlates directly with their higher improbability. Luhmann, *Social Systems*, 26–27. Anthony Giddens considers Althusser's Marxism to be in many ways parallel to Talcott Parsons's (and Luhmann's) systems-functionalism. Giddens, *Central Problems in Social Theory* (Berkeley: U California P, 1979) 52.

84. John Rajchman and Cornell West, eds., *Post-Analytic Philosophy* (New York: Columbia University Press, 1985) xi.

85. Quine, "Two Dogmas of Empiricism," in *From a Logical Point of View*, 2nd ed. (Cambridge: Harvard UP, 1961) 20–46, 41.

86. Quine, "Two Dogmas," in *Logical*, 26.

87. Putnam has put this neatly. To an idea of a fixed world of things, he opposes a conception of "compositional plasticity." To an idea of a closed algorithmic world, he opposes the notion of "computational plasticity." Putnam, *Representation and Reality* (Cambridge: MIT P, 1988) 83–84.

88. Quine, "Two Dogmas," in *Logical*, 42–43. Quine's "underdetermination" can be usefully contrasted with Althusser's "overdetermination"—the two concepts being in a sense flip sides of one coin. As in the underdetermined world of Quine, where no single statement of fact can be contradicted by experience (and vice versa), the world given by a particular Althusserian "structure in dominance" (a concept akin to "system") cannot be specified with respect to a single contradiction. Rather, overdetermination, like Luhmann's "guiding difference," creates unity by referring diverse contradictions to one moment. In Luhmann, this moment is the reproduction of each relatively autonomous (underdetermined) element as part of the system (or not); in Althusser, the identifying moment is the rupture in which relatively autonomous (underdetermined) processes come together in an overdetermined revolutionary conjuncture. Althusser, "Contradiction and Overdetermination," in *For Marx*, 89–116, 100–101.

89. In liberal moral philosophy, there is no unique prudential equilibrium either. Where John Rawls considers "reflective equilibrium" necessary for good judgment, Martha Nussbaum supplements "reflective equilibrium" with "perceptive equilibrium," emphasizing empirical observation of particulars, rather than logical

reflection on categories. Rawls, *Theory of Justice* (Cambridge: Harvard UP, 1971) 48–51; *Political Liberalism* (New York: Columbia UP, 1996) 8; and Nussbaum, "Perceptive Equilibrium: Literary Theory and Ethical Theory, in *Love's Knowledge* (Oxford: Oxford UP, 1990) 168–94.

90. T. C. Koopmans and John M. Montias, "On the Description and Comparison of Economic Systems," in *Comparison of Economic Systems*, ed. Alexander Eckstein (Berkeley: U California P, 1971) 27–78, 28.

91. Johannes R. Becher, "Auf andere Art so große Hoffnung," in *Bekenntnisse, Entdeckungen, Variationen: Denkdichtung in Prosa* (Berlin: Aufbau, 1968) 5–88, 35. The phrase is also famously used as the epigraph to Christa Wolf's *Quest for Christa T*. The second phrase is a repeated motto of Franz Fühmann. "Aus meiner Haut werde ich nicht mehr können und konnte ich nie . . . *Doch* aus seiner Haut herausfahren können." ("I won't be able to get out of my own skin anymore and I never could . . . but *still* to be able to flee out of one's own skin.") Fühmann, *Zweiundzwanzig Tage oder die Hälfte des Lebens* (Suhrkamp: Frankfurt a.M., 1973) 200.

92. See John M. Montias, "Planning with Material Balances in Soviet-type Economies," *American Economic Review* 49 (1959): 963–85.

93. See Don Lavoie, *Rivalry and Central Planning: The Socialist Calculation Debate Reconsidered* (Cambridge: Cambridge UP, 1985).

94. Natural kinds are intuitive classifications grouping similar things together. I take up the question of their existence in Chapter 8. Quine objects to the idea of natural kinds being able to supply any single standard of similarity. Putnam defends a qualified idea of natural kinds: "[W]hat goes on inside people's heads does not fix the reference of their terms. In a phrase due to Mill, 'the substance itself' completes the job of fixing the extension of the term." Neurath connected natural kinds with the possibility of socialism in a manner influential for Lenin's thinking about using material balances to run the new Soviet economy. Otto Neurath, *Through War Economy to Economy in Kind*, excerpted in Neurath, *Empiricism and Sociology*, ed. Marie Neurath and Robert S. Cohen (Dordrecht: D. Reidel, 1973) 123–57. Quine, "Natural Kinds," in *Ontological Relativity*, 114–38. Putnam, "A Problem about Reference," in *Reason, Truth and History* (Cambridge: Cambridge UP, 1981) 22–48, 25. William Shakespeare, *Troilus and Cressida*, iii, 3. Accessed August 28, 2008, at: http://www.gutenberg.org/etext/1790.

95. Ellen Lupton, "Reading Isotype," *Design Issues* 3.2 (autumn, 1986): 47–58, 52.

96. See Paolo Rossi, *Logic and the Art of Memory: The Quest for a Universal Language*, trans. Stephen Clucas (Chicago: U Chicago P, 2000 [1983]).

97. Otto Neurath, "Sociology and Physicalism," in *Logical Positivism*, ed. A. S. Ayer (New York: Free Press, 1959) 282–317, 306.

98. The issue of uniting indexes and icons goes back to the question of what happens to symbolic reference to God in the secular era, when a likeness is no longer held to give evidence of an existence beyond itself. Northrop Frye comments, for example, how "in *Sartor Resartus* Carlyle distinguishes extrinsic symbols, like the cross or the national flag, which are without value in themselves but are signs or indicators of something existential, from intrinsic symbols, which include works of art." Northrop Frye, *Anatomy of Criticism: Four Essays* (Princeton: Princeton UP, 1957) 88. Benjamin, in his work on baroque tragedy, likewise notes that "the unity

of the material and the transcendental object, which constitutes the paradox of the theological symbol, is distorted into a relationship between appearance and essence" in the romantic symbol, which simply prioritized aesthetic appearance over essence. Benjamin, *The Origin of the German Tragic Drama*, trans. John Osborne (London: NLB, 1977) 160. What socialism retains in the face of a lost "beyond" is not a theological, but an indexical, residue. God is dead, but socialist iconography is simultaneously an index pointing to the system equilibrium it strives to mediate.

99. Otto Neurath, *Modern Man in the Making* (New York: Knopf, 1939) 7–8.

100. Jonathan Swift, *Gulliver's Travels*, Part III, Chapter 5. Accessed August 28, 2008, at: http://www.gutenberg.org/etext/829.

CHAPTER THREE

1. Niklas Luhmann, *Social Systems*, trans. John Bednarz, Jr. (Stanford: Stanford UP, 1995) 29. Punctuation slightly modified.

2. "Sovereign is he who decides on the exception." Carl Schmitt, *Political Theology: Four Chapters on the Concept of Sovereignty*, trans. George Schwab (Cambridge: MIT P, 1985 [1922]) 5.

3. C. S. Peirce, "What Is a Sign?" in *The Essential Peirce*, vol. 2, ed. Peirce Edition Project (Bloomington: Indiana UP, 1998) 4–10, 5.

4. By this phrase I mean not so much a specific theory, but a tradition of theories from Peirce to Putnam, with an important place for systems theory (Parsons, Luhmann) along that arc. For Putnam's use of the phrase to describe what he also calls his "internal realism," see Hilary Putnam, *The Many Faces of Realism* (La Salle, IL: Open Court, 1987) 1.

5. These two characteristics of a media would help clarify the debate between Ernesto Laclau and Slavoj Zizek over Zizek's claim that "capital is the real." For Laclau, the real is a hole, a gap, a limit and as such can never be conceived as a system, whereas capital is nothing if not a systemic phenomenon. "The Real cannot be an inexorable spectral logic and even less something that determines what goes on in social reality for the simple reason that the Real is not a specifiable object endowed with laws of movement of its own but, on the contrary, something that only exists and shows itself through its disruptive effects within the Symbolic. It is not an *object* but an internal *limit* preventing the ultimate constitution of any objectivity." Ernesto Laclau, "Why Constructing a People Is the Main Task of Radical Politics," *Critical Inquiry* 32 (summer 2006): 646–80, 657–58. What is striking in this debate is the encounter of traumatic index and emergent medium, the very encounter socialism demands.

6. Giorgio Agamben, "Notes on Politics," in *Means Without End: Notes on Politics*, trans. Vincenzo Binetti and Cesare Casarino (Minneapolis: U Minnesota P, 1992) 116.

7. C. S. Peirce, "The Categories Defended," in *Essential Peirce*, 160–78.

8. Christa Wolf, *Patterns of Childhood*, trans. Ursule Molinaro and Hedwig Rappolt (New York: Farrar, Straus and Giroux, 1980) 253.

9. These words, *tâtonnement* from Léon Walras's GE theory and *Abtasten* from Georg Klaus's cybernetic theory (derived in part from Claude Shannon), refer to

the recursive feedback loop of information by which a system finds a homeostatic balance.

10. Christa Wolf, "The Reader and the Writer," in *The Reader and the Writer: Essays, Sketches, Memories*, trans. Joan Becker (Berlin: Seven Seas, 1977) 177–212, 201. Subsequent page numbers appear parenthetically in the text. The designation of "The Reader and the Writer" as a "founding document" (*Gründungsurkunde*) is cited by Therese Hörnigk in *Christa Wolf* (Göttingen: Steidl, 1989) 132.

11. Jörg Magenau, *Christa Wolf: Eine Biographie* (Berlin: Kindler, 2002); Gail Finney, *Christa Wolf* (New York: Twayne, 1999); Alexander Stephan, *Christa Wolf* (Munich: C. H. Beck, 1991); Therese Hörnigk, *Christa Wolf*; Anna Kuhn, *Christa Wolf's Utopian Vision: From Marxism to Feminism* (Cambridge: Cambridge UP, 1988).

12. Tzvetan Todorov, *The Poetics of Prose*, trans. Richard Howard (Oxford: Basil Blackwell, 1977) 111.

13. Jonathan Culler, Foreword, in Todorov, *The Poetics of Prose*, 8.

14. Plato, "Theaetatus," 152a: "'pantôn chrêmatôn metron' anthrôpon einai," translated as "man is the measure of all things" in the "Theaetatus" of *The Collected Dialogues of Plato*, ed. Edith Hamilton and Huntington Cairns (Princeton: Princeton UP, 1961) 845–919, 856. Such a translation sounds misleadingly Platonic, whereas Protagoras' individualism and relativism were the philosophical basis of Athenian democracy that Plato criticized in the dialogue "Protagoras." I take up Protagoras and Plato again in Chapter 8.

15. Plato, "Theaetatus," 154a10.

16. Plato, "Theaetatus," 157b3.

17. Peirce, in explaining the importance of the category of "Thirdness"—the category of mediation—describes "the most degenerate Thirdness" with such a regression example, imagining a map of a country that showed everything in the country including the map, so that "there will be within the map a map of the map, and within that a map of the map of the map and so on *ad infinitum*." Peirce uses the example to illustrate "pure self-consciousness," which he emphasizes is insufficient without some factual index to the objective world. Peirce, "Categories Defended," in *Essential Peirce*, 161–62.

18. Quine, "Ontological Relativity," in *Ontological Relativity*, 49.

19. This problem, trying to recognize something new, when one does not know the property that would identify it, is known as "Meno's Paradox," and discussed in Chapter 6.

20. Quine, "Ontological Relativity," in *Ontological Relativity*, 39–40.

21. Fühmann, *Zweiundzwanzig Tage oder Die Hälfte des Lebens* (Frankfurt a.M.: Suhrkamp, 1973) 200.

22. There are few monographs on Fühmann's work. Internationally, Dennis Tate has been his most significant exponent and critic. Dennis Tate, *Franz Fühmann: Innovation and Authenticity* (Amsterdam: Rodopi, 1995); Hans Richter, *Franz Fühmann: Ein deutsches Dichterleben* (Berlin: Aufbau, 1992); and Uwe Wittstock, *Franz Fühmann* (Beck: Munich, 1988).

23. Fühmann, *Zweiundzwanzig Tage*, 85. (Subsequent page numbers appear parenthetically in the text.)

24. Quine, "On What There Is," in *Logical Point of View*, 13–15. Quine's observation can be compared to Habermas's critique of hermeneutics. Giving something meaning (and in that sense existence) by referring it back through a recursive hermeneutic spiral of interpretation until it is figured in the whole only secures meaning and existence on the terms of the status quo ante. Jürgen Habermas, "Hermeneutics and the Social Sciences," in *The Hermeneutics Reader*, ed. Kurt Moeller-Vollmer (New York: Continuum, 1985) 293–319. If we hold that there are no unique meanings, then the unifying hermeneutic spiral is helpless for adjudicating our incommensurable plurality. We return to this theme in our discussion of positive law in Chapter 7.

25. Novalis, "Paralipomena," in *Heinrich von Ofterdingen*, ed. Jochen Hörisch (Frankfurt a.M.: Insel, 1982) 173.

26. In the "Athenäumsfragment 116," Friedrich Schlegel famously proclaims that "romantic poetry is a progressive universal poetry." Friedrich Schlegel, *Kritische Friedrich-Schlegel-Ausgabe* II, ed. Ernst Behler (München: Schöningh, 1959) 182.

27. Ingrao and Israel describe the importance of Pareto optimality and efficiency in the ethical debates over centrally planned economies, where they served "as the minimum conditions for the efficient allocation of resources and for consumer sovereignty, which the market guaranteed and which centralized allocation was supposed but perhaps not able to respect." Bruna Ingrao and Giorgio Israel, *The Invisible Hand: Economic Equilibrium in the History of Science*, trans. Ian McGilvray (Cambridge: MIT P, 1990) 254. Late in his career, first as an engineer and then as an economist, Pareto (1848–1923) turned to sociology and elaborated his own social systems theory on the basis of the concept of equilibrium. See Vilfredo Pareto, *Sociological Writings*, selected and introduced by S. E. Finer (New York: Praeger, 1966).

28. Referring to challengers to the inevitability of liberal economics, Jack Amariglio and David Ruccio note that such critics "try in some way or other to establish the prior regime of a key principle . . . in determining the general and specific forms in which economy appears. This is true . . . even when the object is to find a sphere that defies economic logic, such as all those valiant attempts from Deleuze and Guattari to Baudrillard and Bataille and the cultural/economic anthropology organized around Mauss's notion of the gift that seek to escape the constraints of commodity space." Amariglio and Ruccio, "Literary/Cultural 'Economies,' Economic Discourse, and the Question of Marxism," in *The New Economic Criticism: Studies at the Intersection of Literature and Economics*, ed. Martha Woodmansee and Mark Osteen (London: Routledge, 1999) 381–400, 390. Amariglio and Ruccio point out how "literary/cultural economies" often issue in paradoxes that reinforce the belief in the inescapability of neoclassical economic reality. In the spirit of their well-taken point, our *theoretical* starting point is the universal proposition that other systems exist, and our *empirical* starting point is the history of real socialism.

29. Georges Bataille, *The Accursed Share*, vol. 1, trans. Robert Hurley (New York: Zone Books, 1991) 13.

30. Niklas Luhmann, *Die Wirtschaft der Gesellschaft* (Frankfurt a.M.: Suhrkamp, 1988) 265–66. In light of Luhmann's observations, Fühmann's allusion to Lucifer in the West German title of his magnum opus on his experience with the poet Georg

Trakl, *Sturz des Engels* (*The Fallen Angel*), takes on particular significance. As William Blake said of Milton in *Paradise Lost*, Fühmann in his Trakl book is "of the devil's party." It should be emphasized, however, that the heroic romanticism of such an identification was deeply problematic in Fühmann's work. As we see in Chapter 9, in his disturbing essay on E. T. A. Hoffmann's story "Ignaz Denner," Fühmann identifies with the helplessly manipulated peasant Andres rather than the diabolical bandit Denner. "Ignaz Denner," *Essays, Gespräche, Aufsätze, 1964–1981*. In *Autorisierte Werkausgabe 6*. (Rostock: Hinstorff, 1993) 378–99.

31. W. B. Yeats, "Leda and the Swan," 1924. Reprinted with the permission of Scribner, a division of Simon and Schuster, Inc., from *The Collected Works of W. B. Yeats, Volume I: The Poem, Revised*, edited by Richard J. Finneran. Copyright © 1928 by the Macmillan Company. Copyright renewed © 1956 by George Yeats. All rights reserved. Additional electronic permission granted by A. P. Watt Ltd. on behalf of Gráinne Yeats.

32. In his opening essay on the "Definition of Sovereignty," Schmitt repeatedly formulates the defining question around the interrogative "Who?" and repeatedly answers it by evoking the "concrete life" of an individual. Schmitt, *Political Theology*, 15.

33. For a pointed critical reading of Agamben's relation to the Schmittian notion of sovereignty, see William Rasch, "From Sovereign Ban to Banning Sovereignty: Agamben," in *Sovereignty and Its Discontents: On the Primacy of Conflict and the Structure of the Political* (London: Birkbeck Law P, 2004) 89–102.

34. Other influential formulations of this paradox can be found, especially in the nineteenth-century German legal tradition. Thus Otto Gierke noted it was "impossible to make the state logically prior to law [*Recht*] or to make law logically prior to the state, since each exists in, for and by the other." Cited by Frederic William Maitland, Introduction to Otto Friedrich von Gierke, *Political Theories of the Middle Age*, trans. F. W. Maitland (Boston: Beacon, 1958) xliii.

35. Hannah Arendt, *On Revolution* (New York: Viking, 1963) 184.

36. The two paradoxes of sovereignty as beginning and end are embedded in the term *autarchy* or *autarky*, an economic concept that derives its ambiguous meaning from two distinct Greek roots that have long confused its English spelling, *αυτο-αρχη* (self-originating) and *αυτο-αρκη* (self-sufficient). For convenience I will spell the term *autarchy*, but in each case, both senses are intended.

37. Georges Bataille, *The Accursed Share*, vols. 2, 3 (New York: Zone, 1993) 197–98.

38. Bataille, *Accursed*, 2, 3, 198.

39. Ernesto Laclau, *On Populist Reason* (London: Verso, 2005) 162.

40. Laclau, *Populist Reason*, 69.

41. Luhmann, *Social Systems*, 29.

42. Fritz Stern, *The Failure of Illiberalism* (New York: Columbia UP, 1992). Georg Lukács, *Die Zerstörung der Vernunft: Der Weg des Irrationalismus von Schelling zu Hitler* (Berlin: Aufbau, 1955). While Romanticism has relatively clear canonical lines of association, the references of Vitalism and Decisionism might be less apparent, so I would mention Bergson, Nietzsche, and Schopenhauer as the key antecedents of Vitalism, and would associate Decisionism with the influence of Carl Schmitt.

43. See Richard Herzinger, *Masken der Lebensrevolution: Vitalistische Zivilisations- und Humanismuskritik in Texten Heiner Müllers* (Munich: Wilhelm Fink, 1992).

44. Ernst H. Kantorowicz, *The King's Two Bodies: A Study in Mediaeval Political Theology* (Princeton: Princeton UP, 1957) esp. 78–86.

45. Julia Hell, *Post-Fascist Fantasies: Psychoanalysis, History, and the Literature of East Germany* (Durham: Duke UP, 1997) 25–63.

46. Fühmann, "König Ödipus," in *Erzählungen, Autorisierte Werkausgabe 1*, 216–17. Likewise, as we see in Chapter 5, Fühmann's treatment of the Marsyas myth shifts focus from the contest between Apollo and Marsyas to the more subtle role of the Muses in the judgment.

47. Brecht, "Wahrnehmung" (1949) in *Werke. Große kommentierte Berliner und Frankfurter Ausgabe. Band 15 Gedichte 5* (Frankfurt a.M.: Suhrkamp, 1993) 205.

48. Fühmann, "Das mythische Element in der Literatur," in *Essays, Autorisierte Werkausgabe 6*, 82–140, 93. Following page numbers are cited parenthetically in the text.

49. Roland Barthes, *A Lover's Discourse*, trans. Richard Howard (New York: Hill and Wang, 1978) 73.

50. Barthes, *A Lover's Discourse*, 19.

51. Plato, "Symposium," 201b, in *The Collected Dialogues*, 553.

52. Roland Barthes, *Sade/Fourier/Loyola*, trans. Richard Miller (New York: Hill and Wang, 1976).

53. Barthes, *Sade/Fourier/Loyola*, 5.

PART II

EPIGRAPH: Franz Fühmann, "Baubo," *Der Mund des Propheten: Späte Erzählungen* (Berlin: Aufbau, 1991) 176–92, 188.

CHAPTER FOUR

1. Samuel Beckett, et al., *Our Exagmination Round His Factification for Incamination of Work in Progress* (London: Faber and Faber, 1961) 14.

2. Franz Fühmann, "Vademecum für Leser von Zaubersprüchen," In *Essays, Gespräche, Aufsätze 1964–1981. Autorisierte Werkausgabe 6* (Rostock: Hinstorff, 1993) 146–87, 168–69.

3. Christa Wolf, "Für die Franz-Fühmann-Schule in Jeserig, zu ihrer Namensgebung," in Christa Wolf and Franz Fühmann, *Monsieur—Wir Finden Uns Wieder. Briefe 1968–1984* (Aufbau: Berlin, 1995) 151–60, 155.

4. Fühmann to Erich Honecker, May 17, 1979, in Franz Fühmann, *Briefe 1950–1984*, ed. Hans-Jürgen Schmitt (Rostock: Hinstorff, 1994) 292–94, 294.

5. Aristotle, *Nicomachean Ethics*, trans. Martin Ostwald (New York: Macmillan, 1962) 17 (1098a).

6. Michel Foucault, "What Is an Author?" in *Language, Counter-Memory, Practice: Selected Essays and Interviews*, ed. and trans. Donald F. Bouchard (Ithaca, NY: Cornell UP, 1977) 113–38, 125.

7. Fredric Jameson, *Marxism and Form: Twentieth-Century Dialectical Theories*

of Literature (Princeton: Princeton UP, 1971) 50. Dennis Tate also mentions Fühmann's failure to create a novel that might become a literary event or a best-seller. He goes on to chronicle the growing attention and acclaim that Fühmann's work, incomplete as it is, has nevertheless received in the decades since his death. Dennis Tate, *Franz Fühmann: Innovation and Authenticity: A Study of His Prose-Writing* (Amsterdam: Rodopi, 1995) 232.

8. Jameson, *Marxism and Form*, 50. Jameson is describing Adorno's preference for the receptive and provisional quality of the essay form, a form that Adorno sees the stolid German intellectual tradition as having avoided. See Theodor Adorno, "The Essay as Form," in *Notes to Literature I*, ed. Rolf Tiedemann, trans. Shierry Weber Nicholson (New York: Columbia UP, 1991 [1958]) 3–23.

9. Fühmann, "Miteinander reden. Gespräch mit Margarete Hansmann," In *Essays, Autorisierte Werkausgabe 6*, 429–57, 444. For a discussion of Fühmann's preference for the essay genre, see Hans Richter, *Franz Fühmann: Ein deutsches Dichterleben* (Berlin: Aufbau, 1992) 381–88.

10. At the close of a 1997 conference evaluating Fühmann's work and its reception, Margrid Bircken noted the centrality of *Scheitern* to the analyses of Fühmann. Margrid Bircken, "Drei Sätze über das Scheitern. Oder das Dritte ist nicht in Sicht," in *Jeder hat seinen Fühmann: Zugänge zu Poetologie und Werk Franz Fühmanns*, ed. Brigitte Krüger, Margrid Bircken, and Helmut John (Frankfurt a.M.: Lang, 1998) 329–34.

11. Fühmann, "Im Berg: Bericht eines Scheiterns (Fragment, 1983)," in *Im Berg: Texte und Dokumente aus dem Nachlaß*, ed. Ingrid Prignitz (Rostock: Hinstorff, 1991).

12. Fühmann to Christa Wolf, April 29, 1982, in Wolf and Fühmann, *Monsieur*, 126–28, 126.

13. Fühmann, "Auszug aus dem Testament [handschriftlich, 26. Juli 1983]" in *Im Berg*, 307.

14. For this general sense of "progressive," I refer again to Aristotle's *Nicomachean Ethics*, where, in book one he distinguishes his view of the goal of politics from Plato's by arguing that Plato's pure form of goodness allowed for no change or development. Aristotle, by contrast, holds that the good has a prior and posterior and has not only substance but also relation and number.

15. Immanuel Kant, *Critique of the Power of Judgment*, trans. Paul Guyer and Eric Matthews (Cambridge: Cambridge UP, 2000) (§83) 300.

16. Hannah Arendt, *Lectures on Kant's Political Philosophy*, ed. Ronald Beiner (Chicago: U Chicago P, 1982) 54.

17. Uwe Kolbe, "Rede an Franz Fühmanns Grab," in *Renegatentermine: 30 Versuche, die eigene Erfahrung zu behaupten* (Frankfurt a.M.: Suhrkamp, 1998) 9–13, 13.

18. Fühmann felt stymied by the label *Vergangenheitsbewältiger*—someone whose theme is coming to terms with the past—that had been pinned onto him. In 1982 he complained to the editors of a lexicon of GDR authors at the Leipzig Bibliographic Institute that their article on him represented "the typical line of GDR literary scholarship for whom I am the *Vergangenheitsbewältiger* with the nice language, the fine German renditions of foreign poets and the dear children's books. My ever more intensifying struggles over problems and experiences of the society of real socialism remain unmentioned." Cited in the foreword to Krüger, et al., *Jeder*

hat seinen Fühmann, 8. Nonetheless, that label has stuck. See, for example, Jaroslav Kovár, "Antikriegsprosa in Ost und West: Heinrich Bölls Kurzgeschichte *Wanderer, kommst du nach Spa* . . . und Franz Fühmann's Novelle *Kameraden* im Vergleich," *Schuld und Sühne? Kriegserlebnis und Kriegsdeutung in deutschen Medien der Nachkriegszeit*, ed. Ursula Heukenkamp (Amsterdam: Rodopi: 2001) 45–56.

19. Sigmund Freud, *Trauer und Melancholie*, ed. Franz Fühmann and Dietrich Simon (Berlin: Volk und Welt, 1982).

20. Christa Wolf to Fühmann, January 20, 1971, Wolf and Fühmann, *Monsieur*, 7–8, 8.

21. J. Hillis Miller, "Laying Down the Law in Literature: The Example of Kleist," in *Deconstruction and the Possibility of Justice*, ed. Drucilla Cornell, Michel Rosenfeld, and David Gray Carlson (New York: Routledge, 1992) 305–29, 309.

22. Linda Hutcheon, *A Poetics of Postmodernism* (New York: Routledge, 1988); and Harro Müller, *Geschichte zwischen Kairos und Katastrophe* (Frankfurt a.M.: Athenäum, 1988).

23. Fühmann, "Ein paar Nachbemerkungen," in *Das Judenauto, Kabelkran und Blauer Peter, Zweiundzwanzig Tage oder Die Hälfte des Lebens. Autorisierte Werkausgabe 3* (Rostock: Hinstorff, 1993) 517–19, 517.

24. Fühmann, "Das Judenauto," *Das Judenauto, Autorisierte Werkausgabe 3*, 7–172, 166–67.

25. Fühmann, "Das Judenauto," *Das Judenauto, Autorisierte Werkausgabe 3*, 168.

26. For the Joyce reception in Fühmann's work, see Dennis Tate, "Fühmanns heimliche Odyssee: Die Rezeption von James Joyce in seinem Werk," in Krüger et al., *Jeder hat seinen Fühmann,* 185–96. For the Jünger reception, see in the same volume the essay by Dieter Bähtz, "Das Entsetzen—Traumerfahrungen bei Franz Fühmann und Ernst Jünger," 217–29.

27. Georg Lukács, *The Meaning of Contemporary Realism*, trans. John and Necke Mander (London: Merlin, 1963) 20.

28. Lukács, *Meaning of Realism*, 93.

29. Lukács, *Realism*, 25.

30. Fühmann to Wolf, July 23, 1978, Wolf and Fühmann, *Monsieur*, 65–67, 67.

31. For key personal texts, see Barbara Heinze, ed., *Franz Fühmann: Eine Biographie in Bildern, Dokumenten und Briefen* (Rostock: Hinstorff, 1998).

32. Marcel Reich-Ranicki, "Kamerad Fühmann," in *Deutsche Literatur in West und Ost* (Munich: Piper, 1963) 422–33.

33. Franz Fühmann, *Vor Feuerschlünden: Erfahrungen mit Georg Trakls Gedicht* (Rostock: Hinstorff, 2000) 226.

34. Interview with Wilfried F. Schoeller in *Den Katzenartigen wollten wir verbrennen: Ein Lesebuch*, ed. Hans-Jürgen Schmitt (Munich: DTV, 1983) 273–301, 283.

35. §6 of the Law on State Security Documents of the Former GDR (Stasi-Unterlagen-Gesetz, StUG) classifies affected people into four groups: "victim" (*Betroffener*), "collaborator" (*Mitarbeiter*), "beneficiary" (*Begünstigter*), and "third party" *Dritte*). Full text on line at http://bundesrecht.juris.de/stug/index.html.

36. Marianne Birthler, since 2000 the head of the Federal Commission on the Stasi Files, made a striking comment on the complex situation of Fühmann (and

Bertolt Brecht) in her April 4, 2002, assessment of whether a fifth category, "functionary," should be added to the four existing categories of the Stasi-Documents-Law. "Even if supplying information without approval was generally restricted to the much larger circle of 'GDR-functionaries,' the following—completely diverse—groups of people would, according to the Federal Courts, still have to be treated as 'normal' victims or third parties, for example: -church officeholders of the GDR, FRG and foreign countries; -elite athletes, famous artists, and well-known GDR opposition figures; so IM-reports (collaborator reports) which illuminated what intense and vehement disputes Bertold Brecht had with SED-functionaries at the beginning of the 50s would remain sealed. Likewise the whole, very extensive file contents on Franz Fühmann, whom the state security strongly set upon before his death in 1984, is no longer citable[.] . . ." See http://home.snafu.de/domaschk/info89.htm. Accessed July 6, 2003.

37. "Its course correction," Fühmann writes about *Kabelkran* in an afterword to the collected edition of his stories, "came ten years later in a story with the title 'A trifle, largely positive.' I recommend reading it as a complement." Fühmann, "Ein paar Nachbemerkungen," in *Das Judenauto, Autorisierte Werkausgabe 3*, 519. This sort of critical self-reflection on the excesses of socialist realist iconography is famously illustrated by Andrej Wajda's 1976 film *Man of Marble*, which revisits the story of an earlier generation's "hero of socialist labor." Wajda like many artists of his generation in the Eastern bloc had begun his film career making documentaries of such figures at the grand Nowa Hutta industrial construction site. See also Christa Wolf's 1971 satirical story "Kleiner Ausflug nach H." in Christa Wolf, *Gesammelte Erzählungen* (Frankfurt a.M.: Luchterhand, 1981) 124–57.

38. Dennis Tate, *Franz Fühmann*, 87–88; Günther Rüther, "Franz Fühmann: Ein deutsches Dichterleben in zwei Diktaturen," *Aus Politik und Zeitgeschichte* 13 (March 24, 2000): 11–19.

39. Fühmann to Erich Honecker, May 17, 1979, in Walther, Joachim, et al., eds., *Protokoll eines Tribunals: Die Ausschlüsse aus dem DDR-Schriftstellerverband 1979* (Reinbeck: Rowohlt, 1991) 119–21, 121.

40. Géza Csáth, *Opium and Other Stories*, trans. Jascha Kessler and Charlotte Rogers (Harmondsworth: Penguin, 1983). In her introduction, Angela Carter writes of Csáth's fictional children: "[W]ithout conscience, without guilt, they do dreadful things and there is no hope for them, none at all, and hence no hope for the world they might grow up to make. For Csáth, evidently, has no *faith* in children, and, therefore, in the future" (15).

41. Fühmann, Butzbach Interview, May 1984 (Fühmann's last), in Fühmann, *Briefe*, 572–95, 594.

42. Franz Fühmann, "Antwort auf eine Umfrage," in *Zwischen Erzählen und Schweigen* (Rostock: Hinstoff, 1987) 7–11, 8. The same sentence appears in *Zweiundzwanzig Tage*, 161.

43. Georg Lukács, *Die Zerstörung der Vernunft: Der Weg des Irrationalismus von Schelling zu Hitler* (Berlin: Aufbau, 1955) 6.

44. Fühmann, *Zweiundzwanzig Tage*, 159.

45. Franz Fühmann, "König Ödipus," *Erzählungen 1955–1975. Autorisierte Werkausgabe 1* (Rostock: Hinstorff, 1993) 141–217, 216.

46. Fühmann, "Antwort," *Zwischen*, 10.

47. Erich Loest, *Bruder Franz: Drei Vorlesungen über Franz Fühmann gehalten an der Universität Paderborn im Januar 1985* (Paderborn: Schöningh, 1986) 9.

48. Reich-Ranicki, "Kamerad," 424, 426.

49. Rainer Marie Rilke, "Die Weise von Liebe und Tod des Cornets Christoph Rilke," in *Werke in drei Bände*, vol. 3 (Frankfurt a.M.: Insel, 1966) 93–107, 105.

50. Fühmann, *Zweiundzwanzig Tage*, 200.

51. Fühmann, *Zweiundzwanzig Tage*, 129.

52. Fühmann, *Zweiundzwanzig Tage*, 191–92.

53. Fühmann, *Zweiundzwanzig Tage*, 192.

54. Fühmann, *Zweiundzwanzig Tage*, 147.

55. Cited in Andreas Trampe, "Kultur und Medien," in *DDR-Geschichte in Dokumenten*, ed. Matthias Judt (Berlin: Ch. Links, 1997) 300.

56. The phrase "die Delegierbarkeit von Erfahrung" appears in Fühmann, "Ein paar Nachbemerkungen," in *Das Judenauto, Autorisierte Werkausgabe 3*, 518.

57. Catherin Epstein, *The Last Revolutionaries: German Communists and Their Century* (Cambridge: Harvard UP, 2003) 53; 99.

58. Werner Mittenzwei, *Die Intellektuellen: Literatur und Politik in Ostdeutschland von 1945 bis 2000* (Leipzig: Faber und Faber, 2001) 70.

59. Fühmann, *Vor Feuerschlünden*, 107.

60. It is worth remembering Luhmann's distinction between self-reference (consciousness) and other-reference (designation) so as not to assume that emphasis on reference commits one to a naive realism. See, for example, Niklas Luhmann, "The Modernity of Science," in *Theories of Distinction: Redescribing the Descriptions of Modernity*, ed. William Rasch (Stanford: Stanford UP, 2002) 61–75.

61. Fühmann, *Zweiundzwanzig Tage*, 192.

62. "Antwort," *Zwischen*, 10–11.

63. The first quotation is from Fühmann, *Vor Feuerschlünden*, 34. Horace's phrase *tua res agitur* is the culminating refrain of *Zweiundzwanzig Tage*, 215–17.

CHAPTER FIVE

1. Roland Barthes, *A Lover's Discourse*, trans. Richard Howard (New York: Hill and Wang, 1978) 95.

2. Johannes R. Becher, *Der Grosse Plan: Epos des sozialistischen Aufbaus* (Berlin: Agis, 1931) 7.

3. "Was ist eine Novelle anderes als eine sich ereignete unerhörte Begebenheit?" ("What is a novel but a peculiar and as yet unheard-of event?") Goethe to Eckermann, January 29, 1827, *Conversations with Eckermann*, trans. John Oxenford (San Francisco: North Point, 1984 [1850]) 131.

4. Johannes R. Becher, *Auf andere Art so große Hoffnung: Tagebuch 1950* (*Gesammelte Werke*, Vol. 12) (Berlin: Aufbau, 1969). Excerpted in "Auf andere Art so große Hoffnung," in *Bekenntnisse, Entdeckungen, Variationen: Denkdichtung in Prosa* (Berlin: Aufbau, 1968) 5–88, 5.

5. Michel Foucault, "The Discourse on Language," *The Archaeology of Knowledge and the Discourse on Language*, trans. A. M. Sheridan Smith (New York: Pantheon, 1972) 215.

6. Foucault, "Discourse," 215.

7. Foucault, "Discourse," 215.

8. Franz Fühmann, "Marsyas," in *Irrfahrt und Heimkehr des Odysseus. Prometheus. Der Geliebte der Morgenröte und andere Erzählungen. Autorisierte Werkausgabe 4* (Rostock: Hinstorff, 1993) 353–68. Parenthetical page numbers in the text are from this edition.

9. Niklas Luhmann characterizes such theoretical questions as guiding the emergence of a systems theoretical paradigm over the last several hundred years. The question of the part's relationship to the whole, in particular the relationship of an individual to the whole of society, became increasingly vexed in the German idealist tradition, where "the entire world or the totality of humanity as the universal had to be present [. . .] in man." The most significant revision of the question of the part's relationship to the whole came, according to Luhmann, with a conceptual shift of part/whole to system/environment in the 1950s. Niklas Luhmann, *Social Systems*, trans John Bednarz, Jr., with Dirk Baeker (Stanford: Stanford UP, 1995) 5–6.

10. Fühmann, Interview with Margarete Hannsmann, in "Miteinander reden," *Essays, Gespräche, Aufsätze 1964–1981. Autorisierte Werkausgabe 6* (Rostock: Hinstorff, 1993) 429–57, 450.

11. Oscar Wilde, *De Profundis and Other Writings* (Harmondsworth: Penguin, 1973) 182.

12. Thomas Brasch, "Der Zweikampf," in *Vor den Vätern sterben die Söhne* (Berlin: Rotbuch, 1977) 21–26, 23.

13. Georges Bataille, *The Accursed Share*, vols. 2, 3, trans. Robert Hurley (New York: Zone, 1993) 65. Subsequent page numbers are given parenthetically in the text.

14. Alexandre Kojève, *Introduction to the Reading of Hegel*, assembled by Raymond Queneau, ed. Allan Bloom, trans. James H. Nichols, Jr. (New York: Basic Books, 1969) 70.

15. Compare Sigmund Freud, *Totem and Taboo*, trans. James Strachey (New York: Norton, 1950). Freud emphasizes that the dread of incest is not some sort of "innate aversion." Like J. G. Frazer, he holds that the incest prohibition was necessary because "there is a natural instinct in favor of it." Bataille is not suggesting anything innate about either dread or desire for incest. Rather, the natural-human distinction arises as an unstable result, not precondition of the law. Or, to put it in terms of systems theory, the self/other reference of man vs. environment belongs to the emerging system boundary itself.

16. Freud, *Beyond the Pleasure Principle*, trans. and ed. James Strachey (New York: Norton, 1961) 76. Bataille draws upon this late work of Freud for its agonistic theory of competing life and death instincts. Citing Aristophanes' story in Plato's *Symposium* where love is the desire of split subjectivities to return to an original union, Freud suggests an instinctual "need to restore an earlier state of things," "before life was torn apart into small particles" (69–70). The most familiar description of the desire to return to a primordial totality is the "oceanic feeling" that Freud analyzes in *Civilization and Its Discontents*, trans. and ed. James Strachey (New York: Norton, 1961) 11.

17. Freud, *Civilization*, 12–13.

18. G. W. F. Hegel, §89, *Phenomenology of Spirit*, trans. A. V. Miller (Oxford: Oxford UP, 1977) 56–57. For side-by-side translation and original, see *Hegel's Phe-*

nomenology of Spirit, selected and trans. Howard P. Kainz (University Park: Pennsylvania State P, 1994) 22–23. My translation draws from both Miller and Kainz.

19. In his discussion of Bataille's relationship to Hegel, Derrida characterizes Bataille as embracing Hegel's point of Absolute Knowledge as a point of nescience, and the fulcrum of erotic meaning. "The blind spot of Hegelianism, *around* which can be organized the representation of meaning, is the *point* at which destruction, suppression, death and sacrifice constitute so irreversible an expenditure, so radical a negativity [. . .] that they can no longer be determined as negativity in a process or a system." Jacques Derrida, "From Restricted to General Economy," in *Writing and Difference*, trans. Alan Bass (Chicago: U Chicago P, 1978) 251–77, 259.

20. Cited by Foucault, "A Preface to Transgression," in *Language, Counter-Memory, Practice*, ed. Donald F. Bouchard, trans. Donald F. Bouchard and Sherry Simon (Ithaca, NY: Cornell UP, 1977) 33. See Georges Bataille, *Eroticism*, trans. Mary Dalwood (London: Marion Boyars, 1998 [1962]).

21. Foucault, "Transgression," 29–52, 40.

22. Heinrich Heine, "Symbolik des Unsinns," in Heinrich Heine, *Fünfzig Gedichte*, ed. Bernd Kortländer (Stuttgart: Reclam, 1999) 39–41, 40.

23. Jacques Derrida, "Structure, Sign and Play in the Discourse of the Human Sciences," in *Writing and Difference*, 278–93, 280.

24. Herodotus, *The Histories*, trans. Aubrey de Sélincourt (Harmondsworth: Penguin, 1954) 222–23.

25. Richard Rorty, "Pragmatism as Antiauthoritarianism," *Revue Internationale de Philosophie* 207 (1/1999): 7–20, 10. I should point out that, *pace* Rorty, my reading of Peirce focuses more on the "Twoness" associated with his Index, rather than the "Threeness" associated with his Symbol.

26. Aristotle, *Metaphysics*, trans. Hippocrates G. Apostle (Bloomington: Indiana UP, 1966) 1011b23–24. Various versions of formal logic distinguish between the principle of the excluded middle, the principle of noncontradiction, and the principle of bivalence. The issues involved take us beyond our concern here.

27. Derrida, in the second part of his essay "The Force of Law," written for a UCLA conference on representing the Holocaust concentration camps, concedes a limit to the infinite semiosis of evidence in bearing witness to the truth of the Holocaust. The Holocaust in this second part of his essay disqualifies the radical deconstruction of positive law in the Walter Benjamin essay it is criticizing. This rethinking of the first part of the essay was provoked by critiques of Hayden White's strong linguistic turn in historiography. See the editor's note (6) providing the introduction to the UCLA talk in Jacques Derrida, "Force of Law: The Mystical Foundation of Authority," in *Deconstruction and the Possibility of Justice*, ed. Ducilla Cornell, Michel Rosenfeld, and David Gray Carlson (New York: Routledge, 1992) 3–67. See also Hayden White, "Historical Emplotment and the Problem of Truth," in *Probing the Limits of Representation: Nazism and the "Final Solution,"* ed. Saul Friedlander (Cambridge: Harvard UP, 1992) 37–53.

28. The Latin phrase is from Leibniz. Martin Heidegger, *The Principle of Reason*, trans. Reginald Lilly (Bloomington: Indiana UP, 1991) 3.

29. Roland Barthes, *Elements of Semiology*, trans. Annette Lavers and Colin Smith (New York: Hill and Wang, 1967) 43–45.

30. Ferdinand de Saussure, *Course in General Linguistics*, trans. Roy Harris (Chicago: Open Court, 1983) 66–67.

31. Saussure, *Course,* 118.

32. Fühmann is explicit about his critical assessment of the aesthete's posture in his essay on the GDR poet Wolfgang Hilbig, who was forced to publish in the FRG, thus isolating him from an audience and leading to a feeling of impotence that "discourages creativity to the point of drying it up or steering it in a direction [an artist] knows is not worthy and runs contrary to his intentions, towards arrogance or toward l'art pour l'art." "Praxis und Dialektik der Abwesenheit: Eine imaginäre Rede," in *Essays*, 458–74, 463.

33. Franz Fühmann, "Indianergesang," *Erzählungen 1955–1975,* in *Autorisierte Werkausgabe 1* (Rostock: Hinstorff, 1993) 395–407, 402.

34. Franz Fühmann, *Zweiundzwanzig Tage, oder Die Hälfte des Lebens* (Frankfurt a.M.: Suhrkamp, 1973) 190.

35. See the chapter on "The Discovery of Incommunicability" in Niklas Luhmann, *Love as Passion: The Codification of Intimacy*, trans. Jeremy Gaines and Doris L. Jones (Cambridge: Harvard UP, 1986) 121–28.

36. Fühmann, *Zweiundzwanzig Tage*, 102.

37. For a contrasting interpretation of this passage in terms of Fühmann's abject relationship to his fascist past, see Anke Pinkert, "Waste Matters: Defilement and Postfascist Discourse in Works by Franz Fühmann," *Germanic Review* 80.3 (summer 2005): 254–74, 262.

38. Cited in Andreas Trampe, "Kultur und Medien," in *DDR-Geschichte in Dokumenten*, ed. Matthias Judt (Berlin: Ch. Links, 1997) 300.

39. Fühmann, *Zweiundzwanzig Tage*, 165.

40. For Becher's mixture of despair and duty, see Johannes R. Becher, *Der gespaltene Dichter: Gedichte, Briefe, Dokumente 1945–1958*, ed. Carsten Gansel (Berlin: Aufbau, 1991). For Becher's preference for the sonnet, see the articles by Walter Mönch, Alexander Dymschitz, and Anna Seghers in *Sinn und Form. Zweites Sonderheft Johannes R. Becher* (Berlin: Sinn und Form, 1960) 266–85.

41. According to Giorgio Agamben, the sacred human who founds the state is defined as *homo sacer* by the capacity to be killed, but not to be sacrificed. The outcast grounds the state as a state of exception that otherwise relies on reciprocality of sacrifice to produce value. On this view Apollo's senseless destruction of Marsyas outside any economy of moral value might be understood as the founding gesture of sovereign exception—only we are still left with the problem of how this gesture is mediated. Giorgio Agamben, *Homo Sacer: Sovereign Power and Bare Life*, trans. Daniel Heller-Roazen (Stanford: Stanford UP, 1998). See also Agamben's "Notes on Gesture," *Means without End: Notes on Politics*, trans. Vincenza Binetti and Cesare Casarino (Minneapolis: U Minnesota P, 2000).

42. The phrase *unicuique suum* is found in Cicero. See Bloch's discussion of the implications of *suum cuique tribuere* for the perversion of natural law sentiments in the development of Roman positive law in Ernst Bloch, *Natural Law and Human Dignity*, trans. Dennis J. Schmidt (Cambridge: MIT P, 1986) 17–24.

43. Max Horkheimer and Theodor W. Adorno, *The Dialectic of Enlightenment*, trans. John Cumming (New York: Continuum, 1944) 16.

44. For a discussion of Freud's use of *Bahnung*, translated in the standard edition of his works as "facilitation" and by Derrida as "breaching," see Jacques Derrida, "Freud and the Scene of Writing," in *Writing and Difference*, 196–231, esp. 200–205.

45. Heidegger, *Principle*, 51.

46. Barthes, *Lover's Discourse*, 31.

47. Georges Bataille, *Inner Experience*, trans. Leslie Anne Boldt (Albany: SUNY P, 1988) 43.

48. Maurice Merleau-Ponty, *Humanism and Terror: An Essay on the Communist Problem*, trans. John O'Neill (Boston: Beacon, 1969 [1947]) xxxv.

49. Referring to "Marsyas," Dennis Tate writes that "there is a strong sense that Fühmann is setting out to emulate Kafka, by transforming common metaphors into shocking literal truths in the manner Kafka pioneered in stories such as *In der Strafkolonie* and *Die Verwandlung*" (183).

50. Gilles Deleuze and Félix Guattari, *Kafka: Toward a Minor Literature*, trans. Dana Polen (Minneapolis: U Minnesota P, 1986) 22.

51. Franz Fühmann, "Pavlos Papierbuch," in *Saiäns-fiktischen: Erzählungen* (Leipzig: Reclam 1981) 139–57.

52. Niklas Luhmann, *Essays on Self Reference* (New York: Columbia UP, 1990) 116.

53. Luhmann, *Essays*, 12.

54. Derrida, "Structure, Sign and Play," 279.

55. Jacques Derrida, *Dissemination*, trans. Barbara Johnson (Chicago: Chicago UP, 1981) 219.

56. Fühmann, *Zweiundzwanzig Tage*, 104.

57. Fühmann, *Zweiundzwanzig Tage*, 104.

58. Fühmann, *Zweiundzwanzig Tage*, 32.

59. Fühmann, *Zweiundzwanzig Tage*, 174.

CHAPTER SIX

1. Heiner Müller, *Krieg ohne Schlacht: Leben in Zwei Dikatautren*, exp. ed. (Cologne: Kiepenhauer and Witsch, 1994) 364.

2. Charles Baudelaire, "Heauton Timoroumenos," *Poems of Baudelaire: A Translation of* Les Fleurs du mal, trans. Roy Campbell (New York: Pantheon, 1952) 107.

3. Franz Fühmann, *Vor Feuerschlünden: Erfahrung mit Georg Trakls Gedicht* (Rostock: Hinstorff: 2000 [1982]) 27. Subsequent page numbers are given parenthetically in text.

4. Franz Fühmann, "Das Judenauto," in *Das Judenauto, Kabelkran und Blauer Peter, Zweiundzwanzig Tage oder Die Hälfte des Lebens. Autorisierte Werkausgabe 3* (Rostock: Hinstorff, 1993) 7–172, 170–71.

5. Franz Fühmann, "König Ödipus," in *Erzählungen 1955–1975. Autorisierte Werkausgabe 1* (Rostock: Hinstorff, 1993) 141–217, 216.

6. Uta Poiger, in *Jazz, Rock, and Rebels: Cold War Politics and American Culture in a Divided Germany* (Berkeley: U California P, 2000), describes the ideological associations with liberty and pluralism on the one side and permissiveness and deca-

dence on the other in the reception of American occupation culture in both sections of divided Germany. Against the rebellious stylizations of American pop imports, Fühmann's stern 1957 political theses about art and literature in socialism, prepared for the executive board of the National Democratic Party (NDPD), envision a dramatically different direction for literary politics than that being taken by the inferior and derivative West. Arguing in his twelfth thesis for a socialist realism focused on aesthetic quality over ideological obviousness, he states, "I am for socialist realism in the sense that I'm for a great literature by socialist writers that is superior to bourgeois literature and whose range is approximately given by names like Gorki and Brecht." Franz Fühmann, "[Thesen zu Fragen von Literature und Kunst, 26 Februar 1957]," in *Im Berg: Texte und Dokumente aus dem Nachlaß*, ed. Ingrid Prignitz (Rostock: Hinstorff, 1991) 181–245, 233.

7. Lukács uses the term *Schicksalsergebenheit* to criticize the Weimar-era "new sobriety" in Georg Lukács, *Deutsche Literatur im Zeitalter des Imperialismus* (Berlin: Aufbau, 1950) 71–75. Lukács's *Schicksalswende* (Berlin 1956) is cited in Werner Mittenzwei, *Die Intellektuellen: Literatur und Politik in Ostdeutschland von 1945 bis 2000* (Leipzig: Faber und Faber, 2001) 49. Mittenzwei's suggestive discussion of "Denazification instead of national catharsis" (47–56) points to the strong resonance in GDR cultural politics with earlier themes of cathartic intellectual involvement in the World War I.

8. Stefan Wolle, *Die heile Welt der Diktatur: Alltag und Herrschaft in der DDR 1971–1989* (Munich: Econ and List, 1988).

9. Hans Ulrich Gumbrecht, "Die Tränen auf dem Löschpapier," *Frankfurter Allgemeine Zeitung* 258 (November 6, 2001): L14.

10. Wolfgang Schivelbusch, *Entfernte Verwandtschaft: Faschismus, Nationalsozialismus, New Deal 1933–1939* (Munich: Carl Hanser, 2005) 17–18.

11. The failure of the *jus publicum Europaeum*—the system of public European law built on the Peace of Westphalia (1648)—is the theme of Carl Schmitt's *The Nomos of the Earth in the International Law of the Jus Publicum Europaeum*, trans. G. L. Ulmen (New York: Telos, 2003). Causes and consequences of this failure between 1890 and 1918 are threefold: the rise of the spatially unlimited and morally absolute claims of American law, the absolute military partisanship of Bolshevism, and the unlimited destructive potential of modern nuclear technology: all undermine the cultivation of civil limits on warfare. Unlike the argument here, Schmitt posits no specific content to a highly formalized notion of law and spatial politics (camps). For the role of Bolshevism and technology, see Schmitt, *Theory of the Partisan*, trans. G. L. Ulmen (New York: Telos, 2007).

12. The literature on twentieth-century camps is vast—I mention two canonical texts and a website for the sheer, unobservable extent of refugee camps. For the Nazi extermination camps: Raul Hilberg, *The Destruction of the European Jews*, 3rd ed. (New Haven: Yale UP); for the Soviet gulag system: Aleksandr Solzhenitsyn, *The Gulag Archipelago, 1918–1956: An Experiment in Literary Investigation*, trans. Thomas P. Whitney (New York: Harper and Row, 1974–78); for refugee camps: Médicine Sans Frontières/Doctors Without Borders. Accessed August 15, 2008, at: http://www.doctorswithoutborders.org/.

13. Max Horkheimer and Theodor W. Adorno, *Dialektik der Aufklärung* (Frank-

furt a.M.: Fischer, 1969) 158. This translation is my own. Unless otherwise marked, subsequent translations from this work are from Horkheimer and Adorno, *Dialectic of Enlightenment*, trans. John Cumming (New York: Continuum, 1972).

14. Horkheimer and Adorno, *Dialectic of Enlightenment*, 149.

15. Colin Gordon clarifies a counterintuitive distinction in Foucault. "The 'shepherd game' of pastoral care remains incompatible, in Greek political thought, with the 'city game' of the polis and the free citizen. Foucault thinks it is the special accomplishment of the West through the penetration of the pastoral ecclesiastical government of the Church into secular political culture, to have merged or hybridized these two traditions." Colin Gordon, "Introduction," in *Power*, *The Essential Works of Foucault 1954–1984*, vol. 3, ed. James D. Faubion (New York: New Press, 2000), xi–xli, xxvi–xxvii.

16. Giorgio Agamben, *Homo Sacer: Sovereign Power and Bare Life*, trans. Daniel Heller-Roazen (Stanford: Stanford UP, 1998).

17. Giorgio Agamben, "We Refugees," trans. Michael Roscke. Accessed August 15, 2008, at: http://www.egs.edu/faculty/agamben/agamben-we-refugees.html.

18. For a critical study of Arendt's vague and menacing concept of "the social," see Hanna Fenichel Pitkin, *The Attack of the Blob: Hannah Arendt's Concept of the Social* (Chicago: U Chicago P, 1998).

19. Agamben, *Homo Sacer*, 122.

20. Like Agamben, Paul Virilio notably examines politics from the perspective of the technological power of the camp, rather than the rational autonomy of the polis. For Virilio the word camp—*champ*—draws less on the concentration camp and more on military encampments at city walls. Thus, in describing the modern state's genesis from the camp, he cites an early republican military entrepreneur: "[In] 1793 Barere compares the young Republic (the Paris Commune) *to a large city under siege* and he calls for *all of France to be no more than a vast camp*." Paul Virilio, *Speed and Politics: An Essay on Dromology*, trans. Mark Polizzotti (New York: Seimotext(e), 1977) 14.

21. For the meaning of juridification, also variously called judicialization and legalization, see Lars Chr. Blichner and Anders Molander, "What Is Juridification?" in ARENA Working Paper Series 14/2005, Centre for European Studies, University of Oslo. Accessed August 15, 2008, at: http://www.arena.uio.no/publications/working-papers/05_14.xml. Blichner and Molander build explicitly on Georg Jellinek in order to distinguish between pernicious and salutary forms of juridification. Arguing for the ratification of an EU constitution, Jürgen Habermas highlights the contrast he sees between juridification and traditional forms of sovereign state power: "We must attain an effective juridification of international relations, before other world powers are in a position to emulate the power politics of the Bush government in violation of the law of nations." Jürgen Habermas, "The Illusionary "Leftist No": Adopting the Constitution to Strengthen Europe's Power to Act." Accessed on August 15, 2008: http://www.signandsight.com/features/163.html.

22. The most forceful exponent of this position is Gillian Rose, who defends the complexity of traditional legal reasoning as containing the antinomies that poststructuralism believes it uncovers. As she puts it, her *Dialectic of Nihilism: Poststructuralism and Law* (Oxford: Basil Blackwell, 1984) expounds "the declared antinomi-

anism of poststructuralism . . . as a series of regresses to identifiable types or epochs of legal form, and this paradox [is] discovered to be continuous with the difficulty in the conceiving of law since Kant." Gillian Rose, *The Broken Middle: Out of Our Ancient Society* (Oxford: Basil Blackwell, 1992) xiv. Another criticism of deconstruction's supposed dissolution of the antinomies of law is Guyora Binder and Robert Weisberg, *Literary Criticisms of Law* (Princeton: Princeton UP, 2000).

23. For the key legal theoretical issues at the end of the Kaiserreich and beginning of the Weimar Republic, see Peter Caldwell, *Popular Sovereignty and the Crisis of German Constitutional Law: The Theory and Practice of Weimar Constitutionalism* (Durham: Duke UP, 1997); and David Dyzenhaus, *Legality and Legitimacy: Carl Schmitt, Hans Kelsen and Hermann Heller in Weimar* (Oxford: Clarendon P, 1997). Dyzenhaus's book makes the connection to contemporary international legal controversies.

24. See especially Macpherson's seminal study of the theoretical basis of the liberal-democratic state in a seventeenth-century notion of private property. C. B. Macpherson, *The Political Theory of Possessive Individualism: Hobbes to Locke* (Oxford: Oxford UP, 1962).

25. In *The Logic of Sense*, Deleuze calls plan rationality "good sense," which operates in tandem with "common sense," or the logic of identification. Good sense "orients the arrow of time from past to future . . . it assigns the present a directing role in this orientation" (76). Its temporality is that of *chronos*, the measuring time for which "only the present exists; that [. . .] absorbs or contracts in itself the ever greater depth, [and] reaches the limits of the entire universe and becomes a living cosmic present" (61). Gilles Deleuze, *Logic of Sense*, trans. Mark Lester, ed. Constantin V. Boundas (New York: Columbia UP, 1990 [1969]). What I contrast to planning as emergence below would correspond to Deleuze's "becoming" in the infinitive temporality of the *aion* (that is, temporality without past, present, future distinction).

26. Leon Trotsky, "The Soviet Economy in Danger," trans. Max Shachtman (New York: Pamphlet Pioneer Publishers, 1933). Accessed August 15, 2008, at: http://www.marxists.org/archive/trotsky/1932/10/sovecon.htm.

27. G. W. F. Hegel, *Phenomenology of Spirit*, trans. A. V. Miller (Oxford: Oxford UP, 1977) ¶808.

28. Rene Girard, *The Scapegoat*, trans. Yvonne Freccero (Baltimore: Johns Hopkins UP, 1986) 207.

29. The ontological status of the norm itself—the *is* of an *ought*—was a matter of great concern to the Austrian legal formalist Hans Kelsen. Its existence is a matter of its validity (its consistency within a system of norms), not of its effectiveness—that is, the law in this view can be reduced neither to the camp or the plan. Similarly with *Gesetzmäßigkeit*: its existence cannot be reduced to either the origin or the end of a *tendency*.

30. Raymond Aron, *The Opium of the Intellectuals*, trans. Terence Kilmartin (New York: Norton, 1962 [1955]) 3.

31. Niklas Luhmann, "The Modernity of Science," in *Theories of Distinction: Redescribing the Descriptions of Modernity*, ed. William Rasch (Stanford: Stanford UP, 2002) 61–75, 71. The word *reduction* can be confusing here. Philosophical reduc-

tionism is indexing and displacing one phenomenon with another—for example, logic being reduced to material causality. A reduction is thus not the same thing as the collapse of camps, laws, and plans that I am talking about, since this is not a correlation or homologization. Collapse, by dedifferentiating systems, raises complexity (potentially to the level of chaos). Reduction, by linking systems, decreases complexity. My contention is that—as is so often the case with such symmetrical constructions—both can be phases on the path to reorganizing a world. Reduction leads to more internally ramified architecture, collapse to an extensive architectural redesign.

32. I am not suggesting that liberals waited until 1989 to see Soviet sphere socialism as totalitarian. For a history of the concept, see Abbott Gleason, *Totalitarianism: The Inner History of the Cold War* (New York: Oxford UP, 1995). For a literary history of anticommunist dissident intellectuals, see Michael Rohrwasser, *Der Stalinismus und die Renegaten: die Literatur der Exkommunisten* (Stuttgart: Metzler, 1991). When the Soviet Union began to fall, the foreclosure could be applied retrospectively, making the socialist commitment otiose at best, evil at worst. Thus, in the 1980s historians' debate and the 1990s post–Cold War reassessments, historians, most notably Ernst Nolte and François Furet, interpreted fascism and communism as equal and opposite reactions to a normative twentieth-century liberalism: bolshevism an offensive, fascism a defensive formation. Ernst Nolte, *Der europäische Bürgerkrieg, 1917–1945* (Berlin: Propyläen, 1987); and François Furet, *The Passing of an Illusion: The Idea of Communism in the Twentieth Century*, trans. Deborah Furet (Chicago: U Chicago P, 1999).

33. "Something's Missing: A Discussion between Ernst Bloch and Theodor W. Adorno on the Contradictions of Utopian Longing," in Ernst Bloch, *The Utopian Function of Art and Literature: Selected Essays*, trans. Jack Zipes and Frank Mecklenburg (Cambridge: MIT P, 1988) 1–17, 3–4.

34. Dirk Moses describes how left-wing German writers advocating *Vergangenheitsbewältigung* as part of a holistic and pathos-laden critique of West German stabilization ceded ground over the course of the Adenauer administration to those writers who saw *Vergangenheitsbewältigung* as part of a step-by-step reform of German habits of thought leading to an integration of elites into the new social-market state. Dirk Moses, "The Forty-Fivers: A Generation between Fascism and Democracy," *German Politics and Society*, 17.1 (1999): 195–227.

35. Jürgen Habermas, *Between Facts and Norms: Contributions to a Discourse Theory of Law and Democracy*, trans. William Rehg (Cambridge: MIT P, 1996). John Rawls, *The Law of the Peoples* (Cambridge: Harvard UP, 2001) 4.

36. See, for example, Jane Mansbridge, "Fears of Conflict in Face-to-Face Democracies," in *Workplace Democracy and Social Change*, ed. Frank Lindenfeld and Joyce Rothschild Whitt (Boston: Porter Sargent, 1982). The roots of this phenomenon can be found in Lockean possessive individualism, where general and universalizable individual property relations take over the legitimating functions that Hobbes had vested in the political sovereign. For the classic account, see again Macpherson's *Possessive Individualism*.

37. From the Frankfurt School perspective, Habermas discusses this issue compactly, if technically, in *Legitimation Crisis*, trans. Thomas McCarthy (Boston: Bea-

con P, 1975). "Only the relative uncoupling of the economic system from the political permits a sphere to arise in bourgeois society that is free from the traditional ties and given over to the strategic-utilitarian action orientations of market participants . . . replac[ing] value-oriented with interest-guided action" (21).

38. See, Niklas Luhmann, "The Individuality of the Individual: Historical Meanings an Contemporary Problems," in *Essays on Self-Reference* (New York: Columbia, 1990) 107–22.

39. Michel Foucault, "'*Omnes et Singulatim*': Toward a Critique of Political Reason," *Power*, 298–325. In Foucault's later work, it is interesting—because initially counterintuitive—how the pastoral component of caring for the welfare of individuals is put on the "individualization" side, whereas the liberal component of juridification is put on the "totalization" side. See Colin Gordon, "Governmental Rationality: An Introduction," in *The Foucault Effect: Studies in Governmentality*, ed. Graham Burchell, Colin Gordon and Peter Miller (Chicago: U Chicago P, 1991) 1–52.

40. Maurice Merleau-Ponty, *The Visible and the Invisible,* trans. Alphonso Lingis (Evanston: Northwestern UP, 1969) 35.

41. Franz Fühmann, "Antwort auf eine Umfrage," in *Zwischen Erzählen und Schweigen* (Rostock: Hinstoff, 1987) 10.

42. Foucault, "Truth and Power," in *Power*, 111–33, 127–28.

43. Franz Fühmann, "Gespräch mit Horst Simon," in *Essays, Gespräche, Aufsätze, 1964–1981. Autorisierte Werkausgabe 6* (Rostock: Hinstorff, 1993) 475–93, 483.

44. Martin Jay, *Marxism and Totality: The Adventures of a Concept from Lukács to Habermas* (Berkeley: U California P, 1984) 183.

45. Carl Schmitt, *Political Theology: Four Chapters on the Concept of Sovereignty*, trans. George Schwab (Cambridge: MIT P, 1985) 13.

46. As Shapin's and Schaffer's study of the debate between Hobbes and Boyle illustrates, the tension between the religious metaphysics of the leader and the scientific metaphysics of the machine was as present at the beginning of the traditional state order as it is at its end. Steven Shapin and Simon Schaffer, *Leviathan and the Air-Pump: Hobbes, Boyle, and the Experimental Life* (Princeton: Princeton UP, 1985). The figures are dominant again in modernist art; thus in Robert Hughes's canonical survey, *The Shock of the New*, 2nd ed. (New York: McGraw-Hill, 1991), the opening chapters are "The Mechanical Paradise" and "The Faces of Power," documenting the multifarious forms that expressed these two dominant modern metaphors.

47. In the first chapter of his *Philosophical Discourse of Modernity*, trans. Frederick G. Lawrence (Cambridge: MIT P, 1987), Jürgen Habermas approvingly cites Reinhart Koselleck's characterization of modern temporality: "My thesis is that in modern times the difference between experience and expectation has increasingly expanded; more precisely, that modernity is first understood as a new age from the time that expectations have distanced themselves evermore from all previous experience" (12). In this temporalized sense, we could say that innovation opens up a new set of expectations based on rationalization, rather than historical experience.

48. Jean-Jacques Rousseau, *On the Social Contract*, in *The Basic Political Writings*, trans. Donald A. Cress (Indianapolis: Hackett, 1987) 164.

49. "The classical age discovered the body as object and target of power[.] . . .

What was so new in the projects of docility that interested the eighteenth century so much? . . . To begin with, there was the scale of the control." Michel Foucault, *Discipline and Punish: The Birth of the Prison*, 2nd ed., trans. Alan Sheridan (New York: Vintage, 1995) 136.

50. Gilles Deleuze, "Postscript on the Societies of Control," *October* 59 (winter 1992): 3–7.

51. See John P. McCormick's comments in his introduction to Carl Schmitt, *Legality and Legitimacy*, trans. Jeffrey Seitzer (Durham: Duke UP, 2004) n. 8, 120–21.

52. Luhmann, "Modern Sciences and Phenomenology," in *Distinction*, 33–60, 48–49. This distinction between dealing with paradox by shifting meaning frames or temporalizing is discussed by Gillian Rose in terms of nineteenth-century German legal theory. Referring to the neo-Kantian jurists Hermann Cohen and Emil Lask, Rose sees their attempts to overcome the paradoxes of legality as complementary in just Luhmann's sense: "Lask's thinking turns history into logic while Cohen's turns logic into history." Gillian Rose, *Dialectic of Nihilism: Post-Structuralism and Law* (Oxford: Basil Blackwell, 1984) 51.

53. Ernst Bloch, "Inventory of Revolutionary Appearance (1933)," in *Heritage of Our Times*, trans. Neville and Stephen Plaice (Berkeley and Los Angeles: U California P, 1991) 64–69, 64.

54. Ernst Bloch, "Thomas Manns Manifest," *Politische Messungen, Pestzeit, Vormärz* (Frankfurt a.M.: Suhrkamp, 1970) 148–59, 150.

55. Bloch, "Manifest," 149.

56. Bloch, "Manifest," 150.

57. Michael Tratner, *Modernism and Mass Politics: Joyce, Woolf, Eliot, Yeats* (Stanford: Stanford UP, 1995) 10. Tratner discusses the seminal influence of the French theorists of the "mass mind," Gustave Le Bon and Georges Sorel, on modernism, commenting that "Le Bon's contradictions made his theory useful to both the Left and the Right" (23); and "that Sorel's book was written with clearly socialist goals did not disturb [the conservative T. S.] Eliot in the least, possibly because Sorel himself slid back and forth between right-wing and left-wing movements" (37).

58. Jens-Fietje Dwars, *Abgrund des Widerspruchs: Das Leben des Johannes R. Becher* (Berlin: Aufbau, 1998) 534.

59. Franz Fühmann, "Sein Solch-Betrachten war vonnönten," *Sinn und Form. Zweites Sonderheft Johannes R. Becher* (Berlin: Rütten und Loening, 1960) 354–57, 356. Fühmann's closeness to the legacy of Becher's literary loyalty to the state reached its high point with his 1963 receipt of the Johannes-R.-Becher-Prize.

60. For a discussion of the central role played by Vladimir S. Semionov in instigating the hardline campaign against "formalism and decadence," see Mittenzwei, *Die Intellektuellen,* 88–104. In 1948 Abusch wrote the "Task allocation for literature in the propagation of the two-year plan." The official campaign against formalism was announced in 1951 at the fifth plenary session of the Communist Part Central Committee (ZK der SED); see Wolfgang Emmerich, *Kleine Literaturgeschichte der DDR 1945–1988*, expanded ed. (Frankfurt a.M.: Luchterhand, 1989) 98–105.

61. In his study of former communist "renegade literature," Rohrwasser notes that the genre owes its very existence to the fact, "that it is above all 'those affected' [*Betroffene*] who speak and judge the concepts, authors and conditions of this litera-

ture." In this sense, *Betroffenheit* is the generative condition of both communist and former communist literature—but not of bourgeois modernism, which, in the anti-affective current running from, say, Ruskin through Trilling to Karl Heinz Bohrer, constructs itself precisely as a nonaffected literature, whether classical or cool in mood. Rohrwasser, *Stalinismus und die Renegaten,* 2.

62. Contemporary critique of the concept of *Betroffenheit* is tied to the post-1989 criticism of *Gesinnungsliteratur*. A book-length study, calling on Helmuth Plessner's criticism of radical pathos in the Weimar era, is Cora Stephan, *Der Betroffenheitskult: Eine politische Sittengeschichte* (Berlin: Rowohlt, 1993). Norbert Bolz wishes for a new Adorno with "the polemical power to deliver *Betroffenheit* to the crushing laughter to which 'authenticity' was subjected [by Adorno]." Norbert Bolz, "1953—Auch eine Gnade der späten Geburt," in *Texte zur Wirtschaft und zur Wissenschaft* 16 (May 1997). Accessed August 15, 2008, at: http://www.perspektivenmanagement.com/tzw/www/home/article.php?p_id=415. These criticisms focus on a cultivated *Betroffenheit*—something quite distinct from the historically situated *Betroffenheit* to which Fühmann's work gives expression. Heidegger's use of *Betroffenheit* as the "state-of-mind" (*Befindlichkeit*) of encountering a situation that matters conveys our sense of the word. Martin Heidegger, *Being and Time*, trans. John Mcquarrie and Edward Robinson (San Francisco: Harper, 1962) 176; H. 137.

63. "Sufficiently abstract to contain many symbols, sufficiently concrete to offer a convenient object of hatred, the bourgeoisie furnished both Bolshevism and Fascism with their negative pole." Furet, *Passing of an Illusion,* 4.

64. Emmerich, *Kleine Literaturgeschichte,* 233ff. Furet writes that "the fundamental motif of modern society is not, as Marx believed, the struggle of workers against bourgeoisie [. . .] . Much more important is bourgeois self-hatred, and the rent within them that turns them against what they are: all-powerful in economic terms, in control of things but without legitimate power over others and devoid of moral unity deep down inside." Furet, *Passing of an Illusion,* 16.

65. Uwe Wittstock, *Franz Fühmann* (Munich: C. H. Beck, 1988) 79.

66. Christa Wolf to Fühmann, June 27, 1979, Christa Wolf and Franz Fühmann, *Monsieur—Wir Finden Uns Wieder. Briefe 1968–1984* (Aufbau: Berlin, 1995) 95–99, 96.

67. Theodor W. Adorno, "Cultural Criticism and Society," *Prisms*, trans. Samuel and Shierry Weber (Cambridge: MIT P, 1967) 17–34, 34.

68. Horkheimer and Adorno, *Dialectic of Enlightenment*, 120.

69. Bertolt Brecht, "To Those Born Later," in *Poems 1913–1956*, ed. John Willett and Ralph Manheim (London: Meuthen, 1976) 318–20.

70. Fühmann cites the Becher poem in "Sein Solch-Betrachten," 357.

71. Fühmann, *Zweiundzwanzig Tage,* 205. Fühmann's despairing diagnosis of bourgeois society's potential, however closely it hews to the GDR's legitimating narrative, shares more with Frankfurt School pessimism than orthodox Marxism. Thus, in 1924 Lukács argues that "from now on the proletariat is the only class capable of taking the bourgeois revolution to its logical conclusion." Georg Lukács, *Lenin: A Study on the Unity of His Thought*, trans. Nicholas Jacobs (Cambridge: MIT P, 1970 [1924]) 49.

72. For the conservative view, see Konrad-Adenauer-Stiftung, ed., *Der miss-*

brauchte Antifaschismus: DDR-Staatsdoktrin und Lebenslüge der deutschen Linken (Freiburg: Herder, 2002). Even Zizek accepts that "the basic premise of the GDR regime" was "the thesis that the Federal Republic of Germany was a neo-Nazi state, the direct inheritor of the Nazi regime, and that therefore the existence of the GDR as the anti-Fascist bulwark had to be protected at any cost." Slavoj Zizek, *Did Somebody Say Totalitarianism? Five Interventions in the (Mis)use of a Notion* (London: Verso, 2001) 93.

73. Giorgio Agamben, *Means without End: Notes on Politics*, trans. Vincenzo Binetti and Cesare Casarino (Minneapolis: U Minnesota P: 2000) 41. Wolfgang Schivelbusch, without the apocalyptic overtones of Agamben, would likewise see the essential similarity between welfare state capitalism and fascism, less because of the camp than because of a common legacy of fascism, National Socialism, and the New Deal, in which "all three needed an arms race and, ultimately, a war in order to overcome their economic crisis." If not the concentration camp, then the armed camp is the common denominator. See Schivelbusch, *Entfernte Verwandtschaft*, 31.

74. Agamben, *Means*, 40.

75. Agamben, *Means*, 121.

76. Foucault, "'*Omnes et Singulatim*'," *Power*, 298–325, 322–23.

77. Walter Benjamin, "Work of Art in the Age of Mechanical Reproduction," in *Illuminations*, trans. Harry Zohn (New York: Schocken, 1968) 217–51, 242.

78. Franz Fühmann, "Antwort auf eine Umfrage," in *Zwischen Erzählen und Schweigen* (Rostock: Hinstoff, 1987) 8.

79. Theodor Adorno, *Jargon der Eigentlichkeit: Zur deutschen Ideologie* (Frankfurt a.M.: Suhrkamp, 1964) 87.

80. Georg Lukács, *Die Zerstörung der Vernunft: Der Weg des Irrationalismus von Schelling zu Hitler* (Berlin: Aufbau, 1955) 70–71.

81. Walter Benjamin, N3,1, in *The Arcades Project*, trans. Howard Eiland and Kevin McLaughlin, ed. Rolf Tiedemann (Cambridge: Harvard UP, 1999) 463.

82. Benjamin, N10,2, in *Arcades Project*, 474.

83. Alain Badiou, "The Event as Trans-Being," in *Theoretical Writings*, ed. and trans. Ray Brassier and Alberto Toscano (London: Continuum, 2004) 97–102, 101.

84. Lukács, *Lenin*, 11. Zizek emphasizes this point about Lukács's greater appreciation for spontaneism than is usually assumed. Zizek, *Totalitarianism?*, 117. For Laclau and Mouffe, this space between the logic of the figural (or symbolic, as they call it) and the literal is the space where their key concept of "hegemony" operates. "The logic of spontaneism is a logic of the symbol inasmuch as it operates precisely through the disruption of every literal meaning. The logic of necessity is a logic of the literal: it operates through fixations which, precisely because they are necessary, establish a meaning that eliminates any contingent variation." Ernesto Laclau and Chantal Mouffe, *Hegemony and Socialist Strategy: Towards a Radical Democratic Politics* (London: Verso, 1985) 12.

85. Franz Kafka, "A Country Doctor," in *The Metamorphosis and Other Stories*, trans. Donna Freed (New York: Barnes and Nobles, 2004) 121–28, 128.

86. Dennis Tate identifies the lecturer as Prof. Jantzen. Dennis Tate, *Franz Fühmann: Innovation and Authenticity* (Amsterdam: Rodopi, 1995) 21. Bismarck's great grandson, Count Heinrich von Einsiedel, who as a young *Luftwaffe* pilot captured

in 1942 during the battle of Stalingrad helped found the Antifascist Schools, refers to a "Lieutenant Colonel Janson (head of the antifascist school)." Heinrich von Einsiedel, *I Joined the Russians: A Captured German Flier's Diary of the Communist Temptation* (New Haven: Yale UP, 1953) 69. In his history of the Free Germany movement, Bodo Scheurig notes the closeness of a Soviet Professor Janzen to J. R. Becher and Friedrich Wolf, and emphasizes how effective a recruiter he was because together with those émigré writers "they simply addressed themselves to patriotic sentiments." Bodo Scheurig, *Free Germany: The National Committee and the League of German Officers*, trans. Herbert Arnold (Middletown: Wesleyan UP, 1969) 40.

87. G. W. F. Hegel, *Phenomenology of Spirit*, trans. A. V. Miller (Oxford: Oxford UP, 1977) ¶590, 360.

88. Ernst Bloch, *The Spirit of Utopia*, trans. Anthony Nassar (Stanford: Stanford UP, 2000) 255.

89. Plato, *Meno*, 71b, in *The Collected Dialogues of Plato*, ed. Edith Hamilton and Huntington Cairns (Princeton: Princeton UP, 1961) 353–84, 354.

90. Fühmann, *Zweiundzwanzig Tage*, 100.

91. Michael Landmann, "Talking with Enrst Bloch: Korcula, 1968," *Telos* 25 (fall 1975): 178. Cited in Jay, *Marxism and Totality*, 238.

92. Fühmann, "Marsyas," in *Irrfahrt und Heimkehr des Odysseus. Prometheus. Der Geliebte der Morgenröte und andere Erzählungen. Autorisierte Werkausgabe 4* (Rostock: Hinstorff, 1993) 353–68, 365.

93. Friedrich Nietzsche, *The Birth of Tragedy*, in *Basic Writings of Nietzsche*, trans. and ed. Walter Kaufmann (New York: Modern Library, 1966) 1–145, 104.

94. While the interpretations are different, this discussion of Bukharin's trial owes much to Slavoj Zizek's discussion of it in *Totalitarianism?*, 88–140.

95. Rohrwasser, *Stalinismus und die Renegaten*, 1–18.

96. See Jean-Paul Sartre, *Saint Genet: Actor and Martyr*, trans. Bernard Frechtman (New York: George Braziller, 1963) 593ff; Maurice Merleau-Ponty, *Humanism and Terror: An Essay on the Communist Problem*, trans. John O'Neill (Boston: Beacon, 1969); Ernst Bloch, "Bucharins Schlußwort (May 1938)," in *Vom Hasard zur Katastrophe: Politische Aufsätze 1934–1939* (Frankfurt a.M.: Suhrkamp, 1972) 351–59.

97. Bukharin letter to Stalin dated December 10, 1937, in J. Arch Getty and Oleg V. Naumov, *The Road to Terror: Stalin and the Self-Destruction of the Bolsheviks, 1932–39*, trans. Benjamin Sher (New Haven: Yale UP, 1999) 558–60. Cited also in Zizek, *Totalitarianism?* 106–7.

98. Terry Eagleton, *Sweet Violence* (Oxford: Blackwell, 2003) 240.

99. Paul Ricouer, *Time and Narrative*, vol. 2, trans. Kathleen McLaughlin and David Pellauer (Chicago: U Chicago P, 1985) 73.

100. Speech to the Communist Party Central Committee, February 26, 1937. Document 138, in Getty and Naumov, *The Road to Terror*, 399.

101. Bertolt Brecht, "The Epic Theater and Its Difficulties [November 27, 1927]," in *Brecht on Theater: The Development of an Aesthetic,* ed. and trans. John Willett (London: Meuthen, 1964) 22–24, 23.

102. Aristotle, *On the Art of Rhetoric*, trans. John Henry Freese (Cambridge: Harvard UP, 1991) 1356a.

103. Prosecutor Vyshinsky hurls this epithet in his closing statement on March

11, 1938. Peoples Commissariat of Justice of the U.S.S.R., *Report of Court Proceedings in the Case of the Anti-Soviet "Bloc of Rights and Trotskyites"* (New York: Howard Fertig, 1988) 685.

104. Bukharin's last plea, *Report of Court Proceedings*, 778.

105. Getty and Naumov, Doc. 101 (Stalin's speech to December 1936 Central Committee plenum), *Road to Terror*, 322.

106. Ernst Bloch, "Bucharins Schlußwort (May 1938)," in *Vom Hasard zur Katastrophe: Politische Aufsätze 1934–1939* (Frankfurt a.M.: Suhrkamp, 1972) 351–59, 355.

107. Bukharin's last plea, *Report of Court Proceedings*, 779.

108. Georg Lukács, *The Theory of the Novel*, trans. Anna Bostock (Cambridge: MIT P, 1971) 47–48.

109. Virilio, *Speed and Politics*, 33.

110. Rohrwasser, *Stalinismus und die Renegaten*, 30.

111. Laclau and Mouffe, *Hegemony*, 70. Before Laclau and Mouffe, Max Weber noted in the hour of the Soviet Union's emergence its similarity with medieval political (if not confessional) structures. "The 'parties' of the medieval cities, such as those of the Guelfs and the Ghibellines, were pure personal followings. If one considers various things about these medieval parties, one is reminded of Bolshevism and its Soviets." Max Weber, "Politics as Vocation [1919]," in *From Max Weber: Essays in Sociology*, ed. and trans. H. H. Gerth and C. Wright Mills (New York: Oxford UP, 1946) 77–128, 99.

112. Nietzsche, *Birth of Tragedy*, 140.

113. Plato, *Timaeus*, 38b, in *Collected Dialogues*, ed. Hamilton and Cairns, 1151–1211, 1167.

114. Immanuel Kant, *Critique of the Power of Judgment*, trans. Paul Guyer and Eric Matthews (Cambridge: Cambridge UP, 2000) 63.

115. Fühmann, *Zweiundzwanzig Tage*, 210–11.

116. Foucault, *Discipline*, 29.

117. Foucault, *Discipline*, 74.

118. The importance of this "before" and "after" to traditional ethical self identity can be underscored by reference to Aristotle's critique in *Nicomachean Ethics* of Plato's pure form of "the Good"—because the ideal did not refer to "an order involving priority and posteriority," it could not account for development. Aristotle's sequence, however, refers to logic rather than time, but suggests just our problem of trying to solve a paradox in either systemic or historical frameworks. Aristotle, *Nicomachean Ethics*, trans. Martin Ostwald (New York: Macmillan, 1962) 10 (1096a).

119. Agamben discusses temporality in terms of the religious distinction between prophecy and second coming. While it is relevant here, his problem is the end of time, rather than my problem of discrete, but universal sequentiality of time. Agamben equates messianic temporality with figural temporality—the typological relationship that connects, for example, the Hebrew Testament's Adam or Isaiah with the New Testament's Christ by analogy rather than chronology. In this sense, messianic time is neither the end of chronology (this world) nor the arrival of redemption (the beyond), but the time between prophecy and fulfillment, "the time

that is left between time and its ending" (2) or "a contraction of past and present" that is also "a summary judgment pronounced on it" (10). Giorgio Agamben, "The Time that Is Left," *Epoché* 7.1 (fall 2002): 1–14.

120. Fühmann, *Twenty-two Days*, 210.

121. Fühmann, *Twenty-two Days*, 211.

122. Rohrwasser, *Stalinismus und die Renegaten*, 31.

123. For a less religiously themed and more game-theoretical discussion of temporality than in Agamben, see the comparison between Luhmann's and Lacan's notions of temporality in Jonathan Elmer, "Blinded Me with Science: Motifs of Observation and Temporality in Lacan and Luhmann," in *Observing Complexity: Systems Theory and Postmodernity*, ed. William Rasch and Cary Wolfe (Minneapolis: U Minnesota P, 2000) 215–46.

124. Niklas Luhmann, "Autopoiesis of Social Systems," in *Essays on Self-Reference*, 1–20, 13.

125. Luhmann, "Autopoiesis," *Essays*, 13.

126. Frank Kermode describes one aspect of the temporal here by contrasting the organized interval of tick-tock, with the disorganized interval tock-tick. "The fact that we call the second of the two related sounds *tock* is evidence that we use fictions to enable the end to confer organization and form on the temporal structure. The interval between the two sounds, between *tick* and *tock* is now charged with significant duration. The clock's *tick-tock* I take to be a model of what we call a plot, an organization that humanizes time by giving it form; and the interval between *tock* and *tick* represents purely successive, disorganized time of the sort that we need to humanize." Frank Kermode, *The Sense of an Ending: Studies in the Theory of Fiction with a New Epilogue* (Oxford: Oxford UP, 2000) 45. What Kermode's image does not address is the qualitative difference between *tick-tocks* and their various reintegrations of the disorganized successiveness he places into the *tock-tick* interval.

127. Christa Wolf to Fühmann, June 27, 1979, Wolf and Fühmann, *Monsieur*, 97.

128. Maurice Merleau-Ponty, *Signes* (Paris: Gallimard, 1960) 47. Cited in William S. Hamrick, *An Existential Phenomenology of Law: Maurice Merleau-Ponty* (Dordrecht: Martinus Nijhoff, 1987) 103.

CHAPTER SEVEN

1. Ludwig Renn, *Nachkrieg* (Berlin: Das Neue Berlin, 2004) 70.

2. Rosa Luxemburg, *Die Rote Fahne*, January 7, 1919. Accessed on April 3, 2009 at: http://www.marxists.org/deutsch/archiv/luxemburg/1919/01/fuehrer.htm.

3. Fühmann to Wolf, July 19, 1979, Christa Wolf and Franz Fühmann, *Monsieur—Wir Finden Uns Wieder. Briefe 1968–1984* (Berlin: Aufbau, 1995) 101.

4. Wolfgang Emmerich, *Kleine Literaturgeschichte der DDR, 1945–1988*, expanded ed. (Frankfurt a.M.: Luchterhand, 1989) 243.

5. Johannes Raschka, "Militarisierung der Gesetzgebung in der DDR," *Forum Historiae Iuris*, July 11, 2000. Accessed on August 19, 2008, at: http://www.rewi.hu-berlin.de/online/fhi/articles/0007raschka.htm. See also Johannes Raschka, *Justizpolitik im SED-Staat. Anpassung und Wandel des Strafrechts während der Amtszeit*

Honeckers. Schriften des Hannah-Arendt-Instituts für Totalitarismusforschung 13 (Köln: Böhlau, 2000).

6. Fühmann to Wolf, January 31, 1980, *Monsieur*, 106.

7. Fühmann to Wolf, May 15, 1980, *Monsieur*, 109.

8. Bertolt Brecht, *The Threepenny Opera* (1954 New York Cast), Marc Blitzstein's Adaptation (London: Decca Broadway, 1954).

9. Friedrich Engels, *Socialism: Utopian and Scientific* (New York: International, 1935) 42.

10. Georg Klaus, *Die Macht des Wortes: Ein Erkenntnistheoretisch-pragmatisches Traktat* (Berlin: Deutscher Verlag der Wissenschaften, 1964) 167–68.

11. Georg Klaus and Hans Schulze, *Sinn, Gesetz und Fortschritt in der Geschichte* (Berlin: Dietz, 1967) 141.

12. Klaus, *Macht des Worts*, 145.

13. H. L. A. Hart, *The Concept of Law* (Oxford: Oxford UP, 1961) 87.

14. Hart, *Concept*, 87–88.

15. Hart's philosophical mentor (and Carl Schmitt's antagonist), Hans Kelsen criticizes how Marxist legal doctrine deprives law of this independent dimension of experience. In Marxist legality, he argues, law is not qualitatively different from state compulsion and requires no separate theory. "It is based on the assumption that the economic production and the social relationships constituted by it [. . .] determine the coming into existence as well as the disappearance of state and law." Hans Kelsen, *The Communist Theory of Law* (New York: Praeger, 1955) 1.

16. Zizek claims that Wolf's *The Quest for Christa T.*, "by expressing the subjective complexities, inner doubts and oscillations of the GDR subject, actually provided a realistic literary equivalent of the ideal GDR subject, and was as such much more successful in her task of securing political conformity than the open naïve propagandist fiction depicting ideal subjects sacrificing themselves for the Communist Cause." Slavoj Zizek, "Class Struggle or Postmodernism? Yes, Please!" in *Contingency, Hegemony, Universality: Contemporary Dialogues on the Left,* ed. Judith Butler, Ernesto Laclau, and Slavoj Zizek (London: Verso, 2000) 90–135, 104.

17. Klaus and Schulze, *Sinn, Gesetz und Fortschritt*, 229.

18. Lewis Carroll, *Alice in Wonderland,* 2nd ed., ed. Donald J. Gray (New York: Norton, 1992) 96.

19. Franz Fühmann, *Der glückliche Ritter von Trinitat oder Wie wird man Oberdiskutierer. Ein Puppenspiel für Kinder* (Rostock: Hinstorff, 1999) 27.

20. In 1967 Fühmann had published translations of Miklos Radnoti's poetry under the title *Ansichtskarten* (*Postcards*).

21. Charles Sanders Peirce, "Logical Tracts, No. 2," in *Collected Papers of Charles Sanders Peirce*, vol. 4, ed. Charles Hartshorne and Paul Weiss (Cambridge: Harvard UP, 1933) para. 418–509, 447.

22. Klaus, *Macht des Wortes*, 137; Klaus and Schulze, *Sinn, Gesetz und Fortschritt*, 139.

23. Klaus, *Macht des Wortes*, 142.

24. Christian Metz, "Instant Self-Contradiction," In *On Signs*, ed. Marshall Blonsky (Baltimore: Johns Hopkins UP, 1985) 259–66. For Metz the humor of such apparently self contradicting statements is in the uncomfortable, partial identification of a subject with contradictory ego ideals.

25. Klaus, *Macht des Wortes*, 173.

26. Klaus, citing Ota Weinberger, *Macht des Wortes*, 172.

27. Charles Sanders Peirce, "Dictionary of Philosophy and Psychology," *Collected Papers of Peirce*, vol. 1, 305.

28. Franz Fühmann, "Gespräch mit Horst Simon," in *Essays, Gespräche, Aufsätze 1964–1981. Autorisierte Werkausgabe 6* (Rostock: Hinstorff, 1993) 475–93, 491–92.

29. Kurt Batt, publisher's evaluation of *Erfahrung und Widersprüche*, December 3, 1974, in *Franz Fühmann: Eine Biographie in Bildern, Dokumenten und Briefen*, ed. Barbara Heinze (Rostock: Hinstorff, 1998) 192.

30. Franz Fühmann, "Antwort auf eine Umfrage," in *Essays. Autorisierte Werkausgabe 6*, 28–33, 30.

31. Letter to Kurt Batt, July 9, 1972, in *Franz Fühmann Briefe 1950–1984*, ed. Hans-Jürgen Schmitt (Rostock: Hinstorff, 1994) 110–11.

32. Wolf Biermann, *Deutschland: Ein Wintermärchen* (Berlin: Wagenbach, 1972) 22–23.

33. "Protokoll der Sitzung des Politbüros des ZK der SED, 16 Nov.1976," in *In Sachen Biermann: Protokolle, Berichte und Briefe zu den Folgen einer Ausbürgerung*, ed. Roland Berbig et al. (Berlin: Ch. Links, 1994) 69.

34. "Mitteilung der SED-Bezirksleitung Berlin, 19 Nov. 1976," in Berbig, *In Sachen Biermann*, 289.

35. Cited in Roland Berbig and Holger Jens Karlson, "'Leute haben sich eindeutig als Gruppe erwiesen': Zur Gruppenbildung bei Wolf Biermanns Ausbürgerung," in Berbig, *In Sachen Biermann*, 11–28, 11.

36. Berbig and Karlson, "Gruppenbildung," in *In Sachen Biermann*, 11.

37. Walter Ulbricht, "Die Staatslehre des Marxismus-Leninismus und ihre Anwendung in Deutschland," in *DDR-Geschichte in Dokumenten*, ed. Matthias Judt (Berlin: Ch. Links, 1997) 79.

38. Kurt Hager, the politburo member responsible for culture and ideology, delivered a series of prominent talks on the "scientific-technical revolution," cultural policy, and social science in order to elucidate the SED conception of "developed socialist society" announced at the 8th Party Convention in 1971. See Kurt Hager, *Erinnerungen* (Leipzig: Faber and Faber, 1996). In 1974 the Honecker regime revised Ulbricht's new constitution of 1968. According to Thomas Friedrich, the constitutional revisions corresponded to Honecker's new course and "strengthened the instrumentalization of the state for the SED-led political system" as well as introducing the unity of social and economic policy as a constitutional goal. Thomas Friedrich, "Das Verfassungslos der DDR—die verfassungslose DDR," in *Rechtserfahrung DDR: Sozialistische Modernisierung oder Entrechtlichung der Gesellschaft?* ed. Gerhard Dilcher (Berlin: Berlin Verlag, 1997) 33–68, 57.

39. Carl Schmitt, *The Concept of the Political*, trans. George Schwab (New Brunswick: Rutgers UP, 1976) 26.

40. Fühmann to Willi Stoph, Chair of the Council of Ministers of the GDR, November 16, 1976, *Monsieur*, 19.

41. Gerhanrd Hotz-Baumert, Protocol of the Party Meeting of the Berlin Writers' Union, 23 Nov. 1976, Berbig, in *In Sachen Biermann*, 72. Peter Hohendahl calls this truncated public, the "party public sphere" (*Parteiöffentlichkeit*). Peter Uwe Hohendahl, "Recasting the Public Sphere," *October* 73 (summer 1995): 27–54, 45.

42. Stasi file page from October 5, 1977, reprinted in Heinze, ed., *Franz Fühmann*, 246.

43. Habermas draws out the functionalist nature of a legitimation crisis: "The political system requires an input of mass loyalty that is as diffuse as possible. The output consists in sovereignly executed administrative decisions. Output crises have the form of a rationality crisis in which the administrative system does not succeed in reconciling and fulfilling the imperative received from the economic system. Input crises have the form of a legitimation crisis; the legitimizing system does not succeed in maintaining the requisite level of mass loyalty [. . .]. The legitimation crisis . . . is directly an identity crisis." Jürgen Habermas, *Legitimation Crisis*, trans. Thomas McCarthy (Boston: Beacon, 1975) 46.

44. Peter Caldwell, *Popular Sovereignty and the Crisis of German Constitutional Law: The Theory and Practice of Weimar Constitutionalism* (Durham: Duke UP, 1997) 42.

45. Jacques Derrida, "The Force of Law: The 'Mystical Foundation of Authority,'" in *Deconstruction and the Possibility of Justice*, ed. Drucilla Cornell, Michel Rosenfeld, and David Gray Carlson (New York: Routledge, 1992) 3–67, 6. Hans Kelsen contests this view by distinguishing sharply between law's mode of existence as "validity" versus it empirical "effectiveness."

46. Carl Schmitt understands these terms, *polemios* and *hostis*, as specifically political, not private, intimate definitions of the enemy. "The enemy is *hostis*, not *inimicus* in the broader sense; πολεμιος, not εχθρος." Schmitt, *Concept*, 28.

47. H. L. A. Hart, *The Concept of Law*, 88.

48. The process of discovery is the part of a trial in which it is determined whether a law exists to cover the alleged crime. Hans-Georg Gadamer sees the task of legal hermeneutics "to discover law—i.e., to so interpret the law that the legal order fully penetrates reality." *Truth and Method*, 2nd rev. ed., trans. Joel Weinsheimer and Donald G. Marshall (New York: Continuum, 1989) 517.

49. Schmitt, *Concept*, 46.

50. Tape transcription of the presentation of the Secretary for Culture of the Central Committee of the SED to the steering committee of the Writers Union of the GDR, March 11, 1977, in Berbig, *In Sachen Biermann*, 331.

51. Fühmann to Wolf, September 4, 1977, *Monsieur*, 38.

52. Fühmann to Hans Joachim Bernhard, November 16, 1976, *Briefe*, 207.

53. Fühmann to Wolf, [end of November 1976] and December 11, 1976, *Monsieur*, 21, 23.

54. Fühmann to Kurt Batt, [February 23] 1971, *Briefe*, 92–98, 96.

55. David Bathrick, *The Powers of Speech: The Powers of Culture in the GDR* (Lincoln: U Nebraska P, 1995), 234.

56. Franz Fühmann, "Antwort auf eine Umfrage," in *Zwischen Erzählen und Schweigen* (Rostock: Hinstoff, 1987) 7–11, 10.

57. Fühmann, *Zweiundzwanzig Tage*, 210–11.

58. Fühmann, "Marsyas," in *Irrfahrt und Heimkehr des Odysseus; Prometheus; Der Geliebte der Morgenröte und andere Erzählungen*, *Autorisierte Werkausgabe* 4, ed. Ingrid Prignitz (Rostock: Hinstorff, 1993) 353–68, 361–62.

59. Uwe Kolbe, "Meinem Lehrer Franz Fühmann," in *Renegatentermine: 30 Ver-*

suche, die eigene Erfahrung zu behaupten (Frankfurt a.M.: Suhrkamp, 1998) 70–81, 74.

60. Gerog Trakl, "Psalm," 2nd version, in Franz Fühmann, *Vor Feuerschlünden: Erfahrung mit Georg Trakls Gedicht* (Rostock: Hinstorff: 2000 [1982]) 310–12, 312.

61. Fühmann to Wolf, July 24, 1979, *Monsieur*, 102.

62. As evidence of the presence of a disjuncture, Fühmann's aestheticization could not differ more from that discerned by Christoph Hein as the Wall fell in 1989: "I now see indications that newspapers will concern themselves with politics, relieving art of that duty. So art will be led back to its proper task." Cited by Paul Cooke, *Speaking the Taboo* (Amsterdam: Rodopi, 2000) 222.

63. Fühmann to Konrad Reich, October 13, 1972, cited by Ingrid Prignitz, foreword to Franz Fühmann, *Urworte Deutsch: aus Steputats Reimlexikon gezogen* (Rostock: Hinstorff, 1995) 9.

64. "Zustand manchen Staates: Mittelmäßig/verfassungsmäßig," in Fühmann, *Urworte*, 25.

65. Franz Fühmann, *Die dampfenden Hälse der Pferde im Turm von Babel* (Berlin: Kinderbuchverlag, 1978) 237.

66. Fühmann quotes several pages of Galletti's sentences, *Dampfenden Hälse*, 238–41, 240.

67. Klaus, *Macht des Wortes*, 142.

68. Martin Heidegger, "The End of Philosophy and the Task of Thinking," in *Basic Writings*, ed. David Farrell Krell (San Francisco: HarperCollins, 1977) 369–92, 376.

69. Heidegger, "The End of Philosophy," 443, 447.

70. Heidegger, "The End of Philosophy," 443.

71. Fühmann to Honecker, May 17, 1979, *Briefe*, 292–94, 292.

72. Stasi file page, October 5, 1977, reprinted in Heinze, ed., *Franz Fühmann*, 246.

73. Document N. 6, Concluding Report on OV "Filou," April 24, 1989, *Briefe*, 596–98.

74. Hans-Jürgen Schmitt, Afterword, in *Briefe*, 545–62, 556.

75. Fühmann, *Dampfenden Hälse*, 245.

76. Fühmann to Wolf, June 20, 1978, *Monsieur*, 63.

77. Fühmann to Wolf, July 3, 1979, *Monsieur*, 100.

78. Schmitt, Afterword, in *Briefe*, 556.

79. Klaus Michael, citing a discussion between Fühmann and Günther Rücker, the director of poetry and language of the GDR Academy of Arts, "Eine verschollene Anthologie: Zentralkomitee, Staatssicherheit und die Geschichte eines Buches," in *MachtSpiele: Literatur und Staatssicherheit im Fokus Prenzlauer Berg*, ed. Peter Böthig and Klaus Michael (Leipzig: Reclam, 1993) 202–16, 204.

80. Fühmann to Konrad Wolf, December 22, 1981, *Briefe*, 396–401, 400 and 396.

81. Fühmann to K. Wolf, December 22, 1981, *Briefe*, 398.

82. Cited in Michael, "Eine verschollene Anthologie," 204.

83. Cited in Michael, "Eine verschollene Anthologie," 205.

84. Franz Fühmann, "Miteinander reden: Gespräch mit Margarete Hannsmann," in *Essays, Autorisierte Werkausgabe 6*, 429–57, 448.

85. Fühmann, Protocol of the Divisional Meeting for Literature and Language, February 1, 1984, in Heinze, ed., *Franz Fühmann*, 271.

86. Fühmann to K. Wolf, December 22, 1981, *Briefe*, 399.

87. Michel Foucault, *The Order of Things* (New York: Vintage, 1970) xvi.

88. Fühmann to the GDR Supreme Court President, October 22, 1981, *Briefe*, 386–89, 387.

89. Fühmann, "Canto ami et non mourier," in Franz Fühmann and Dietmar Riemann, *Was für eine Insel in was für einem Meer: Leben mit geistig Behinderten* (Rostock: Hinstorff, 1985) 147–51, 150.

90. Stasi file page from March 17, 1982, reprinted in Heinze, ed., *Franz Fühmann*, 315.

CHAPTER EIGHT

1. Georg Klaus, "Kybernetik und ideologischer Klassenkampf," *Einheit* 25.9 (1970): 1180–89, 1181.

2. Johannes R. Becher, *Der Grosse Plan: Epos des sozialistischen Aufbaus* (Berlin: Agis, 1931) 9.

3. Lothar Kreiser, "Logik—Lehre und Lehrinhalte an den philosophischen Fakultäten der Universitäten in der SBZ/DDR (1945–1954)," in *Anfänge der DDR-Philosophie: Ansprüche, Ohnmacht, Scheitern*, ed. Volker Gerhardt and Hans-Christoph Rauh (Berlin: Links, 2001) 119–59, 125.

4. Jérôme Segal, "Die Einführung der Kybernetik in der DDR: Begegnung mit der marxistischen Ideologie." Accessed August 29, 2008, at: http://jerome-segal.de/Publis/Kyb-DDR.htm. See also Heinz Liebscher, "Georg Klaus—Ein unbequemer Marxist," in Gerhardt and Rauh, *Anfänge der DDR-Philosophie*, 406–19; and Peter C. Caldwell, *Dictatorship, State Planning, and Social Theory in the German Democratic Republic* (Cambridge: Cambridge UP, 2003) 149–59.

5. These accusations are cited in Caldwell, *Dictatorship*, 134.

6. Martha Nussbaum and Amartya Sen, "Introduction," in *The Quality of Life*, ed. Martha Nussbaum and Amartya Sen (Oxford: Oxford UP, 1993) 4.

7. As Imre Lakatos, otherwise very close to Karl Popper, has pointed out, Popper is inconsistent precisely with respect to the question of the failure or refutation of Marxism, which leads Popper to make "such confusing formulations as 'Marxism is irrefutable' and, at the same time, 'Marxism has been refuted.'" Imre Lakatos, "Falsification and the Methodology of Scientific Research Programmes," in *Criticism and the Growth of Knowledge*, ed. Imre Lakatos and Alan Musgrave (Cambridge: Cambridge UP, 1970) 91–196, n119. The point might be made more clearly outside of the Popperian program of falsifiability. In the same volume, Thomas Kuhn ("Logic of Discovery of Psychology of Research?" in *Criticism and the Growth of Knowledge*, ed. Imre Lakatos and Alan Musgrave [Cambridge: Cambridge UP, 1970] 1–23) argues that rival models of knowledge (paradigms)—and, more fundamentally, the communities that support their respective frameworks—are mutually incomprehensible. They cannot be tested, and thus cannot fail, in each other's terms (13, and for Lakatos's characterization, 179). The failure, then, of the GDR, must be seen, as I suggest below, as a failure of historical state socialism to establish persuasive criteria for its own effective and legitimate *self*-description.

8. Max Weber, "Science as a Vocation," in *From Max Weber: Essays in Sociology*, trans. H. H. Gerth and C. Wright Mills (New York: Oxford UP, 1946) 129–56. The classic statement of Popper's position, centrally engaged with Cold War ideological struggle, is *The Open Society and Its Enemies* (Princeton: Princeton UP, 1971).

9. For an overview of the 1930s debates (and defense of von Mises's position) see Don Lavoie, *Rivalry and Central Planning: The Socialist Calculation Debate Reconsidered* (Cambridge: Cambridge UP, 1985).

10. Loren R. Graham makes a somewhat different point about the study of Soviet science. He points out that because Soviet society was "based on principles—economic, social, philosophical—strikingly different from those of other industrial nations," those aspects of it that were similar to Western nations, in particular its science, reveal a lot about the way science and society relate. He concludes his overview of the Soviet experience by saying that "we can understand how much *our* science and *our* culture are conditioned by *our* society only if we have another society and another culture with which we can appropriately draw comparisons. The Soviet Union may well have been one of the last modern alternatives to dominant Western patterns with which such comparisons of science can be made. In that sense, the study of Soviet science is also a study of *our* science." *What Have We Learned About Science and Technology from the Russian Experience?* (Stanford: Stanford UP, 1998) 135.

11. Walter Benjamin, "The Task of the Translator," in *Illuminations*, ed. Hannah Arendt (New York: Schocken, 1969) 69–82.

12. Georg Klaus, *Kybernetik—eine neue Universalphilosophie der Gesellschaft?* (Berlin: Akadamie, 1973) 16.

13. Plato, "Protagoras," 352a–362a, in *The Collected Dialogues of Plato*, ed. Edith Hamilton and Huntington Cairns (Princeton: Princeton UP, 1961) 308–52. See also all of book seven of Aristotle, *Nicomachean Ethics*, trans. Martin Oswald (New York: Macmillan, 1962). Also important here are Martha Nussbaum, "Plato on Commensurability and Desire," in *Love's Knowledge* (Oxford: Oxford UP, 1990) 106–24; and Donald Davidson, "How Is Weakness of the Will Possible?" in *Essays on Actions and Events*, 2nd ed. (Oxford: Oxford UP, 2001) 21–42.

14. Such well-ordering is a key idea also in interstate relationships. In John Rawls, *The Law of Peoples* (Cambridge: Harvard UP, 1999), Rawls argues that only those states based on a reasonably well-ordered deliberative framework can be admitted to self-jurisdiction in a system of international law. Non-well-ordered (rogue) states are subject to military enforcement.

15. The debate over the incommensurability of "paradigms" in Kuhn's work is a more recent, but now classic, locus for the discussion of incommensurability. "The point-by-point comparison of two successive theories demands a language into which at least the empirical consequences of both can be translated without loss or change [. . . .] [No] such vocabulary is available [. . . .] Successive theories are thus, we say, incommensurable." Kuhn, "Reflections on My Critics," in *Criticism and the Growth of Knowledge*, ed. Lakatos and Musgrave, 231–78, 266–67.

16. Martha Nussbaum distinguishes four constituent claims in Plato's ethical science of measurement (*metretike techne*). Metricity implies that in a situation of choice there is a common value, varying only in quantity, to each choice. Singleness implies that there is one metric for all situations of choice. Consequentialism

implies that these comparable values reside in the outcome of the choice. Maximalization implies that there is a value that (either in each case, or—for example happiness or pleasure—in all cases) can and should be maximized. Martha Nussbaum, "The Discernment of Perception: An Aristotelian Conception of Private and Public Rationality," in *Love's Knowledge*, 54–105, 56. One ambiguity of *akrasia* distinguishes between criteria as universal standards "outside" of a situation being decided, and criteria that themselves are effective causes of a situation of choice in the first place and thus cannot be adduced as independent (third party) standards.

17. Jean-Pierre Dupuy emphasizes how the modern liberal version of the enkratic subject differs from that found in Aristotle's ethics since it does away with traditional morality and the strong hand of a ruler. "Since sovereignty is the problem, let us do without sovereignty: being diluted throughout the social body it will be boiled down to the self-sufficiency of individuals, i.e., of independent atoms that have no other relationships besides economic exchange." Jean-Pierre Dupuy, "Shaking the Invisible Hand," in *Disorder and Order: Proceedings of the Stanford International Symposium*, ed. Paisley Livingston (Saratoga, CA: Anima Libri, 1984) 129–45, 133.

18. This doubling of the criteria of reasoning—how does one choose, how does one evaluate the choice made—addresses one problem of decisionism. Even if a choice cannot be rationally decided, so that the event is motivated by what might be called "private" preferences, its outcomes might nonetheless be retrospectively evaluated. That two sets of criteria, and two arguments, apply to the same event, is something described by Davidson, "Actions, Reasons, Causes," in *Actions and Events*, 1–19.

19. "This can be called the *forced adjustment equilibrium*. The aggregate demand of all households for all products, adjusted to supply, can be satisfied from the entire supply available to households. Emergence of this forced adjustment equilibrium is compatible with a persisting sense of frustration in the buyer, since she is unable to satisfy her notional demand and obliged to spend her money on forced substitutes. . . . [This] might be called the paradox of the shortage economy. On the one hand, consumers are highly dissatisfied and rightly complain about the items in short supply. On the other, 'global equilibrium' . . . can arise after all. The buyer's painful process of forced adjustment allows both sides of the paradox to apply." Janos Kornai, *The Socialist System* (Princeton: Princeton University Press, 1992) 238.

20. W. V. Quine, "Natural Kinds," in *Ontological Relativity and Other Essays* (New York: Columbia UP, 1969) 114–38, 117.

21. See, for example, Otto Neurath, "Economics in Kind, Calculation in Kind and Their Relation to War Economics" (1916), in *Economic Writings: Selections 1904–1945*, ed. Robert S. Cohen and Thomas E. Uebel (Dordrecht: Kluwer, 2004) 299–311.

22. Among the better known statements of qualitative incommensurability to appear since the end of the Cold War are Samuel Huntington, *The Clash of Civilizations and the Remaking of the World Order* (New York: Simon and Schuster, 1996); and Benjamin Barber, *Jihad vs. McWorld* (New York: Times Books, 1995).

23. Bloch, Ernst, *Erbschaft dieser Zeit* (Frankfurt a.M.: Suhrkamp, 1962) 104ff.

24. Edmund Husserl, *The Crisis of the European Sciences: An Introduction to Phe-*

nomenological Philosophy, trans. David Carr (Evanston: Northwestern UP, 1970) 15–16.

25. Caldwell, *Dictatorship, State Planning, and Social Theory*, 1–2.

26. Otto Neurath, "Economic Plan and Calculation in Kind: On the Socialist Order of Life and the Human Beings of the Future" (1925), in *Economic Writings*, 405–65, 406.

27. Hubert Laitko, "The Reform Package of the 1960s: The Policy Finale of the Ulbricht Era," in *Science under Socialism*, ed. Kristie Macrakis and Dieter Hoffmann (Cambridge: Harvard UP, 1999) 44–63, 47; Raymond G. Stokes, *Constructing Socialism: Technology and Change in East Germany 1945–1990* (Baltimore: Johns Hopkins UP, 2000) 131–52.

28. Walter Ulbricht at the VII Party Congress, cited in Günter Mittag, "Sozialistische Ökonomie und wissenschaftlich-technische Revolution meistern," *Einheit* 22.8 (1967): 972–82, 972.

29. Mittag, "Sozialistische Ökonomie," 978.

30. See Steven Heims, *The Cybernetics Group* (Cambridge: MIT P, 1991).

31. The words *in principle* are key here. I am not claiming that the party ever came close to relinquishing tight ideological control over the various social subsystems. Most revealing here would be the 11th Party Plenum of 1965, in which the cultural liberalization promised with the Wall suffered a heavy blow (the nickname for the Plenum was *das Kahlschlag-Plenum*) at the same time as the NÖS program struggled to keep itself in place.

32. These words are all entries in Georg Klaus, ed., *Wörterbuch der Kybernetik* (Berlin: Dietz, 1969). See *Selbstorganisation*, 556–57; *Selbstreproduktion*, 559–60; *selbsttätige Regelung*, 560; *selbsttätige Steuerung*, 560; *Zielstrebigkeit*, 727–29.

33. Klaus, "Zielstrebigkeit," in *Wörterbuch*, 729.

34. See William Rasch, *Niklas Luhmann's Modernity* (Stanford: Stanford UP, 2000) 36, for a discussion of the significance of this idea for contemporary systems theory.

35. Klaus, "Trial and Error," in *Wörterbuch*, 660–62, 661.

36. The *Dictionary* describes the difference between "internal" and "external" contradiction in the entry for "Wechselwirkung," in Klaus, *Wörterbuch*, 713–15.

37. Klaus, "Dialektischer Widerspruch," in *Wörterbuch*, 141–43, 143.

38. Sigrid Meuschel, *Legitimation und Parteiherrschaft in der DDR* (Frankfurt a.M.: Suhrkamp, 1992), esp. 221–41, here 231.

39. Klaus, "Selbstorganisation," in *Wörterbuch*, 556–57.

40. Georg Klaus, "Regelkreise und Organismen," *Neues Deutschland* (October 15, 1960): 15.

41. Klaus, "Regelkreise," 15.

42. Klaus, "Regelkreise," 15.

43. "Determinate Being is Being with a character or mode—which simply *is*; and such unmediated character is **Quality**." §90. G. W. F. Hegel, *Hegel's Logic*, trans. William Wallace (Oxford: Oxford UP, 1975) 134.

44. §104, Hegel, *Logic*, 153.

45. §107, Zusatz, Hegel, 157.

46. Cited in Harvey Leff and Andrew Rex, overview, in *Maxwell's Demon: En-*

tropy, Information, Computing, ed. Harvey Leff and Andrew Rex (Princeton: Princeton UP, 1990) 4.

47. Heinz von Foerster, "Disorder/Order: Discovery or Invention?" in *Disorder and Order*, 177–89, 183–84.

48. Georg Klaus, "Die Entwicklung des sozialistischen Denkens und Handelns in philosophischer Sicht," *Einheit* 22.2 (1967): 165–73, 168.

49. Klaus, "Entwicklung," 168.

50. §9, Husserl, *Crisis*, 33.

51. Klaus, "Qualität," in *Wörterbuch*, 503–4, 504.

52. Klaus, "Entwicklung," 170.

53. Klaus, "Entwicklung," 170.

54. For one formulation of this paradox, see Husserl, §53. "The paradox of human subjectivity: being a subject for the world and at the same time being an object in the world," *Crisis*, 178.

55. This succession of paradoxes applies to Hegel's *Logic* as well. Thus, the introduction of "Quantity" in §99 is followed by the distinction between "Continuous" and "Discrete" in §100. Hegel, *Logic*, 145, 148.

56. Klaus, "Qualität," in *Wörterbuch*, 504.

57. Klaus Dieter Wüstneck, "Die Bedeutung der Kybernetik für die Führungstätigkeit der Partei," *Einheit* 22.8 (1967): 983–92, 992.

58. Klaus, "Qualität," in *Wörterbuch*, 504.

59. "This motto came about when the deputy planning chief responsible for prognoses cited it in November 1968, in the presence of Ulbricht, from an *Izvestia* article by the Soviet cybernetician Glushkov." André Steiner, *Von Plan zu Plan: Eine Wirtschaftsgeschichte der DDR* (Munich: Deutsche Verlags-Anstalt, 2004) 142.

60. Karl Popper, "Normal Science and its Dangers,"in *Criticism and the Growth of Knowledge*, eds. Lakatos and Musgrave, 51–58, 57. Similarly, Lakatos in "Falsification" criticizes Kuhn's model of paradigm shifts by calling it "a mystical conversion which is not and cannot be governed by rules of reason" (93).

61. Klaus, *Kybernetik—eine neue Universalphilosophie?* 12.

62. Klaus, "Kybernetik und ideologischer Klassenkampf," 1181.

63. Klaus, "Kybernetik und ideologischer Klassenkampf," 1181.

64. Plato, "Theatatus," 160d, in *Collected Dialogues*, 866.

65. Klaus, "Kybernetik und ideologischer Klassenkampf," 1180.

66. Kuhn, "Reflections," 261.

67. Plato, "Gorgias," 474d, in *Collected Dialogues*, 229–307, 257.

68. Plato, "Gorgias," 453a, 455a, in *Collected Dialogues*, 236; 238.

69. See the pioneering analysis of rhetoric and *kairos* in James L. Kinneavy, "Kairos in Classical and Modern Rhetorical Theory," in *Rhetoric and Kairos: Essays in History, Theory, and Praxis*, ed. Phillip Sipiora and James S. Baumlin (Albany: SUNY P, 2002).

70. Albrecht von Haller, cited by Hegel, §104 Zusatz, in *Logic*, 154.

71. Galen, *On Medical Experience* 16.1–17.3, in *Vagueness: A Reader*, ed. Rosanna Keefe and Peter Smith (Cambridge: MIT P, 1996) 58–59, 58.

72. Franz Fühmann, "Der Haufen," *Saiäns-fiktschen: Erzählungen* (Rostock: Hinstorff, 1981) 34. Page numbers for this story are subsequently cited parenthetically in the text.

73. For a discussion of methodological individualism, associated with the critique of Marxism in the work of F. A. Hayek and Karl Popper, see Richard W. Miller, "Fact and Method in the Social Sciences," in *The Philosophy of Science*, ed. Richard Boyd, Philip Gasper, and J. D. Trout (Cambridge: MIT P, 1991) 743–62. Kuhn, in contrast to Popper's a priori rationalism, believes that any explanation of scientific progress must "be a description of a value system, an ideology, together with an analysis of the institutions through which that system is transmitted and enforced." Kuhn, "Logic of Discovery," 21.

74. Franz Fühmann, *Zweiundzwanzig Tage oder Die Hälfte des Lebens* (Frankfurt: Suhrkamp, 1978) 127.

75. Fühmann, *Saiäns-fiktschen*, 6–7.

76. Bertrand Russell, "Vagueness," in *Vagueness*, 61–68.

77. Max Black, "Vagueness: An Exercise in Logical Analysis," in *Vagueness*, 69–81, 74.

78. Black, "Vagueness," 76.

79. Russell, "Vagueness," 62–63.

80. Russell, "Vagueness," 65.

81. Here we can also see how a satire of cybernetic reasoning such as Christa Wolf's 1970 story "Neue Lebensansichten eines Katers" played a misguided role against the NÖS. Bitterly repressed at the 11 Party Plenum ("Kahlschlag Plenum"), humanists like Wolf did not recognize that their enemies were not directly the technocrats then in favor with the Ulbricht regime. They equated the state with technocratic reasoning, which presumably spurned humanist values such as quality, and thus when the state struck back with the qualitative force of party sovereignty, they had lost their chance for an alliance with quantity. Fühmann's story, in contrast to Wolf's, sees the merits of quantity and the dangers of quality. Christ Wolf, "Neue Lebensansichten eines Katers," in *Gesammelte Erzählungen* (Frankfurt: Luchterhand, 1981) 97–123.

82. Franz Fühmann to Kurt Batt, August 22, 1971, *Briefe 1950–1984. Eine Auswahl*, ed. Hans-Jürgen Schmitt (Rostock: Hinstorff, 1994) 102.

83. Fühmann to Batt, August 22, 1971, *Briefe*, 104.

84. Fühmann to Batt, September 9, 1971, *Briefe*, 105. The text shows $1/x^2$—I have corrected the typo by logic of Fühmann's argument.

85. "This infinity [of endless negation] is the wrong or negative infinity: it is only a negative of a finite: but the finite rises again the same as ever, and is never got rid of or absorbed." Hegel, §94, *Logic*, 137. In the Zusatz to §94 Hegel elaborates the good infinity by contrast. "Such a progression to infinity is not the real infinite. That consists in being at home with itself in its other, or, if enunciated as a process, in coming to itself in its other." Hegel, *Logic*, 137.

86. Quine considers negative predicates "non-projectible," by which he means that they do not tend to confirm an induction. Thus, each black raven tends to confirm the claim that all ravens are black, but a nonblack nonraven does not tend to prove anything about ravens, because it is not a "natural kind." Quine, "Natural Kinds," 114ff.

CHAPTER NINE

1. Roland Barthes, *A Lover's Discourse*, trans. Richard Howard (New York: Farrar, Straus and Giroux, 1978) 202.

2. Roland Barthes, "Twenty Key Words for Roland Barthes," in *The Grain of the Voice: Interviews 1962–1980*, trans. Linda Coverdale (New York: Farrar, Straus and Giroux, 1985) 205–32, 206.

3. Franz Fühmann, "Der Haufen," in *Saiäns-fiktschen* (Leipzig: Reclam, 1990 [1981]) 32–57, 57.

4. From *Inner Experience*, cited in Denis Hollier, *Against Architecture: The Writings of Georges Bataille*, trans. Betsy Wing (Cambridge: MIT P, 1989 [1974]) 46.

5. Franz Fühmann, "Die Straße der Perversionen," *Saiäns-fiktschen*, 69–78, 69. Page numbers for this story will subsequently be cited parenthetically in the text.

6. Georges Bataille, *The Impossible*, trans. Robert Hurley (San Francisco: City Lights, 1991) 33.

7. Franz Fühmann, "Anhang: 'Ignaz Denner,'" in *Essays, Gespräche, Aufsätze 1964–1981. Autorisierte Werkausgabe 6* (Rostock: Hinstorff, 1993) 378–99, 380. Page numbers for this essay will subsequently be cited parenthetically in the text.

8. G. W. F. Hegel, *Phenomenology of Spirit*, trans. A. V. Miller (Oxford: Oxford UP, 1977).

9. Plato, "Parmenides" 130c6–130d5, in *The Collected Dialogues of Plato*, ed. Edith Hamilton and Huntington Cairns (Princeton: Princeton UP, 1961) 924. See the discussion of this passage in Chapter 2.

10. G. W. F. Hegel, *Reason in History: A General Introduction to the Philosophy of History*, trans. Robert S. Hartman (Indianapolis: Bobbs-Merrill, 1953) 44.

11. Franz Fühmann to Kurt Batt, August 22, 1971, Fühmann, *Briefe 1950–1984: Eine Auswahl*, ed. Hans-Jürgen Schmitt (Rostock: Hinstorff, 1994) 101–4, 102.

12. Julia Kristeva, *Powers of Horror: An Essay on Abjection*, trans. Leon S. Roudiez (New York: Columbia UP, 1982) 5.

13. Fühmann, *Zweiundzwanzig Tage oder Die Hälfte des Lebens* (Frankfurt a.M.: Suhrkamp, 1973) 200.

14. Fühmann to Wolf, July 23, 1978, in Christa Wolf and Franz Fühmann, *Monsieur—Wir Finden Uns Wieder: Briefe 1968–1984* (Berlin: Aufbau, 1995) 64–67, 67.

15. Hegel, *Philosophy of History*, 48.

16. Hegel, *Phenomenology*, ¶206, 126.

17. "Every citizen of the German Democratic Republic has the right to help comprehensively shape the political, economic, social and cultural life of the socialist state. The principle is valid: 'Work together, plan together, govern together!'" Article 21, paragraph 1 of the GDR Constitution of 1968 (1974 revision).

18. Hegel, *Phenomenology*, ¶113, 68.

19. Hegel, *Phenomenology*, ¶195, 118 (translation modified).

20. Hegel, *Phenomenology*, ¶120, 72–73.

21. Franz Fühmann, "Gespräch mit Wilfried F. Schoeller," in *Den Katzenartigen wollten wir verbrennen: Ein Lesebuch*, ed. Hans-Jürgen Schmitt (Hamburg: Hoffmann und Campe, 1983) 349–84, 378.

22. Fühmann, "Schoeller," 372.

23. Fühmann to Wolf, July 23, 1978, *Monsieur*, 67.

24. Georg Trakl, *Sämtliche Werke und Briefwechsel: historisch-kritische Ausgabe,* ed. Eberhard Sauermann und Hermann Zwerschina (Basel: Stroemfeld/Roter Stern, 1995).

25. Fühmann, "Das mythische Element in der Literatur," in *Essays*, 82–140, 93.

26. According to Terry Castle the notion of phantasmagoria appears at the moment when conventional society's credulity gives way to scientific rationalism. A slippage then marks the term as it moves from designating the artificial appearance of a ghost (for example, a magic lantern) to the real subjective imagining of a ghost (a mental state). Terry Castle, "Phantasmagoria and the Metaphorics of Modern Reverie," in *The Horror Reader*, ed. Ken Gelder (New York: Routledge, 2000).

27. Tzvetan Todorov, *The Fantastic: A Structural Approach to a Literary Genre*, trans. Richard Howard (Ithaca, NY: Cornell UP, 1975) 25.

28. Donald Davidson, "What Metaphors Mean," in *Philosophical Perspectives on Metaphor*, ed. Mark Johnson (Minneapolis: U Minnesota P, 1981) 200–220.

29. Martin Heidegger, *The Principle of Reason*, trans. Reginald Lilly (Bloomington: Indiana UP, 1991) 46–47.

30. Heidegger, *Principle of Reason*, 47.

31. Heidegger, *Principle of Reason*, 48.

32. Heidegger, *Principle of Reason*, 48.

33. Heidegger, *Principle of Reason*, 48. For *das Ereignis*, see the discussion in "Das Ding," in Heidegger, *Vorträge und Aufsätze* (Frankfurt a.M.: Klostermann, 2000) 165–87, 180–82.

34. Franz Fühmann, "Marsyas," in *Irrfahrt und Heimkehr des Odysseus. Prometheus. Der Geliebte der Morgenröte und andere Erzählungen. Autorisierte Werkausgabe 4* (Rostock: Hinstorff, 1993) 353–68, 365.

35. Franz Fühmann, *Vor Feuerschlünden: Erfahrung mit Georg Trakls Gedicht* (Rostock: Hinstorff: 2000 [1982]) 230.

36. Franz Fühmann, "Praxis und Dialektik der Abwesenheit: Eine imaginäre Rede," in *Essays, Autorisierte Werkausgabe 6*, 458–74, 463.

37. Franz Fühmann, "Der Traum von Moira," from "Dreizehn Träume," in *Vor Feuerschlünden: Erfahrung mit Trakls Gedicht. Unter den Paranyas: Traum-Erzählungen und –Notate. Autorisierte Werkausgabe 7* (Rostock: Hinstorff, 1993 [1985]) 245–46. © Hinstorff Verlag GmbH, Rostock 1993. Translated with permission Hinstorff Verlag.

Bibliography

Adorno, Theodor W. "Cultural Criticism and Society." In *Prisms*, trans. Samuel and Shierry Weber, 17–34. Cambridge: MIT P, 1981.

——. "The Essay as Form." In *Notes to Literature*, vol. 1, ed. Rolf Tiedemann, trans. Shierry Weber Nicholson, 3–23. New York: Columbia UP, 1991.

——. *Jargon der Eigentlichkeit: Zur deutschen Ideologie*. Frankfurt a.M.: Suhrkamp, 1964.

——. *Prisms*. Trans. Samuel and Shierry Weber. Cambridge: MIT P, 1967.

——. "Reconciliation under Duress." In *Aesthetics and Politics*, ed. Ernst Bloch et al., 151–76. London: Verso, 1977.

Agamben, Giorgio. *Homo Sacer: Sovereign Power and Bare Life*. Trans. Daniel Heller-Roazen. Stanford: Stanford UP, 1998.

——. *Means without End: Notes on Politics*. Trans. Vincenzo Binetti and Cesare Casarino. Minneapolis: U Minnesota P, 2000.

——. "The Time that Is Left." *Epoché* 7.1 (fall 2002): 1–14.

Althusser, Louis. *For Marx*. Trans. Ben Brewster. London: Verso, 1969.

Althusser, Louis and Étienne Balibar. *Reading Capital*. Trans. Ben Brewster. London: Verso, 1979.

Amariglio, Jack, and David F. Ruccio, "Literary/Cultural 'Economies,' Economic Discourse, and the Question of Marxism." In *The New Economic Criticism: Studies at the Intersection of Literature and Economics*, ed. Martha Woodmansee and Mark Osteen, 381–400. London: Routledge, 1999.

Anderson, Benedict. *Imagined Communities*, rev. ed. London: Verso, 1991.

Anderson, Perry. *In the Tracks of Historical Materialism*. London: Verso, 1983.

Arendt, Hannah. *Lectures on Kant's Political Philosophy*. Ed. Ronald Beiner. Chicago: U Chicago P, 1982.

——. *On Revolution*. New York: Viking, 1963.

Aristotle, *Metaphysics*. Trans. Hippocrates G. Apostle. Bloomington: Indiana UP, 1966.

——. *Nicomachean Ethics*. Trans. Martin Ostwald. New York: Macmillan, 1962.

———. *On Interpretation*. In *The Categories; On Interpretation; Prior Analytics*, trans. Harold P. Cooke. Cambridge: Harvard UP, 1938.

———. *On the Art of Rhetoric*. Trans. John Henry Freese. Cambridge: Harvard UP, 1991.

Arnold, Heinz Ludwig, and Frauke Meyer-Gosau, eds. *Literatur in der DDR: Rückblicke*. München: edition text + kritik, 1991.

Aron, Raymond. *The Opium of the Intellectuals*. Trans. Terence Kilmartin. New York: Norton, 1962.

Badiou, Alain. *Being and Event*. Trans. Oliver Feltham. London: Continuum, 2005.

———. "Eight Theses on the Universal." In *Theoretical Writings*, ed. and trans. Ray Brassier and Alberto Toscano. London: Continuum, 2004.

———. "One Divides into Two." Trans. Alberto Toscano. http://culturemachine.tees.ac.uk/Cmach/Backissues/j004/Articles/Badiou.htm.

———. *Saint Paul: The Foundation of Universalism*. Trans. Ray Brassier. Stanford: Stanford UP, 2003.

———. *Theoretical Writings*. Ed. and trans. Ray Brassier and Alberto Toscano. London: Continuum, 2004.

Bahro, Rudolf. "Abdankung des Grashüpfers?" *Forum* 10 (1966): 23.

Barber, Benjamin. *Jihad vs. McWorld*. New York: Times Books, 1995.

Barthes, Roland. *Elements of Semiology*. Trans. Annette Lavers and Colin Smith. New York: Hill and Wang, 1967.

———. *The Grain of the Voice: Interviews 1962–1980*. Trans. Linda Coverdale. New York: Farrar, Straus and Giroux, 1985.

———. *A Lover's Discourse*. Trans. Richard Howard. New York: Hill and Wang, 1978.

———. *Sade/Fourier/Loyola*. Trans. Richard Miller. New York: Hill and Wang, 1976.

Bataille, Georges. *The Accursed Share*, vol. 1. Trans. Robert Hurley. New York: Zone Books, 1991.

———. *The Accursed Share*, vols. 2 and 3. Trans. Robert Hurley. New York: Zone, 1993.

———. *Eroticism*. Trans. Mary Dalwood. London: Marion Boyars, 1998.

———. *The Impossible*. Trans. Robert Hurley. San Francisco: City Lights, 1991.

———. *Inner Experience*. Trans. Leslie Anne Boldt. Albany: SUNY P, 1988.

Bateson, Gregory. *Steps to an Ecology of Mind*. San Francisco: Chandler, 1972.

Bathrick, David. *The Powers of Speech: The Powers of Culture in the GDR*. Lincoln: U Nebraska P, 1995.

Baudelaire, Charles. "Heauton Timoroumenos." In *Poems of Baudelaire: A Translation of* Les Fleurs du Mal, trans. Roy Campbell. New York: Pantheon, 1952.

Baudrillard, Jean. *For a Critique of the Political Economy of the Sign*. Trans. Charles Levin. St. Louis: Telos, 1981.

Becher, Johannes R. *Auf andere Art so große Hoffnung: Tagebuch 1950. Gesammelte Werke*, vol. 12. Berlin: Aufbau, 1969.

———. *Bekenntnisse, Entdeckungen, Variationen: Denkdichtung in Prosa*. Berlin: Aufbau, 1968.

———. *Der gespaltene Dichter: Gedichte, Briefe, Dokumente 1945–1958*. Ed. Carsten Gansel. Berlin: Aufbau, 1991.

——. *Der Grosse Plan: Epos des sozialistischen Aufbau*. Berlin: Agis, 1931.
Beckett, Samuel, et al. *Our Exagmination Round His Factification for Incamination of Work in Progress*. London: Faber and Faber, 1961.
Benjamin, Walter. *The Arcades Project*. Trans. Howard Eiland and Kevin McLaughlin, ed. Rolf Tiedemann. Cambridge: Harvard UP, 1999.
——. *Illuminations*. Trans. Harry Zohn, ed. Hannah Arendt. New York: Schocken Books, 1968.
——. *The Origin of the German Tragic Drama*. Trans. John Osborne. London: NLB, 1977.
Berbig, Roland, et al., eds. *In Sachen Biermann: Protokolle, Berichte und Briefe zu den Folgen einer Ausbürgerung*. Berlin: Ch. Links, 1994.
Biermann, Wolf. *Deutschland: Ein Wintermärchen*. Berlin: Wagenbach, 1972.
Binder, Guyora, and Robert Weisberg. *Literary Criticisms of Law*. Princeton: Princeton UP, 2000.
Bloch, Ernst. *Erbschaft dieser Zeit*. Frankfurt a.M.: Suhrkamp, 1962.
——. *Heritage of Our Times*. Trans. Neville and Stephen Plaice. Berkeley and Los Angeles: U California P, 1991.
——. *Natural Law and Human Dignity*. Trans. Dennis J. Schmidt. Cambridge: MIT P, 1986.
——. *Politische Messungen, Pestzeit, Vormärz*. Frankfurt a.M.: Suhrkamp, 1970.
——. *The Principle of Hope*. Cambridge: MIT Press, 1986.
——. *The Spirit of Utopia*. Trans. Anthony Nassar. Stanford: Stanford UP, 2000.
——. *The Utopian Function of Art and Literature: Selected Essays*. Trans. Jack Zipes and Frank Mecklenburg. Cambridge: MIT P, 1988.
——. *Vom Hasard zur Katastrophe: Politische Aufsätze 1934–1939*. Frankfurt a.M.: Suhrkamp, 1972.
Bloom, Harold. *Agon: Towards a Theory of Revisionism*. Oxford: Oxford UP, 1982.
Bohrer, Karl Heinz. "Kulturschutzgebiet DDR." *Merkur* 500 (October–November 1990): 1015–18.
Bolsinger, Eckard. *The Autonomy of the Political: Carl Schmitt's and Lenin's Political Realism*. Westport, CT: Greenwood, 2001.
Borneman, John. *Settling Accounts: Violence, Justice, and Accountability in Postsocialist Europe*. Princeton: Princeton UP, 1997.
Brasch, Thomas. "Der Zweikampf." In *Vor den Vätern sterben die Söhne*, 21–26. Berlin: Rotbuch, 1977.
Brecht, Bertolt. "The Epic Theater and Its Difficulties [November 27, 1927]." In *Brecht on Theater: The Development of an Aesthetic*, ed. and trans. John Willett, 22–24. London: Meuthen, 1964.
——. *The Threepenny Opera*. 1954 New York Cast. Marc Blitzstein Adaptation. London: Decca Broadway, 1954.
——. "To Those Born Later." In *Poems 1913–1956*, ed. John Willett and Ralph Manheim. London: Meuthen, 1976.
——. "Wahrnehmung." In *Werke. Große kommentierte Berliner und Frankfurter Ausgabe. Band 15 Gedichte 5*, ed. Werner Hecht, Jan Knopf, Werner Mittenzwei, and Klaus-Detlef Müller, 205. Berlin: Aufbau and Frankfurt a.M.: Suhrkamp, 1993.
Burchell, Graham, Colin Gordon, and Peter Miller, eds. *The Foucault Effect: Studies in Governmentality*. Chicago: U Chicago P, 1991.

Burns, Rob, ed. *German Cultural Studies*. Oxford: Oxford UP, 1995.
Butler, Judith, Ernesto Laclau, and Slavoj Zizek. *Contingency, Hegemony, Universality: Contemporary Dialogues on the Left*. London: Verso, 2000.
Caldwell, Peter C. *Dictatorship, State Planning, and Social Theory in the German Democratic Republic*. Cambridge: Cambridge UP, 2003.
———. *Popular Sovereignty and the Crisis of German Constitutional Law: The Theory and Practice of Weimar Constitutionalism*. Durham: Duke UP, 1997.
Carnap, Rudolf. "Empiricism, Semantics and Ontology," Supplement, in *Meaning and Necessity: A Study in Semantics and Modal Logic*, enl. ed., 205–21. Chicago: U Chicago P, 1956.
Carroll, Lewis. *Alice in Wonderland*. 2nd ed. Ed. Donald J. Gray. New York: Norton, 1992.
Castle, Terry. "Phantasmagoria and the Metaphorics of Modern Reverie." In *The Horror Reader*, ed. Ken Gelder, 29–46. New York: Routledge, 2000.
Cooke, Paul. *Speaking the Taboo*. Amsterdam: Rodopi, 2000.
Csáth, Géza. *Opium and Other Stories*. Trans. Jascha Kessler and Charlotte Rogers. Harmondsworth: Penguin, 1983.
Culler, Jonathan. Foreword to *The Poetics of Prose* by Tzvetan Todorov, trans. Richard Howard, 7–13. Oxford: Basil Blackwell, 1977.
Davidson, Donald. "How Is Weakness of the Will Possible?" In *Essays on Actions and Events*, 2nd ed., 21–42. Oxford: Oxford UP, 2001.
———. "What Metaphors Mean." In *Philosophical Perspectives on Metaphor*, ed. Mark Johnson, 200–220. Minneapolis: U Minnesota P, 1981.
Davis, John B. "Agent Identity in Economics." In *The Economic World View: Studies in the Ontology of Economics*, ed. Uskali Mäki, 114–31. Cambridge: Cambridge UP, 2001.
Deleuze, Gilles. *The Logic of Sense*. Trans. Mark Lester. New York: Columbia UP, 1990.
Deleuze, Gilles, and Félix Guattari. *Kafka: Toward a Minor Literature*. Trans. Dana Polen. Minneapolis: U Minnesota P, 1986.
Derrida, Jacques. *Dissemination*. Trans. Barbara Johnson. Chicago: Chicago UP, 1981.
———. "Force of Law: The Mystical Foundation of Authority." In *Deconstruction and the Possibility of Justice*, ed. Ducilla Cornell, Michel Rosenfeld, and David Gray Carlson, 3–67. New York: Routledge, 1992.
———. *Specters of Marx*. Trans. Peggy Kamuf. New York: Routledge, 1994.
———. *Writing and Difference*. Trans. Alan Bass. Chicago: U Chicago P, 1978.
Domdey, Horst. "Die DDR-Literatur als Literatur der Epochenillusion." In *Deutschland Archiv. Sonderheft: Die DDR im vierzigsten Jahr*, ed. I. Spittmann and G. Helwig, 141–49. Cologne: Deutschland Archiv, 1989.
Dupuy, Jean-Pierre. "Shaking the Invisible Hand." In *Disorder and Order: Proceedings of the Stanford International Symposium*, ed. Paisley Livingston, 129–45. Saratoga, CA: Anima Libri, 1984.
Dwars, Jens-Fietje. *Abgrund des Widerspruchs: Das Leben des Johannes R. Becher*. Berlin: Aufbau, 1998.
Dyzenhaus, David. *Legality and Legitimacy: Carl Schmitt, Hans Kelsen and Hermann Heller in Weimar*. Oxford: Clarendon P, 1997.

Eagleton, Terry. *Sweet Violence*. Oxford: Blackwell, 2003.
Edgeworth, Francis Ysidro. *Mathematical Psychics and Further Papers on Political Economy*. Ed. Peter Newman. Oxford: Oxford UP, 2003 [1881].
Einsiedel, Heinrich von. *I Joined the Russians: A Captured German Flier's Diary of the Communist Temptation*. New Haven: Yale UP, 1953.
Eley, Geoff. *Forging Democracy: The History of the Left in Europe, 1850–2000*. Oxford: Oxford UP, 2002.
———. "Reviewing the Socialist Tradition." In *The Crisis of Socialism in Europe*, ed. Christiane Lemke and Gary Marks, 21–60. Durham: Duke University Press, 1992.
Emmerich, Wolfgang. *Kleine Literaturgeschichte der DDR 1945–1988*. Exp. ed. Frankfurt a.M.: Luchterhand, 1989.
Engels, Friedrich. *Socialism: Utopian and Scientific*. New York: International, 1935.
Ensikat, Peter. *Hat es die DDR überhaupt gegeben?* Berlin: Eulenspiegel, 1998.
Epstein, Catherine. *The Last Revolutionaries: German Communists and Their Century*. Cambridge: Harvard UP, 2003.
Finney, Gail. *Christa Wolf*. New York: Twayne, 1999.
Fischer, Ernst. *Art against Ideology*. New York: George Brazillier, 1969.
Foerster, Heinz von. "Disorder/Order: Discovery or Invention?" In *Disorder and Order: Proceedings of the Stanford International Symposium*, ed. Paisley Livingston, 177–89. Saratoga, CA: Anima Libri, 1984.
Foucault, Michel. *The Archaeology of Knowledge and the Discourse on Language*. Trans. A. M. Sheridan Smith. New York: Pantheon, 1972.
———. *Discipline and Punish: The Birth of the Prison*. 2nd ed. Trans. Alan Sheridan. New York: Vintage, 1995.
———. "Governmentality." In *The Foucault Effect: Studies in Governmentality*, ed. Graham Burchell, Colin Gordon, and Peter Miller. 87–104. Chicago: U Chicago P, 1991.
———. *The Order of Things*. New York: Vintage, 1970.
———. "What Is an Author?" In *Language, Counter-Memory, Practice: Selected Essays and Interviews*, ed. and trans. Donald F. Bouchard, 113–38. Ithaca: Cornell UP, 1977.
Fox, Thomas C. *Border Crossings: An Introduction to East German Prose*. Ann Arbor: U Michigan P, 1993.
Fraser, Nancy. *Justice Interruptus: Critical Reflections on the "Postsocialist" Condition*. New York: Routledge, 1997.
Freud, Sigmund. *Beyond the Pleasure Principle*. Trans. and ed. James Strachey. New York: Norton, 1961.
———. *Civilization and Its Discontents*. Trans. and ed. James Strachey. New York: Norton, 1961.
———. *Totem and Taboo*. Trans. and ed. James Strachey. New York: Norton, 1950.
Friedlander, Saul, ed. *Probing the Limits of Representation: Nazism and the "Final Solution."* Cambridge: Harvard UP, 1992.
Friedman, Milton. *Essays in Positive Economics*. Chicago: U Chicago P, 1953.
Friedrich, Thomas. "Das Verfassungslos der DDR—die verfassungslose DDR." In *Rechtserfahrung DDR: Sozialistische Modernisierung oder Entrechtlichung der Gesellschaft?* ed. Gerhard Dilcher, 33–68. Berlin: Berlin Verlag, 1997.

Frye, Northrop. *Anatomy of Criticism: Four Essays*. Princeton: Princeton UP, 1957.
Fühmann, Franz. *Autorisierte Werkausgabe*. 8 Vols. Rostock: Hinstorff, 1993 [1977–88].
——. *Briefe 1950–1984*. Ed. Hans-Jürgen Schmitt. Rostock: Hinstorff, 1994.
——. *Die dampfenden Hälse der Pferde im Turm von Babel*. Berlin: Kinderbuchverlag, 1978.
——. *Der glückliche Ritter von Trinitat oder Wie wird man Oberdiskutierer. Ein Puppenspiel für Kinder*. Rostock: Hinstorff, 1999.
——. *Im Berg: Texte und Dokumente aus dem Nachlaß*. Ed. Ingrid Prignitz. Rostock: Hinstorff, 1991.
——. *Den Katzenartigen wollten wir verbrennen: Ein Lesebuch*. Ed. Hans-Jürgen Schmitt. Munich: DTV, 1983.
——. "Marsyas." In *Irrfahrt und Heimkehr des Odysseus; Prometheus; Der Geliebte der Morgenröte und andere Erzählungen*, *Werkausgabe 4*, ed. Ingrid Prignitz. Rostock: Hinstorff, 1993.
——. *Der Mund des Propheten: Späte Erzählungen*. Berlin: Aufbau, 1991.
——. *Saiäns-fiktschen: Erzählungen*. Leipzig: Reclam, 1981.
——. "Sein Solch-Betrachten war vonnönten." In *Sinn und Form. Zweites Sonderheft Johannes R. Becher*, ed. Deutsche Akademie der Künste, 354–57. Berlin: Rütten und Loening, 1960.
——. *Twenty-two Days, or, Half a Lifetime*. Trans. Leila Vennewitz. London: Jonathan Cape, 1992.
——. *Urworte Deutsch: aus Steputats Reimlexikon gezogen*. Rostock: Hinstorff, 1995.
——. *Vor Feuerschlünden: Erfahrung mit Georg Trakls Gedicht*. Rostock: Hinstorff, 2000 [1982].
——. *Zweiundzwanzig Tage oder die Hälfte des Lebens*. Suhrkamp: Frankfurt a.M., 1973.
Fühmann, Franz, and Dietmar Riemann. *Was für eine Insel in was für einem Meer: Leben mit geistig Behinderten*. Rostock: Hinstorff, 1985.
Furet, François. *The Passing of an Illusion: The Idea of Communism in the Twentieth Century*. Trans. Deborah Furet. Chicago: U Chicago P, 1999.
Gadamer, Hans-Georg. *Truth and Method*. 2nd rev. ed. Trans. Joel Weinsheimer and Donald G. Marshall. New York: Continuum, 1989.
Gerhardt, Volker, and Hans-Christoph Rauh, eds. *Anfänge der DDR-Philosophie: Ansprüche, Ohnmacht, Scheitern*. Berlin: Links, 2001.
Getty, J. Arch, and Oleg V. Naumov. *The Road to Terror: Stalin and the Self-Destruction of the Bolsheviks, 1932–39*. Trans. Benjamin Sher. New Haven: Yale UP, 1999.
Geyer, Michael, ed. *The Power of Intellectuals in Contemporary Germany*. Chicago: U Chicago P, 2001.
Giddens, Anthony. *Central Problems in Social Theory*. Berkeley: U California P, 1979.
——. *The Third Way: The Renewal of Social Democracy*. Cambridge: Polity, 1998.
Gide, Charles, and Charles Rist. *A History of Economic Doctrines*. Trans. R. Richards. Boston: D. C. Heath, 1948 [1915].
Gierke, Otto Friedrich von. *Political Theories of the Middle Age*. Trans. F. W. Maitland. Boston: Beacon, 1958.

Girard, Rene. *The Scapegoat*. Trans. Yvonne Freccero. Baltimore: Johns Hopkins UP, 1986.

Gleason, Abbott. *Totalitarianism: The Inner History of the Cold War.* New York: Oxford UP, 1995.

Goethe, Johann Wolfgang von. *Conversations with Eckermann*. Trans. John Oxenford. San Francisco: North Point, 1984.

———. *Faust: Part I*, trans. Anna Swanwick. Vol. 19, part 1 of The Harvard Classics. New York: P. F. Collier, 1909–14. Bartleby.com, 2001. www.bartleby.com/19/1/.

Gordon, Colin. Introduction to *Power, The Essential Works of Foucault 1954–1984*, vol. 3, ed. James D. Faubion, xi–xli. New York: New Press, 2000.

Goux, Jean-Joseph. *Symbolic Economies: After Marx and Freud*. Trans. Jennifer Curtiss Gage. Ithaca: Cornell UP, 1990.

Graham, Loren R. *What Have We Learned about Science and Technology from the Russian Experience?* Stanford: Stanford UP, 1998.

Groys, Boris. *Das kommunistische Postskriptum*. Frankfurt a.M.: Suhrkamp, 2006.

Guillory, John. *Cultural Capital*. Chicago: U Chicago P, 1993.

Habermas, Jürgen. *Between Facts and Norms: Contributions to a Discourse Theory of Law and Democracy*. Trans. William Rehg. Cambridge: MIT P, 1996.

———. "Hermeneutics and the Social Sciences." In *The Hermeneutics Reader*, ed. Kurt Moeller-Vollmer, 293–319. New York: Continuum, 1985.

———. *Knowledge and Human Interests*. Trans. Jeremy J. Shapiro. Boston: Beacon P, 1971.

———. *Legitimation Crisis*. Trans. Thomas McCarthy. Boston: Beacon P, 1975.

———. "A Letter to Christa Wolf." In *A Berlin Republic: Writings on Germany*, trans. Steven Rendall, 95–105. Lincoln: U Nebraska P, 1997.

———. *Philosophical Discourse of Modernity*. Trans. Frederick G. Lawrence. Cambridge: MIT P, 1987.

Hager, Kurt. *Erinnerungen*. Leipzig: Faber and Faber, 1996.

Hamrick, William S. *An Existential Phenomenology of Law: Maurice Merleau-Ponty.* Dordrecht: Martinus Nijhoff, 1987.

Hannsmann, Margarete, ed. *Protokolle aus der Dämmerung: 1977–1984; Begegnung und Briefwechsel zwischen Franz Fühmann, Margarete Hannsmann und HAP Grieshaber.* Rostock: Hinstorff, 2000.

Hart, H. L. A. *The Concept of Law*. Oxford: Oxford UP, 1961.

Hawkes, Terrence. *Structuralism and Semiotics*. Berkeley: U California Press, 1977.

Hayek, Friedrich A. von. *The Road to Serfdom*. London: Routledge, 1944.

Hegel, G. W. F. *Hegel's Logic*. Trans. William Wallace. Oxford: Oxford UP, 1975.

———. *Hegel's Philosophy of Right*. Trans. T. M. Knox. Oxford: Oxford UP, 1952.

———. *Phenomenology of Spirit*. Trans. A. V. Miller. Oxford: Oxford UP, 1977.

———. *Reason in History: A General Introduction to the Philosophy of History*. Trans. Robert S. Hartman. Indianapolis: Bobbs-Merrill, 1953.

Heidegger, Martin. *Being and Time*. Trans. John Macquarrie and Edward Robinson. San Francisco: Harper and Row, 1962.

———. "The End of Philosophy and the Task of Thinking." In *Basic Writings*, ed. David Farrell Krell, 369–92. San Francisco: HarperCollins, 1977.

———. *The Principle of Reason*. Trans. Reginald Lilly. Bloomington: Indiana UP, 1991.

——. *Vorträge und Aufsätze*. Frankfurt a.M.: Klostermann, 2000.

Heims, Steven. *The Cybernetics Group*. Cambridge: MIT P, 1991.

Heine, Heinrich. *Fünfzig Gedichte*. Ed. Bernd Kortländer. Stuttgart: Reclam, 1999.

Heinze, Barbara. *Franz Fühmann: Eine Biographie in Bildern, Dokumenten und Briefen*. Rostock: Hinstoff, 1998.

Hell, Julia. *Post-Fascist Fantasies: Psychoanalysis, History, and the Literature of East Germany*. Durham: Duke UP, 1997.

Hell, Julia, Loren Kruger, and Katie Trumpener. "Dossier: Socialist Realism and East German Modernism—Another Historians' Debate." *Rethinking Marxism* 7.3 (fall 1994): 37–79.

Herodotus. *The Histories*. Trans. Aubrey de Sélincourt. Harmondsworth: Penguin, 1954.

Herzinger, Richard. *Masken der Lebensrevolution: Vitalistische Zivilisations- und Humanismuskritik in Texten Heiner Müllers*. Munich: Wilhelm Fink, 1992.

Heukenkamp, Ursula. "Ortsgebundenheit: Die DDR-Literatur als Variante des Regionalismus in der deutschen Nachkriegsliteratur." *Weimarer Beiträge* 42.1 (1996): 30–53.

——, ed. *Schuld und Sühne? Kriegserlebnis und Kriegsdeutung in deutschen Medien der Nachkriegszeit*. Amsterdam: Rodopi: 2001.

Hilberg, Raul. *The Destruction of the European Jews*. 3rd ed. New Haven: Yale UP.

Hohendahl, Peter, ed. *Reappraisals: Shifting Alignments in Postwar Critical Theory*. Ithaca: Cornell UP, 1991.

——. "Recasting the Public Sphere." *October* 73 (summer 1995): 27–54.

Hollier, Denis. *Against Architecture: The Writings of Georges Bataille*. Trans. Betsy Wing. Cambridge: MIT P, 1989.

Horkheimer, Max. "Traditional and Critical Theory." In *Critical Theory: Selected Essays*, 188–243. New York: Seabury P, 1972.

Horkheimer, Max, and Theodor Adorno. *The Dialectic of Enlightenment*. Trans. John Cumming. New York: Continuum, 1972.

Hörnigk, Therese. *Christa Wolf*. Göttingen: Steidl, 1989.

Hughes, Robert. *The Shock of the New*. 2nd ed. New York: McGraw-Hill, 1991.

Huntington, Samuel. *The Clash of Civilizations and the Remaking of the World Order*. New York: Simon and Schuster, 1996.

Husserl, Edmund. *The Crisis of the European Sciences: An Introduction to Phenomenological Philosophy*. Trans. David Carr. Evanston: Northwestern UP, 1970.

Hutcheon, Linda. *A Poetics of Postmodernism*. New York: Routledge, 1988.

Ingrao, Bruna, and Giorgio Israel. *The Invisible Hand: Economic Equilibrium in the History of Science*. Trans. Ian McGilvray. Cambridge: MIT P, 1990.

Jameson, Fredric. *Marxism and Form: Twentieth-Century Dialectical Theories of Literature*. Princeton: Princeton UP, 1971.

——. *A Singular Modernity: Essay on the Ontology of the Present*. London: Verso, 2002.

Jarausch, Konrad H. *Dictatorship as Experience: Toward a Socio-Cultural History of the GDR*. Trans. Eve Duffy. New York: Berghahn, 1999.

Jay, Martin. *Marxism and Totality: The Adventures of a Concept from Lukács to Habermas*. Berkeley: U California P, 1984.

Judt, Mathias, ed. *DDR-Geschichte in Dokumenten*. Berlin: Ch. Links, 1997.

Kafka, Franz. "Ein Landarzt." In *Das Urteil und andere Erzählungen*, ed. Friedrich Ani, 55–66. Munich: Deutscher Taschenbuchverlag, 2003.

——. *The Metamorphosis and Other Stories*. Trans. Donna Freed. New York: Barnes and Nobles, 2004.

Howard P. Kainz, ed. and trans. *Hegel's Phenomenology of Spirit*. University Park: Pennsylvania State P, 1994.

Kant, Immanuel. *Critique of the Power of Judgment*. Trans. Paul Guyer and Eric Matthews. Cambridge: Cambridge UP, 2000.

Kantorowicz, Ernst H. *The King's Two Bodies: A Study in Mediaeval Political Theology*. Princeton: Princeton UP, 1957.

Keefe, Rosanna, and Peter Smith, eds. *Vagueness: A Reader*. Cambridge: MIT P, 1996.

Kelsen, Hans. *The Communist Theory of Law*. New York: Praeger, 1955.

Kermode, Frank. *The Sense of an Ending: Studies in the Theory of Fiction with a New Epilogue*. Oxford: Oxford UP, 2000.

Kinneavy, James L. "Kairos in Classical and Modern Rhetorical Theory." In *Rhetoric and Kairos: Essays in History, Theory, and Praxis*, ed. Phillip Sipiora and James S. Baumlin, 58–76. Albany: SUNY P, 2002.

Klaus, Georg. "Die Entwicklung des sozialistischen Denkens und Handelns in philosophischer Sicht." *Einheit* 22.2 (1967): 165–73.

——. *Kybernetik und Gesellschaft*. 2nd ed. Berlin: Verlag der Wissenschaften, 1965.

——. "Kybernetik und ideologischer Klassenkampf." *Einheit* 25.9 (1970): 1180–89.

——. *Kybernetik—eine neue Universalphilosophie der Gesellschaft?* Berlin: Akadamie, 1973.

——. *Die Macht des Wortes: Ein Erkenntnistheoretisch-pragmatisches Traktat*. Berlin: Deutscher Verlag der Wissenschaften, 1964.

——. "Regelkreise und Organismen." *Neues Deutschland* (October 15, 1960): 15.

——, ed. *Wörterbuch der Kybernetik*. Berlin: Dietz, 1969.

Klaus, Georg, and Hans Schulze. *Sinn, Gesetz und Fortschritt in der Geschichte*. Berlin: Dietz, 1967.

Kojève, Alexandre. *Introduction to the Reading of Hegel*. Assembled by Raymond Queneau, ed. Allan Bloom, trans. James H. Nichols, Jr. New York: Basic Books, 1969.

Kolbe, Uwe. *Renegatentermine: 30 Versuche, die eigene Erfahrung zu behaupten*. Frankfurt a.M.: Suhrkamp, 1998.

Konrad-Adenauer-Stiftung, ed. *Der missbrauchte Antifaschismus: DDR-Staatsdoktrin und Lebenslüge der deutschen Linken*. Freiburg: Herder, 2002.

Koopmans, T. C., and John M. Montias. "On the Description and Comparison of Economic Systems." In *Comparison of Economic Systems*, ed. Alexander Eckstein, 27–78. Berkeley: U California P, 1971.

Kornai, János. *Anti-equilibrium: On Economic Systems Theory and the Tasks of Research*. Amsterdam: North-Holland, 1971.

——. *Contradictions and Dilemmas*. Cambridge: MIT P, 1986.

——. *The Socialist System: The Political Economy of Communism*. Princeton: Princeton UP, 1992.

Krause, Günter. "Economics in Eastern Germany, 1945–90." In *Economic Thought in Communist and Post-Communist Europe*, ed. Hans-Jürgen Wagener, 264–328. London: Routledge, 1998.

Kreiser, Lothar. "Logik—Lehre und Lehrinhalte an den philosophischen Fakultäten der Universitäten in der SBZ/DDR (1945–1954)." In *Anfänge der DDR-Philosophie: Ansprüche, Ohnmacht, Scheitern*, ed. Volker Gerhardt and Hans-Christoph Rauh, 119–59. Berlin: Links, 2001.

Kristeva, Julia. *Powers of Horror: An Essay on Abjection*. Trans. Leon S. Roudiez. New York: Columbia UP, 1982.

Krüger, Brigitte, Margrid Bircken, and Helmut John, eds. *Jeder hat seinen Fühmann: Zugänge zu Poetologie und Werk Franz Fühmanns*. Frankfurt a.M.: Lang, 1998.

Kuhn, Anna. *Christa Wolf's Utopian Vision: From Marxism to Feminism*. Cambridge: Cambridge UP, 1988.

Kuhn, Thomas. "Logic of Discovery of Psychology of Research?" In *Criticism and the Growth of Knowledge*, ed. Imre Lakatos and Alan Musgrave, 1–23. Cambridge: Cambridge UP, 1970.

Laclau, Ernesto. *On Populist Reason*. London: Verso, 2005.

———. "Why Constructing a People Is the Main Task of Radical Politics." *Critical Inquiry* 32 (summer 2006): 646–80.

Laclau, Ernesto, and Chantal Mouffe. *Hegemony and Socialist Strategy: Towards a Radical Democratic Politics*. London: Verso, 1985.

Laitko, Hubert. "The Reform Package of the 1960s: The Policy Finale of the Ulbricht Era." In *Science under Socialism*, ed. Kristie Macrakis and Dieter Hoffmann, 44–63. Cambridge: Harvard UP, 1999.

Lakatos, Imre. "Falsification and the Methodology of Scientific Research Programmes." In *Criticism and the Growth of Knowledge*, ed. Imre Lakatos and Alan Musgrave, 91–196. Cambridge: Cambridge UP, 1970.

Lakoff, George. *Women, Fire, and Dangerous Things*. Chicago: University of Chicago Press, 1987.

Lange, Oskar, and Fred M. Taylor. *On the Economic Theory of Socialism*. Ed. Benjamin E. Lippincott. Minneapolis: U Minnesota P, 1938.

Latour, Bruno. *We Have Never Been Modern*. Trans. Catherine Porter. Cambridge: Harvard UP, 1993.

Lavoie, Don. *Rivalry and Central Planning: The Socialist Calculation Debate Reconsidered*. Cambridge: Cambridge UP, 1985.

Leeder, Karen. *Breaking Boundaries: A New Generation of Poets in the GDR*. Oxford: Oxford UP, 1996.

Leff, Harvey, and Andrew Rex. *Maxwell's Demon: Entropy, Information, Computing*. Princeton: Princeton UP, 1990.

Lemke, Christiane, and Gary Marks, eds. *The Crisis of European Socialism*. Durham: Duke University Press, 1992.

Lenin, Vladimir Ilyich. *The Lenin Anthology*. Ed. Robert C. Tucker. New York: Norton, 1975.

Lévi-Strauss, Claude. *Introduction to the Work of Marcel Mauss*. Trans. Felicity Baker. London: Routledge and Kegan Paul, 1987.

Liebscher, Heinz. "Georg Klaus—Ein unbequemer Marxist." In *Anfänge der DDR-Philosophie: Ansprüche, Ohnmacht, Scheitern*, ed. Volker Gerhardt and Hans-Christoph Rauh, 406–19. Berlin: Links, 2001.

Lindenfeld, Frank, and Joyce Rothschild Whitt, eds. *Workplace Democracy and Social Change.* Boston: Porter Sargent, 1982.
Loach, Ken. *Land and Freedom*, VHS. New York: Polygram, 1996.
Loest, Erich. *Bruder Franz: Drei Vorlesungen über Franz Fühmann gehalten an der Universität Paderborn im Januar 1985*. Paderborn: Schöningh, 1986.
Luhmann, Niklas. *Essays on Self-Reference*. New York: Columbia UP, 1990.
——. *Love as Passion: The Codification of Intimacy*. Trans. Jeremy Gaines and Doris L. Jones. Cambridge: Harvard UP, 1986.
——. *Social Systems*. Trans. John Bednarz, Jr., with Dirk Baecker. Stanford: Stanford UP, 1995.
——. *Theories of Distinction: Redescribing the Descriptions of Modernity*. Ed. William Rasch. Stanford: Stanford UP, 2002.
——. *Die Wirtschaft der Gesellschaft*. Frankfurt a.M.: Suhrkamp, 1988.
Lukács, Georg. *Deutsche Literatur im Zeitalter des Imperialismus*. Berlin: Aufbau, 1950.
——. *Lenin: A Study on the Unity of His Thought*. Trans. Nicholas Jacobs. Cambridge: MIT P, 1970.
——. *The Meaning of Contemporary Realism*. Trans. John and Necke Mander. London: Merlin 1963.
——. *The Theory of the Novel*. Trans. Anna Bostock. Cambridge: MIT P, 1971.
——. *Die Zerstörung der Vernunft: Der Weg des Irrationalismus von Schelling zu Hitler*. Berlin: Aufbau, 1955.
Lupton, Ellen. "Reading Isotype." *Design Issues* 3.2 (autumn 1986): 47–58.
Lyotard, Jean-Francois. *Libidinal Economy*. Trans. Iain Hamilton Grant. Bloomington: Indiana UP, 1993.
Maaz, Hans-Joachim. *Der Gefühlsstau: Ein Psychogram der DDR*. Berlin: Argon, 1990.
Macpherson, C. B. *The Political Theory of Possessive Individualism: Hobbes to Locke*. Oxford: Oxford UP, 1962.
Magenau, Jörg. *Christa Wolf: Eine Biographie.* Berlin: Kindler, 2002.
Mandel, Ernest. Introduction to Karl Marx, *Capital*, vol. 1, trans. Ben Fowkes, 9–86. New York: Vintage,1977.
Mannheim, Karl. *Ideology and Utopia*. Trans. Louis Wirth and Edward Shils. San Diego: Harcourt Brace Jovanovich, 1968.
Marcuse, Herbert. *One Dimensional Man*. Boston: Beacon P, 1964.
Maron, Monica. *Nach Maßgabe meiner Begreifungskraft*. Frankfurt: S. Fischer, 1993. First published in 1991.
Marx, Karl. *Karl Marx: Selected Writings*. Ed. David McLellan. Oxford: Oxford UP, 1977.
——. *The Marx-Engels Reader.* 2nd ed. Ed. Robert C. Tucker. New York: W. W. Norton, 1978.
——. *Pre-Capitalist Economic Formations*. Ed. Eric J. Hobsbawm. New York: International, 1965.
Medovoi, Leerom, Shankar Raman, and Benjamin Robinson. "Can the Subaltern Vote?" *Socialist Review* 20.3 (1990): 133–49.
Merleau-Ponty, Maurice. *Humanism and Terror: An Essay on the Communist Problem*. Trans. John O'Neill. Boston: Beacon, 1969.

——. *Signes*. Paris: Gallimard, 1960.
——. *The Visible and the Invisible*. Trans. Alphonso Lingis. Evanston: Northwestern UP, 1969.
Metz, Christian. "Instant Self-Contradiction." In *On Signs*, ed. Marshall Blonsky, 259–66. Baltimore: Johns Hopkins UP, 1985.
Meuschel, Sigrid. *Legitimation und Parteiherrschaft in der DDR*. Frankfurt a.M.: Suhrkamp, 1992.
Michael, Klaus. "Eine verschollene Anthologie: Zentralkomitee, Staatssicherheit und die Geschichte eines Buches." In *MachtSpiele: Literatur und Staatssicherheit im Fokus Prenzlauer Berg*, ed. Peter Böthig and Klaus Michael, 202–16. Leipzig: Reclam, 1993.
Michaels, Walter Benn. *The Gold Standard and the Logic of Naturalism*. Berkeley: U California P, 1987.
Miller, J. Hillis. "Laying Down the Law in Literature: The Example of Kleist." In *Deconstruction and the Possibility of Justice*, ed. Drucilla Cornell, Michel Rosenfeld, and David Gray Carlson, 305–29. New York: Routledge, 1992.
Miller, Richard W. "Fact and Method in the Social Sciences." In *The Philosophy of Science*, ed. Richard Boyd, Philip Gasper, and J. D. Trout, 743–62. Cambridge: MIT P, 1991.
Mises, Ludwig von. "Economic Calculation in the Socialist Commonwealth." In *Collectivist Economic Planning*, ed. F. A. Hayek, 87–130. London: Routledge and Kegan Paul, 1935.
——. *Socialism*. New Haven: Yale University Press, 1951.
Mittag, Günter. "Sozialistische Ökonomie und wissenschaftlich-technische Revolution meistern." *Einheit* 22.8 (1967): 972–82.
Mittenzwei, Werner. *Die Intellektuellen: Literatur und Politik in Ostdeutschland von 1945 bis 2000*. Leipzig: Faber und Faber, 2001.
Montias, John M. "Planning with Material Balances in Soviet-type Economies." *American Economic Review* 49 (1959): 963–85.
Mortley, Raoul. "The Fundamentals of the Via Negativa." *American Journal of Philology* 103.4 (winter 1982): 429–39.
Moses, Dirk. "The Forty-Fivers: A Generation between Fascism and Democracy." *German Politics and Society* 17.1 (1999): 195–227.
Müller, Harro. *Geschichte zwischen Kairos und Katastrophe*. Frankfurt a.M.: Athenäum, 1988.
Müller, Heiner. *Gesammelte Irrtümer 3: Texte und Gespräche*. Frankfurt a.M.: Verlag der Autoren, 1994.
——. *Krieg ohne Schlacht: Leben in Zwei Dikatautren*, exp. ed. Cologne: Kiepenhauer and Witsch, 1994.
Neurath, Otto. "Economics in Kind, Calculation in Kind and Their Relation to War Economics." In *Economic Writings: Selections 1904–1945*, ed. Robert S. Cohen and Thomas E. Uebel, 299–311. Dordrecht: Kluwer, 2004.
——. *Empiricism and Sociology*. Ed. Marie Neurath and Robert S. Cohen. Dordrecht: D. Reidel, 1973.
——. *Modern Man in the Making*. New York: Knopf, 1939.
——. "Sociology and Physicalism." In *Logical Positivism*, ed. A. S. Ayer, 282–317. New York: Free Press, 1959.

Nietzsche, Friedrich. *The Birth of Tragedy*. In *Basic Writings of Nietzsche*, trans. and ed. Walter Kaufmann, 1–145. New York: Modern Library, 1966.

Nolte, Ernst. *Der europäische Bürgerkrieg, 1917–1945*. Berlin: Propyläen, 1987.

Novalis. "Paralipomena." In *Heinrich von Ofterdingen*, ed. Jochen Hörisch. Frankfurt a.M.: Insel, 1982.

Nove, Alec. *The Economics of Feasible Socialism Revisited*. London: HarperCollins, 1991.

Nussbaum, Martha. *Love's Knowledge*. Oxford: Oxford UP, 1990.

Nussbaum, Martha, and Amartya Sen, eds. *The Quality of Life*. Oxford: Oxford UP, 1993.

Orwell, George. *Homage to Catalonia*. San Diego: Harcourt Brace, 1952.

Pareto, Vilfredo. *Sociological Writings*. Ed. S. E. Finer. New York: Praeger, 1966.

Parker, Ralph. *How Do You Do Tovarish?* London: George G. Harrap, 1947.

Peirce, Charles Sanders. *Collected Papers of Charles Sanders Peirce*, vols. 1–6, ed. Charles Hartshorne and Paul Weiss; vols. 7–8, ed. Arthur W. Burks. Cambridge: Harvard University Press, 1931–58.

——. *The Essential Peirce: Selected Philosophical Writings*, vol. 2 (1893–1913), ed. the Peirce Edition Project. Bloomington: Indiana UP, 1998.

Peoples Commissariat of Justice of the U.S.S.R. *Report of Court Proceedings in the Case of the Anti-Soviet "Bloc of Rights and Trotskyites."* New York: Howard Fertig, 1988.

Pinkert, Anke. "Waste Matters: Defilement and Postfascist Discourse in Works by Franz Fühmann." *Germanic Review* 80.3 (summer 2005): 254–74.

Pitkin, Hanna Fenichel. *The Attack of the Blob: Hannah Arendt's Concept of the Social*. Chicago: U Chicago P, 1998.

Plato. *The Collected Dialogues of Plato*. Ed. Edith Hamilton and Huntington Cairns. Princeton: Princeton UP, 1961.

Poiger, Uta. *Jazz, Rock, and Rebels: Cold War Politics and American Culture in a Divided Germany*. Berkeley: U California P, 2000.

Popper, Karl. "Normal Science and its Dangers," in *Criticism and the Growth of Knowledge*, ed. Imre Lakatos and Alan Musgrave, 51–58. Cambridge: Cambridge UP, 1970.

Power, Michael, ed. *Accounting and Science: Natural Inquiry and Commercial Reason*. Cambridge: Cambridge UP, 1994.

Putnam, Hilary. *The Many Faces of Realism*. LaSalle, IL: Open Court, 1987.

——. *Reason, Truth and History*. Cambridge: Cambridge University Press, 1981.

——. *Representation and Reality*. Cambridge: MIT P, 1988.

Quine, W. v. O. *From a Logical Point of View*. 2nd ed. Cambridge: Harvard UP, 1961.

——. *Ontological Relativity and Other Essays*. New York: Columbia UP, 1969.

Rajchman, John, and Cornell West, eds. *Post-Analytic Philosophy*. New York: Columbia University Press, 1985.

Rasch, William. *Niklas Luhmann's Modernity*. Stanford: Stanford UP, 2000.

——. *Sovereignty and Its Discontents: On the Primacy of Conflict and the Structure of the Political*. London: Birkbeck Law P, 2004.

Rasch, William, and Cary Wolfe, eds. *Observing Complexity: Systems Theory and Postmodernity*. Minneapolis: U Minnesota P, 2000.

Raschka, Johannes. *Justizpolitik im SED-Staat. Anpassung und Wandel des Strafrechts während der Amtszeit Honeckers.* Schriften des Hannah-Arendt-Instituts für Totalitarismusforschung 13. Köln: Böhlau, 2000.

Rawls, John. *The Law of the Peoples.* Cambridge: Harvard UP, 2001.

——. *Political Liberalism.* New York: Columbia UP, 1996.

——. *A Theory of Justice.* Cambridge: Harvard UP, 1971.

Reich-Ranicki, Marcel. "Kamerad Fühmann." In *Deutsche Literatur in West und Ost*, 422–33. Munich: Piper, 1963.

Renn, Ludwig. *Nachkrieg.* Berlin: Das Neue Berlin, 2004.

Resnick, Stephen, and Richard Wolff. "Between State and Private Capitalism: What Was Soviet 'Socialism'?" *Rethinking Marxism* 7.1 (spring 1994): 9–30.

Richter, Hans. *Franz Fühmann: Ein deutsches Dichterleben.* Berlin: Aufbau, 1992.

Ricouer, Paul. *Time and Narrative*, vol. 2. Trans. Kathleen McLaughlin and David Pellauer. Chicago: U Chicago P, 1985.

Rilke, Rainer Marie. *Werke in drei Bände*, vol. 3. Frankfurt a.M.: Insel, 1966.

Rohrwasser, Michael. *Der Stalinismus und die Renegaten: die Literatur der Exkommunisten.* Stuttgart: Metzler, 1991.

Rorty, Richard. "The End of Leninism and History as Comic Frame." In *History and the Idea of Progress*, ed. Arthur M. Melzer, Jerry Weinberger, and M. Richard Zinman, 211–26. Ithaca: Cornell UP, 1995.

——. "Pragmatism as Antiauthoritarianism." *Revue Internationale de Philosophie* 207.1 (1999): 7–20.

Rose, Gillian. *The Broken Middle: Out of Our Ancient Society.* Oxford: Basil Blackwell, 1992.

——. *Dialectic of Nihilism: Post-Structuralism and Law.* Oxford: Basil Blackwell, 1984.

Rossi, Paolo. *Logic and the Art of Memory: The Quest for a Universal Language.* Trans. Stephen Clucas. Chicago: U Chicago P, 2000.

Rousseau, Jean-Jacques. *On the Social Contract.* In *The Basic Political Writings*, trans. Donald A. Cress. Indianapolis: Hackett, 1987.

Rüther, Günther. "Franz Fühmann: Ein deutsches Dichterleben in zwei Diktaturen." *Aus Politik und Zeitgeschichte* 13 (March 24, 2000): 11–19.

Salisbury, Harrison E. *The 900 Days: The Siege of Leningrad.* New York: Harper and Row, 1969.

Sartre, Jean-Paul. *Saint Genet: Actor and Martyr.* Trans. Bernard Frechtman. New York: George Braziller, 1963.

Saussure, Ferdinand de. *Course in General Linguistics.* Trans. Roy Harris. Chicago: Open Court, 1983.

Schabowski, Günter. *Abschied von der Utopie: Die DDR—das deutsche Fiasko des Marxismus.* Stuttgart: Franz Steiner, 1994.

Scheurig, Bodo. *Free Germany: The National Committee and the League of German Officers.* Trans. Herbert Arnold. Middletown: Wesleyan UP, 1969.

Schirrmacher, Frank. "Dem Druck des härteren, strengeren Lebens standhalten." In *Der deutsch-deutsch Literaturstreit oder "Freunde, es spricht sich schlecht mit gebundener Zunge,"* ed. Karl Deiritz and Hannes Krauss, 127–36. Hamburg and Zurich: Luchterhand, 1991. Reprinted from *Frankfurter Allgemeine Zeitung*, June 2, 1990.

Schivelbusch, Wolfgang. *Entfernte Verwandtschaft: Faschismus, Nationalsozialismus, New Deal 1933–1939*. Munich: Carl Hanser, 2005.
Schlegel, Friedrich. *Kritische Friedrich-Schlegel-Ausgabe*, vol. 2. Ed. Ernst Behler. München: Schöningh, 1959.
Schlink, Bernhard. "Rechtsstaat und revolutionäre Gerechtigkeit," Inaugural Lecture, Humboldt University Law School, April 14 1994. *Öffentliche Vorlesungen* 61 (1996).
Schmitt, Carl. *The Concept of the Political*. Trans. George Schwab. New Brunswick: Rutgers UP, 1976.
——. *Legality and Legitimacy*. Trans. Jeffrey Seitzer. Durham: Duke UP, 2004.
——. *The Nomos of the Earth in the International Law of the Jus Publicum Europaeum*. Trans. G. L. Ulmen. New York: Telos, 2003.
——. *Political Theology: Four Chapters on the Concept of Sovereignty*. Trans. George Schwab. Cambridge: MIT P, 1985.
——. *Theorie des Partisanen: Zwischenbemerkung zum Begriff des Politischen*. Berlin: Dunker and Humblot, 1963.
Schmitt, Hans-Jürgen, ed. *Franz Fühmann Briefe 1950–1984*. Rostock: Hinstorff, 1994.
Schneider, Peter. *Extreme Mittellage: Eine Reise durch das deutsche Nationalgefühl*. Reinbeck: Rowohlt, 1990.
Sen, Amartya. *Reason before Identity: The Romances Lecture for 1998*. Oxford: Oxford UP, 1999.
Shapin, Steven, and Simon Schaffer. *Leviathan and the Air-Pump: Hobbes, Boyle, and the Experimental Life*. Princeton: Princeton UP, 1985.
Shell, Marc. *The Economy of Literature*. Baltimore: Johns Hopkins UP, 1978.
Simmel, Georg. *The Philosophy of Money*. 2nd ed. Trans. Tom Bottomore and David Frisby. London: Routledge, 1990.
Simon, Horst, and Barbara Richter, eds. *Zwischen Erzählen und Schweigen: Ein Buch des Erinnerns und Gedenkens. Franz Fühmann zum 65*. Rostock: Hinstorff, 1987.
Solzhenitsyn, Aleksandr. *The Gulag Archipelago, 1918–1956: An Experiment in Literary Investigation*. Trans. Thomas P. Whitney. New York: Harper and Row, 1974–78.
Spivak, Gayatri. "Scattered Speculations on the Question of Value." *Diacritics* 15.4 (winter 1985): 73–93.
Staniszkis, Jadwiga. *The Ontology of Socialism*. Ed. and trans. Peggy Watson. Oxford: Oxford UP, 1992.
Steiner, André. *Von Plan zu Plan: Eine Wirtschaftsgeschichte der DDR*. Munich: Deutsche Verlags-Anstalt, 2004.
Stephan, Alexander. "Die wissenschaftlich-technische Revolution in der Literatur der DDR." *Der Deutschunterricht* 2 (1978): 18–34.
——. *Christa Wolf*. Munich: C. H. Beck, 1991.
Stephan, Cora. *Der Betroffenheitskult: Eine politische Sittengeschichte*. Berlin: Rowohlt, 1993.
Stern, Fritz. *The Failure of Illiberalism*. New York: Columbia UP, 1992.
Stokes, Raymond G. *Constructing Socialism: Technology and Change in East Germany 1945–1990*. Baltimore: Johns Hopkins UP, 2000.
Storey, John. *An Introduction to Cultural Theory and Popular Culture*. 2nd ed. Athens: U of Georgia P, 1998.

Tate, Dennis. *Franz Fühmann: Innovation and Authenticity*. Amsterdam: Rodopi, 1995.

Tocqueville, Alexis de. *Democracy in America*, 2 vols. Ed. Phillips Bradley and trans. Henry Reeves as revised by Francis Bowen. New York: Knopf, 1945.

Todorov, Tzvetan. *The Fantastic: A Structural Approach to a Literary Genre*. Trans. Richard Howard. Ithaca: Cornell UP, 1975.

——. *The Poetics of Prose*. Trans. Richard Howard. Oxford: Basil Blackwell, 1977.

Trakl, Georg. *Sämtliche Werke und Briefwechsel: historisch-kritische Ausgabe*. Ed. Eberhard Sauermann und Hermann Zwerschina. Basel: Stroemfeld/Roter Stern, 1995.

Tratner, Michael. *Modernism and Mass Politics: Joyce, Woolf, Eliot, Yeats*. Stanford: Stanford UP, 1995.

Tucker, Robert C., ed. *The Lenin Anthology*. New York: Norton, 1975.

Virilio, Paul. *Speed and Politics: An Essay on Dromology*. Trans. Mark Polizzotti. New York: Seimotext(e), 1977.

Wagener, Hans-Jürgen, ed. *Economic Thought in Communist and Post-Communist Europe*. London: Routledge, 1998.

Walther, Joachim, et al., eds. *Protokoll eines Tribunals: Die Ausschlüsse aus dem DDR-Schriftstellerverband 1979*. Reinbeck: Rowohlt, 1991.

Weber, Max. "Politics as Vocation [1919]." In *From Max Weber: Essays in Sociology*, ed. and trans. H. H. Gerth and C. Wright Mills, 77–128. New York: Oxford UP, 1946.

——. "Science as a Vocation." In *From Max Weber: Essays in Sociology*, ed. and trans. H. H. Gerth and C. Wright Mills, 129–56. New York: Oxford UP, 1946.

Wehler, Hans-Ulrich. *Modernisierungstheorie und Geschichte*. Göttingen: Vandenhoeck and Ruprecht, 1975.

Werckmeister, Otto Karl. *Icons of the Left*. Chicago: U Chicago P, 1999.

Wilde, Oscar. *De Profundis and Other Writings*. Harmondsworth: Penguin, 1973.

Williams, Raymond. *The Long Revolution*. New York: Columbia UP, 1961.

Wittgenstein, Ludwig. *Philosophical Investigations*. 3rd ed. Trans. G. E. M. Anscombe. Oxford: Basil Blackwell, 1953.

Wittstock, Uwe. *Franz Fühmann*. Beck: Munich, 1988.

Wolf, Christa. *Die Dimension des Autors: Essays und Aufsätze, Reden und Gespräche, 1959–1985*. Darmstadt and Neuwied: Luchterhand, 1987.

——. "Neue Lebensansichten eines Katers." In *Gesammelte Erzählungen*,Christa Wolf, 97–123. Frankfurt a.M.: Luchterhand, 1981.

——. *Parting from Phantoms: Selected Writings, 1990–1994*. Trans. Jan van Heurck. New York: Farrar Straus Giroux, 1993.

——. *Patterns of Childhood*. Trans. Ursule Molinaro and Hedwig Rappolt. New York: Farrar, Straus and Giroux, 1980.

——. *The Reader and the Writer: Essays, Sketches, Memories*. Trans. Joan Becker. Berlin: Seven Seas, 1977.

Wolf, Christa, and Franz Fühmann. *Monsieur—Wir Finden Uns Wieder. Briefe 1968–1984*. Berlin: Aufbau, 1998.

Wolle, Stefan. *Die heile Welt der Diktatur: Alltag und Herrschaft in der DDR 1971–1989*. Munich: Econ and List, 1988.

Woodmansee, Martha, and Mark Osteen, eds. *The New Economic Criticism: Studies at the Intersection of Literature and Economics*. London: Routledge, 1999.
Wüstneck, Klaus Dieter. "Die Bedeutung der Kybernetik für die Führungstätigkeit der Partei." *Einheit* 22.8 (1967): 983–92.
Yeats, William Butler. *The Tower: A Facsimile Edition*. Ed. Richard J. Finneran. New York: Scribner, 2004.
Zizek, Slavoj. *Did Somebody Say Totalitarianism? Five Interventions in the (Mis)use of a Notion*. London: Verso, 2001.
——. "Eastern Europe's Republics of Gilead." In *Dimensions of Radical Democracy*, ed. Chantal Mouffe, 193–207. London: Verso, 1992.

Index

The authorized representative in the EU for product safety and compliance is:
Mare Nostrum Group
B.V Doelen 72
4831 GR Breda
The Netherlands

www.ingramcontent.com/pod-product-compliance
Lightning Source LLC
Chambersburg PA
CBHW030812310726
48980CB00006B/473/J

* 9 7 8 0 8 0 4 7 6 2 4 7 2 *